PRAGMATISM
&
DEMOCRACY

PRAGMATISM & DEMOCRACY

Studies in History, Social Theory, and Progressive Politics

Dmitri N. Shalin

Routledge
Taylor & Francis Group

LONDON AND NEW YORK

First published 2011 by Transaction Publishers

2 Park Square, Milton Park, Abingdon, Oxfordshire OX14 4RN
711 Third Avenue, New York, NY 10017

Routledge is an imprint of the Taylor & Francis Group, an informa business

First issued in paperback 2017

Copyright © 2011 Taylor & Francis

Library of Congress Catalog Number: 2010046168

Library of Congress Cataloging-in-Publication Data

Shalin, Dmitri N.
  Pragmatism and democracy : studies in history, social theory, and progressive politics / Dmitri N. Shalin.
        p. cm.
  Includes bibliographical references and index.
  ISBN 978-1-4128-1126-2 (alk. paper)
    1. Sociology--United States--History. 2. Pragmatism. 3. Progressivism (United States politics) I. Title.

HM477.U6S53 2011
306.201--dc22

                                                        2010046168

ISBN 13: 978-1-4128-1126-2 (hbk)
ISBN 13: 978-1-138-51350-1 (pbk)

For Igor S. Kon,
Teacher, Colleague, Friend

Contents

Introduction

In 1967, during my second year of undergraduate studies at the University of Leningrad, I met Professor Igor S. Kon, a leading Russian sociologist and my future mentor. Professor Kon gave me a book by an American philosopher whose name, George Herbert Mead, was unfamiliar to me. I did not know English at the time, but the prospect of working with Igor Kon was too enticing to turn down the invitation to study the volume and write a report on it. *Mind, Self, and Society* was the first book I read in English. This assignment launched a lifelong project that would occupy me for several decades, beginning with a senior thesis on George Mead and Lev Vygotsky, a Ph.D. on early American sociology, followed by a series of studies exploring the impact of pragmatist philosophy on politics, culture, and society.

In 1976, I immigrated to the United States and enrolled in the graduate program at Columbia University where I set out to write a thesis on "Romanticism, Pragmatism, and Interactionism," tracking the genesis of American pragmatism and its impact on interactionist sociology. A three hundred-page manuscript covering the first part of the proposed research did not impress Robert Merton, my dissertation advisor. The project was indeed over-ambitious and not altogether suitable for a sociology department. My dissertation committee changed thereafter, but I would never complete the thesis (Columbia eventually awarded me a Ph.D. *extra muros* on the basis of my publications). Meanwhile, I continued the same line of inquiry that produced a range of studies on the interfaces between pragmatism, romanticism, interactionism, progressivism, and hermeneutics.

In the mid-1990s I received word from an editor who told me that his university press was interested in bringing out a collection of my essays. I was excited about the prospect but felt that the planned volume could benefit from a few more papers expanding my research. Meanwhile, other projects took precedence, and by the time I had enough material for an anthology, I felt reluctant to resubmit the collection to the same editorial board. The invitation from Professor Irving Louis Horowitz to bring out a volume of my essays for Transaction Publishers was as welcome as it was unexpected. This is yet another example of serendipity — without this fortuitous development this book might never have seen the light of day.

The nine essays selected for this volume examine the roots of pragmatist imagination and trace the influence of American pragmatism in diverse areas of politics, law, sociology, political science, and transitional studies. Chapter 1 deals with Romanticism, a protean intellectual movement whose adherents critically appropriated the legacy of the French Revolution, upholding its emancipatory ideals while decrying its violent excesses. My thesis is that the dialectical tenets of romantic philosophy reflected a search for a compromise between the conservative and radical political agendas of the day, and that the quest for a synthesis that animated transcendental idealists had a lasting impact on progressive politics, modern hermeneutics, and interpretive sociology.

Chapter 2 explores the interfaces between the Progressive movement and American pragmatism. Focusing on George H. Mead, I try to show how early twentieth-century progressivism influenced the pragmatism's philosophical agenda and how pragmatists, who took an active part in the politics of the day, helped articulate a theory of progressive reform. An argument is made that through pragmatism, the progressive aspirations shaped a key branch in early American sociology.

Chapter 3 takes up pragmatism and interactionist sociology and illuminates the cross-fertilization between these two fields of studies. Special emphasis is placed on the interactionists' predilection for a logic of inquiry sensitive to the objective indeterminacy of the situation. It is my believe that the paucity of contemporary interactionist studies addressing the issues of power and inequality reflects not their uncritical reliance on pragmatism, as some critics allege, but their failure to follow pragmatist tenets and fulfill the political commitments of pragmatist philosophers.

Chapter 4 addresses the theory of democracy as it evolved in the Frankfurt School and pragmatist philosophy. The discussion focuses on Habermas's critique of the Continental tradition denigrating pragmatism and his effort to incorporate Anglo-Saxon philosophy into his theoretical framework. While Habermas deftly uses pragmatist insights into communicative rationality and admirably reconstructs its radically democratic ethos, he shows little sensitivity to other facets of pragmatism, notably to its concern for embodied experience and objective uncertainty.

I urge incorporating the pragmatist perspective on experience and inde-terminacy as a corrective to the emancipatory agenda championed by critical theorists.

Chapter 5 takes up the encounter between postmodernism and pragma-tist sociology. It tracks the (dis)continuities that mark these two projects, offering a critique of deconstructive engagement as a research practice and a political strategy. I argue that postmodernists err in equating mo-dernity with the Enlightenment and identifying counter-Enlightenment chiefly with Nietzsche. This reading ignores Romanticism, a vibrant counter-Enlightenment current that eschewed both hyperrationalism and irrationalism and that paved the way to pragmatist philosophy and sociol-ogy which combined the Enlightenment's commitment to rational inquiry with Romanticism's critique of rationalism and capitalist modernity.

Chapter 6 articulates a research program of pragmatist hermeneutics and biocritique. I begin with the classical hermeneutics which is focused exclusively on discursive products and then show how the interpretation theory informed by pragmatism can reconstruct a meaningful occasion as an embodied semiotic process through an indefinite triangulation of symbols, icons, and indices. The chapter shows that the tension between various types of signifying media is unavoidable, that the pragmatic-discursive misalignment is an ontological condition, and that bridging the gap between our discursive, behavioral, and affective outputs is at the heart of ethical life.

Chapter 7 examines the pragmatist perspective on law. It reviews the range of discursive and nondiscursive practices associated with the pragmatic perspective on law and democracy. Starting with Kant's le-gal philosophy and its peculiar relevance for pragmatism as a negative reference frame, I reconstruct how philosophers responded to Kant and jurists' reacted to the pragmatist challenge. The discussion zeroes in on the place of principles in pragmatic jurisprudence, efforts to reclaim juridical moralism in the discourse theory of law, and the growing interest in the legacy of Dewey and Mead as theoreticians of the fully embodied democratic process.

Chapter 8 explores the vital link between democracy, civility, and affect. Its central thesis is that democracy is an embodied process that binds affectively as well as rhetorically and that flourishes in places where civic discourse is not an expedient means to be discarded when it fails to achieve a proximate goal, but an end in itself, a source of vitality and social creativity sustaining an emotionally intelligent democratic community. The discussion starts with a blueprint for democratic polity formulated in ancient Greece and its critical reception at the time, then moves on to the difficulties that fledgling democracies encounter on the way to civil society. I go over cases demonstrating why civic discourse is hobbled by the civic body that has been misshapen by past abuses. Drawing on Norbert Elias's work on the civilizing process, I speculate about the emotion, demeanor, and the body language of democracy and explore from this angle the prospects for democratic transformation in countries struggling to shake their totalitarian past.

Chapter 9 tracks the controversy over policy engagement and national sociology in cotemporary Russia. It shows that the heated polemics splitting the Russian sociological community over the issues of patriotic social science reflects the struggle for power in contemporary Russia, that theoretical monism advocated by nationalist sociologists is incompatible with a scientific ethos, and that the contempt for pragmatism evinced by both the nationalist right and the illiberal left undercut prospects for reform in emerging democracies.

The debate about advocacy, national sociology, and pragmatism is then placed in a comparative perspective, with the focus shifting to American sociology and C. Wright Mills in particular.

Most papers collected in this volume were previously published in a wide range of social science, humanities, and law journals, some of which are less known and accessible than others. I am grateful to the publishers for their permission to reproduce my work in this volume. A few stylistic changes and occasional clarifications were made in the course of preparing these materials for publication, but editorial work centered on eliminating redundancies and repetitions. Some overlap in source material and formulations is inevitable, and perhaps necessary, to spotlight the thematic continuity of the present research agenda.

I was tempted to add fresh insights to my early works, but chose not to do so. Inserting such into papers written a decade or two ago risks creating an impression that there was more prescience in my thoughts than there actually was. It is harder to justify the absence of a conclusion that would provide a grand synthesis of the insights developed over time. Somehow, I don't feel like I have much to say in addition to what I have already written, and providing stale summaries of chapter findings (beyond what is found in this preface) seems superfluous. It is my hope that readers sampling the essays in this volume will share my fascination with the probing humanity and continuing relevance of American pragmatism.

This volume is dedicated to my teacher, colleague, and friend, Igor S. Kon. I owe him a profound debt of gratitude for nurturing my interest in pragmatism and sociology. When I teach seminars on classical theory and pragmatist hermeneutics, I return in my thoughts to Igor Kon, whose taste for intellectual inquiry, willingness to cross disciplinary lines, and the ability to intercut exegesis with present-day concerns I try to cultivate in my students.

I wish to thank my colleagues who supported a project that did not fit squarely into any disciplinary mold. The explorations featured in this tome variously benefited from my exchanges with scholars hailing from different parts of academia —Mitchell Aboulafia, Robert Antonio, Edward Beliaev, Peter Berger, Herbert Blumer, Vincent Colapietro, Gary Fine, David Franks, Eugene Halton, Ruth Horowitz, Hans Joas, Erkki Kilpinen, Bruce Mazlish, Richard Shusterman, Norbert Wiley, and Vladimir Yadov.

I am also grateful to my wife, Janet S. Belcove-Shalin, who cheered me up at turning points in my career and offered valuable comments on the assembled papers at various stages of their development.

November 2, 2009
Las Vegas

1

Empowering the Self:
Romanticism, the French Revolution,
and the Rise of Sociological Hermeneutics

Although biblical exegesis and rhetoric, from which modern hermeneutics derived its first principles, are ancient arts, an effort to establish hermeneutics as a universal science, and especially to extend its principles to the science of society, is of decidedly recent origin. "There is little doubt," states Gouldner, "that hermeneutics' roots in the modern era are traceable to Romanticism."[1] Why is this so, what makes romanticism fertile ground for hermeneutical speculations? Hans-Georg Gadamer, a leading authority on hermeneutics, makes this intriguing suggestion about its origins:

> The hermeneutical problem only emerges clearly when there is no powerful tradition present to absorb one's own attitude into itself and when one is aware of confronting an alien tradition to which he has never belonged or one he no longer unquestioningly accepts…. Historically it is worth of note that while rhetoric belongs to the earliest Greek philosophy, hermeneutics came to flower in the Romantic era as a consequence of the modern dissolution of firm bonds with tradition.[2]

Gadamer does not pursue the argument much further, yet his remark offers a clue for a potentially fruitful line of inquiry.

Indeed, the onset of romanticism was marked by the breakdown of a century-old tradition. Precipitated by the French Revolution of 1789, a

Originally presented at the 1983 Annual Meeting of the American Sociological Association, this paper was published as "Romanticism and the Rise of Sociological Imagination" in *Social Research*, 1986, Vol. 53, pp. 77-123. I wish to express my gratitude to Professors Peter Berger, Ira Cohen, David Zaret, and Lon Shelby for their comments on an earlier draft of this chapter.

major upheaval swept over Europe, leaving its indelible mark on virtually every form of practical and spiritual life. The romantic movement was in great measure an attempt, inconclusive and contradictory as it might seem, to come to grips with the legacy of the French Revolution. The revolution compelled the reappraisal of the past and made imperative a conscious stance with regard to the present. It underscored the historicity and fragility of the tradition. Most frighteningly, the revolution revealed the constitutive role of reason, its uncanny ability to revamp the natural order of things that establishes man as a participant observer in the drama of history. The realization that man is a producer as much as the product of society—this major insight of sociological hermeneutics—was first formulated by the romantic thinkers in response to the promise and the threat of the French Revolution.

A few preliminary remarks on the meaning of "romanticism" as employed in this paper are in order. The term has been the subject of an ongoing controversy since the beginning of this century.[3] Some critics see little use in it because "it has come to mean so many things that, by itself, it means nothing"[4] —too many different authors are lumped together under the heading "romanticism," too antithetical are the ideas stamped "romantic," too uncertain is the time span encompassing the "romantic movement." What useful purpose, indeed, may serve bringing under one head such unlikely bedfellows as Goethe, Tieck, E. T. A. Hoffman, Fichte, F. Schlegel, Novalis, Hegel, Schopenhauer, Kierkegaard, A. Müller, and Marx? Lovejoy's unhappiness with the term and his preference for the plural form "romanticisms"[5] are understandable. Still, his argument overestimates the uniqueness of the case. What is peculiar about them, as Gouldner rightly noted, is that "ever since Hegel, romantics have expressed their distance from others by condemning them as 'romantics.'"[6] It may be prudent to distinguish those consciously advancing the romantic cause (we can call them "romantics") from those partaking in it without openly subscribing to its tenets or accepting some of its forms (they may be called "romanticists"), but to deny Goethe, Hegel, or Marx a place in the history of romanticism on account of their ambivalence about it is to engage in the "petty politics of cultural history."[7] Barzun hardly overstates the case when he calls *Faust* "a bible of Romanticism" in spite of Goethe's deliberate attempts to put distance between himself and the romantics.[8] Hegel's contempt for everything romantic notwithstanding, his *Phenomenology of Mind* is an outstanding piece of romantic philosophy, deservedly included by Peckham among the required readings on romanticism.[9] Gouldner's interest in "Marx's

Romanticism"[10] does no violence to the historical realities, even though it flies in the face of Marx's well-known antiromantic sentiments. And certainly a long list of romantic writers compiled by Isaiah Berlin,[11] which features among others Chateaubriand, Kierkegaard, Stirner, and Nietzsche, is no sign of his indifference to the diversity of their respective views. The greater the stature of a thinker, the more likely he is to be in a class by himself; classing him together with other romanticists is not meant to suggest that he is nothing but romantic, only that he took part in the romantic discourse, shared in the romantic problematics, and wittingly or unwittingly contributed to the vast field of idioms and meanings which sprang to life in the aftermath of the French Revolution and signified a break with the Age of Reason.

All this is not to belittle the formidable task facing the student of romanticism seeking to unravel the unity of the romantic movement. This task is exacerbated by the violently contradictory statements emanating from alleged romanticists. In the same breath we find them asserting the autonomy of the individual and the primacy of the whole, the right to self-determination and the duty to the state, personal responsibility for the future and the inviolability of tradition. These contradictions cannot be simply charged to the factional divisions within the romantic movement, for they are endemic to every genuinely romantic thinker; rather, they should be seen as a manifestation of the "contradictoriness, dissonance and inner conflict of the Romantic mind."[12] It is to the credit of such students of romanticism as Kluckhohn and Barzun, Peckham and Abrams, Wasserman and Schenk that they endeavored to grasp the unity underlying the romantic movement without glossing over the artistic, intellectual, and ideological diversity of its protagonists.

The following account focuses on the tension inherent in the premises of romantic thought. Several of these premises are central to the present study. The first one concerns the romanticists' political commitment and is predicated on the idea that "Romanticism as well as Revolution … were united in their impassioned striving for freedom."[13] Deploring revolutionary violence, the romanticists remained committed to the Revolution's emancipatory goals. The novel element in their political reasoning was the contention that individual freedom is not antithetical to social order, that the former is grounded in the latter and can be fully realized only in and through society. The second premise has to do with the philosophical assumptions of romanticism and is based on the precept that "the romantic reaction was a protest on behalf of value."[14] Whereas rationalist philosophy sought to minimize the value component in human understanding, the romantic thinkers proclaimed it to be the very condition of objective knowledge. The notion that knowledge devoid of interest and a priori assumptions is a contradiction in terms is quintessentially romantic. The third idea contained in romanticism is that of organic unity. "The paradigm of 'organic' unity," according to Higonnet, is central to "romantic hermeneutics."[15] I will also argue that it is central to the entire romantic tradition in sociology, insofar as it entails a new image of society as *Gemeinschaft* or free discourse. The above precepts do not exhaust the list of romantic premises; arguably, they form the core of the romantic teaching and are signally important for the understanding of romantic sociology and the hermeneutical perspective endemic to its premises. The principle task of this chapter is to place these in a proper historical, social, and political context. I begin with the examination of the romanticists' attitude toward the French Revolution. After reconstructing the premises of romantic hermeneutics, I discuss the circular nature of reasoning in romantic social thought. Next, I analyze the notion of *Gemeinschaft* as an epitome of the romantic ideal of the future community. And finally, I zero in on the continuity between romantic theory and twentieth-century interpretative sociology.

Political Underpinnings of the Romantic Movement

The history of the romantic movement is inexorably tied to the Revolution of 1789, which continued to evoke passionate response throughout the nineteenth century. The first generation of romanticists greeted the news about the fall of the Bastille with cheers and applause. To commemorate the happy events of July 14, young students in Gottingen—Hegel, Schlegel and Hölderlin — planted a liberty tree. Friedrich Schlegel ranked the French Revolution with "the greatest tendencies of the age," along with Fichte's philosophy and Goethe's *Meister*.[16] Fichte praised the *valeur* of the French and claimed to have laid the philosophical foundation for what they selflessly fought for in practice.[17] Wordsworth, deploring "the baleful influence of aristocracy and nobility upon human happiness and virtue," declared himself a supporter of the republic.[18] The feeling of euphoria, however, did not survive the third year of the Revolution. The terror struck, and almost overnight the mood of the romanticists changed: enthusiasm gave way to depression, hope to despair, acclamation to denunciation. The awakening was particularly rude for the German romanticists, who saw in the French Revolution the best hope for the liberty in their country, still deeply ensconced in the feudal tradition. Even in England, where a good many liberties espoused by the French revolutionaries were in place for more than a century, the judgment of the three years of revolutionary violence was strongly negative. "*I* abandoned France and her rulers," explained Wordsworth, "when *they* abandoned the struggle for liberty, gave themselves up to tyranny, and endeavored to enslave the world."[19] By the end of the century this sentiment prevailed among the romantic thinkers. The first decade of the nineteenth century witnessed the romanticists' turning away from cosmopolitanism to patriotism, from republicanism to monarchism, from scientific rationality to Christianity and revelation.

It is this metamorphosis that accounts for a still predominant view of romanticism as a soundly conservative movement. Thus in his study of Goethe and his age, Lukács rarely refers to romanticism without a qualifier "reactionary"; Cobban uses the terms "romantic" and "conservative" as virtually synonymous; Zeitlin speaks about "the Romantic-Conservative reaction" to the French Revolution; Ruggiero scolds romanticism for "promoting a reactionary type of thought inspired by the pure Junkerism"; and Briefs deplores romantic idealism as "the philosophy of counter-revolution."[20] Mannheim makes perhaps the most elaborate case for romanticism as a paragon of conservative thinking. In his important inquiry into the styles of social thought, Mannheim identifies conservatism with the distrust of reason and formal logic, preference for qualitative thinking and dialectics, penchant for irrationalism and mysticism, and above all, with the idealization of the past: "Acting along conservative lines ... means that the individual is consciously or unconsciously guided by a way of thinking and acting which has its own history behind it, before it comes into contact with the individual."[21] Romanticism, or "feudalistic romanticism" as Mannheim sometimes refers to it, with its preoccupation with medieval institutions, abhorrence of radical change, and the support of reactionary governments, does then appear to be the purest species of conservatism.

Whatever the merit of the above interpretation—and it certainly succeeds in bringing into focus romantic stylistics—it cannot be accepted in its original form. Mannheim's scheme fails to account for other facets of romantic thought that cannot be forced under the heading "conservatism." Too perceptive a thinker to simply ignore the inconsistencies, Mannheim acknowledges "the infiltration of liberal ideas into the conservative system of thought" and admits that "liberalism allowed itself to be penetrated by conservative elements."[22] By and large, however, he chooses to explain away anomalous manifestations rather than to admit the deficiency of his schema. Yet the whole scheme needs to be overhauled if we are to understand the unique position of romanticism in postrevolutionary Europe. The uniqueness of romanticism is not to be seen in its furnishing a rallying point for the forces of the past, but in the romanticists' ingenuous effort to enlist tradition in service of the revolutionary objectives of the present. An interpretation that paints romanticism as "a one-dimensional negation of liberalism and bourgeois society,"[23] an interpretation first fully articulated in Mannheim's *Habilitation* thesis and still enjoying wide currency, fails to grasp the peculiar status of the past in romantic literature. A simple return to the past was not seriously contemplated by the romantic thinkers, certainly not as a practical option for the future. An ideal past—an organic state of feudal Europe, an amiable polis of Greek antiquity, or a harmonious community of prehistoric past—was to be regained on a higher level, through the negation of the present. The past of the romantics is clearly an extension of the present, a resource skillfully manipulated to advance contemporary cause. As Mead observed in his vastly underestimated study of romantic thought, the romanticists "created a different past from that which had been there before, a past ... into which a value has been put which did not belong there before."[24] The values the romanticists found in medieval Europe were their own, conspicuously modern values of autonomy, freedom, and dignity of man. Combined with the ancient virtues of courage, honesty, and duty, these values were thought to produce the noble, harmonious order. Never mind that the idyllic picture of the past was chiefly the phantom of the romantic imagination; its function was to furnish a convenient vantage point for an attack on the ills of modern society:

> The romantics were no fools. They recognized the great accomplishments of the Enlightenment and saw the powerful potential of early capitalist technology. But they saw how these advances in thinking and industry were being used to affect and enslave their own consciousness and behavior as well as those of the people in general. And the[y] ... sought to recover the revolutionary potential of new inventions and fought for the in-formation and formation of a new social order which was still in transition.[25]

This is not to gainsay that criticism couched in nostalgic terms lends itself handily to reactionary ideologies. Whatever the intent of the early romantics, they did provide ammunition to the ideologists of Prussian Junkerism; their attacks on the institutions of revolutionary France delayed the advancement of civil rights; and their rejection of capitalism helped to prolong the agony of industrial transformation in Germany and elsewhere. Still, it is imperative to refrain from sitting in judgment on the ideological nature of romanticism outside the historical context. It is hardly an accident that Hegel, a model of romantic conservatism in the eyes of some contemporary critics, was considered in his own time a liberal and an agent of revolution, his political writings being denied posthumous publication, his influence in German universities condemned to eradication by Frederick William IV. Nor is it totally fortuitous that the proponents of Stein-Hardenberg liberal reforms were sympathetic to the romantic cause. As to the romanticists' vociferous opposition to the Enlightenment, we should remember that, in the nineteenth century, the latter's universalism and cosmopolitanism were transformed into a progressively coercive Napoleonic imperialism, deeply resented throughout Europe. The ideological underpinnings of the Romantic movement are "neither of the Right nor of the Left."[26] The romanticists looked to the past for a model of the future that would be "neither bourgeois nor feudal."[27] It is telling that the thinkers of such impeccably radical credentials as William Morris, Gustav Landauer, and Georg Lukács have a strong romantic background. All in all, romanticism defies an unambiguous political identification and resists attempts to put it squarely on one side of the ideological battles of the day. Can we say, then, that it lacks a unifying political theme? By no means. Löwy misses this point, I believe, when he denigrates the ideological multifariousness of romanticism as "ideological hermaphroditism"[28] ("ideological ambivalence" would be a more fitting term). What he fails to appreciate is that the very attempt to rise above the ideological extremes of the Right and the Left is a unifying principle of romantic thought. The romanticists' craving for tradition and social order is inseparable from their commitment to self-determination and freedom. This commitment survived the decades of reaction and remained as strong in the second generation of romantic thinkers—the generation of Feuerbach and Kierkegaard, Stirner and Marx, Emerson and Thoreau—as it was at the inception of the Romantic era, when Schelling first proclaimed that "freedom is the beginning and the end of all philosophy."[29] On this score the romanticists proved to be true heirs of the Enlightenment and the classical liberal tradition. Where they parted company with their predecessors was on the question of the relationship between individual freedom and society.

For the philosophers of the Enlightenment and their revolutionary heirs, freedom was indigenous, servitude was man-made; humans came before society and made it possible through a social contract. Freedom was defined here as the freedom from, as negative freedom or liberty that should be continuously guarded against the encroaching influence of authority, state, and society. The romanticists retained this preoccupation with freedom, but after a brief period of enthusiasm for the French Revolution, they abandoned the premises of *jus naturae* and embarked on a path toward a new theory, which stipulated that "a firm government is indispensable to freedom."[30] Brutal and often patently random violence in the later years of the Revolution (as exemplified in the September massacre of 1792) planted the seeds of doubt in the romantic mind as to the inherent rationality of reason. Liberated from external constraints and left to its own devices, reason showed irrational, if not downright suicidal, tendencies which were conspicuously at odds with the lofty assumptions of the philosophers of the Enlightenment. This traumatic experience compelled the rejection of the system of natural rights and precipitated a thorough revision of the notion of freedom. Reinterpreted as positive freedom or "freedom for," liberty was proclaimed an end product of human history, rather than its starting point. Equally radical was the change in outlook on the relevance of tradition. Caught between the ancien régime they deemed obsolete and the new order they found inimical to freedom, the romanticists turned to a distant past. The medieval past of the romantic fancy had little to do with the stagnant society in which the individual was permanently locked into his estate; this past was passé for those who believed that every man is entitled "to make oneself a member of one of the moments of civil society by one's own act, through one's energy, industry and skill,"[31] that "no man whatever ought to be compelled to any particular class, nor shut from any."[32] The past order which the romanticists came to praise and against which they learned to judge the present was both harmonious, or in the terminology of the epoch "organic," and at the same time perfectly conducive to individual freedom. No one is forced here to comply; everyone follows one's native genius; society remains forever malleable, though changes in it come not through the abrupt termination of tradition but through the gradual expansion of its confines. It is a permanent (r)evolution, accomplished through the continuous self-rejuvenation of reason.

One can readily see why these romantic musings appealed to the reactionary politicians in post-revolutionary Europe. No less apparent, however, is the liberating component of romanticism, which proved compatible with the socialist and liberal currents of nineteenth century political discourse. The ideological perspective unifying nineteenth-century romanticism grows out of the romanticists' determination to realize radical objectives by conservative means. Romanticism was as much "a negation of the philistine substance and life style of the emerging bourgeoisie and a protest against the utilitarian ordering of life" as it was "a *reaction against* the backward feudal ideology and conditions of authoritarianism."[33] The romanticists were "innovators and revolutionists" as well as "great restorers and wise conservatives."[34] Their dialectical commitment to liberty and order is the broadest common denominator that unites otherwise diverse and openly antagonistic thinkers identified with the romantic movement. To be a romantic, we can say, is to believe that freedom can coexist with necessity, diversity with unity, and self-determination with social order. Romantic philosophy, with its critical—hermeneutical—thrust, was an attempt to work out a theoretical foundation for the practical resolution of these antinomies.

Romantic Philosophy and Hermeneutics

Whitehead defined the romantic attitude as "a protest against the exclusion of value from the essence of matter of fact."[35] This formula captures the gist of the romantic revolt against the dominant rationalist philosophy. Man, according to the rationalists, is handicapped in his quest for knowledge by innate as well as acquired biases, prejudices, or in Bacon's terminology, "idols," which obscure the shape of things in the knower's mind. The understanding process succeeds only when the knower purges himself from preconceptions. The rational mind, urged Descartes, is active to the extent that is necessary to curtail its own unwanted interference with the pre-established order. The universal science of the future, as the rationalists envisioned it, called for faithful observance, not for participant observation; it stressed the activity of *res extensa*, not that of *res cogitans*. Once the mind fulfilled its purgatory function, it was to assume its proper role, that is, to record faithfully the preordained movement of matter, as it revealed itself to a disinterested scientific observer. It was this impersonal, mechanical universe that provoked the romantic revolt against rationalism and mechanicism of the preceding era. The romanticists rejected the idea that knowledge can be freed from the contaminating influence of the process that engendered understanding. Scientific endeavor, according to them, is not a quest for things themselves and their primordial order; the scientific method is not an expedient way of getting around the distortions incurred by man's presence in the universe. Quite to the contrary, science's true aim is to humanize nature, to make it more rational; the scientist is a participant observer whose imprint on the outside world is irradicable and whose proper role is to restore man's responsibility for the world out there. The determination of mechanistic philosophy to do away with "idols" resulted in the dehumanization of the process of understanding. Along with human bias, the rationalists excised the active side of knowing, reducing knowledge to passive reflection. "The overcoming of all prejudices," contends Gadamer, "this global demand of the enlightenment, will prove to be itself a prejudice..."[36]

Herein lies the significance of the revolution in philosophy initiated by Kant and continued by his romantic successors. The process of knowledge, for Kant, is selective, in that it chooses among many elements before it shapes them into an object. The selection is guided by our beliefs, preconceptions, values, and prejudices—literally prejudgments, without which cognition would be impossible. What it means is that rationalists overlooked an irreducible element of faith or value permeating our knowledge. "I had therefore to remove *knowledge*," explains Kant, "in order to make room for *belief*."[37] The secret of the transcendental judgment a priori—the heart of Kant's system—is that it is value judgment, that is, a judgment whose objective validity presupposes prior commitment to certain beliefs and values. The task of philosophical analysis, then, is not to expunge value from understanding and to eliminate all biases but to render them conscious, to turn them into premises. This is exactly the task of philosophical hermeneutics, the task of becoming reflexive, of uncovering prejudices through which our understanding participates in the production of reality as objective and meaningful. When Goethe insists that "every fact is already a theory"; when Hegel exposes as self-deception the unreflexive mind's insistence on dealing with "bare facts"; when Emerson scolds reason that separates "fact" from "value"; when Schlegel takes to task an empiricist for his unconscious reliance on a transcendental outlook—when all these giants of the romantic era raise their objections to unreflexive reasoning and urge the inescapability of prejudgments, they speak the language of hermeneutics: "This recognition that all understanding inevitably involves some prejudice gives the hermeneutical problem its real thrust."[38]

Romantic hermeneutics, as one can gather from the above, is an extension of romantic philosophy. Dilthey takes note of this fact when he points out that Schleiermacher "was specifically trained in transcendental philosophy which was the first to provide adequate means for stating the problem of hermeneutics in general terms and solving it."[39] The principles of romantic hermeneutics—the constitutive nature of understanding, the a priori foundation of knowledge, the unreflexivity of consciousness, the dialectics of part and whole—belong to the general fund of ideas developed by romantic idealism. Transcendentalism furnished a new foundation for romantic hermeneutics, moving it away from the traditional concern with the inherent properties of the text toward the examination of the concealed interaction between the interpreter and his object. It helped to broaden the scope of the hermeneutical analysis by including in its orbit the entire range of cultural and natural objects, by treating all objective reality as a text waiting to be interpreted. The old hermeneutics urged the interpreter unraveling the meaning of the past to free oneself from the contaminating influence of the present; the romantic hermeneutics claimed that "the past exists only through the present." The former insisted that the interpreter should approach his task unbiased and presuppositionless; the latter assumed that bias is an unacknowledged premise. Where one aimed outward, focusing the interpreter's undivided attention on the object, the other turned inward, postulating self-reflection as a precondition of successful interpretation. All understanding which is not dogmatic must begin with self-understanding. This romantic premise gives modern hermeneutics its peculiar flavor. It also points to a distinctly critical thrust of modern—romantic—hermeneutics.

The Project of Sociological Hermeneutics

Paul Ricouer once observed that we live "in a hermeneutical age,"[40] by which he meant modern man's extraordinary preoccupation with self-reflection, demystification, and criticism. The roots of this now ubiquitous attitude can be traced to the Romantic era, or if you will, to 1781, when Kant first proclaimed that "our age is, in every sense of the word, the age of criticism, and everything must submit to it."[41] The same sentiment we find in Kant's successors who declared a war on "dogmatism as a way of thinking,"[42] on "the dogmatic tendency in man,"[43] and demanded "*a ruthless criticism of everything existing,*"[44] "a strenuous reacquisition of that which has once been acquired,"[45] "putting to the test what has long since passed as established truth."[46] Such were the opening salvos of the age of criticism, the hermeneutical age. Not surprisingly, this was also the dawning of the new political era. It was the time when philosophical disquisitions were nourished by the flames of revolution, when self-reflection bred criticism and criticism inspired open insurrection. The specter of democratic revolutions rising over Europe spurred the romantic imagination and encouraged sociological hermeneutics whose impact would be felt well beyond the century that brought it into being.

A great accomplishment of the French Revolution was the doubt it cast over the divine nature of the social order and man's place in it. In a dramatic fashion the revolution demonstrated that man's social qualities as well as the social order of which he finds himself a part are emergent. Whether it consists of slaves and masters, noblemen and commoners, capitalists and laborers, the social order is not ordained by God; nor are its members earmarked by nature for their station in life; rather, individuals themselves generate their social order in the very process of knowing, by subsuming each other under a priori categories and forcing upon reality taken-for-granted nomenclatures. The institutions of society established in this manner only appear to be "noumenal," subsisting on their own; in truth, they are "phenomenal," that is, emergent, historical, contingent on the rational activities of its members. It is the mind that imposes the structure on the world and assures its objective reality, and it is entirely in man's power to destroy his own creation, to supplant the old order with a new one. The realization that mind is a constitutive force was itself an offshoot of the revolutionary era:

> That was an age of great destructions. When the Revolution came, many institutions which long seemed to be things in themselves, showed that they were nothing but phenomena. And when new constitutions and new social orders had to be planned, the spirit of the age emphasized the fact that, at least in the social world, it is the office of human intelligence to impose its own forms upon the phenomena, and to accept no authority but that of the rational self.[47]

The critical mode of thinking engendered in romantic social thought predicates that society owes its objective reality to consciousness. A fine-spun network of a priori assumptions and categories, according to this premise, serves as a ground plan following which the understanding generates the social world. The understanding does its job without being aware of its awesome accomplishment—it is perennially unreflexive, yet this unreflexivity is the very stuff of which social facts are made. Social reality presents itself to the mind as a noumenon, an object unrelated to the subject or "bare fact," yet this facticity is apparent: social facts and the social orders they comprise are brought into being through the labor of our collective understanding. The paradox of the social world is that society confronting us in all its glorious externality and unyielding thinghood is the work of our (un)conscious activity. The whole edifice of social institutions rests on the exceedingly shaky foundation of transcendental beliefs and values. "Ultimately everything rests on a postulate," intones Kierkegaard,[48] even if this postulate remains incomprehensible to the subject. An element of incomprehensibility, opaqueness, and un-reflexivity is at the core of social being—expose it, and the whole order will collapse.

> But is incomprehensibility really something so unmitigatedly contemptible and evil? Methink the salvation of families and nations rests upon it. If I am not wholly deceived, then states and systems, the most artificial productions of man, are often so artificial that one simply can't admire the wisdom of their creator enough. Only an incredibly minute quantity of it suffices: as long as its truth and purity remain inviolate and no blasphemous rationality dares approach its sacred confines. ... [Every system] depends in the last analysis ... on some such point of strength that must be left in the dark, but that nonetheless shores up and supports the whole burden and would crumble the moment one subjected it to rational analysis.[49]

It should be clear by now that social institutions are not immune to the hermeneutical analysis, that social facts are perfectly amenable to the interpretative understanding. Moreover, it is quite plausible, as Rickert argued decades ago,[50] that the romantic idealists derived their general problematics chiefly from the social domain, on which they modeled their treatment of nature. Transcendentalism was inspired by the travails of the revolutionary age in which the task of recapturing one's authorship first emerged as a practical problem. Dogmatism or the unreflexive mode of being in the world decried by the romantic thinkers is coterminous with the institutions of the ancien régime which, toward the end of the nineteenth century, ceased to be perceived as natural and inherently rational and were increasingly subjected to critical debunking by the subjects rediscovering the constitutive power of reason. "Thing in itself" is a philosophical epitome of the world in which the individual is no longer at home, where he is not a master of himself but an exile, condemned to inauthentic existence by his own unreflexivity. He is surrounded by social facts—customs, institutions, estates, each weighing heavily on his consciousness, demanding unequivocal respect, threatening to sub-due anyone who dares to question their authenticity. Alas, this unhappy state of affairs is itself the work of the mind unconscious of its agency. To break the mold of pseudo-facticity in which the institutions present themselves to the mind, the latter must become self-reflexive. When the understanding becomes transparent to itself and acquires a hermeneutical insight into its role as a participant observer in the order of things, social facts lose their impenetrability and submit to rational change.

The project of sociological hermeneutics is fundamentally that of rediscovery and emancipation—rediscovery of authorship and emancipation from the oppressive weight of obsolete institutions. The first impetus to this project came from Kant's *Critique of Pure Reason* and the French Declaration of the Rights of Man and Citizen. We find an unmistakable imprint of these two pillars of modernity in Schelling's attacks on dogmatism and Fichte's belief in the primacy of self-determination; in the contempt for philistinism professed by Novalis, Schlegel and Tieck; in the critique of the various forms of alienation by Hegel, Feuerbach, Stirner, and Marx; as well as in the transvaluation of values attempted by Nietzsche at the close of the Romantic era. When Marx announced that "self-understanding (equals critical philosophy) by our age ... is a task for the world" and promised to reform society "through the analysis of mystical consciousness that is not clear to itself,"[51] he did not break new ground—he simply stated in explicitly sociological terms the mission of romantic hermeneutics. Marx's iconoclastic attitude is characteristic of the second generation of romantic thinkers, who were determined to put "the searching knife of criticism" to every institution of yesteryear. Their diction, expressly political and self-consciously defiant, differed markedly from the studiously metaphysical language of their romantic predecessors, but their message remained essentially the same: man is an author of the historical drama, responsible for his social world and capable of reclaiming authority over his creations through the systematic exercise of self-reflection.

The Dialectic of Rationality and Sociality

The enthusiasm with which the romanticists greeted the breakdown of the old regime, intense and sincere as it was in the opening days of the Revolution, faded rapidly as the news about the increasingly bloody turn of events in Paris spread throughout Europe. And when the measured staccato of the guillotines heralded to the world the arrival of the Terror, most of the early supporters of the revolution turned against it, feeling betrayed and loudly denouncing the dangerous shortcut to freedom taken by the French. Something went terribly wrong with the way the heirs of the Enlightenment set out to reclaim the natural rights of man. The dawn of the Age of Reason was marred by exemplary irrationality and seemingly random violence which made a mockery of the optimistic forecasts of the prophets of the Enlightenment. Freed from the restraints of society, reason looked nothing like the benign and constructive force in the service of natural law it was hailed to be; instead, it showed itself to be arrogant, vindictive, and utterly self-destructive. In the wake of the Terror the veracity of a theory that pictured society as derivative and incidental to the affairs of reason was suspect. Toward the end of the century it came under close scrutiny by the romantic thinkers, who gave a decidedly new—sociological—turn to the traditional discourse on the nature of reason.

According to the rationalist mode of thinking, reason precedes society and needs no help from it to do the job it was entrusted with by the Almighty. Society contaminates reason with prejudices—idols—which only muddle the picture of the preestablished harmony. To fulfill its mission, reason must break through the veils of society and open itself to the natural purity of things themselves and their primordial order. By contrast, the romanticists conceived of reason as socially embedded and historically emergent. Consciousness is permeated with prejudices and a priori assumptions, but it is only because it is so informed and guided by society that it is the consciousness of man. Humans act consciously and rationally when they raise themselves above their immediate existence, place themselves in the perspective of the community, and, armed with a priori categories and values, transform the flux of things themselves into an orderly flow of objective reality. Sociality is implicit in every rational act. "*Gemeinschaft*, pluralism is our innermost essence,"[52] exclaims Schlegel. What this means is that only those forces in man are truly rational that are mediated by the community. Rationality without sociality, mind outside of the human community, is unthinkable.

Already in Kant we find a hint that reason may be social, at least in form if not in substance. The transcendental domain contains cognitive constructs which have no existence apart from the individual mind but which nevertheless transcend personal experience and claim universal validity. Drawing on these transcendental schemes of understanding, the subject can induce objectivity into things without visible recourse to any authority beyond himself, yet each time he raises the claim that the reality in question is objective and meaningful, he presupposes, however tacitly, that it is universally—intersubjectively—valid. When man hazards a universal judgment, "he disregards the subjective private conditions of his own judgment ... and reflects upon it from a universal standpoint (which he can only determine by placing himself at the standpoint of others)."[53] Kant would not say of course that a priori categories of reason come from society and change with time (he thought these to be innate and unalterable), but the very fact that they possess a power transcending individual experience and binding on every rational member of the community invites a sociological interpretation.

With Kant's romantic followers the social and historical nature of reason is already a matter of unshakable conviction. Reason evolves historically, along with the human community, and embodies the collective forces of society, even though its immediate expression is individual. The transcendental power of mind, the power to convert things in themselves into objects, is social in form and content. Beyond the transcendental judgment a priori stands a community (real or potential) which delegates its authority to its members and gives them confidence to treat the reality in question as objective and meaningful. Every thought, precept, or deed that passes the test of rationality has its beginning and end in society. Even the most intimate notion of self, according to romantic thinkers, is of social origins: "The self perceives itself at the same time that it is perceived by others.... Self-consciousness exists in itself and for itself ... by the very fact that it exists for another self-consciousness; that is to say, it is only by being acknowledged or recognized."[54] "Only by meeting with, so as to be resisted by, *Another*, does the Soul become a *Self*. What is Self-consciousness but to know myself at the same moment that I know another, and to know myself by means of knowing another, and vice versa."[55]

It would be wrong to infer from the above that, while reason needs society to perform its function, society endures on its own, independently from individual minds. Each society has an enormous stake in cultivating its members' rational faculties—suppress them, and it withers away along with the reasoning powers of individuals. Society is a perpetually renewed community of minds accomplished through the rational activities of individuals. The thesis of the inherent sociality of reason, consequently, requires a dialectical inversion: just as reason is social through and through, so is society permeated with reason. The individual is a responsible member of society to the extent that he acts rationally, and society is an objective and meaningful whole as long as its members share rationales for action. External and petrified as the social order may seem, it remains a product of ongoing rationalization at every moment of its existence. In the language of philosophical hermeneutics this proposition reads as follows: "What is rational is actual and what is actual is rational."[56] In the sociological parlance it can be stated this way: "Activity and mind, both in their content and in their mode of existence, are social: social activity and social mind."[57] Rendered freely, this means that society persists as long as it is projected into the meaningful actions of its members and ceases to exist as an objective whole when individuals deny its inherent rationality and refuse to abide by the a priori schemes of understanding in which it has been traditionally cast.

There is a body of opinion, both popular and scholarly, that depicts romantics as narcissistic, oblivious to the problems of community at large, antisocial in their basic impulses. This view is hopelessly one-sided. Much closer to the truth, I think, are those commentators who contend that "the longing for community is one of the most important themes in Romanticism,"[58] that "in every definite sense we can speak of this philosophy ... as one which is social in its character."[59] True, the romanticists are preoccupied with self-reflection and place an inordinate emphasis on subjectivity, but this romantic concern does not imply an asocial bias; if anything, it is due to the romanticists' acute sense of responsibility for the fate of the community and reflects their belief that the actions of the individual count. This goes not only for the champions of public causes such as Fichte, Hegel, and Marx, but also for the "archindividualists" like F. Schlegel, Kierkegaard, and Emerson. Even Max Stirner, the prophet of modern egoism, reserves his most eloquent rhetoric for the description of "union"—the future community of free spiritual beings. Concern for society is embedded in the romantic frame of mind. What is different about the romanticists' treatment of society and reason is the radical manner in which they welded the two into one continuum. The romanticists found the seeds of society at the nub of consciousness and discerned the imprint of reason on the fabric of the social order. They discovered a new domain—they called it "transcendental"—where reason and society meet, becoming one, a realm of what we now call values, the locus of which is intraindividual but the substance of which is extrapersonal and intersubjective. This is a paradoxical realm comprising all those prelogical and largely taken-for-granted categories in terms of which we make sense of the world and which tie us together into a community. Through this domain society enters the individual, leaving a deposit of rationality that makes man truly human. Both reason and society appear to be sui generis, yet neither can exist by itself, and each is inexorably tied to its other. The two grow together, sometimes locked in bitter dispute, sometimes peacefully coexistent, always mutually constitutive. This reasoning was a methodological expression of the romanticists' political ambivalence, of their desire to mediate between the conservative thesis and the radical antithesis. "Dialectical" and "mediatory" are virtually synonymous in romantic idealism.

The whole approach could be seen as a deft attempt to safeguard the emancipatory legacy of the French Revolution from its violent excesses by substituting hermeneutical philosophy for the shallow contractarianism of the Enlightenment. Rejecting the political ideology of the Left, the romanticists contended that human society is not a mechanical aggregate of individuals but an organic whole the members of which are bound together by a continuous thread of tradition, a way of thinking and feeling that is ingrained in every individual mind and that cannot be dislodged by revolutionary decrees. At the same time, they shunned the reactionary ideologies and urged the inevitability of social change, thereby serving notice on the ideologists of the old regime that the traditional ways of doing things cannot be petrified by the repressive measures any more than they can be legislated by the overzealous guardians of natural rights. An offshoot of this dual political agenda was the hermeneutically grounded social theory with its dialectical, mediatory stance and a characteristic emphasis on the organic nature of the relationship between reason and society, liberty and order, tradition and social change.

Romantic Organicism and the Hermeneutical Circle

In the Occidental tradition, society was often compared to an organism and treated as a whole which, as the saying goes, is always more than the sum of its parts. To be sure, the will of the individual was instrumental in setting society in motion, but once established, it was to persist as a collective body charged with ultimate power to coerce its members in the interests of the whole. From Plato and Aristotle, through Augustine and Aquinas, to Hobbes and Saint-Simon, this metaphor provided a guiding light to theorists searching for an ideal of social peace and harmony. The message it conveyed was a simple one: there would be no peace and harmony until individuals are subordinated to society, as parts of an organism are subordinated to the whole. A healthy society, as seen in this perspective, is the one that is insulated from the will of its individual members.

The image of organic society we find in romantic literature is of a strikingly different nature. The individual is cast here not only as an actor but also as an author, a self-conscious and critical being endowed with a right—and duty—to judge for himself the matters of state. A healthy society is not the one where the will of the individual is subordinated to the will of society, but where the will of the whole coincides with the will of the individual. The whole is more than the sum of its parts, romanticists concede, but it is also less than any of its individual members. For the human individual is a social being, "he belongs to more than one world ... traverses many systems and encircles many a sun."[60] He is "the living species," the knower and the subject who "treats himself as a universal and therefore free being";[61] "to him his species, his essential nature, and not merely his individuality, is an object of thought."[62] To cast him as a part indifferent to the whole is therefore to deprive the individual of his true dignity. The organic analogy thus loses much of its customary biological connotation, becoming more akin to the metaphor of the micro- and macrocosm: "The individual lives in the whole, the whole in the individual.... Society is nothing but social life: an invisible, thinking, and feeling person. Each man is a small society."[63] "Man is no abstract being squatting outside the world. Man is the world of man, the state, society.... Man, much as he may therefore be a *particular* individual, ... is just as much a *totality*—the ideal society—the subjective existence of thought and experienced society for itself.[64]

The thing that strikes one most about these creedal statements of romantic organicism is their circular character: the whole is looked at here through the prism of its parts, while the properties of the part are explicated through the whole. The circle involved in this reasoning is not vicious, nor is it unintended. It can be understood as a special case of what Schelling called "the circle of knowledge," or what is now better known under the name popularized by Schleiermacher as "the hermeneutical circle." The term refers to a circular path the mind is forced to travel in pursuit of meaning. Thus the exact sense of a word becomes clear to an interpreter through its context; the meaning of a sentence transpires in reference to the whole text; the text is understood when the author's intent and a priori assumptions come to the fore, which, in turn, presuppose the knowledge of a school of thought and a cultural tradition that shaped the author's imagination.

To comprehend the total cultural context, we have to travel in the opposite direction, starting with the larger whole and making our way to the individual parts. The understanding en route to full knowledge of the objects invested with meaning henceforth travels in circles: "Complete knowledge always involves an apparent circle that each part can be understood only out of the whole to which it belongs, and vice versa. All knowledge that is scientific must be constructed in this way."[65] Schleiermacher did not explore the implications of this principle for the study of society, nor did his sociologically minded contemporaries draw on his hermeneutical writings. Still, we can say with confidence that Schleiermacher's theory of the hermeneutical circle and romantic sociology share a common heritage of transcendental idealism and help illuminate each other. The principle of the hermeneutical circle, Schleiermacher contends, covers all forms of intercourse, past and present, where people make sense, exchange meaning, and produce order out of seemingly incongruous individual acts. Social intercourse, as seen in this perspective, is the hermeneutical process whereby individuals achieve a sense of the whole and generate the universe of meaning intelligible to every participant.

By the same token, society is a universe of discourse. The term "universe"—literally, one verse—favored by the romantic thinkers is very indicative in this respect: it hints at the Logos, the Word that unites disparate individuals into a social whole. To be grasped hermeneutically, this whole must be "lived through [erlebt] and not just apprehended and explained [erkannt und erlernt]"; it must be studied by the knower with "a feeling for value and meaning."[66] The hermeneutical scholar appropriates as his own the universe of meaning generated by others. He learns to discern the meaningful actions of individuals behind the most rigid institutions of the state. Cut down to size by his interpretative gaze, the state will no longer awe him with its Leviathanic vastness—he will see it as a living reality. Society will unfold before his eyes as a process of articulation in the course of which individuals grasp their identities as members of the same universe of meaning. The successive generations of individuals partake in this process, bound by a common heritage of language and meaning, yet never failing to leave a mark on it. While they continue to rely on customary terms and apply time-honored nomenclatures, society persists as a pattern or structure with all the appearance of an eternal thing-in-itself. This is just an appearance, however. Society's customary being is routine, not extemporaneous; it is perpetuated by the participants who are not bound irrevocably to the terms of their discourse. New nomenclatures are devised and brought to bear on the familiar situations, assuring the flow of change. And so we can say with the romantic thinkers that "just as society produces man as man, so is society produced by him."[67]

If there is a single ideological imperative underlying the circular mold of romantic thought, it is the determination to place the individual and society on equal footing. Behind the organic imagery of romantic social theory one senses the craving for freedom qualified by responsibility, the longing for continuity punctuated by change. Man-the-microcosm, the part coequal to the whole, the species being—these romantic idioms bear the markings of the postrevolutionary era. It reflects the sentiment of those who rejected the arrogance of revolutionaries determined to impose their will on society, and yet refused to endorse the self-serving ideology of reactionaries forever bent on stalling social change. The language of romanticism confers on the individual a crushing responsibility for the well-being of the whole society. At the same time, it stipulates that man's liberty is contingent on his ability to embrace the whole, to incorporate its ways into his self. In choosing this language, the romanticists consciously break with the classical dichotomy of the individual and society, for which they substitute a dialectical view that posits the two as a thesis and antithesis, as aspects of the same process of production of social reality. The species being celebrated by the romanticists is a conscious being, willingly submitting to the necessity of law, and not just because this law is ordained and enforced by an external authority but because it stands to reason. He accepts the law as a moral imperative which he legislates for himself. A sovereign and citizen at the same time, he is, above all, a self, a subjective being of society conscious of itself: "...The Romantic philosophy pointed out that the self, while it arises in the social experience, also carries with it the very unity that makes society possible ... that society is nothing but an organization of selves."[68]

Gemeinschaft as an Ideal of Free Discourse

The image of *Gemeinschaft* formed in many a head by the prolific literature on the subject is that of a community of individuals bound together by personal, emotional ties, going leisurely about the business of life, insulated from the hustle and bustle of industrial civilization, and generally antithetical to the spirit of modernity. The impression of an antimodernist bias is exacerbated by the medieval symbolism that sometimes crops up in the rhetoric of *Gemeinschaft*. Contrasted to the latter is the image of an impersonal, money-bound, legalistic *Gesellschaft* symbolizing the modern way of life. The final conclusion seems inevitable: one is dealing with a solidly conservative idea, masquerading as a historical description but intended chiefly as ideological ammunition against the forces of modernity and social change. This common view, much of which originates in neoromantic literature, does not withstand a critical examination.

That the romanticists spoke in hostile terms about the age of the machine, despised utilitarianism, and scorned bourgeois philistinism is the fact. It is also true that they praised the virtues of medieval culture and bemoaned the passing of the organic state. It is emphatically not true that the romanticists entertained serious hopes for the revival of medieval institutions, or that they rejected modernity as such. The romantic notion of *Gemeinschaft* was a normative construct whose critical edge was directed against the reified conditions of modern life. The unfolding of bourgeois society accorded ill with romantic ideals, and as the gulf between these ideals and bureaucratic realities widened, the romanticists did not hesitate to denounce what they perceived to be a perversion of social intercourse. The romantic idealists longed for a social order that would be neither bourgeois nor feudal. Their views were anti-capitalist, insofar as the capitalism of the time was synonymous with the degradation of human conditions, but they were also anti-authoritarian and therefore inimical to the spirit of the Middle Ages. Their mistrust of industrialism and capitalism did not blind them to the emancipatory potential of the machine. And their contempt for bourgeois philistinism was more than offset by their deep respect for the freedoms of conscience and religion that were bourgeois to the core. Call them utopian, idealistic, romantic, if you will, but not reactionary. Even the label "conservative" does not fully apply to the proponents of *Gemeinschaft*, whose commitment to the ideal of a free discourse where everybody has a say was nothing short of revolutionary, and whose target—bureaucratic ossification—was as sure a sign of modernity as the anti-statist strictures of Marx and Weber.

The reification of the state was the main target of the romantic critique in the 1830s and 1840s. So strong was the anti-state sentiment in this period that it is sometimes taken as a sign of a break between the first and second generations of romanticists. This split is largely apparent. All romanticists were propelled by the same longing for an organic relation between man and society. The romanticists of the 1840s turned against the state only after their hopes for its imminent transformation into an organic whole were dashed. The iconoclastic attitude toward the state and bureaucracy, common among the romanticists of the second generation, was already evident in early romantics who lived long enough to witness the distortion of their ideal of the organic whole in the Napoleonic and Prussian states. As early as 1823 Schlegel lamented that the modern state resembles "an all-directing and all-ruling law machine—and decree factory—whose sovereign power should subjugate all things divine and human..."[69] An echo of these jeremiads can be heard in Marx's attack on "the spirit of the bureaucracy" permeating modern society, Stirner's philippics against the state as a "true personality" more real than the individual, as well as in the antiestablishment declarations of Emerson. The target of this criticism was not so much the state as the stifling effect of the bureaucratic social order on the individual. A specimen, a member of a class, modern man seemed to the romanticists of the second generation a bitter caricature of the image of "the living species" they cherished so much: "The individuals have only the value of specimens of the same species or genus ... what you are ... as a unique person must be—suppressed.[70] "The individuals of a class [exist] only as average individuals, only in so far as they lived within the conditions of existence of their class—a relationship in which they participate not as individuals but as members of a class.[71] "Our age has forsaken the individuals.... There are no more individuals but only specimens.... Man's kinship with deity [is forgotten]."[72]

Underlying all these lamentations is a theme that has become closely associated with romantic thought—the theme of alienation and reification. Reification is a pathological symptom of the modern age, a state in which society appears to its members as a noumenon, an external and coercive entity, and not as a living whole responsive to its members' needs and wishes. The state confronts one here as an omnipotent being to be revered, obeyed, and feared by mere mortals. In this reified conditions, free discourse is greatly impeded: it grows compulsive, is marred by deep enmity between the participants, and is subject to frequent breakdowns. The individual is forced to take part in this discourse against his will, producing sense that makes little sense to him personally, generating a reality he experiences as a threat. Alienated from his universal essence, he is reduced to a cog in a superhuman machine. Life, reason, power—everything that belongs to the individual—is delegated to this lifeless automaton that hovers in the Platonic realm of everlasting beings, exhorting men to selfless efforts on its behalf. The root of the modern predicament, as romanticists saw it, is reason's unreflexivity, the fact that "we first share the life by which things exist and afterwards see them as appearances in nature and forget that we have shared their causes."[73] The weight of social facts, magnified by the power of tradition, prevents the individual from seeing his own imprint on the way things are. To challenge the reality of social facts, he would have to question the rationality and good judgment of other beings with whom he partakes in the same social intercourse. The wider the social discourse and the community of assumptions behind it, the more thinglike the social reality and the greater the fear of committing *lapsus judicii*. No wonder "mankind is shy of self-analysis, and many people tremble slavishly when they can no longer dodge the question ... what they have become, and who they really are.... The spell of life and of the world is upon them."[74]

It is against the backdrop of this heartless world that we should judge the ideal of an organic community, whose roots the romanticists sought in the past but whose full realization they tied to the future. The term *Gemeinschaft* did not yet acquire its common meaning, but the vision of a harmonious community it had come to signify was already in place.

Fichte called it "the universal commonwealth," Schleiermacher "the community of free spiritual beings," Müller "an organic state," Marx "communism," Stirner "union," Thoreau "perfect and glorious state," Emerson "a nation of men unanimously bent on freedom." Differing in a number of important respects, the authors of these projects agreed on one key point: the society of the future should be a universal community, an ever-expanding universe of discourse that exists for its own sake, excludes no one, and draws every human being in its orbit. The foundation of this social order is not a social contract of the *philosophes* "but an ever-originating Social Contract," an alliance that is "perpetually and at every moment renewed and thereby reestablished through new freedoms that spring to life along the old ones."[75] "It is not another State ... that men aim at, but their Union, this ever-fluid uniting of everything standing ... *intercourse* or *union*."[76] The new social order creates "the real basis for rendering it impossible that anything should exist independently of individuals, in so far as things are only a product of the preceding intercourse of individuals themselves."[77]

How can this ideal be realized? A basic premise of romantic hermeneutics—reason is social, society is rational—suggest an answer. If it is true that reified social institutions are nothing but "thoughts [that] had become corporeal on their own account," that the state is "a fixed idea ... that has subjected man to itself,"[78] then to bring down ossified social reality reason must recognize its involvement in the objectivity of the social world—it must become self-reflexive. The knower conquers the Leviathan of the state when he appropriates social reality as his own and refuses to identify himself with it. The species being, a subjective being of society conscious of itself, man only needs to alter his self-consciousness to bring about changes in society: "The idols exist through me; I need only refrain from creating them anew, then they exist no longer."[79] The foremost task of the day is "self-examination: becoming conscious of oneself, not as individuals but as mankind."[80] This task of critical self-reflection is first accomplished by a great man. A seer, a prophet, a rebel—a great man is always an individual who manages before others to break the spell of oppressive social reality. What distinguishes him from other disaffected individuals is his ability to penetrate the sacred domain of the transcendental a priori, to cast a shadow on the taken-for-granted rationality of a tradition, to effect the "transvaluation of all values."[81] The romantic hero is a virtuoso of self-reflection and self-transcendence. He does not merely forecast the future—he casts the future by casting doubt on reified realities, recasting old schemes of thought, and broadcasting the new ones. Single-handedly he can supply the verses for the future universe of discourse: "The given actuality has completely lost its validity [for him]; it has become for him an imperfect form which everywhere constrains.... [He] has advanced beyond the reach of his age and opened a front against it."[82] His task is not fully accomplished until he is joined by others, that is, until the awakening from the dogmatic slumber spreads throughout society. That is when self-reflection and self-change translate into revolutionary change, when "the coincidence of the changing of circumstances and of human activity or self-changing [transpires] as *revolutionary practice*."[83] A genuine revolution is a crisis of objectivity on a mass-scale, a practical accomplishment of an army of alienated human beings, refusing to subsume themselves under the customary classifications and to lend their faces to dramatizing the familiar social reality as objective and meaningful. Revolutionary labor denaturalizes the social order, converts things in themselves back into concrete historical phenomena, and it accomplishes this feat not through physical force but through the power of reason.

It is striking how thoroughly convinced the romantic idealists were in the peaceful nature of their endeavor. The most hot-headed of them were at pains to emphasize the peaceful character of their revolution. The radical transformation of society, insisted Marx while he was still under the sway of romantic idealism, involves nothing else but the

> reform of consciousness, [which] consists solely in letting the world perceive its own consciousness by awakening it from dreaming about itself, in explaining to it its own actions.... Reform of consciousness not through dogmas, but through analysis of mystical consciousness that is not clear to itself.... Self-understanding ... is the task for the world and for us. It can only be the result of united forces. What is at stake is a confession, nothing more. To get its sins forgiven, humanity only needs to describe them as they are.[84]

Just that—the confession and the reform of consciousness—and the whole of society will be transformed, as if by magic, into something more rational and infinitely more humane. Thoreau and Emerson could not agree more. "Peaceable revolution" is the term Thoreau aptly used to describe the revolt of reason against society that has become impervious to the wishes of its members ("civil disobedience" is its other, more familiar name). "In fact, I quietly declare war with the state, after my fashion.... I simply wish to refuse allegiance to the state, to withdraw and stand aloof from it effectually."[85] In the language of Emerson, one should be a "nonconformist" in order to effect social change, that is, one must stop "conforming to usages that have become dead to you," refuse to play the "game of conformity."[86] For Kierkegaard, revolution is also chiefly an affair of the mind; it is begun by an ironist, a master of self-transcendence, who endeavors to throw off "the weight of objectivity" and destroy "the actuality he hostilely opposes"; his role is "prophetic ... for he constantly points to something future," but he cannot achieve his task of tearing down the obsolete actuality alone; this is the task for a people.[87] Of all the romantics, Stirner takes perhaps the most radical scalpel to the reified social institutions, vowing to destroy "fixed ideas" whatever form they take—"people," "party," "society" itself. Radical as his ends are, Stirner is convinced, they can be achieved by the same "peaceable" means of self-awakening and self-transcendence: "...'Higher powers' exist only through my exalting them and abasing myself.... All slaves become free men as soon as they no longer respect their master as master."[88]

With all their iconoclasm and extremism, spurred by the upsurge of public discontent in the 1830s and 1840s, the late romantic thinkers remained true to the spirit of idealism, sharing their predecessors' belief in the constitutive power of reason, man's potential for self-renewal, and the possibility of evolutionary change. Behind their rhetoric we find the same abhorrence of revolutionary violence and desire to transform the world peacefully that informed the political sensibilities of early romantics who suffered the trauma of the Terror. The image of "true *Gemeinschaft*" was a guiding light in the romanticists' quest for a society that makes violence and compulsion obsolete in all its forms, and it is this quest that led them to rediscover the value of tradition and social order. Far from being an expression of the reactionary ideology of the forces defeated in the French Revolution and marching crabwise into the future, the notion of *Gemeinschaft* was an attempt at creative reappraisal of the past with an eye to securing the emancipatory goals of the future. Reflecting the romanticists' unshakable conviction in the dignity of man, these goals were as modern, as the means of furthering them were peaceful and idealistic. All reason had to do to secure its ends was to realize its constitutive power and break the veil of facticity surrounding obsolete social institutions. The battle for the community of the future had to be fought and won not on the barricades but in the minds of individuals. Ultimately, it was to be a battle of reason against itself, "the battle of reason ... to break the rigidity to which understanding has reduced everything."[89]

The romantic quest for an organic community brings into clear relief what Ricoeur calls the "double edge" of hermeneutics: its penchant for suspicion and its longing for certitude.[90] It also brings to the fore a quixotic, utopian element in romantic hermeneutics, manifested in its proponents' reliance on reason as a sole means of social reconstruction. The romanticists vastly underestimated the resilience of the bureaucratic state and the readiness of the extant powers to heed the demands of reason. Their confidence in the ability of all people, regardless of class, culture, and ethnic heritage, to come together on ideologically neutral grounds of reason was badly shattered by the flow of history. The logistics of awakening and self-transcendence proved to be far more complex than their optimistic declarations implied. And when the revolutionary tide of the 1840s subsided without bringing down the much-despised institutions, romantic thought was bound to plunge into a crisis. The decline of romanticism in the mid-nineteenth century was in large measure a product of a disillusionment in the efficacy of idealism as a means of social reconstruction. The mood of hopelessness and despair palpable everywhere in Europe at this time accelerated the dissolution of romanticism, which, in the second half of the nineteenth century, broke into several divergent, ideologically incompatible currents of thought. Marx's historical materialism, Morris's guild socialism, and Bakunin's anarchism represented the movement to the left from the romantic center; the *völkish* mysticism and racial theories of Lagarde, Langbehn, and List reflected the parallel movement to the right. The materialist, urban, and internationalist views of the former contrasted with the conservative, nationalist, and militantly anti-modernist leanings of the latter. Both the left- and right-wing successors of the romantic movement turned away from the mediatory proclivities of romantic hermeneutics, embracing the spirit of partisanship and showing an increasing readiness to employ violence as a vehicle of social change. And the heritage of romantic hermeneutics? It received a new lease on life in the late nineteenth and early twentieth centuries, thanks to the efforts of Wilhelm Dilthey and a brilliant pleiade of his German and American disciples who resurrected the measured spirit of romantic idealism in the tradition of interpretative social science.

Romanticism and Early-Twentieth Century Interpretative Sociology

The impact of romantic ideas on modern social thought was facilitated by the revival of interest in transcendental idealism, which shaped much of the intellectual landscape in the late nineteenth and early twentieth centuries, in both Europe and the United States. This impact was felt most immediately in the program of cultural studies initiated by Dilthey and popularized by Windelband, Rickert, Simmel, and Max Weber. It is also clearly discernible in early American sociology, which derived its inspiration at least in part from its German counterpart. "The purest vein of Romanticism in American sociology," points out Gouldner, "is ... to be found in the 'Chicago School,' which had the most concentrated exposure to the German tradition and was, in fact, established by many (A. W. Small, W. Y. Thomas, and R. E. Park) who were directly trained in it."[91] We may add to this that Mead, a life-long student of romantic philosophy, was exposed to Dilthey while studying in Germany and at one time contemplated writing a dissertation under his guidance, while Cooley, himself not a Chicagoan but a figure influential among the Chicago interactionists, was a strong advocate of "sympathetic under-standing"—a procedure resembling the method of *Verstehen*.

The proponents of cultural science and social interactionism shared ground with a contemporaneous current of thought sometimes referred to as neoromanticism.[92] Neoromanticism was particularly strong in Germany, although some elements of it can be detected in the Populist and the Progressive movement in the United States. Its distinguishing characteristics included a keen concern for the ossifying propensities of bureaucratic rationalization, the aversion to rationalism and dualism, and a strong interest in romantic organicism, all of which contributed to the makings of interpretative sociology. The affinity between the two was only partial, however, as the interpretative thinkers refused to endorse the irrationalism and anti-modernism that became the mainstream of neo-romanticism in this century, remaining closely attuned to the mediatory spirit of romantic idealism. Dilthey credited Schleiermacher's herme-neutics as an inspiration for his own cultural studies. Simmel quoted extensively and approvingly from the romantic sources and traced his notion of "qualitative individuality" to the romantic premise that the in-dividual is "a 'compendium' of mankind." Rickert repeatedly stressed that cultural sciences derived their concepts from the German idealist philosophers. Weber endorsed romantic epistemology in his theory of ideal type. And Mead credited romantic idealists with the pioneering insight into the dialectic of self and other.

Philosophically, interpretative sociology can be seen as a systematic application of romantic idealism to social reality. The very form of Simmel's famous query "How is society possible?" reminds us of Kant's "How is nature possible?" His answer, inspired by transcen-dentalist philosophy, was that the objective structure of the social world is isomorphous with, and incomprehensible without, the a priori forms of the mind, although in the case of social reality the mind in question is not just that of an external observer, of a sociologist, but the mind of historical individuals comprising a given society. In Simmel's words, "Societal unification needs no factors outside its own component elements, the individuals.... The unity of society is directly realized by its own elements because these elements are themselves conscious and synthesizing units."[92] The object of interpretative social science is "the mind-constructed world" or social reality insofar as it is brought into existence through the constitutive work of individuals generating the social world with an aid of their taken-for-granted beliefs. This object calls for a special method of inquiry, the method of *Verstehen*, which is rooted in the assumption that "knowledge of *cultural* events is inconceivable except on a basis of the *significance* which the concrete constellations of reality have for us in certain concrete individual situations."[93] The American interactionists sounded a similar note when they contended that a key question for a sociologist studying human behavior—"What does it mean?"—can be answered only through "an imaginary reconstruction of life,"[94] that sociologists should not "follow ... uncritically the example of the physical sciences, [for] while the effect of a physical phenomenon depends exclusively on the objective nature of this phenomenon ... the effect of the social phenomenon depends in addition on the subjective standpoint taken by the individual or the group..."[95]

The interpretative approach follows the hermeneutical thesis according to which the whole must be understood in terms of its individual parts, individual parts in terms of the whole. Like their romantic predecessors, the interpretative thinkers sought to bring into one continuum mind, self, and society, to posit the historical human being as a product and producer of society, to grasp society as social intercourse or a universe of discourse. Following the principles of romantic hermeneutics, the interpretative thinkers shifted the focus of sociological inquiry from the macro- to the microsocial phenomena. They did not thereby abandon the study of macro-social formations, as Weber's analysis of Western capitalism readily testifies; they simply endeavored to telescope these into the meaningful actions of individuals:

> Such concepts as 'state,' 'association,' 'feudalism,' and the like designate certain categories of human actions. Hence it is the task of sociology to reduce those concepts to 'understandable' action, that is, without exception to the actions of participating individual men.[96]

Society is certainly not a substance, nothing concrete but an *event* ... The relation between society and the individual is an organic relation.... The mind is social ... society is mental ... society and the mind are aspects of the same whole...[97]

Given these conceptual parallels, one should not be surprised to find an ideological affinity between the proponents of interpretative social science and their romantic predecessors. The mediatory spirit of romantic hermeneutics permeates the entire edifice of interpretative and interactionist thought. It is evident in Weber's rejection of the "ethics of ultimate ends" with its belief in the efficacy of the last violent deed and his undivided commitment to the "ethics of responsibility." It bulks large in Dewey's ethics of means and his crusade on behalf of "great community." It shows in Simmel's criticism of "negative freedom," and Mead's advocacy of "international mindedness." Inherent in these thinkers' ideological stance is longing for social change free of violence and revolutionary upheavals, a desire to undermine the political appeal of the Right and the Left that was on the rise at the time in both the Old and the New Worlds. We may recall that the principle task of the *Verein für Sozialpolitik* which had the backing of the interpretative thinkers in Germany was "to achieve by more conservative means the social justice at which the Marxists aimed..."[98] The same desire to rectify the injustices endemic to laissez faire liberalism informs the progressive agenda of American interactionists. To combat the ills of modernity, the latter resorted to the familiar tactic of juxtaposing the idealized past to the conditions of the present. The community of the past they chose as a point of reference was, of course, not the medieval social order, but the native, rural, Jeffersonian community, yet the virtues they ascribed to it—liberty, participation, cooperation—were the romantic virtues of free discourse, of *Gemeinschaft*. German interpretative thinkers were less apt to invoke the vision of the golden past as an antidote to the wretched conditions of the present (in part because of the indiscriminate use made of it by the neoromantics), but their critique of the "iron cage" of modern bureaucratic civilization had more than a tinge of nostalgia for the bygone era of the true *Gemeinschaft*.

Whatever the differences, it was clearly the ideal of free discourse that inspired the political imagination of interpretative thinkers on the Continent and in the United States. What these authors strained to assert is that, however alienated the social intercourse, it is still our discourse, and it is up to us, the participants in this discourse, to change its course and to transform it into a truly "'universal' discourse." We can do so, the interpretative thinkers believed, and we can do so without recourse to violence, by subjecting to critical examination the rational grounds of our discourse, by reevaluating the old values, and supplanting them with the new and more rational ones.

Two sum up, early twentieth-century interpretative sociology was an attempt to extend the principles of romantic hermeneutics to the entire domain of the social sciences. Its object was the production of social reality as objective and meaningful; its major premise—the interdeterinination of reason and society; its methodological tool—interpretative understanding; and its ideal—free discourse. With this shift in perspective, the focus of sociological analysis became microscopic, not in the sense that society as a whole moved out of the reach of interpretative thinkers, but in the sense that the whole of society was to be systematically translated into the predicative activities and rational schemes of understanding employed by its members. A priori categories and values are the means of production of social reality as objective and meaningful; using them skillfully and knowledgeably, members of society impart rational-logical qualities to reality, wade through the uncertainties of daily life, confer on each other social status, and in the process of doing so perpetuate the social order. To the participants of social intercourse this order appears as a thing in itself, a superhuman entity beyond their control and power. But this is only an appearance. With all its rigidities and inequities, the social order is a product of human intercourse which produces individuals as historical individuals at the same time that it is produced by them as the historical universe of discourse. The structure of the social order is periodically exploded by prophets and charismatic leaders whose reflexive power lifts the veils thrown over the transcendental domain of a priori beliefs and values and forces humans to realize their responsibility for the way things are. The task of interpretative sociology is to aid in this process of demystification. But since this process never ends—bringing down old reifications clears the way for the new ones—the task of interpretative sociology is a never-ending one. That is to say, demystification is a Sisyphean labor that must begin anew the moment it is completed, and so the task of hermeneutically grounded social-science is to ensure that this transcendence remains an ongoing endeavor.

There is a characteristic fusion of the normative and the descriptive endemic to the project of sociological hermeneutics and manifested in its idealistic approach that first imputes a "true" essence to the individual and society and then proceeds to demonstrate how this essence, perverted in the existent reality, can be recovered through self-conscious efforts of individuals. The individual, according to this mode of reasoning, is a species being, albeit reduced to a specimen; society is discourse, albeit reified and compulsive. What is, is judged here by the standards of what ought to be, and what ought to be, is proffered as an ideal that is bound to come about when humans begin to live up to their true essence. This fusion of the normative and the descriptive is the legacy of transcendental idealism, the legacy inherited by twentieth-century interpretative thinkers and amply manifested in their abhorrence of violence, commitment to liberty and order, and a penchant for political mediation and meliorism. The interpretative thinkers did not abandon their trust in reason and peaceful means of social reconstruction when revolutions swept over Europe and violence seemed the only solution to the vexing problems of modernity. We have every reason to call this thinking "utopian" in the sense in which the term was used by Mannheim, but it is hard to deny its humanism or its relevance to contemporary political discourse. The hermeneutical perspective on society as a universe of discourse perpe-tuated by self-conscious individuals reflects the profound trust in the freedom and dignity of man. It is an outlook whose humanistic values are shared today by those who believe in the possibility of a community that combines unity and diversity.

It is also an outlook that is flawed by certain biases, a perspective with blind spots of its own. If the social process is fundamentally a process of production of social reality as objective and meaningful, as interpretative sociologists imply, then the questions to ponder are: What are the means of production of social reality as objective and meaningful? Who controls these means of production? How is the participation in social discourse affected by one's status and class? How is the process of universalization and generation structured? Which are the historically specific modes of production of social reality as objective and meaningful? All these ques-tions are of paramount sociological importance. The failure to meet them head-on typical of much of interpretative sociology makes it vulnerable to the charges of astructural and conservative bias.

Is this failure a legacy of romantic idealism? That the idealistic ten-dency to exaggerate the claims of reason, to mix the real with the ideal, and to treat the subject of the historical process as a unitary phenomenon might have contributed to it seems undeniable. That hermeneutically grounded social theory is inherently incapable of answering these perti-nent sociological questions is far from certain. A reexamination of Marx's romantic heritage now under way suggest that romantic hermeneutics is not incompatible with class analysis.[99] The current debate about Lukács' romantic period also points in this direction.[100] Anthony Giddens' work is one more example of recent attempts to combine structural and hermeneutical analysis.[101] It is too early to tell whether these efforts will bear fruit. One thing is clear, however: if interpretative sociology is to succeed as a full-fledged sociological theory it has to address these questions directly, that is, it has to deal with issues of inequality and exploitation, and it has to maintain a fruitful dialogue with alternative sociological perspectives.

Notes

1. Alvin W. Gouldner, *For Sociology: Renewal and Criticism in Sociology* (New York: Basic Books, 1974), p. 336.
2. Hans-Georg Gadamer, *Philosophical Hermeneutics* (Berkeley: University of California Press, 1976), pp. 46, 21.
3. The history of this controversy is reviewed in Rene Wellek, *Concepts of Criticism* (New Haven, CT: Yale University Press, 1963), and Lilian R. Furst, *Romanticism* (London: Methuen, 1969). The best substantive discussion is still Jacques Barzun's *Classic, Romantic, and Modern* (New York: Anchor Books, 1961).
4. A.O. Lovejoy, "On the Discrimination of Romanticisms," in *English Romantic Poets: Modern Essays in Criticism* (New York: Oxford University Press, 1960), p. 6.
5. Ibid.
6. Gouldner, *For Sociology*, p. 336.
7. Barzun, *Classic*, p. 8.
8. Ibid.
9. Morse Peckham, "On Romanticism," *Studies in Romanticism* 9 (1970): 218.
10. Gouldner, *For Sociology*, p. 339; see also *The Two Marxisms* (New York: Oxford University Press, 1980), p. 192.
11. Isaiah Berlin, "Preface," in H. G. Schenk, *The Mind of the European Romantics* (New York: Anchor Books, 1969), p. xv.
12. Schenk, *Mind*, p. 10.
13. Ibid., p. 10.
14. Alfred N. Whitehead, *Science and the Modern World* (Middlesex: Penguin Books, 1938), p. 115.
15. M. R. Higonnet, "Organic Unity and Interpretative Boundaries: Friedrich Schlegel's Theories and Their Application in His Critique of Lessing," *Studies in Romanticism* 19 (1980): 164.
16. Friedrich Schlegel, *Friedrich Schlegel's Lucinde and the Fragments* (Minneapolis: University of Minnesota Press, 1971), p. 190.
17. "Fichtean Baggesen Antwort, April, 1795," in *Johann Gottlieb Fichte Briefwechsel* (Leipzig: Haesselverlag, 1925), pp. 449-450.
18. William Wordsworth, "A Letter to the Bishop of Landoff, 1793," in *The Prose Works of William Wordsworth* (Oxford: Clarendon Press), 3: 46.
19. William Wordsworth, "Letter to a Friend, 1821," in *The Prose Works*, 3: 269.
20. Georg Lukács, *Goethe and His Age* (New York: Grosset & Dunlap, 1969); Alfred Cobban, *Aspects of the French Revolution* (New York: W. W. Norton, 1968), p. 26;

Irving M. Zeitlin, *Ideology arid the Development of Sociological Theory* (Englewood Cliffs, N.J.: Prentice-Hall, 1968), p. 39; Goetz A. Briefs, "The Economic Philosophy of Romanticism," *Journal of the History of Ideas* 2 (1941): 279.

21. Karl Mannheim, "Conservatism," in *From Karl Mannheim* (New York: Oxford University Press, 1971), p. 153.
22. Ibid., pp. 167, 139.
23. Steven Seidman, *Liberalism and the Origin of European Social Theory* (Berkeley: University of California Press, 1983), p. 101.
24. George H. Mead, *Movements of Thought in the Nineteenth Century* (Chicago: University of Chicago Press, 1936), p. 64. On the interfaces of Mead and romanticism, see Dmitri N. Shalin, "The Romantic Antecedents of Meadian Social Psychology," *Symbolic Interaction* 7 (1984): 43-65.
25. J. Zipes, "The Revolutionary Rise of the Romantic Fairy Tale in Germany," *Studies in Romanticism* 16 (1977): 450.
26. Henri Brunschwig, *Enlightenment and Romanticism in Eighteenth Century Prussia* (Chicago: University of Chicago Press, 1974), p. 183.
27. Gouldner, *For Sociology*, p. 324.
28. Michael Lowy, *Georg Lukács. From Romanticism to Bolshevism* (Thetford: Lowe & Brydon Printers, 1976), p. 46.
29. F. W. J. Schelling, *Vom Ich als Prinzip der Philosophie* (1795) (Leipzig: Verlag von Felix Meiner, 1911), p. 29.
30. G.W. F. Hegel, "The German Constitution" (1779-1802), in *Hegel's Political Writings* (Oxford: Clarendon Press, 1964), p. 234.
31. G. W. F. Hegel, *Hegel's Philosophy of Right* (1821) (London: Oxford University Press. 1977), p. 133.
32. J. G. Fichte, "The Vocation of the Scholar" (1794), in *The Popular Works of Johann Gottlieb Fichte* (London: Trubner, 1889), 1: 179.
33. Zipes, "Revolutionary Rise," p. 421.
34. Talmon, *Romanticism*, p. 136.
35. Whitehead, *Science*, p. 115.
36. Hans-Georg Gadamer, *Truth and Method* (New York: Crossroad, 1982), p. 244.
37. Immanuel Kant, *Critique of Pure Reason* (1781) (New York: Anchor, 1966), p. xxxix.
38. Gadamer, *Truth and Method*, p. 239.
39. Wilhelm Dilthey, *Selected Writings* (London: Cambridge University Press, 1976), p. 258.
40. Paul Ricoeur, *The Philosophy of Paul Ricoeur* (Boston: Beacon Press, 1978), p. 221.
41. Kant, *Critique of Pure Reason*, p. xxiv.
42. G.W. F. Hegel, *The Phenomenology of Mind* (1807) (New York: Harper & Row, 1967), p. 99.
43. J. 0. Fichte, *Science of Knowledge* (1794) (New York: Appleton, 1970), p. 161.
44. Karl Marx, "Letter to Arnold Ruge, September 1843," in Robert C. Tucker, ed., *The Marx-Engels Reader* (New York: W. W. Norton, 1972), p. 8.
45. F. W. J. Schelling, *System of Transcendental Idealism* (1800) (Charlottesville: University of Virginia Press, 1978), p. 1.
46. S. Kierkegaard, *Concluding Unscientific Postscript* (1846) (Princeton, NJ: Princeton University Press, 1941), p. 35.
47. Josiah Royce, *Lectures on Modern Idealism* (New Haven, CT: Yale University Press, 1919), p. 65.
48. S. Kierkegaard, *The Journals of Kierhegaard* (New York: Harper & Row, 1959), p. 45

49. Schlegel, *Friedrich Schlegel's Lucinde*, p. 268.
50. Heinrick Rickert, *Science and History: A Critique if Positivist Epistemology* (1902) (New York: D. Van Nostrand Co., 1962), p. 102.
51. Karl Marx, "A Correspondence of 1843." In *Karl Marx: Ealy Texts* (New York: Harper R. Row, 1972), p.82.
52. Quoted in *Kluckhohn, Personlichkeit und Gemeinschaft: Studien zur Staats Auffassung der Deutschen Romantik* (Halle/Saale: M. Niemeyer Verlag, 1925), p. 5.
53. Immanuel Kant, *Critique of Judgment* (1790) (New York: Bobbs-Merrill, 1951), p. 137.
54. Hegel, *Phenomenology*, pp. 661, 229.
55. S. T. Coleridge, quoted in K. Coburn, *The Self-Conscious Imagination* (London: Oxford University Press, 1974), p. 32.
56. Hegel, *Philosophy of Right*, p. 10.
57. Karl Marx, *Economic and Philosophic Manuscripts of 1844* (New York: International Publishers, 1964), p. 138.
58. H. Staten, "Newman on Self and Society," *Studies in Romanticism* 18 (1979): 69.
59. Mead, *Movements of Thought*, p. 147.
60. F. D. E. Schleiermacher, *Schleiermacher's Soliloquies* (1800) (Chicago: Open Court, 1957), p. 47.
61. Marx, *Economic and Philosophic Manuscripts*, p. 112.
62. P. J. A. von Feuerbach, *The Essence of Christianity* (1841) (New York: Harper & Row. 1957), p. 2.
63. Novalis, *Schriften: Das Philosophische Werke* (Stuttgart: W. Kohlhammer Verlag, 1960), p. 66.
64. Karl Marx, *Critique of Hegel's Philosophy of Right* (Cambridge: Cambridge University Press, 1967), p. 131; *Economic and Philosophic Manuscripts*, p. 138.
65. F. D. E. Schleiermacher, *Hermeneutics: The Handwritten Manuscripts* (1805-33) (Missoula, MT: Scholars Press, 1977), p. 42.
66. Adam H. Muller, *Die Elemente der Staatskunst* (1809) (Jena: Verlag von Gustav Fischer, 1922). p. 16.
67. Marx, *Economic and Philosophic Manuscripts*, p. 137.
68. Mead, *Movements of Thought*, pp. 125, 101.
69. Quoted in H. G. Schenk, "Leviathan and the European Romantics," *Cambridge Journal* 1 (1948): 247.
70. Max Stirner, *The Ego and His Own* (1845) (New York: Harper & Row, 1971), p. 215.
71. Kark Marx, *The German Ideology* (New York: International Publishers, 1947), p. 75.
72. Sören Kierkegaard, The *Point of View of My Work as an Author: A Report to History* (1848) (New York: Harper & Row, 1962), p. 111.
73. R. W. Emerson, *Emerson's Essays* (New York: Thomas Y. Crowell, 1961), p. 46.
74. Schleiermacher, *Soliloquies*, p. 26.
75. Coleridge, in *Kathleen Coburn, Inquiring Spirit* (Toronto: University of Toronto Press), p. 316 and Mülller, *Elemente*, p. 147.
76. Stirner, *Ego*, pp. 138, 212.
77. Marx, *German Ideology*, p. 70.
78. Stirner, *Ego*, pp. 237, 59.
79. Ibid., p. 223.
80. Friedrich Nietzsche, *The Will to Power* (1901) (New York: Vintage Books, 1968), p. 316.
81. Friedrich Nietzsche, "The Genealogy of Morals," in *The Birth of Tragedy and The Genealogy of Morals* (1887) (New York: Doubleday, 1956), p. 296.

82. Søren Kierkegaard, The Concept of Irony (1841) (Bloomington: Indiana University Press, 1965), p. 278.
83. Marx, *German Ideology*, p. 198.
84. Marx, "A Correspondence of 1843," p. 81.
85. Henry David Thoreau, "Civil Disobedience " (1847), in *The Portable Thoreau* (New York: Viking Press, 1947), pp. 123, 131.
86. Emerson, *Essays*, pp. 35, 2-3.
87. Kierkegaard, Concluding. p. 62; *Concept of Irony*, p. 278.
88. Stirner, *Ego*, pp. 223, 168.
89. G. W. F. Hegel, *Hegel's Logic: Being Port of the Encyclopedia of the Philosophical Sciences* (1817) (London: Oxford University Press, 1975), p. 53.
90. Ricoeur, *Philosophy*, p. 234.
91. Gouldner, For Sociology, p. 345. The impact of idealist thought on interactionist sociology is discussed in Dmitri N. Shalin, "The Genesis of Social Interactionism and Differentiation of Macro- and Microsociological Paradigms," *Humboldt Journal of Social Relations* 6 (1978): 3-38, and "Pragmatism and Social Interactionism," *American Sociological Review* 51(1986).
92. Georg Simmel, *Georg Simmel on Individuality and Social Forms* (Chicago: University of Chicago Press, 1970), p. 7.
93. Max Weber, *The Methodology of the Social Sciences* (New York: Free Press, 1949), p. 80.
94. C. H. Cooley, "The Roots of Social Knowledge," *American Journal of Sociology* 32 (1926): 68, 77.
95. W. I. Thomas, *W. I. Thomas on Social Organization and Social Personality: Selected Papers* (Chicago: University of Chicago Press, 1966), p. 272.
96. Max Weber, *From Max Weber: Essays in Sociology* (New York: Oxford University Press, 1946), p. 55.
97. Charles Horton Cooley, *Human Nature and the Social Order* (1902) (New York: Schocken Books, 1964), pp. 35, 81.
98. H. Stewart Hughes, *Consciousness and Society: The Reorientation of European Social Thought*, 1890-1930 (New York: Vintage Books, 1261), p. 294.
99. P. Breines, "Marxism, Romanticism, and the Case of Georg Lukacs: Notes on Some Recent Sources and Situations," *Studies in Romanticism* 16 (1971).
100. Breines, "Marxism"; Lowy, Goerg Lukács.
101. Anthony Giddens, New Rules of Sociological Method: A Positive Critique of Interpretative Sociologies (New York: Basic Books, 1976).

2

Reforming American Democracy: Socialism, Progressivism, and Pragmatic Reconstruction

The image of Mead many sociology students form in the years of their apprenticeship is that of an armchair philosopher, dispassionately discoursing on the nature of mind, self, and society and largely removed from the practical concerns of the day. It is usually later that they learn that Mead was at the forefront of the contemporary movement for social reform and at some point seriously contemplated a career as professional reformer. The publications by Diner (1975, 1980), Deegan and Burger (1978), and, more recently, Joas (1985) alert us to this less-known facet of Mead's life. The extent of Mead's involvement in the Progressive movement and the effect it had on his social theory, however, are still far from being fully appraised.

One reason Mead's political views and engagements have until recently escaped close scrutiny is that the relevant publications, some unmentioned in any standard bibliography, appeared mostly in limited-circulation magazines and local newspapers, while a portion of his

This chapter is part of a project on Progressivism and Chicago Sociology supported by a grant from the American Sociological Association's Committee on the Problems of the Discipline. The second section of the paper was presented at the annual meeting of the Midwest Sociological Society, Des Moines, 1986. The full version appeared as "G. H. Mead, Socialism, and the Progressive Agenda" in *American Journal of Sociology*, 1988, Vol. 93, pp. 913-951. I wish to thank my colleagues at Southern Illinois University for the generous responses they gave me during the discussion of this paper at the departmental seminar; Norbert Wiley for directing me to Mead's early publications in the *Oberlin Review*; and Janet S. Belcove-Shalin for substantive comments and her help in deciphering some intractable passages from Mead's correspondence.

political writings—notably on socialism and the human cost of industrialization—were never published and are available only in manuscript form.[1] The impression one draws from these writings, reinforced by Mead's private correspondence, is that of a man of radically democratic convictions, keenly aware of social inequality, and deeply concerned with the effect of the division of labor on the working man. Like many other progressives of his time, Mead was engaged in a lifelong polemic with socialists. He accepted without reservation their humanitarian ends but took issue with them on the question of means, fully embracing the basic progressivist tenet that the historically unique framework of American democracy provides the best available leverage for social reconstruction. Mead's life can be seen as an attempt to prove in both theory and practice that revolutionary objectives can be achieved by essentially conservative means.

This chapter examines Mead's political beliefs, public engagements, and theory of progressive reform as representative of the concerted effort to revamp American democracy at this critical juncture of American history. I begin with the sociohistorical context of the Progressive movement. After tracing Mead's path to Progressivism, I analyze his theory of the reform process. Next, I explore the relationships between his political beliefs and substantive ideas. And finally, I discuss the contribution of the pragmatist intellectuals aligned with the Progressive movement to the theory and practice of American democracy.

The Sociohistorical Context of Progressivism

> We plow new fields, we open new mines, we found new cities; we drive back the Indian and exterminate the buffalo; we girdle the land with iron roads and lace the air with telegraph wires; we add knowledge to knowledge, and utilize invention after invention; we build schools and endow colleges; yet it becomes no easier for the masses of our people to make a living. On the contrary, it becomes harder. The wealthy class is becoming more wealthy; but the poor class is becoming more dependent. The gulf between the employed and the unemployed is growing wider; social contrasts are becoming sharper; as liveried carriages appear, so are barefooted children.

These words were written in 1879 by Henry George ([1879] 1926, pp. 309-91), the prophet of American reform, and are excerpted from his book *Progress and Poverty*. Serialized in the United States, translated into the major European languages, and selling some two million copies in the next two decades, this book left an indelible impression on the generation of progressive thinkers in America. In retrospect, the enthusiastic response the book elicited from clergy, businessmen, academics, professionals, and philanthropists seems all the more startling in view of the author's expressed commitment to socialism: "The ideal of socialism is grand and noble; and it is, I am convinced, possible of realization" (George 1926, p. 319). That was written at a time when the spirit of laissez-faire reigned supreme and the principle of "the survival of the fittest" enjoyed the status of unassailable truth. The book's phenomenal success is testimony to the sweeping change in popular mood that the country underwent within two decades and that marked the transition to the Age of Reform in American politics (Aaron 1951, p. 67; Hofstadter 1955; Goldman 1956, p.76; Resek 1967, p. xxi).

The best indicator of the new mood in the land was the change in mainstream Protestantism. Toward the end of the nineteenth century, the predominantly individualistic evangelicalism of the pre-Civil War era yielded to socially conscious and reform-oriented forms of Christianity. Throughout the country, evangelical establishments, such as Mead's alma mater, Oberlin College, were spreading the word that shaping man in the image of God meant not only purifying his soul through the gospel of Jesus but also changing the environment that corrupted his spirit and bred social ills. Henry King's *Theology and the Social Consciousness* and John Commons's *Social Reform and the Church* are just two examples of the voluminous literature of the 1890s that spurred municipal reforms, the survey of immigrants, and the formation of settlements, and that helped to shape the idea of Christian social work as a practical way of improving society (Smith 1957; Barnard 1969). The Christian socialism of this period was but a radical expression of the Social Gospel movement that challenged the Christian establishment in the last decade of the nineteenth century. When the Rev. W. D. P. Bliss ([1890] 1970, p. 352-53) demanded "the ownership, or at least, the control of, city railways; the immediate cessation of giving away or selling valuable street franchises to private monopolists" and insisted that "Christian socialists should teach by fact and not by sentiment; by fact about city gas works, not by mere talk about city brotherhood," he was pursuing to the end the logic of new evangelicalism.

The reformers of the Progressive Era owed much of their inspiration to the critical ferment stirred by the Social Gospel. Their arguments against old-school liberals, for whom government interference in the free market economy was a crime against nature, bore a particularly strong resemblance to the rhetoric of Christian socialists. Along with the latter, the progressives cast aside still-potent social Darwinism and embraced George's argument that, unless ways were found to check the relentless drive toward monopoly and the growing polarization of wealth and poverty, America would soon find itself in the same sorry state as the injustice-ridden regimes of the Old World. The most important progressive reforms—the establishment of the Interstate Commerce Commission, the Conservation Act, the Federal Reserve Act, the food and drug law, the federal workmen's compensation program, the Adamson Act mandating an eight-hour working day on interstate railroads, the electoral reforms, including the initiative, the referendum, the direct election of U.S. senators, and women's suffrage—demonstrate the break with the old liberalism that occurred in the Progressive Era. To be sure, the reforms in question fell short of the social legislation adopted around the same time in Europe, notably in England (Orloff and Skocpol 1984), but they were precipitous enough to provoke the charges—from both the political Right and Left—that Progressivism is the first step toward socialism.

If the critics on the Right saw progressive reforms as a dangerous interference with natural market forces, for the critics on the left these were but half measures. For the very success of progressive reform, socialists charged, furnished proof that state control does work, that equalizing opportunity is indeed the government's business. That is what the socialist critics of laissez-faire capitalism had been saying all along. The progressive reforms, they were quick to point out, were palliatives designed to stem the irreversible movement toward a social and industrial democracy, half-hearted attempts to refurbish the capitalist system that needed to be revamped on a fundamentally new—socialist—basis. The appeal of this argument was considerably enhanced by moderation within the socialist movement. Emboldened by their electoral successes and the growing interest from respectable middle-class audiences, socialists all over the world were eager to assure the public that they had "no intention of appealing to force," that the time had come "to free Socialism from the Marxian system," which in the long run turned out to be "more of a hindrance than a help"(Sombart [1909] 1968, pp. 225, 90). "I am opposed to any tactics which involve stealth, secrecy, intrigue, and necessitate acts of industrial violence for their execution," declared Eugene Debs (1912, p. 483), the pragmatic leader of the Socialist Party of America. No wonder that by 1912 he could claim the support of five daily papers, 250 weeklies, fifty mayors, and one congressman and was polling close to a million votes in the presidential election—not enough to become a mainstream party but sufficient to make opponents worry (Pease 1962, p. 216; Fried 1970, pp. 377-90).

There is a long-standing debate about the causes of the failure of socialism in America. According to one school of thought, socialism never had a chance in this country because it is incompatible with the individualistic American creed. Others argue that socialism did strike roots in America and that its effect on the political scene here is vastly underestimated (for an overview of this debate, See Laslett and Lipset 1974). There is also a third opinion, expressed most cogently by Albert Fried: "Socialism was not an alien but an integral part of the American past. Here, in fact, lay the root of its 'failure,' of its inability to develop into an independent sturdy movement. In Europe, Socialism, with its radically egalitarian ethic, stood in militant opposition to, or at war with, established authority.... But the ideals of American Socialism were embodied, implicitly at least, in the creation of America itself" (1970, p. 2). Although this statement cannot be accepted without qualifications, it does contain a kernel of truth, and it certainly helps understand the progressive thinkers' well-known ambivalence toward socialism (Goldman 1956, p. vii; McNaught 1974, p. 415). Indeed, Woodrow Wilson was not simply using scare tactics when he reminded his audience during his first presidential campaign, "I need not tell you how many men were flocking over to the standard of the Socialists, saying neither party any longer bears aloft an ancient torch of liberty" ([1912] 1962, p. 375). Nor did Theodore Roosevelt exaggerate much when he said, "I am well aware that every upholder of privilege, every hired agent or beneficiary of the special interests, including many well-meaning parlor reformers, will denounce this [Progressive platform] as Socialism'" ([1912] 1962, p. 318).

Herbert Croly, the founding editor of the *New Republic* and a staunch supporter of the Bull Moose Party, was even bolder in his recognition of the affinity between the socialist and progressivist programs: "The majority of good Americans will doubtless consider that the reconstructive policy, already indicated, is flagrantly socialistic both in its method and its objects; and if any critic likes to fasten the stigma of socialism upon the foregoing conception of democracy, I am not concerned with dodging the odium of the term" (1909, p. 209). One can also detect the imprint of socialist ideas in Jane Addams's resolute denunciation of "the overaccumulation at one end of society and the destitution at the other" and in her keen awareness of the paradox of a "large and highly developed factory [that] presents a sharp contrast between its socialized form and its individualistic aim" (1910, p. 126; 1902, p. 139). Socialism was very much on the minds of the progressives. The latter often sounded defensive in front of their socialist opponents (e.g., Roosevelt 1909), but they also shared with them humanitarian objectives. Progressive reforms reflected their desire to socialize American democracy, their "passion for the equalization of human joys and opportunities" (Addams 1910, p. 184). Much as they wished for the socialism of opportunity, however, progressives were leery of the socialism of property, endorsing it chiefly in areas like municipal services and public transportation. The massive nationalization advocated by orthodox socialists, according to progressives, was a false solution, for it would only dampen the entrepreneurial spirit so essential to American life, undermine its basic freedoms, and eventually stifle the opportunity it aimed to promote. The solution to the problem was reform not revolution, a program of reconstruction that would build on the strengths of the American democratic tradition yet would not hesitate to dispense with the old institutions standing in the way of socializing opportunity.

To sum up, the progressive agenda was shaped in the course of the polemics with the proponents of unrestrained capitalism and the adherents of socialist teaching. It also reflected the considerable influence of social Christianity. Progressivism represented an attempt to come to grips with "some of the more glaring failures of capitalism" (White 1957, p. 46). It was "plainly influenced by socialism" (Goldman 1956, p. vii), which served the progressives as both a negative and positive frame of reference. In substance, Progressivism represented "a dual agenda of economic remedies designed to minimize the dangers from the extreme left and right" (Hofstadter 1955, p. 236). This dual agenda called for a new outlook, a philosophy in a different key. It was to be conservative and radical, pragmatic and principled, faithful to the nation's democratic heritage yet critical of its political and economic practices. This dual agenda of American Progressivism found expression in the life and work of George Herbert Mead.

The Making of a Reformer: Mead's Path from Evangelicalism to Progressivism

Few American reformers on the path to Progressivism escaped the influence of liberal Christian theology, and Mead in this respect was no exception. His father, Hiram Mead, a minister in the Congregational church and a prominent educator, taught homiletics at Oberlin Theological Seminary. Mead's mother, Elizabeth Storrs Billing, was a strong-willed, dignified, very religious woman; for a number of years, she served as president of Mount Holyoke College and later taught at

Oberlin College. With a background like this it was logical to expect that Mead—a rather shy, serious, well-behaved boy—would take up the ministry. Oberlin College, where Mead matriculated in 1879, was a perfect place to start such a career. Founded by clergy and renowned for its piety and abolitionist sentiments, Oberlin was a stronghold of the spirit of old New England Puritanism, which for decades filled its students with "a zeal for bettering the life of mankind as the highest expression of religious duty" (Barnard 1969, p. 126). Yet just around the time when Mead was ready to enter college, the winds of change swept through American institutions of higher learning. Darwin's theory of evolution, reinforced by German historical criticism of the Bible, was winning converts among the public, making a revision of Christian dogma a necessity. The Social Gospel movement burst onto the scene, propelled by its proponents' ardent belief in the power of Christian social work to cure society's ills. About this time, various reform schemes started attracting followers among students and faculty in colleges and universities all over the country. Oberlin College was at the center of the new currents of theological, political, and social thought. In the 1880s and 1890s, it was the site of several conferences in which the Rev. Washington Gladden, Walter Rauschenbusch, Lyman Abbot, Richard T. Ely, Carroll D. Wright, and scores of other liberal theologians and reformers debated topics ranging from Darwinism and Scripture, to intemperance and crime, to immigration and poverty. In later years, an array of progressive and socialist thinkers were invited to speak directly to student audiences, including such luminaries as Robert M. La Follette, Jane Addams, Lincoln Steffens, Jack London, and John Spargo. Among the people most talked about at Oberlin during this period was Henry George. In 1887, he visited the campus and spoke on the issues of reform to an enthusiastic audience of faculty and students (Barnard 1969, p.62).

Mead's early correspondence documents the depth of his religious feelings, the earnest commitment to spreading the word of God inculcated in him during the college years. "I believe Christianity is the only power capable of grappling with evil as it exists now," wrote Mead to his college friend Henry Castle (MP April 23 and March 16, 1884, b1, f1).[2] "There can be no doubt of the efficacy of Christ as a remedial agent and so I can speak of him as such.... The moral realities of the world are powerful enough to stimulate me and Christianity lays the strongest hold upon me." There were also some indications that Mead was affected by the critical currents of the day. These indications are not to be found in the four signed articles that Mead (1881, 1882a, 1882b,

1882c) published in the *Oberlin Review* and that deal with conventional literary and philosophical subjects, but rather in the unsigned editorials that he and his co-editor, Henry Castle, wrote during their last year in college and that point to the influence of liberal theology on Mead's thinking.[3] Noting with satisfaction that "the religious craze against evolutionary theories is dying out," the editors urged a rapprochement between church dogma and the theory of evolution (Editorial 1882). A long editorial (1883) drew attention to the growing number of students passing up the ministry as a vocation because of their doubts about the veracity of church doctrine and insisted that "this doubt is, as an almost universal rule, honest doubt." At Oberlin, Mead also acquired his political allegiance. As his letter to the editor of the *Nation* (Mead 1884) suggests, his political views in the college years followed middle-class Republicanism, which was then prevalent at Oberlin and which Mead was ready to defend against the attacks of its critics. Despite his later ambivalence about Roosevelt and admiration for Wilson, Mead would remain loyal to the Republican Party throughout his life.

After college, Mead confronted a difficult career choice. Two possibilities appealed to him—Christian social work and teaching philosophy. What he liked most about the former was the chance to work for people and somehow to make the world a better place. The latter career attracted Mead because of the secure academic environment and an opportunity to continue his philosophical speculations, which he had grown increasingly fond of in his last year of college. There were problems with both lines of work. A career in Christianity required belief in God, which over the years Mead found difficult to sustain. To follow this path, wrote Mead in a letter to Henry Castle (MP March 16, 1884, b1, f1), "I shall have to let persons understand that I have some belief in Christianity and my praying be interpreted as a belief in God, whereas I have no doubt that now the most reasonable system of the universe can be formed to myself without a God. But notwithstanding all this I cannot go out with the world and not work for men. The spirit of a minister is strong with me and I come fairly by it." The alternative career had problems of its own. "There is a great deal of good work that needs to be done in popularizing metaphysics among common people," wrote Mead in the same letter, but this option did not appear to satisfy his passion for commitment: "I want to give myself to that which I can give my whole self to…" For several years, Mead remained troubled by this choice. He would weigh the arguments, assess his chances, extol the virtues of the Christian faith, and then confess his inability to follow suit. "I need the strength of religion in my work," confided Mead to his friend (MP February 23, 1884, b1, f1). "Nothing could meet the wants of mankind as Christianity, and why not have a little deception if need be?... And yet as I look at it now, there is hardly any position I would not rather occupy than that of a dogmatic theologian. I would rather be a school teacher than a Joseph Cook dabbling in metaphysics."

No one knows how long this torturous quest would have continued had it not been for Henry Castle,[4] who finally convinced Mead to join him in Cambridge, Massachusetts, where he had settled earlier to study law. Once his mind was made up, Mead threw himself into the study of philosophy. Of all possible specializations available to him when he enrolled in the Department of Philosophy at Harvard, he selected the one most peripheral to the discipline's traditional concerns—physiological psychology. The reason for this choice, according to Castle ([1889] 1902, p. 579), was Mead's belief that he had found "a harmless territory in which he [could] work quietly without drawing down upon himself the anathema and excommunication of all-potent Evangelicism." The spirit of a minister, however, was too strong in Mead, and it was not long before the longing to serve people reasserted itself.

In the fall of 1888, after successfully completing a year at Harvard, Mead won a scholarship and went to Germany, ostensibly to continue his studies toward a doctoral degree. Yet his mind would soon turn to politics, stimulated by the burgeoning reform movement in Germany. The extent of government involvement in the issues of social security, the popularity of the Social Democratic Party, and particularly the respect socialism commanded in academic circles deeply impressed Mead, who found the situation in Germany to be in sharp contrast to the one back home, where the idea of state involvement in labor-management relations was still suspect and the term "socialism" had a somewhat odious connotation. A few months after settling in Germany, Mead experienced something akin to conversion. His letters of this period are brimming with enthusiasm for social reforms and the prospect of transplanting them to the States. He talks about "opening toward everything that is uplifting and satisfying in socialism" (MP August 1890, b1, f3), urges Henry "to get a hold upon the socialistic literature—and the position of socialism here—in Europe" (MP October 21, 1890, b1, f3), and deplores in the most sweeping terms American politics: "American political life is horribly idealess.... Our government in ideas and methods belongs so to the past.... We had never had a national legislature in which corrupt motives in the most pecuniary form could be more shamelessly used than in the present" (MP October 21 and 19, 1890, b1, f3).[5]

Somewhere along the way doubts about his career choice came to haunt Mead again. Invoking his abiding need for commitment, he declared a readiness to go into politics, at least on a trial basis: "Life looks like such an insignificant affair that two or three or more years of utterly unsuccessful work would not seem to me in the slightest dampening, and the subjective satisfaction of actually doing what my nature asked for of infinitely more importance than anything else.... I mean that I am willing to go into a reform movement which to my eyes may be a failure after all; simply for the sake of the work" (MP October 19, 1890, b1, f3). Soon a plan was hatched in Mead's head, in which he envisioned himself and his friend, Henry Castle, after a thorough study of the German scene, coming back to the States, securing control of a newspaper, and launching a crusade for social reform:

> The immediate necessity is that we should have a clear conception of what forms socialism is taking in [the] life of European lands, especially of the organisms of municipal life—how cities sweep their streets, manage their gas works and street cars, their *Turnvereins*, their homes of prostitution, their poor, their minor criminals, their police, etc., etc., that one may come with ideas to the American work. Now Henry you must come and at least get such a share in these subjects and hold of the social political literature that you can go right on when we are back. I must teach at first for I must earn money, but I shan't keep it long. I want more active life.... My vague plan now is that I go to the university of Minnesota as a teacher—and you to Minneapolis as lawyer and that we finally get control of the Minneapolis Tribune. This is of course hazy but Minneapolis has very large attractions for this work—it is young, not sunk into the meshes of any traditional machine, and yet beyond the boom period. But this is entirely superfluous castle building but to go to some city we must and to go to work and fail if need be, but work in any case and work satisfactorily. (MP August 1890, b1, f3)

What is particularly impressive in Mead's thinking of those years is his clear understanding that the city is bound to play a special role in future reforms. City Hall, insisted Mead in a manner reminiscent of Christian socialists, is the true focus of the reform movement, and city politics is the place where the reconstruction of America should start: "We must get into politics of course—city politics above all things, because there we can begin to work at once in whatever city we settle, because city politics need men more than any other branch, and chiefly because, according to my opinion, the immediate application of principle of corporate life—of socialism in America must start from the city.... If we can purify there, we can throughout, if we could not there, we could not anywhere. If we can give American institutions the new blood of the social ideal, it can come in only at this unit of our political life and from this starting point it will naturally spread" (MP October 21 and 19, 1890, b1, f3).

Unlike Mead, Castle was a man of more practical bent. He shared many of Mead's ideals and was strongly affected by the reform currents in Germany, where he traveled extensively,[6] yet he thought Mead's plans of going into politics and reforming America via city hall somewhat utopian and did not hesitate to impress this on Mead. Without Castle's financial backing and his editorial skills, Mead had to put his plans on the back burner. Meanwhile, his life took a decidedly new turn. In 1891, Mead was appointed an instructor at the University of Michigan, where he met his future colleague and friend, John Dewey. An academic of no small renown even in those days, Dewey shared Mead's passion for social democracy and philosophical disquisition. As early as 1888, Dewey ([1888] 1969, p. 246) speculated about the "tendency of democracy toward socialism, if not communism" and claimed that "there is no need to beat about the bush in saying that democracy is not in reality what it is in name until it is industrial, as well as civil and political ... a democracy of wealth is a necessity." The two pursuits that Mead was trying to reconcile were united in the life of this remarkable man. Indeed, Dewey was the foremost example of an American academic successfully combining research and political engagement, and, as such, he was bound to become a role model for Mead.

Not much is known about Mead's stay at Ann Arbor. He still seemed to have harbored some hopes for direct political engagement, as indicated, for instance, by his enthusiastic response to the idea of a socialist weekly which Dewey, Mead, and Park were contemplating for a while (MD February 28, 1892, b1, f3; see also Raushenbush 1979, pp. 18-21; Joas 1985, p. 21). What is clear is that Dewey and Mead formed a friendship that each of them would later claim was his most precious possession. When Dewey was offered the chairmanship at the University of Chicago he made his acceptance contingent on the appointment of Mead (who never completed his doctoral thesis) as an assistant professor in his department. It was at the University of Chicago that Mead's career as a reformer began to flourish. In the years following his move to Chicago Mead joined the City Club, an organization of reform-minded professionals and businessmen, of which he became president in 1918. Mead worked in close association with such people as Graham Taylor and Jane Addams, and for more than a decade he served as treasurer of the University of Chicago settlement.[7] Along with Dewey, Mead was keenly interested in reform of the Chicago school system and at some point headed the Chicago Educational Association and the Vocational League. He was vice president of the Immigrants Protective League of

Chicago. On several occasions, he served as a member of the settlement committees. By 1910, Mead was generally recognized as one of the leaders of the Progressive movement in the city of Chicago.

The first expressly political publications of Mead—a review of Le Bon's *Psychology of Socialism* and an article "The Working Hypothesis in Social Reform"—testify to Mead's continued preoccupation with socialism. In his words, "Socialism, in one form or another, lies back of the thought directing and inspiring reform" (Mead 1899a, p. 367). But one can also detect a new critical note in Mead's treatment of socialism, or rather a "doctrinaire" and "utopian" version of it, to which Mead juxtaposes the "pragmatic" and "opportunist" approach of progressive reformers. Indicative in this respect is Mead's review of Le Bon's book. He agrees with the author that socialist teaching has a tendency to become dogmatic insofar as it lays claim to a priori validity. He also renounces all versions of socialism that sanction violence and expresses skepticism about Marx's economic analysis, which he finds at odds with modern economic and political realities. Nevertheless, he resolutely parts company with Le Bon and other critics of socialism who confuse its doctrinaire form with its humanistic content. The programmatic and apocalyptic aspects of socialist teaching may be obsolete, Mead argues, but its quest for justice is not. This quest is now taken over by social democrats who have denounced revolutionary violence and turned into reformers: "The socialists are becoming opportunists. They are losing confidence in any delineation of the future conditions of society—any 'vision given on the mount'.... Socialistic thinking may be different in France and England, but it is the same great force and cannot be studied in the camp of the programmist alone. It is coming to represent, not a theory, but standpoint and attitude.... We have, in general, given up being programmists and become opportunists. We do not build any more Utopias, but we do control our immediate conduct by the assurance that we have the proper point of attack, and that we are losing nothing in the process. We are getting a stronger grip on the method of social reform every year, and are becoming proportionately careless about our ability to predict the detailed result" (Mead 1899b, pp. 405-6, 409).

Mead's political beliefs at this point, and specifically his emphasis on pragmatism and opportunism, are reminiscent of Eduard Bernstein's brand of social democracy, with its motto, "The movement is everything, the goal is nothing." That is to say, Mead is cognizant of socialism's historical import and sympathetic to its humanitarian objectives: "Socialism presented at least for some decades the goal that society must contemplate, whether it will or not [be] a democratic society in which the means of social expressions and satisfactions are placed at the disposal of the members of the whole community" (MP b2 addenda, f27). Nonetheless, Mead grows skeptical about socialist means. He continues to stress socialism's historical importance but mostly in the past tense, viewing it as a movement that shook the world from its dogmatic slumber but that had now outlived its usefulness, at least in the United States. By the early 1900s, Mead fully identified himself with the Progressive creed, to which he remained faithful the rest of his life.[8]

It would not be appropriate to speak about Mead's movement away from socialism, for there is not enough evidence to assert that he ever was a card-carrying socialist to begin with. The question that one may pose is, why did Mead not embrace more openly socialist premises? Part of the answer to this query can be gleaned from the status of politically engaged scholarship in this period. The marriage of scholarship and advocacy in American academia at the time was far from peaceful and harmonious (Furner 1975). The professor's right to speak on controversial issues was acknowledged, albeit within limits. An outright endorsement of socialism was pretty much out of the question.[9] Instructors willing to take a political stance had to make sure that their views bore the imprimatur of science and dovetailed with the democratic creed. Bemis, Ross, and some other instructors who lost their jobs in the late nineteenth century because of their political engagements did, in one way or another, overstep the boundaries of what most in academia then thought were the standards of objectivity and disinterestedness. Others, such as Richard T. Ely, Charles Zueblin, and Thorstein Veblen, had to go through endless explanations and humiliating denials concerning their alleged pro-socialist sentiments.[10] Still, quite a few academics with various degrees of commitment to the ideals of social democracy, such as Seligman, Commons, Bird, and Dewey, found a formula that seemingly reconciled scholarship and advocacy. The common denominator that united these otherwise disparate characters was an unswerving commitment to reform, combined with a vigorous renunciation of violence as the means of social reconstruction. That, of course, was the basic creed of Progressivism, which had just started coming into its own. It is this rising current in American politics that provided legitimation for the incipient fusion of scholarship and advocacy and that helped to secure a niche for all those who sought to partake in the reform of American society without jeopardizing their academic positions. Mead's political views, or at any rate his public stance, showed that he understood the limits of the possible for an academic in the Progressive Era.

Still, we need to bear in mind that Mead's regard for socialism remained unchanged throughout his life. He greeted with enthusiasm the democratic February Revolution in Russia (Mead 1917d), and he supported the program of the British Labour Party (Mead 1918). "What has been said [about socialism]," wrote Mead in a characteristic passage, "has been said with a profound realization of the past and future import of its economic gospel, even if it has been a gospel only according to Marx" (MP b3 addenda, f7). Mead's highest praise, however, was reserved not for socialists but for people like Jane Addams and R. F. Hoxie, radical democrats thoroughly committed to the struggle for the rights of the underprivileged (Mead 1907, 1916-17). What attracted Mead to these people was that, without wrapping themselves in the revolutionary flag, they were searching for ways of realizing the revolutionary ideals that inspired socialist critics of society. This quest for peaceful revolution provides a key to Mead's own theory of the reform process.

To sum up, Mead's intellectual and political growth was marked from the beginning by the tension between his evangelical desire to serve people and his predilection for an academic career. This tension was resolved when the emerging movement for social reform legitimized the fusion of scholarship and advocacy in the academic setting. Along with some other social scientists of his day, Mead was influenced by socialism, or rather a social democratic version of it, that renounced all forms of revolutionary violence and endorsed strictly democratic and political means of effecting social change. After establishing himself in academia, Mead embraced the Progressivist creed, yet even then he did not cease to see the historical importance of socialism or to acknowledge his debt to it. By the end of the nineteenth century, Mead emerged as a "radically democratic intellectual" (Joas 1985, p. 10), a reformer deeply involved in progressive cases, and a budding academic searching for a theoretical rationale for a far-reaching yet peaceful reconstruction of American society.

Institutionalizing Revolution:
Mead's Theory of the Reform Process

Progressive reformers differed among themselves on the etiology of current problems, the ultimate objectives of reform, and the best strategies for social reconstruction, but they all agreed that the gap between democratic ideals and American reality had grown intolerably wide. The founding fathers envisioned the United States as a community of civil-minded and well-informed citizens consciously shaping their destiny under the protection of constitutionally guaranteed freedoms. The reality, with its predominance of poorly educated workers and illiterate immigrants, made a mockery of this Jeffersonian ideal of popular democracy. Like all progressives, Mead was very much aware of "the chasm that separates the theory and practice of our democracy," yet he went farther than most in delineating "the tragedy of industrial society" with its "routine and drudgery of countless uninterested hands" and "the blind production of goods, cut off from all the interpretation and inspiration of their common enjoyment" ([1923] 1964, p. 263, [1925-26] 1964, pp. 295-96). The plight of workers caught in the meshes of the modern factory system attracted his special attention.

The Industrial Revolution, according to Mead, makes the worker's participation in the democratic process problematic, because it minimizes his educational needs, cheapens his labor, and dehumanizes his life. The modem worker is in some sense worse than his medieval counterpart, whose skills, slowly acquired and hard to replace, "made of him an admirable member of the older community.... It is the machine that has taken possession of the trades, has displaced the artisan, and has substituted for the artisan, who makes an entire article, a group of laborers who tend the machine. The effect of this upon the training of the laborer has been most deplorable. The more the machine accomplishes the less the workman is called upon to use his brain, the less skill he is called upon to acquire.... The man who tends one of these machines becomes a part of the machine, and when the machine is thrown away the man is thrown away, for he has fitted himself into the machine until he has become nothing but a cog" (1908-9a, pp. 370-71; 1908, p. 20). The machine is a product of the social forces over which no individual has control, yet its devastating effects have been multiplied by the callous attitude of its owners: "Thus the machine is a social product for which no individual can claim complete responsibility. Its economic efficiency is as dependent on the presence of the laborer and the market for its products as mechanical structure is dependent upon the inventor, and its exploitation upon the capitalist. But the group morality under which the community suffers, recognizes no responsibility of the exploiter to the laborer, but leaves him free to exhaust and even maim the operator, as if the community had placed a sword in his hand with which to subjugate" (1907, p. 127).

The situation is further exacerbated by the current educational system, which perpetuates the division between the two kinds of skills—one for laborers and the other for higher orders of society. An investment into the future worker's education beyond what is necessary to fulfill his role as a laborer is considered a luxury, and so he rarely moves beyond elementary school and is often compelled to start work even earlier. The wealth of cultural goods that belongs to everyone in the community remains closed to him: "Cultured classes in some sense have an access to this wealth, which is denied to masses in the community.... We are encouraging a class distinction which must be destructive of American democracy if it persists.... " ([1930] 1964, p. 403; 1908-9b, p. 157). Bad as the position of the American-born worker is, it is worse for the immigrant. He is brought to the United States as a source of cheap labor and, lacking English and education, becomes easy prey for employers. The latter, Mead concluded from his many encounters with Chicago businessmen, "had absolutely no feeling of responsibility to the immigrant, or the sense of debt which Chicago owes to the immigrant.... He [the immigrant] comes ignorant and helpless before the system of exploitation which enwraps him before he leaves the old country and may last for two generations after he enters our gates. Our government has nothing to offer him by way of protection but the doctrine of the abstract human rights of man, a vote he cannot intelligently exercise, and the police to hold him in his place" (1909, pp. 222-23; 1907, p. 123). Whatever American democracy has to offer the well-to-do, Mead concludes, falls far short of its promise when it comes to the millions of working-class people effectively excluded from meaningful participation in the life of the community. If modern America is to fulfill the democratic aspirations of its founding fathers, it has to "eliminate the evils to which economic inferiority exposes great masses of man," it has to provide equal access to cultural goods for all members of the community, and it must imbue the laborer's work with meaning: "In the bill of rights which a modem man may draw up and present to the society which has produced and controls him, should appear the right to work both with intelligent comprehension of what he does, and with interest. For the latter one must see the product as a whole..." (1908-9a, pp. 381,378).

Many of the above themes, as one can readily see, run parallel to the familiar socialist critique of capitalist society. The likeness is particularly striking if we think about the young Marx's philippics against the effects of the division of labor on the working man. Indeed, both Marx and Mead deplored the dehumanizing consequences of the factory system, both sought to restore the producer's sense of the product as a whole, and both resisted a wholesale renunciation of modernity and invested much hope in the future of science and technology. Beyond these parallels, however, one finds differences that set Marx's socialism sharply apart from Mead's progressivism. For Marx, the real culprit is capitalism, with its private ownership of the means of production, inherently unstable economy, and that perennial scourge—alienated labor. Capitalism must be abolished, if necessary by revolutionary force, and, if the dictatorship of the proletariat means curtailing individual freedoms, that is no great loss, since the civil liberties guaranteed by bourgeois society are a sham anyhow. When the considerations of justice and equality collide with those of freedom and democracy, the former are to be given higher priority in Marx's system. Not so in Mead's book. Democracy gets the top billing there. To be sure, justice is important for Mead, as it is for any progressive—it is a vital condition of genuine democracy—yet, if pursued for its own sake, radical equality is bound to impinge on civil liberties and undermine democratic institutions. Justice must be pursued as far, and only as far, as necessary to secure for every member of society an opportunity to participate in the democratic process. This last point needs further elaboration.

Underlying the Progressive movement was the realization that economically unregulated and socially unconstrained democracy flourishing under laissez-faire capitalism creates an underclass that is, de jure, free yet, de facto, excluded from meaningful participation in the democratic process. The United States, a country that prided itself on its commitment to democracy, was willing to tolerate degrading human conditions, including the shameful exploitation of woman and child labor. In the name of freedom of contract and freedom of trade, employers were able to impose on workers the terms of contract they wished to, even when this meant paying starvation wages. Clearly, progressives concluded, civil rights alone could not guarantee personal dignity and ensure the realization of human potential to which every member of society is entitled. A measure of economic well-being and educational opportunity is imperative for a democratic society. This is what Mead had in mind when he declared that "abstract human rights" offer little protection to immigrant workers, and what Dewey meant when he urged that "actual and concrete liberty of opportunity and action is dependent upon equalization of the political and economic conditions under which individuals are alone free *in fact*, not *in some metaphysical way*" (1946, p. 116). This progressive stance had far-reaching implications. It implied that "poverty is a result of a faulty organization of society, and the organization of society can be changed" (MP b2 addenda, f26). It led to the conclusion that "community has a right to exert control over corporation" (MP b7, f8). And, by bringing to light "singular evils which have resulted from corporate property" (MP b7, f8), it hastened the end of laissez-faire capitalism in the United States.

As one could imagine, this attack on nineteenth-century capitalism met stiff resistance from die-hard defenders of the old ways, who decried the progressive program as an unconstitutional abridgment of democratic liberties. Yet most progressives stood firm and did not waver in their conviction that society's interference in the market process is both justifiable and necessary, that is, insofar as this interference makes democracy more equitable and to the extent that it leaves the core of civil liberties intact. The last point is particularly important, for it underscores the fact that progressives had more faith in bourgeois democracy than Marxists did. They thought that civil liberties, constitutionally guaranteed and when necessary expanded, could provide a firm foundation for social reconstruction. Radical and revolutionary as this reconstruction might be, it had to be carried out by constitutional means, its success to be judged by the degree to which democratic values were preserved.

There is a phrase that crops up in Mead's writings—institutionalizing of revolution. Says Mead: "Revolutions might be carried out by methods which would be strictly constitutional and legal"; "Government by the will of the people means that orderly revolution is a part of the institution of government itself"; "When you set up a constitution and one of the articles in it is that the constitution may be changed, then you have, in a certain sense, incorporated the very process of revolution into the order of society" ([1915] 1964, pp. 150-51; MP b3 addenda, f29; 1936, p. 361). These statements, so emblematic of Mead's political thought, illuminate the widely held progressivist belief that radical change can be accomplished without recourse to violence, by legitimate constitutional means. Revolution is not in itself a bad thing, according to Mead; it is "a summary reconstruction" that takes place when "a whole population is able to assume, for a time, the larger or more universal attitude" (MP Mead to Irene Tufts Mead, September 16, 1916, b1a, f13). As such, it represents a constructive force that must be harnessed by progressive legislation and directed by enlightened public opinion. This peaceful democratic revolution naturally presupposes that the democratic machinery is already in place, as, for instance, in the United States. The democratic alternative is very much in doubt where bourgeois democracy has not yet been established, which, Mead pointed out, was the case in most of Europe at the time. The appeal of socialism is strongest precisely in those countries where the struggle for bourgeois democracy is still going on: "Socialism abroad has been the outcome of popular struggle against governments which have been in the hands of privileged classes.... It has been democracy's fighting formation when opposed to a modern feudalism" (Mead 1917d). Once democratic institutions are secured, socialism has done its job and must merge with other reform currents.

And what about capitalism? It must be transformed but not necessarily into socialism. The future social order will be a radically democratic society that encourages personal initiative, equalizes opportunity in every sphere of life, and makes social reconstruction an ongoing concern. If capitalism is a thesis, then socialism is more in the nature of an antithesis—not a synthesis, as socialists would have it. If such a synthesis is possible at all, it is likely to be provided by progressivism. Here is how Mead laid out this idea in his course on the logic of the social sciences that he gave at the apex of the Progressive Era in the academic year 1911-12, as jotted down by one of his students: "Take case of Socialism vs. Individualism. Individualism owns capital, and Socialism asks that community shall on property—here [is] a clash. Solution involves say this form: individual initiative, individual control must be preserved and on the other hand public control must be preserved to protect the individual. How [can we] deal practically with this? Any number of schemes now appearing—interstate commerce, control of wages, control of conditions of labor, pensions, old age, out of work, sickness [benefits]. These statements are present solutions so that the clash is done away with" (MP 14, f8).

It would be a mistake to infer from this that Mead conceived the institutionalizing of revolution as a legalistic affair, some sort of never-ending legislative process supervised by politicians and professional reformers. The legislative measures introduced by the progressive administrations were valuable, and Mead was enthusiastic about them, particularly about the platform of the Wilson administration,[11] yet these legislative initiatives, he thought, were not in themselves sufficient to bring about a radical democracy, nor did they go to the heart of the reform movement. The ongoing reconstruction, as Mead envisioned it, was a multifaceted process designed to further the common interests of all groups and individual members of society. It required (1) the mobilization of public opinion; (2) persistent attention of the press; (3) cooperation of labor and business organizations; (4) reorganization of the school; and (5) direct participation of the scientific community and public intellectuals.

1. It was an article of faith with Mead, and a starting point in his theory of the reform process, that underneath the conflicting interests of

groups, classes, and nations lies a public good, waiting to be discovered and realized. "The real assumption of democracy inside the society of a nation and within the society of different nations," wrote Mead in an article from his little-known series of essays on democracy and war, "is that there is always to be discovered a common social interest in which can be found a solution of social strifes.... Democratic advance, therefore, has always been in the direction of breaking down the social barriers and vested interests which have kept men from finding the common denominators of conflicting interests" (1917d; see also 1917a, 1917b, 1917c, 1917e). Mead did not specify what the public good is or how it is to be determined, nor was he ready to identity it with majority vote.[12] Yet he was convinced that some notion of public good must be a guiding force in the reform movement, and he vested the responsibility for its articulation in the general public. No government, elected body of representatives, or group of professional reformers in a democratic society could successfully complete its task without ordinary citizens, organized into voluntary associations. "The whole work of legislation," asserted Mead (1899a, p. 368), "is not only dependent upon public senti-ment, at least in democratic countries, but it is finding constantly fuller expressions in other channels of publicity.... If only it becomes possible to focus public sentiment upon an issue in the delicate organism of the modem community, it is as effective as if the mandate came from leg-islative halls, and frequently more so." The public, as Mead, following Dewey, understood it, is a body of citizenry, well informed, conscious of its interests, and ready to take the problems of society as their own. This body is distinguished by its members' willingness to consider the interests of all groups and individuals from the standpoint of what is good for the community as a whole. The success of the reform process ultimately depends on how thoroughly the public is mobilized and how long it can sustain interest in the critical issues of the day.

2. A vital role in mobilizing public opinion belongs to the press, which has the power to focus attention on the ills of society and to keep them in the news until a consensus is reached regarding ways of dealing with the problem: "The newspaper, in its various forms of journal and magazine, is effecting changes that are assumed to be those which follow governmental action" (1899a, p. 368). So far, however, the overall perfor-mance of the press had been less than satisfactory. One serious problem, according to Mead, was that "our newspapers represent frequently, or generally, political parties, instead of bringing together the common in-terests of all of us—that they represent only single parts" (1912, p. 215).

Another scourge, especially characteristic of the progressive press, was its pervasive "sensationalism [which] is the expression of a fundamental social conflict which the community feels but is not willing to come to terms with" (MP b4 addenda, f1). To fulfill its mission, the press needs to curb its partisan bias and serve as a unifying force.

3. Mead had similar advice for the leaders of labor and business organizations. He gave his full support to labor unions, whose combative spirit "is amply explained by the simple American demand for what one has confessedly earned, and the American determination to fight, if necessary, to get one's fair rights" (1907-8, p. 133). He urged business leaders to do their share in improving the conditions of labor and get directly involved in the issues of minimum wage, working hours, workmen's compensation, and so on. Yet, he did not hesitate to chastise both labor and capital when he thought that intransigence on either side prevented a fair resolution of labor-management disputes (see MP Mead to Irene Tufts Mead, July 16 and 20, 1919, bl, f17; see also Diner 1980, pp. 148-51). The solution to labor strife Mead personally favored was arbitration, to be conducted with expert mediators and under the eye of the public. The important thing was to keep searching for common ground, which, Mead was convinced, could always be found if only businessmen assumed their full responsibility as members of the community and workers aimed at "immediately possible achievements, with a vivid sense of the present reality of the means used and their necessary parity with the methods of the employers. Gradually the sense of community of interest between both arises, and with it growing interest in the actual struggle and a feeling of intense meaning that does not have to be projected into the future to get reality" (1899b, p. 411).

4. Schools have a vital part to play in humanizing American society. Progressive education, mandatory and free for all children, could at least partially offset "social restrictions which limit the development of children of poorer classes," and it could aid the progressive cause by bringing cultural goods to the poor and "freeing ... culture of its class connotation" (1964, pp. 405-6). Progressive education could also help to counteract the negative effects of the division of labor by furnishing the worker with knowledge of the industrial process as a whole. That, in turn, would require the elimination of the two-tier schooling system that gives liberal education to some and industrial training to others. "Industrial training in this century should aim to give to the laborer not only professional efficiency but the meaning of his vocation, its historical import, and some comprehension of his position in the democratic

society out of this will arise an interest in the whole product which may lay the foundation for that intelligence which can in some measure resist the narrowing influence of the specialized labor in the factory.... American industrial education must be a liberal education" (1908-9b, p. 157; l908-9c, p. 213).

5. Finally, the success of reform depends on tapping the vast resources of science and mobilizing the energies of public intellectuals. The traditional reliance on charity and philanthropy is no longer adequate to the task in hand. A path to contemporary reform is a "path from impulsive charity to social reconstruction"; to be successful, it has to lead "not only to efforts of amelioration but also to judgments of value and plans for social reforms" (1964, p. 399). Members of the academic community can make a large contribution to charting the reform program and formulating the means of social reconstruction. This is not simply because university professors possess specialized knowledge but also because they combine scientifically trained intelligence with the knowledge of the problems of the community at large. "The university is not an office of experts to which the problems of the community are sent to be solved; it is a part of the community within which the community problems appear as its own" (1915, p. 351). What sets scientific intelligence apart and makes its contribution to the reform process signally important is its impartial character, its "disinterestedness in existing structures, social and intellectual, and willingness to continually reconstruct these substituting for them other structures at any point and to any extent" (MP b3 addenda, f16). A scientifically trained mind can rise above conflicting values and find a solution that reconciles disparate claims in the best interests of the community as a whole. In the search for a solution, scientific intelligence is likely to be guided not by a ready-made blueprint of a future society, "a vision given on the mount," but by the sense of the possible, a realistic account of available means, and a habit of dealing methodically and rationally with the problem at hand. This habit of impartiality does not mean that progressive scholars have no interest in the outcome, no values of their own. They are after all on the side of progress, and so, when their job is done, the old social order will be replaced with a new one that is more universal, rational, and humane: "The rational solution of the conflicts, however, calls for the reconstruction of both habits and values, and this involves transcending the order of the community. A hypothetically different order suggests itself and becomes the end in conduct ... it is a social order that includes any rational being who is or may be implicated in the situation with which thought deals. It sets up

an ideal world, not of substantive things but of proper method" (1964, p. 404).

In summary, Mead's theory of the reform process stems from his belief, widely shared by the progressive reformers of his time, that a crying gap separates contemporary American society from the Jeffersonian ideal of popular democracy, that capitalism and democracy are presently working at cross purposes, and that, unless a way is found to humanize laissez-faire capitalism, the future of democracy in America will be imperiled. One road to a more humane and equitable society lies in the institutionalization of revolution—the term by which Mead meant that radical reforms can be carried out within the constitutional framework of democracy and that social reconstruction must be an ongoing concern rather than an all-out, one-time effort to set up a perfect society. Mead refused to spell out the exact nature of the future social order aside from general statements that it should be based on public good, take account of the interests of all social groups, and broaden the scope of economic and social opportunity for disadvantaged members of the community. He focused, instead, on methods and means of social reconstruction, the most salient of which are the mobilization of the general public, continued attention of the press, arbitration of labor-management disputes, the fusion of academic and vocational education, and the participation of members of the academic community. There was no gap between Mead's rhetoric and practical action. Whether he was marching with Jane Addams on the streets of Chicago in support of women's suffrage, surveying the homes of immigrants from Eastern Europe, writing editorials on the dispute between the Board of Education and the Chicago Teachers' Federation, giving public support to the beleaguered reformers at the University of Wisconsin, or serving on the citizens' committee investigating labor grievances in the Chicago garment workers' strike—he was doing exactly what he thought a member of the public should do to stay politically engaged and to further the cause of reform. The interplay between Mead's political beliefs and his other intellectual pursuits was great indeed, and it comes into clear relief in his pragmatist philosophy and interactionist social theory.

Socializing Human Intelligence:
Mead's Theory of Social Process

The parallels between pragmatist and progressivist thought have been frequently noted (White 1957; Featherstone 1972; Levine 1969; Cremin 1969; Shalin 1986a), yet their sociological implications have not been fully spelled out. My argument in the present section is that there is a far-reaching elective affinity between Progressivism and pragmatism, particularly the social pragmatism of Dewey and Mead. Indeed, the pragmatist vision of the world-in-the-making—the world that is perennially indeterminate, continuously emergent, and wonderfully malleable—is a metaphysics tailor-made for the age of reform. The traditional world of rationalist thought, the world of natural law and order, left little room for conscious efforts to make it more rational and humane. In contrast, the world confronting pragmatists was crying out for reform; it had to be transformed, and not just by the impersonal forces of evolution but by human intelligence. The latter, according to pragmatist philosophers, was not a mirror faithfully reflecting natural laws but an active force capable of transforming matter according to a logic of its own. Nowhere is the transformative, constitutive power of reason more evident or urgently needed than in the social domain: "In the physical world we regard ourselves as standing in some degree outside the forces at work, and thus avoid the difficulty of harmonizing the feeling of human initiative with the recognition of series which are necessarily determined. In society we are the forces that are being investigated, and if we advance beyond the mere description of the phenomena of the social world to the attempt at reform, we seem to involve the possibility of changing what at the same time we assume to be necessarily fixed" (Mead 1899a, pp. 370-71). It seems logical, therefore, that, to make room for reform, pragmatists would postulate a measure of indeterminacy, proclaim that "uncertainty does not belong simply to the values, it belongs to the facts as well" (MP b8, fl), and urge that "the individual and environment—the situation—mutually determine each other" (Mead [1908] 1964, p. 86). If one were to assert the possibility of reform, one had to decry the morality that pictured the existing order of things as inherently rational and to replace it with a new ethics, according to which "moral advance consists not in adapting individual natures to the fixed realities of a moral universe, but in constantly reconstructing and recreating the world as the individuals evolve" (Mead [1908] 1964, p. 90). These philosophical tenets found their expression in the pragmatism-inspired—interactionist—theory of society.

In one of the posthumously published volumes of Mead's works appears a telling passage in which he formulates the central problem of modem society: "How can you present order and structure in society and bring about the changes that need to take place, are taking place? How can you bring those changes about in orderly fashion and yet preserve order? To bring about change is seemingly to destroy the given order, and yet society does and must change. That is the problem, to incorporate the methods of change into the order of society itself" (1936, pp. 361-62). This question is paradigmatic to the conception of sociology as the science of social reconstruction or the science of social control that gained wide currency among American sociologists in the Progressive Era (Faris 1967; Fisher and Strauss 1978; Janowitz 1978; Shalin 1986a). It was commonly held at the time that sociology dealt with the problems of society undergoing transformation, that the "process of reconstructing social conditions is the process with which the social sciences deal" (MP b7, f8). It was also widely assumed that sociology could aid in efforts to minimize the more disruptive consequences of social change. Indicative of the community of assumptions underlying sociological thinking of this period was the concept of social control. More than a technical term, social control was also a theoretical expression of progressive ideology. How can we exercise intelligent control over social processes? was the burning question of the Progressive Era, and it was in response to this query that sociologists came up with an ingenuous answer: Intelligent control over human society requires social control over human intelligence. What this meant was that the fortunes of society did not have to be decided on the barricades and in the flames of revolutions, for the real battle was for people's minds. To influence the direction in which society grows, one had to *reform* or, what is the same, to *inform* the consciousness of its members. That is to say, the answer to the modern predicament was not coercion and violence but social control—not in a sense that every member of society will be issued a standard set of beliefs, but that everybody will be given a chance to develop critical intelligence necessary for public discourse and social reconstruction. This answer, along with other precepts of social interactionism, was consistent with the political climate of the age of reform. Again, Mead's writings offer us insight into the interplay between ideological beliefs and substantive theorizing in the Progressive Era.

As we have seen before, Mead acknowledged the socialists' role in exposing capitalism's seedier sides and raising the workers' awareness of the need to fight for their rights. There was one more, and not so obvious, thing for which Mead was ready to credit socialism—its role in striking down the then prevalent concept of man as an asocial being. In addition to exposing the economic institutions of laissez-faire capitalism, the socialist critique exposed its ideological fallacies, including the utilitarian idea of mind as biological endowment and of action as an instrument for maximizing personal pleasure. Socialist thinkers rejected this utilitarian view, substituting for it the idea of the perennially social nature of man. "But the essence of man is no abstraction inherent in each separate individual. In its reality it is the *ensemble* (aggregate) of social relations" (Marx [1846] 1963, p. 198). Now Mead was not familiar with all the sociologically relevant works of Marx, certainly not with the writings of the young Marx, which appeared in print for the first time after Mead's death, yet he had an acute sense of socialism's sociological import. Socialist teaching is ultimately concerned with socializing man's action and thought, argued Mead: "Its reality lies in the essentially social character of all conduct, and the gospel, according to socialism, is the recognition that all self-seeking has and must have a social end, if it belongs inside a social organism. What society is struggling to accomplish is to bring this social side of our conduct out so that it may, in some conscious way, become the element of control" (1899b, p. 406). This insight, maintained Mead, is socialism's most useful contribution to the diagnosis of modern conditions.

Indeed, as long as our motives remain private and we act without regard for other members of society, democracy will continue to breed injustice and misery. It is only when the individual takes into account the larger social context, when he "takes the role of the other," that social control becomes a guiding force in society and democracy realizes its potential as a political system: "Social control depends, then, upon the degree to which the individuals in society are able to assume the attitudes of the others who are involved with them in common endeavor" (Mead [1924-25] 1964, p. 291). This, according to Mead, is the sociological essence of socialism, and this, I should add, is when his own sociological ideas intersect with those of the young Marx and romantic thinkers. Mead's premise that "the whole nature of our intelligence is social to the very core" (1934, p. 141) is consistent with Marx's view that "activity and mind, both in their content and in their *mode of existence*, are social, *social* activity and *social* mind" [1844] 1964, p. 138). The same is true of Mead's (1935-36, p. 70) contention that "the individual is no thrall to society. He constitutes society as genuinely as society constitutes the individual," which reminds us of Marx's (1964, p. 137) motto, "*Just as* society produces *man as man*, so is society *produced* by him." There is a family resemblance between Mead's assertion that "the unity and structure of the complete self reflects the unity and structure of the social process as a whole" (1934, p. 144) and Marx's thesis that "man, much as he may therefore be a *particular* individual ... is just as much a *totality*—the ideal society—the subjective existence of thought and experienced society for itself" (1964, p. 138). And, finally, Mead's (1934, p. 309) insight that the "relations between social reconstruction and self or personality reconstruction are reciprocal and internal" reflects the same dialectical pattern that is embedded in Marx's idea of revolutionary practice as "the coincidence of changing of circumstances and of human activity or self-changing" (1963, p. 198).

It would be a mistake to push the parallels between Mead and Marx too far, and it would be equally mistaken to ignore them. These parallels reflect the same determination to overcome the opposition between public and private, social and individual, society and man, the determination to bring into one continuum mind, self, and society that marked the thought of romantic philosophers, progressive reformers, and pragmatist thinkers. I wish to stress that Mead's interactionism is closest to Marx's romanticism, that is, to that early period in Marx's intellectual career when he was close to the idealism of Hegel and Fichte, when he did not yet break with bourgeois democratism and still had high regard for the curative powers of self-conscious reason (Gouldner 1973, pp. 337-40; Shalin 1986b, pp. 112-13). As Marx became increasingly disillusioned with the prospects for the peaceful transformation of society, the romantic-idealist themes gave way in his writings to a new emphasis on economic factors and revolutionary force. Mead, on the other hand, like most progressive thinkers, retained his youthful idealism as well as his romantic organicism with its root metaphor of man-the-microcosm (Shalin 1984, pp. 55-58). What is signally important about romantic organicism is that it compels one to see man and society not as opposed entities but as aspects of the same process of the production of social reality as objective and meaningful. The individual appears here not just as one organ or part of the social whole but as a social self, or, to use the language of romantic organicism, a "species being" reflecting in unique fashion the totality of social relations. By the same token, society loses in this scheme its externality and thinglike character, as it is dissolves into a series of interactions in the course of which it is continuously regenerated as a social universe or universe of discourse. It is very important from the interactionist standpoint that the individual embraces within his self the whole of society, that he "takes the attitude of the generalized other." It is equally important that the individual does not become a passive receptacle of social norms and values but develops a critical attitude toward his social self and the society that provided him with this self.[13] The individual is both "Me" and "I"—a responsible member of various social groups and a unique personality capable of transcending a given order, a law-abiding citizen and a critic of society.

Insofar as the individual successfully integrates these two aspects of his social existence, the relationship between the individual and society can be judged organic, which is exactly what progressives wished it to be. Here is a sample of statements expressing this romantic theme, as formulated by different progressive thinkers:

> The organization and unification of a social group is identical with the organization and unification of any one of the selves arising within the social process.... Each individual self within this process, while it reflects in its organized structure the behavior pattern of that process as a whole, does so from its own particular or unique standpoint.... (Mead 1934, pp. 144, 201)

> But human society represents a more perfect organism. The whole lives truly in every member, and there is no longer the appearance of physical aggregation, or continuity. The organism manifests itself as what it truly is, an ideal or spiritual life, a unity of *will*. If then, society and the individual are really organic to each other, then the individual is society concentrated. He is not merely its image or mirror. He is the localized manifestation of its life. (Dewey 1969, p. 237)

> A national structure which encourages individuality as opposed to mere particularity is one which creates innumerable special niches, adapted to all degrees and kinds of individual development. The individual becomes a nation in miniature, but devoted to loyal realization of a purpose peculiar to himself. The nation becomes an enlarged individual whose special purpose is that of human amelioration, and in whose life every individual should find some particular but essential functions. (Croly 1909, p. 414)

These utterances should not be taken to mean that progressives saw contemporary American society as an actual embodiment of organic interaction. A contemporary industrial society, as Mead (1934, p. 307) and other progressives repeatedly stated, is ridden with contradictions: "Within such a society, conflicts arise between different aspects or phases of the same individual self ... as well as between individual selves [that must be] settled or terminated by reconstructions of particular social situations, or modifications of the given framework of social relations, wherein they arise or occur." Rather, the above statements should be seen as an attempt to lay down a standard for judging contemporary reality, an ideal and a theory that indicated the direction of social reconstruction and the method of social control. As an ideal, the future society envisioned by the progressive imagination was somewhat akin to the romantic notion of *Gemeinschaft*, in that it accentuated the virtues of the "Great Community," "free and enriching communion," or free intercourse, whose participants are "the constant makers of a continuously new society" (Dewey [1927] 1954, p. 115-17; [1929] 1962, p. 143). A formal model of this future society was "the universe of discourse, a community based simply on the ability of all individuals to converse with each other through use of the same significant symbols"; its actualization requires an understanding that "the brotherhood of men ... is the basis for a universal society" (Mead 1934, pp. 282-83). As a method, interactionist theory extolled the advantages of intelligent social control over force as a means of effecting social change. Its preference for peaceful, non-coercive forms of social reconstruction was already implied in its basic premises: If mind, self, and society belong to one continuum and are indeed aspects of the same social intercourse, then the reconstruction of society is largely a matter of reconstructing the human mind. "An institution is, after all, nothing but an organization of attitudes which we all carry in us" (Mead 1934, p. 211), and so, abolishing obsolete institutions means reforming our attitudes, our ways of thinking. That is, to change society, we have to change ourselves: "Thus the relation between social reconstruction and self or personality reconstruction by the individual members of any organized human society entails self or personality reconstruction in some degree or other by each of these individuals.... In both types of reconstruction the same fundamental material of organized social relations among human individuals is involved, and is simply treated in different ways, or from different angles or points of view, in the two cases respectively; or in short, social reconstruction and self or personality reconstruction are the two sides of a single process—the process of human social evolution" (Mead 1934, p. 309).

To sum up, there is an elective affinity between Mead's social philosophy and his political beliefs. Along with other pragmatists, Mead abandoned the rationalist universe of natural order, replacing it with a world brimming with possibilities and open to social reform. Translated into the language of sociological theory, this world-in-the-making yielded a peculiar version of "sociological progressivism" (Fisher and Strauss 1978, p. 488), with its dynamic picture of society as ongoing social interaction. Every individual appears in this picture as simultaneously a product and producer of society, whereas society transpires as both an antecedent and outcome of social interaction. Mind, self, and society are bound here together as parts of one continuum, or aspects of the same process of production, of social reality as objective and meaningful, which makes it imperative that each be understood in terms of the other. The circle involved in the interactionist mode of reasoning is not unintentional; it is the dialectical or hermeneutical circle that requires that each part be explained through the whole and the whole in terms of its parts. This dialectical approach, characteristic of nineteenth-century romanticism and twentieth-century Progressivism, accentuates the possibility of peaceful social transformation and predicates the reconstruction of society on the reconstruction of the human mind. The ultimate goal of social reconstruction envisioned in social interactionism is a democratic community embodying the ideal of free discourse or organic interaction (Habermas 1981, pp. 11-68). When the self-consciousness of all individuals is so altered that each can rejoice with the successes, empathize with the miseries, and help meet the needs of others, that is, when everyone assumes the attitude of the whole society, then the latter is transformed into a truly universal and democratic community.

Conclusion: Mead and the Progressive Legacy

Many observers have commented on the contradictions inherent in the Progressive movement, on its "profound internal dialectic" (Conn 1933, p. 1; see also Hofstadter 1955, pp. 5, 236; White 1957, p. 46; Noble 1958). There is indeed a great deal of tension in progressive ideology. Its adherents extolled the virtues of entrepreneurial individualism and at the same time stressed the need for public control; they longed for a socialism of opportunity yet defended the capitalism of property; they urged a radical break with the present and reached deep into the past for an ideal of the future; above all, they were determined to escape the twin dangers of radicalism and conservatism. "There is the conflict between the old and the new, between the radical and the conservative," wrote Mead about the dominant mood of this time, "but ... we may not wish to be either radical or conservative. We may wish to comprehend and to do justice to the changing valuations" (1938, p. 480). It is this desire to rise above the political extremes of the Right and the Left that brought on the scorn for the progressives from some contemporary and modem critics. Those on the Right have charged that Progressivism ultimately leads to socialism. For critics on the Left, Progressivism has been little more than an episode in the ongoing effort to stem the inexorable decline of corporate capitalism. Yet historical Progressivism defies attempts to subsume it under a neat ideological label.

Progressive reformers were democrats of a new breed. These were "men and women longing to socialize their democracy" (Addams 1910, p. 116), working for "a more balanced, a more equal, even, and equitable system of human liberties" (Dewey 1946, p. 113) and determined "to limit and control private economic power as the Founders had limited political power" (Graham 1967, p. 5). It is arguable whether, as Scott (1959, pp. 697,690) claims, "the Progressive Era was more original than the New Deal and more daring as well," but he is right to stress its historical importance, and he is justified in his critique of persistent attempts in modern historiography "to conservatize Progressivism." Kolko's thesis (1963) that progressive reforms constituted "the triumph of conservatism" flies in the face of the progressives' democratic aspirations. The very term "social reconstruction" adopted by progressives was indicative of their values. It harked back to the Civil War era, when Lincoln invoked it to describe the need to break cleanly with the past and to start the country on a radically new path. With an equal sense of urgency, progressives faced up to the task of social reconstruction, which on the eve of the twentieth century meant bringing government into the marketplace, broadening the scope of economic opportunity, democratizing education, and transforming the public into an agent of social control. Far from a monolithic movement, Progressivism was championed by the people who, regardless of their many differences, shared the belief that the key to transforming society is to be found in public discourse rather than in the skills of professional politicians. In their fight against laissez-faire capitalism, progressives borrowed many an insight from socialism. Some claimed that "we are in for some kind of socialism, call it by whatever name we please" (Dewey 1962, p. 119). Nevertheless, there were important points of theory and method on which progressives and socialists parted company. Progressives endorsed socialism's emancipatory goals but rejected its revolutionary means. Their attempt, unsuccessful as it might have been, to work out a scheme for securing these goals without breaking the constitutional framework of democracy—an attempt that is at the core of the progressive agenda—is the most enduring legacy of the Progressive movement. It is also a source of perennial tension and contradiction in Progressivism as well as in the kindred pragmatist and interactionist movements.

Progressives recognized that democracy would self-destruct unless it provided room for justice, that society must secure minimum economic and social standards for every one of its members. But how much democracy, how much justice? Does it include socialized medicine, guaranteed employment, free college education? Both Mead and Dewey were likely to include these among the standards of social decency required for the development of each individual's creative potential, but there is nothing in progressive ideology that would help to resolve this matter in principle. More important, one has to wonder whether full equality of opportunity can be accomplished under private ownership of the means of production. The critics on the Left had reasons to doubt that the efforts of the progressives to socialize opportunity would ever bring about the socialism of opportunity in a capitalist America, but the socialists' wholesale dismissal of Progressivism was far too hasty. They did not understand the progressives' preoccupation with the means of social reconstruction and specifically with their concern for the fate of democracy in a society where economic power was radically centralized. The highest value for socialists was economic equality; once it was achieved, Marx thought, human rights would take care of themselves, and universal democracy would naturally ensue. But more recent socialist thinkers have become increasingly aware (Lynd 1974, p. 773; Giddens 1981, pp. 172-73; Lukes 1985) that this outcome is far from assured. All radical attempts to nationalize the means of production in this century have resulted in the breakdown of democratic institutions—the more radical the scope of nationalization, the more deleterious effect it seems to have on human rights; the more successful the efforts to do away with bourgeois democracy, the less room left for radical social criticism. This is not to say that capitalism guarantees human rights (think of Chile or South Africa), only that human rights have invariably been a casualty of attempts to substitute a socialist (in Marx's sense of the word) for a capitalist society. In light of this historical experience, progressives' concern for democracy and the means-ends relationship in social reconstruction is entirely justified. There is a dialectical tension between justice and democracy, equality and freedom, that is inherent in Western liberalism (Lasch 1983; Gutmann 1983) and that the progressives failed to resolve, but this is a creative tension, and progressives did the right thing by bringing it to light and illuminating the need to balance the considerations of justice with those of democracy.

The amorphous notion of public good is another source of difficulty and confusion in progressive theory. Mead consistently refused to enunciate what he meant by "public good" or to spell out the values that would help one judge a policy or a program as being in the "interests of the community as a whole." Like other reformers of his time, he was confident that each contentious issue lends itself to public adjudication and that every social conflict could be amicably resolved. Critics have been attacking the excessive optimism, deliberate ambiguity, and opportunistic tendencies in pragmatist and progressive thought (Bourne 1915; Smith 1931; Niebuhr [1932] 1960; Novack 1975). What they are less likely to see is that these tendencies are not without a rationale. Pragmatists and progressives refused to specify the exact nature of a future democratic society because they believed that "every generation has to accomplish democracy over and over again," that "the very idea of democracy has to be constantly discovered, and rediscovered, remade and reorganized" (Dewey 1946, pp. 31, 47). Any overarching scheme, "a vision given on the mount," is likely to turn into a straitjacket if followed rigidly and unswervingly, as numerous attempts in recent decades to impose a shining revolutionary ideal on an unyielding reality readily testify. It is not true that progressives had no vision of the future or that all their values were ad hoc. The failure of the progressives to endorse the comprehensive social security program, caused by their fear of patronage politics and federal bureaucracy, does not undermine their commitment to spreading social justice. Their emphasis on regulatory reforms and public control instead of state-run and government-supervised programs was also far from disingenuous and class-motivated, as it is sometimes portrayed. Progressives were essentially right in leaving it to the public to define and redefine continuously what shape their ideal of a more democratic and humane society should assume in a given historical setting. There will always be much bickering and plenty of tactical mistakes, but in the long run a public forum is the best one for articulating the public good. The idea of a democratic public, as Janowitz (1952, 1978) points out, that is, the idea of "the passing of functions which are supposed to inhere in the government into activities that belong to the community" (Mead 1899a, p. 369), is an enduring contribution of pragmatism and interactionism to contemporary social thought.

Another facet of philosophical and sociological progressivism that has drawn criticism is tied to the belief in scientific method as an instrument of social reform. Mead's insistence that "scientific method ... is nothing but a highly developed form of impartial intelligence," that "science has become the method of social progress, and social progress itself has become a religion" ([1923] 1964, p. 256; 1918, p. 639) is sure to invite criticism. Charges of scientism and positivism are frequently leveled against pragmatism in this connection (Selsam 1950). Much of this criticism, in my view, stems from a misconception of the pragmatist idea of science. It is not true that pragmatists saw scientific knowledge as being value neutral and scientists as standing above society. "Knowing, including most emphatically scientific knowledge," stressed Dewey (1946, p. 17), "is not outside social activity, but is itself a form of social behavior, as much as agriculture or transportation." Moreover, as Mead ([1930]

1964, p. 406) claimed, "It is not until science has become a discipline to which the research ability of any mind from any class in society can be attracted that it can become rigorously scientific." Pragmatists did not seek value neutrality, nor did they espouse value partisanship. Their position is best described as value tolerance or value-added politics, in that it advocates "taking the value perspective of the other" and seeks truth at "the intersection of conflicting values" (Shalin 1979, 1980).[14] Mead and his fellow pragmatists did not trust the magic powers of scientific intelligence to resolve the burning issues of the day. Rather, they valued science as a form of rational discourse in which every participant has a say, all claims are subject to testing, and each solution undergoes continuous revision. It is not a perfect institution, but, warts and all, science offers the best available model of democracy in action, and we should credit pragmatists for focusing attention on the operations of value-tolerant science and the contribution it could make to rational discourse in society at large.

One final issue that needs to be addressed here concerns the progressives' trust in democratic institutions and peaceful revolution in America. As many critics (Bates 1933; Selsam 1950; Purcell 1973; Schwedinger and Schwedinger 1974; Karier 1975; Novack 1975) have argued, correctly in my view, pragmatists tended to exaggerate both the potential for and the actual extent of social change in America. They confused the normative and the descriptive in their accounts by, on the one hand, criticizing contemporary democracy and, on the other, insisting that the institutional framework of democracy necessary for social reconstruction was already in place. This confusion is clearly visible in the indifference of Mead and most of the progressives to the plight of blacks. They spoke eloquently on behalf of immigrants, women, and children, but the institutionalized exclusion of blacks from American democracy did not seem to bother progressive reformers much. I should also note that Mead, along with other progressives, held a rather naive view of business leaders' readiness to heed the voice of reason and jump on the bandwagon of reform. "While a good part of the program of socialism is being put into practice," wrote Mead (MP b2, addenda, f27), "the striking difference lies in the fact that it [is] being undertaken not by the proletariat but by the whole community under the eager guidance of captains of industry, community generals, research scientists and conservative statesmen." This statement flies in the face of the long war with trade unions and dogged opposition to labor reforms that "captains of industry" waged, as they still do, using more or less preposterous excuses. It took a large-scale rebellion at Homestead and elsewhere to convince big business that reforms were unavoidable, perhaps even useful, after all. We may add that it took a massive campaign of civil disobedience in the 1960s to bring blacks into American democracy. All of which suggests that American society, certainly in the Progressive Era, was far from the institutional democracy in which revolution could have been carried out by peaceable means alone.

Having said this, I take issue with those critics who see pragmatists and progressives as dreamy idealists at best and apologists for corporate capitalism at worst. "These men were progressives and meliorists of their day, but they were realists and skeptics as well" (Janowitz 1970, p. xii). They fought hard battles in Congress for progressive legislation, they were doing tangible things to improve the lot of immigrants and the poor, and they were prepared to change the very system if necessary to make room for meaningful reform: "In order to endure under present conditions, liberalism must become radical in the sense that, instead of using social power to ameliorate the evil consequences of the existing system, it shall use social power to change the system" (Dewey 1946, p. 132). There is every reason to believe that Mead would have endorsed this statement.

Notes

1. One should also bear in mind that Mead's articles gathered in a widely used volume edited by Reck (1964) sometimes appear there in an abridged form and that typically left out are the politically relevant sections.

2. The letters "MP" stand here and elsewhere in the text for the George H. Mead papers, a collection of letters and manuscripts by Mead in the Special Collections Department of the Joseph Regenstein Library, University of Chicago. The letters "b" and "f" followed by a number indicate, respectively, box number and folder number where a particular document is located. Mead's letters to Castle are gathered in box 1, folders 1-4. Editorial changes in the following excerpts from Mead's letters and manuscripts are limited to typographical errors and punctuation. Two of the letters pertaining to Mead's interests in socialism and reform have been transcribed by the author and are published in the Fall 1987 issue of *Symbolic Interaction* (see Shalin 1987).

3. In his senior year, Mead was elected an editor of the *Oberlin Review* and charged with the responsibility of assisting Henry Castle, his close friend and fellow editor, in the editorial department. Most of the editorials published during the academic year of 1882-83 were probably written by Castle, but some, judged by their style and other telltale signs, were penned by Mead, and virtually all must have had at least his tacit approval.

4. Mead's difficulties of those years were financial as much as intellectual. After college, Mead had to support himself and possibly his mother first by working as a school teacher and then as a member of a survey team of the Wisconsin Central

Railroad Company. It does appear that Henry Castle, the son of wealthy American missionaries in Hawaii, furnished Mead with some financial assistance during the latter's studies at Harvard and later in Germany. In 1891, Mead married Castle's sister, Helen, and eventually inherited, through her, part of the Castle family fortune. The influence of Henry Castle on Mead's personal and intellectual growth was great indeed, and one can only hope that the story of this beautiful friendship, which ended in 1895 with Castle's tragic death, will one day be told.

5. Mead's criticism of this period, and particularly his lamentations about the lack of a "national feeling" in America (MP October 19, 1890, b1, f1), bears a startling resemblance to the criticism of the American scene developed by the members of the Nationalist Club—a reform organization established by the followers of Bellamy, the author of the popular utopia, *Looking Backward*, which advocated the cause of socialism in the United States.

6. The importance of social democracy here is tremendous, but not in the least alarming," wrote Castle ([1894] 1902, p. 784) to his parents while on a trip to Germany. "It simply stands as a protest against the existing conditions, not merely on their economical but also on their political side. The leaders are men of brains and education, whose influence is on the side of the general democratic movement after all, and as such useful and necessary."

7. Graham Taylor, a social worker with long experience in the Chicago reform department, wrote to Mead's son on the death of his father, "More than he or any of us know the social settlement and city movements owed much to his enlistment and guidance" (MP Taylor to Henry Mead, September 26, 1931, b1a, f7).

8. In a letter to his daughter-in-law, Mead, (MP March 10, 1919, b1, f16) refers to his duty as president of the City Club to nominate a few of its members as candidates for its leading positions: "Now I will spend hours on the phone securing the consent of the five—well balanced between the radicals and conservatives—which means two reds, two blues and one Menshevik." Somehow, one gets the impression that Mead's sympathies were, at this time, with the Mensheviks, i.e., with the moderate social democrats committed to democracy, reform, and the rule of law.

9. Even in the heyday of Progressivism, teaching socialism in colleges was seen as a disloyal act. Here is a statement on the subject adopted in 1914 by the state of Wisconsin Republican Convention: "We favor the principle of *Lehrfreiheit*. The truth must and shall he taught. However, Socialism is not a demonstrated truth and we regard it as destructive of every principle of government that is dear to the American people and the mind of the student should he kept free from its misleading theories" (quoted in Mead 1915, p. 351).

10. One of Mead's letters to his wife contains a interesting reference to Veblen: "Had a pleasant call upon Veblen, who is pained because the Socialist Review says his doctrine is good socialism" (MP May 13, 1901, b1, f5). Veblen was no socialist, but his precarious position at the University of Chicago must have made him sensitive to such suggestions.

11. In 1916, Mead wrote to his daughter-in-law, Irene Tufts Mead: "It is good that there is likely to be a popular majority for Wilson as well as the majority of the Electoral College, though I wish it had been larger, that is I wish that the country had swung further in the direction of progressivism...." (MP November 12, 1916, b1, f3). While sympathetic to Wilson's program, Mead appeared to be a life-long member of the Republican Party. In 1919, he took issue with the senator Medill McCormick over the League of Nations, but in his exchange with the senator he identified himself as "a member of the Republican party" and expressed concern for the party's fate (MP b1, f16).

12. In one place, Mead refers to "a real democracy in which the theoretical political power is not simply in the hands a voting majority, but in which the community life expresses the interests of all..." (MP b2 addenda, f27).

13. "Human society, we have insisted, does not merely stamp the pattern of its organized social behavior upon any one of its individual members, so that this pattern becomes likewise the pattern of the individual's self; it also, at the same time, gives him a mind.... And his mind enables him in turn to stamp the pattern of his further developing self (further developing through his mental activity) upon the structure or organization of human society, and thus in a degree to reconstruct and modify in terms of his self the general pattern of social or group behavior in terms of which his self was originally constituted" (Mead 1934, p. 363). I have examined elsewhere (Shalin 1978) the macrosociological implications of this thesis.

14. There is a interesting parallel between the way pragmatists and contemporary German scholars searched for a proper mix of science and ethics. Thus, both Dewey and Weber expressed considerable regard for scientific procedures, both thought that objective knowledge is grounded in values, and both rejected the "ethics of ultimate ends" and opted for the "ethics a responsibility" or "ethics of means." Ultimately, however, Weber praised value neutrality as a stance befitting scientific workers, whereas Dewey and the pragmatists were more in tune with the idea of value tolerance.

References

Aaron, D. 1951. *Men of Good Hope: A Story of American Progressives*. New York: Oxford University Press.

Addams, Jane. 1902. *Democracy and Social Ethics*. New York: Macmillan.

_____.1910. *Twenty Years at Hull-House*. New York: Macmillan.

Barnard, John. 1969.*From Evangelicalism to Progressivism at Oberlin College, 1866-1917*. Columbus: Ohio State University Press.

Bates, E. S. 1933. "John Dewey: America's Philosophic Engineer." *Modern Monthly* 7:387-96.

Bliss, W. D. P. (1890) 1970. "What to Do Now?" Pp.350-54 in *Socialism in America: From the Shakers to the Third International*, edited by Albert Fried Garden City, NY: Doubleday.

Boume, R. S. 1915. "John Dewey's Philosophy." *New Republic* 13:154-56.

Castle, Henry N. (1889) 1902. "Letter of Henry Castle to George H. Mead, February 3, 1899," pp. 578-81 in *Henry Northrup Castle: Letters*. London: Sands.

_____. 1902. "Letter of Henry Castle to Mabel, Helen, and Mother, November 27, 1894." Pp.783-85 in *Henry Northrup Castle: Letters*. London: Sands.

Conn, Peter. 1983. *The Divided Mind: Ideology and Imagination in America, 1898-1917*. Cambridge: Cambridge University Press.

Cremin, L. A. 1969. "John Dewey and the progressive Education Movement," *Antioch Review* 67:160-73.

Croly, Herbert. 1909. *The Promise of American Life*. New York: Macmillan.

Debs, Eugene. 1912. "Sound Socialist Tactics." *International Socialist Review* 12:481-86.

Deegan, M. J., and J. S. Burger. 1978. "George Herbert Mead and Social Reform: His Work and Writings." *Journal of the History of the Behavioral Sciences* 14:362-73.

Dewey, John. (1888)1969. "The Ethics of Democracy." Pp. 227-49 in *John Dewey, the Early Works, 1882-1889*, Vol.1. Carbondale: Southern Illinois University Press.

_____. (1927) 1954. *The Public and Its Problems*. New York: Holt.

_____. (1929) 1962. *Individualism, Old and New*. New York: Capricorn.

_____. (1938) 1950. "What I Believe, Revised." Pp.32-35 in *Pragmatism and American Culture*, edited by Gail Kennedy. Boston: D. C. Heath.

_____. 1946. *The Problems of Men*. New York: Philosophical Library.

Dewey, John, and John L. Childs. 1933. "The Underlying Philosophy of Education." Pp.287-319 in *The Educational Frontier*, edited by W. H. Kilpatrick. New York: Appleton-Century.

Diner, S. J. 1975. "Department and Discipline: The Department of Sociology at the University of Chicago, 1892-1920." *Minerva* 13:514-53.

_____. 1980. *A City and its Universities, Public Policy in Chicago, 1892-1919*. Chapel Hill: University of North Carolina Press.

Editorial. 1882. *Oberlin Review* 10:55.

_____. 1883. *Oberlin Review* 10:175-76.

Faris, Robert E. 1970. *Chicago Sociology, 1920-1932*. Chicago: University of Chicago: University of Chicago Press.

Featherstone, J. 1972. "John Dewey." *New Republic* 8:27-32.

Fisher, Berenice M., and Anselm L. Strauss. 1978. "Introduction." Pp.457-98 in *A History of Sociological Analysis*, edited by Tom Bottomore and Lewis A. Coser. New York: Basic Books.

Fried, Albert, ed. 1970. *Socialism in America: From the Shakers; to the Third International*. Garden City, NY: Doubleday.

Furner, Mary 0. 1975. *Advocacy & Objectivity. A Crisis in the Professionalization of American Social Sciences, 1865-1905*. Lexington: University Press of Kentucky.

George, Henry. (1879) 1926. *Progress and Poverty*. New York: Doubleday, Page.

Giddens, Anthony. 1981. *A Contemporary Critique of Historical Materialism*, Vol. 1. Berkeley and Los Angeles: University of California Press.

Goldman, Eric. 1956. *Rendezvous with Destiny: A History of Modern American Reform*. New York: Vintage.

Gouldner, Alvin A. 1973. "Romanticism and Classicism: Deep Structures in Social Science." Pp. 323-66 *in For Sociology: Renewal and Criticism in Sociology Today*, by Alvin A. Gouldner. New York: Basic Books.

Graham, Otis L. 1967. *An Encore for Reform: The Old Progressive and the New Deal*. New York: Oxford University Press.

Gutmann, Amy. 1983. "How Liberal is Democracy?" Pp.25-50 in *Liberalism Reconsidered*, edited by Douglas MacLean and Claudia Mills. Totowa, NJ: Rowman & Allanheld.

Habermas, Jargen. 1981. *Theorie des Kommunihativen Handelns*. Band 2. Frankfurt: Suhrkamp.

Hofstadter, Richard. 1955. *The Age of Reform: From Byron to FDR*. New York: Alfred A. Knopf.

Janowitz, Morris. 1952. *The Community Press in an Urban Setting*. Chicago: University of Chicago Press.

_____. 1970. "Preface." Pp. xi-xii in *Introduction to the Science of Sociology*, by Robert Park and Ernest W. Burgess. Chicago: University of Chicago Press.

_____. 1978. *The Last Half Century: Societal Change and Politics in America*. Chicago: University of Chicago Press.

Joas, Hans. 1985. *G. H. Mead: A Contemporary Reexamination of His Thought*. Cambridge, MA: Polity Press.

Karier, C. J. 1975. "John Dewey and the New Liberlism." *History of Education Quarterly* 15:417-43.

Kolko, Gabriel. 1963. The *Triumph of Conservatism: A Reinterpretation of American History*, 1900-1916. New York: Free Press.

Lasch, Christopher. 1983. "Liberalism in Retreat" Pp. 105-16 in *Liberalism Reconsidered*, edited by Douglas MacLean and Claudia Mills. Totowa, NJ: Rowman & Allanheld.

Laslett, John H. M., and Seymour Martin Lipset, eds. 1974. *Failure of a Dream? Essays in the History of American Socialism*. Garden City, NY: Anchor.

Levine, D. 1969. "Randolph Bourne, John Dewey, and the Legacy of Liberalism." *Antioch Review* 29:234-44.

Lukes, Steven. 1985. *Morality and Marxism*. London: Oxford University Press.

Lynd, Staughton. 1974. "The Prospects of the New Left." Pp. 713-38 in *Failure of a Dream? Essays in the History of Amercan Socialism*, edited by John H. M. Laslett and Seymour Martin Lipset. Garden City, NY: Anchor.

McNaught, Kenneth. 1974. "Comment." Pp.409-20 in *Failure of a Dream? Essays in the History of Amercan Socialism*, edited by John H. Laslett and Seymour Martin Lipset. Garden City, NY: Anchor.

Marx, Karl. (1844) 1964. *The Economic & Philosophic Manuscripts of 1844*. New York: International.

_____. (1846) 1963. *The German Ideology. Parts 1 and 3*. New York: International

Mead, George H. (n.d.) *George Herbert Mead Papers*. University of Chicago Archives.

_____. 1881. "The Relation of Art to Morality." *Oberlin Review* 9:63-64.

_____. 1882a. "Charles Lamb." *Oberlin Review* 10:15-16.

_____. 1812b. "De Quincey." *Oberlin Review* 10:50-52.

_____. 1882c. "John Locke." *Oberlin Review* 10:217-19.

_____. 1884. "Republican Persecution, Letter to the Editor." *Nation* 39:519-20.

_____. 1899a. "The Working Hypothesis in Social Reform." *American Journal of Sociology* 5:367-71.

_____. 1899b. "Review of Le Bon, Psychology of Socialism." *American Journal of Sociology* 5:404-12.

_____. 1907. "Review of Jane Addam's The Newer Ideals of Peace." *American Journal of Sociology* 13:121-28.

_____. (1908) 1964. "The Philosophical Basis of Ethics." Pp. 82-93 In *Selected Writings: George Herbert Mead*, edited by A. J. Reck. New York: Bobbs-Merrill.

_____. 1907-8. "The Educational Situation in the Chicago Public Schools." *City Club Bulletin* 1:131-38.

_____. 1908. "Educational Aspects of Trade Unions." *Union Labor Advocate* 8: 19-20.

_____. 1908-9a. "Industrial Education, the Working Man, and the School." *Elementary School Teacher* 9:369-83.

_____. 1908-95. "Editorial Notes." *Elementary School Teacher* 9:156-57.

_____. 1908-9c. "Editorial Notes." *Elementary School Teacher* 9:212-14.

_____. 1909. "The Adjustment of Our Industry to Surplus and Unskilled Labor." Proceedings of the National Conference of Charities and Corrections 34:222-25.

_____. 1912. "Remarks on Labor Night concerning Participation of Representatives of Labor in the City Club." *City Club Bulletin* 5:9.

_____. 1915. "Madison: The Passage of the University of Wisconsin through the State Political Agitation of 1914; the Survey by William H. Allen and His Staff and the Legislative Fight of 1915, with the Indications These Offer of the Place the State University Holds in the Community." *Survey* 35:349-61.

_____.(1915) 1964. "Natural Rights and the Theory of the Political Institution." Pp. 150:-70 in *Selected Writings: George Herbert Mead*, edited by A. J. Reck. New York: Bobbs-Merrill.

_____. 1916-17."Professor Hoxie and the Community." University of Chicago Magazine 9:114-17.

_____. 1917a. "Germany's Crisis—Its Effect on Labor. Part I." *Chicago Herald*, Thursday, July 26.

_____. 1917b. "Germany's Crissis—Its Effect on Labor. Part II." *Chicago Herald*, Friday, July 27.

_____. 1917c. "War Issues to U.S. Forced by Kaiser." *Chicago Herald*, Thursday, August 2.

_____. 1917d. "Democracy's Issues in the World War." *Chicago Herald*, August 4.

_____. 1917e. "American Ideals and the War." *Chicago Herald*, Friday, August 3.

_____. 1918. "Social Work, Standards of Living and the War." Proceedings of the National Conference of Social Work 45:637-44.

_____.(1923) 1964. "Scientific Method and the Moral Sciences." Pp.248-66 in *Selected Writings: George Herbert Mead*, edited by A. J. Reck. New York: Bobbs-Merrill.

_____.(1924-25) 1964. "The Genesis of the Self and Social Control." Pp. 267-93 in *Selected Writings: George Herbert Mead*, edited by A. J. Reck. New York: Bobbs-Merill.

_____.(1925-26) 1964. "The Nature of Aesthetic Experience." Pp. 294~305 in *Selected Writings: George Herbert Mead*, edited by A. J. Rock. New York: Bobbs-Merrill.

_____. (1930) 1964. "Philanthropy from the Point of View of Ethics." Pp.392-407 in *Selected Writings: George Herbert Mead*, edited by A. J. Rock. New York: Bobbs-Merrill.

_____. 1934. *Mind, Self, and Society*. Chicago: University of Chicago Press.

_____. 1935-36. "The Philosophy of John Dewey." *International Journal of Ethics* 46:64-81.

_____. 1936. *Movements of Thought in the Nineteenth Century*. Chicago: University of Chicago Press.

_____. 1938. *The Philosophy of the Act*. Chicago: University of Chicago Press.

Niebuhr, Reinhold. (1932) 1960. *Moral Man and Immoral Society*. New York: Charles Scribner's Sons.

Noble, David W. 1958. *The Paradox of Progressive Thought*. Minneapolis: University of Minnesota Press.

Novack, George. 1975. *Progmatism versus Marxism*. New York: Pathfinder.

Orloff, Ann Shola, and Theda Skocpol. 1984. "Why Not Equal Protection? Explaining the Politics of Public Social Spending in Britain, 1906-1911, and the United States, 1880s-1920." *American Sociological Review* 49:726-50.

Pease, Otis, ed. 1962. *The Progressive Years: The Spirit and Achievement of American Reform*. New York: Braziller.

Purcell, Edward A., Jr. 1973. *The Crisis of Democratic Theory*. Lexington: University Press of Kentucky.

Raushenbush, Winifred. 1979. *Robert E. Park: Biography of a Sociologist*. Durham, NC: Duke University Press.

Reck, A. J., ed. 1964. *Selected Writings: George Herbert Mead*. New York: Bobbs-Merrill.

Resek, Carl. 1967. *The Progressives*. Indianapolis: Bobbs-Merrill.

Roosevelt, Theodore. 1909. "Socialism." *Outlook* 41:619-23.

_____. (1912) 1962. "A Confession of Faith." Pp. 310-41 in *The Progressive Years: The Spirit and Achievement of American Reform*, edited by Otis Pease. New York: Braziller.

Schwedinger, Herman, and Julia R. Schwedinger. 1974. *The Sociologists of the Chair*. New York: Basic Books.

Scott, A. M. 1959. "The Progressive Era in Perspective." *Journal of Politics* 21: 685-701.

Selsam, Howard. 1950. "Science and Ethic." Pp.81-92 in *Pragmatism and American Culture*, edited by Gail Kennedy. Boston: D. C. Heath.

Shalin, D. N. 1978. "The Genesis of Social Interactionism and Differentiation of Macro- and Microsociological Paradigms." *Humboldt Journal of Social Relations* 6:3-38.

_____. 1979. "Between the Ethos of Science and the Ethos of Ideology." *Sociological Focus* 12:275-93.

_____. 1980. "Marxist Paradigm and Academic Freedom." *Social Research* 47: 361-82.

_____. 1984. "The Romantic Antecedents of Meadian Social Psychology." *Symbolic Interaction* 7:43-65.

_____. 1986a. "Pragmatism and Social Interactionism." *American Sociological Review* 51:9-29.

_____. 1986b. "Romanticism ad the Rise of Sociological Hermeneutics." *Social Research* 53:77-123.

_____. 1987. "Socialism, Democracy and Reform: A Letter and an Article by George H. Mead." *Symbolic Interaction*, Vol. 10, no. 2.

Smith, T. V. 1931. "The Social Philosophy of George Herbert Mead." *American Journal of Sociology* 37:368-85.

Smith, Timothy L. 1957. Revivalism *and Social Reform in Mid-Nineteenth Century America*. New York: Abington.

Sombart, Werner. (1909) 1968. *Socialism and Social Movement*. New York: Kelley.

Wilson, Woodrow. (1912) 1962. "Address at Duquesne Garden." Pp. 372-78 in *The Progressive Years: The Spirit and Achievement of American Reform*, edited by Otis Pease. New York: Braziller.

White, Morton C. 1957. *Social Thought in America: The Revolt against Formalism*. Boston: Beacon.

3

Envisioning Pragmatist Sociology: Philosophical Sources, Methodological Principles, and Political Underpinnings of Social Interactionism

Present-day commentators agree about the impact of pragmatist philosophy on social interactionism, although the exact nature of this impact is hotly disputed. Some critics, mostly outside the interactionist perspective proper, charge interactionism with an astructural, subjectivist, and status-quo bias and blame pragmatism for the fact (Kanter 1972; Huber 1973; Reynolds and Reynolds 1973). Others argue that there is nothing inherently astructural, subjectivist, or conservative about either interactionism or pragmatism (Hall 1972; Stone et al. 1974; Maines 1977; Stryker 1980; Johnson and Schifflet 1981). Still others detect a fissure among social interactionists, tracing it to the division within the pragmatist tradition between the nominalist and subjectivist pragmatism of Dewey and James and the realist and objectivist pragmatism of Peirce and Mead (Lewis 1976; McPhail and Rexroat 1979: Lewis and Smith 1980). The question these polemics are likely to raise in many a head is, "Shouldn't the whole matter be left for professional philosophers to decide?"

The first section of this chapter was presented in 1985 at the Annual Meeting of the Midwest Sociological Society. The paper was later published as "Pragmatism and Social Interactionism" in *American Sociological Review* 1986, Vol. 51, pp. 9-20. I thank Herbert Blumer, Thomas Burger, Lewis A. Coser, Lon R. Shelby and two anonymous reviewers for their comments on an earlier draft of this paper. I wish to acknowledge a special debt of gratitude to Professor Igor S. Kon for nurturing my interest in pragmatism and social interactionism.

One answer to this question is suggested by Kuhn's theory of paradigms. Along with substantive theories and research procedures, according to Kuhn, scientific schools include "metaphysical paradigms" or "metaphysical parts of paradigms." Normally, philosophical assumptions underlying research practice in a given area are taken for granted, but in periods of crisis "scientists have turned to philosophical analysis as a device for unlocking the riddles of their field" (Kuhn 1970: 184, 83). Whether sociology is currently undergoing a crisis is beyond the scope of this chapter, yet Kuhn's argument is relevant for the present study in one important respect: It assigns the task of philosophical self-reflection to practitioners in the field rather than to professional philosophers. The prodigious output in speculative writings by Bohr, Heisenberg, de Broglie, Born, Schrodinger, Eddington, Jordan, Pauli, Weizsacker, and Oppenheimer, to mention only some better-known names in modern physics, should convince the skeptics in our field that the reflection on the a priori foundations of science is more than a self-indulgent practice of wayward sociologists. As Whitehead (1938: 29) put it, "if science is not to degenerate into a medley of *ad hoc* hypotheses, it must become philosophical and must enter upon a thorough criticism of its own foundations." The present inquiry into the paradigmatic unity of pragmatist and interactionist thought accepts this judgment and is undertaken in the hope that such an inquiry will help illuminate the problems facing modern interactionism. More specifically, this study is intended to show that since its formative years, interactionist sociology contained a structural component, although its pragmatism-inspired approach to the problem of social order significantly diverged from the traditional one. The present inquiry also aims to demonstrate that interactionist methodology has a strong predilection for participatory forms of research, reflecting its paramount concern, again directly influenced by pragmatist ideas, with the objective indeterminacy of the situation. Finally, I will argue that the relative paucity of interactionist research on the issues of power, class, and inequality is not so much a reflection of the conservative bias that the interactionists allegedly inherited from pragmatism as the result of their failure to embrace fully the political commitments of pragmatist philosophers.

The terms "pragmatism," "pragmatist sociology," and "social interactionism" are used here inclusively. That is, Peirce, James, Dewey, and Mead, despite their divergent views, are all considered pragmatists insofar as they took a common stance against rationalist philosophy. Correlatively, Cooley, Thomas, Park, Ellwood, Blumer, and a number of other kindred yet disparate writers are treated here as interactionists for the sake of contrasting their views to those of functionalist thinkers. Pragmatist philosophers, it is further held, formulated important sociological ideas, while interactionists have something to contribute to the discourse of philosophical pragmatism.

Without claiming to have exhausted the premises of social interactionism, I will examine the following tenets central to interactionist thought: (1) the philosophical perspective on reality as being in the state of flux; (2) the sociological view of society as emergent interaction; (3) the methodological quest for a logic of inquiry sensitive to the objective indeterminacy of the situation; (4) and the ideological commitment to ongoing social reconstruction as a goal of sociological practice. The four paradigm-setting features of social interactionism are addressed in this order.

Studying the World-in-the-Making:
The Philosophical Premises of Social Interactionism

"For rationalism reality is ready-made and complete from all eternity while for pragmatism it is still in the making" (James [1907] 1955: 167). This cherished precept of pragmatist philosophy—one of "the philosophies of flux" (Dewey [1929] 1958: 50) that became popular in the late nineteenth and early twentieth centuries—conveys an image of the world brimming with indeterminacy, pregnant with possibilities, waiting to be completed and rationalized. The fact that the world out there is "still" in the making does not augur its completion at some future point: the state of indeterminacy endemic to reality cannot be terminated once and for all. It can be alleviated only partially, in concrete situations, and with the help of a thinking agent. The latter has the power to carve out an object, to convert an indeterminate situation into a determinate one, because he is an active being. The familiar world of color, sound, and structure is his practical accomplishment: He hears because he listens to, he sees because he looks at, he discerns a pattern because he has a stake in it, and when his attention wavers, interest ceases, and action stops—the world around him sinks back into the state of indeterminacy.

There is more than a tinge of post-Kantian idealism in this mode of reasoning, which should come as no surprise, given the prominent role transcendentalism played in the pragmatists' formative years. Traces of transcendentalism can be detected in Dewey's celebration of the mind as "the constitutive author of the whole scheme" ([1929] 1960: 33), James' preoccupation with the world "anchored in the Ego" ([1890] 1950 11:

297), and Mead's conviction that "what a thing is in nature depends not simply on what it is in itself, but also on the observer" (1929: 428). Transcendentalist overtones are unmistakable in the pragmatist view of cognition, which harks back to the idealist metaphor of knowing as artistic carving. From transcendentalism pragmatists learned to distrust the rhetoric of "bare facts" which, in Mead's words (1938: 98), "are not there to be picked out. They have to be dissected out, and the data are the most difficult of abstractions..." Pragmatists' resistance to behaviorism as incompatible with the active and conscious mode of man's being in the world, no doubt, reflected the aversion to materialism bred into their bones in the years of apprenticeship. Salient as the elective affinity of idealist and pragmatist thought is, it does not signify an uncritical acceptance of the idealist legacy. Pragmatism is a post-Darwinian philosophy in which the principle of subject-object relativity was replaced with that of the relativity of organism and environment, the constitutive activity of Absolute Mind with the tool-aided, transformative activity of organized individuals, and the dialectical logic of self-propelling concepts with the experimental logic of situation. Pragmatists parted company with idealists on the issue of the primacy and the constitutive power of thought, which, according to them, needs to be explained, not presupposed. The root of knowledge is not to be found in knowledge itself—it is to be sought in action. The latter intervenes in the relationship between the subject and object, giving rise to the phenomenon of "emergence" which, in simplest terms, refers to "a certain environment that exists in its relationship to the organism, and in which new characters can arise by virtue of the organism" (Mead 1934: 330). Pragmatists conceded that subject and object are bound to each other by the fundamental relationship of relativity, yet they placed this relationship in a broader context suggested by the Darwinian theory of evolution. The individual continuously adapts to his environment, changing his action to meet the exigencies of the situation and transforming the situation to satisfy his practical needs. In that sense pragmatists speak of "a relativity of the living individual and its environment, both as to form and content. The individual and environment—the situation—mutually determine each other" (Mead [1924-25] 1964: 278; [1908] 1964: 86). A key word in this statement is "mutual." Action is constituted by, as much as it constitutes, the environment, and it is in the course of this mutual constitution that reality opens itself up to the knower. Knowing does not exist for its own sake, but for the sake of doing. Whatever doubts the knower has about the nature of things, he alleviates practically, by manipulating his objects,

putting them to different uses, literally forcing these objects to conform
to his notion of them, and in the process of doing so establishing—*in
situ*—whether a thing in question is what it is thought to be. The very
mode of handling things is part and parcel of their objective being. Said
Peirce ([1877] 1955: 29), "thought is essentially an action." "The unit
of existence is the act," concurred Mead (1938: 65). The only reality
available to us," in James's words, is "practical reality" ([1890] 1950,
II: 295). "Reality which is not in any sort of use, or bearing upon use,"
bristled Dewey ([1931] 1963: 41), "may go hang, so far as knowledge
is concerned."

As action took precedence over thought in pragmatist analysis, the old
question of thing in itself emerged in a new light. "Reality in itself, or in
its uninterpreted nakedness," observes Thayer (1973: 68), "is a pragmatically meaningless notion..." The problem for pragmatists is not so much
that the thing in itself is unknowable in principle, but that it can be known
in so many ways. One thing can function as many different objects, and
one object can be represented by many different things. Which role a
thing assumes in a given situation, which determinate object it is made
to impersonate, depends not only on its inherent qualities, but also on the
interests, assumptions, and practical skills of the actor. A thing we call
paper can be used for building a fire, writing a letter, covering the floor,
making a mask, as it can be put to many other uses, every one of which
brings into existence a new situation and a different object. Moreover, as
Mead (1936: 158 155) stressed, our very treatment of things as definite
objects involves an abstraction, in that it requires an active selection
of certain elements from among the many encompassed in our field of
experience. The status of a thing as a determinate object is problematic;
it is established in the course of interaction between the thing in question and other things: "Everything that exists in as far as it is known and
knowable is in interaction with other things.... Interaction is a universal
trait of natural existence" (Dewey [1929] 1958: 175; [1929] 1960: 244).
Among the things involved in the interaction producing a determinate
object is the knower. Things emerge as objectively meaningful when
they encounter the knower with all his practical skills and the power to
symbolize: "Symbolization constitutes objects not constituted before....
Language does not simply symbolize a situation or object which is
already there in advance; it makes possible the existence or the appearance of that situation or object, for it is a part of the mechanism whereby
that situation or object is created" (Mead 1934: 78). Thus, *situation* in
the pragmatist lexicon always presupposes an actor and a transaction

between the knower and the known, or as Gouinlock (1972: 8) put it, "if there were no human beings (or comparably sentient creatures) there would be no situations in nature."

This pragmatist reasoning is ripe with interesting, if unsettling, implications. It suggests the possibility of multiple realities, or to use James's favorite expression, "the pluralistic universe," comprised of many worlds, each one rational in its own way, each reflecting alternative lines of action, ends, and situations. "Other sculptors, other statues from the same stone!" exclaims James ([1890] 1950, I: 289). "Other minds, other worlds from the same monotonous and inexpressive chaos! My world is but one in a million alike embedded, alike real to those who may abstract them." This argument runs into a problem, however. If the world is as fluent and indeterminate as James wants us to believe, how do we go about deciding which course of action to follow, which world to cut out of the primordial chaos of unmediated being? Are we not heading for a solipsism when we adopt this mode of reasoning? These are the questions that critics posed to the pragmatists and that consumed so much of James's time in the last ten years of his life. His claim that "the fons et origo of all reality, whether from the absolute or the practical point of view, is thus subjective, is ourselves" ([1890] 1950, II: 296-7), exposed him to the charges of subjectivism, which, despite all his efforts, James was not able to refute resolutely. This cannot be said about Dewey, who came to appreciate without reservation that "meaning is objective as well as universal," that "significant things are things actually implicated in situations of shared or social purpose and execution," that "communication is a condition of consciousness" ([1929] 1958: 188-9 180-1 187). The charges of subjectivism are also inapplicable to Peirce and Mead who saw the process of terminating indeterminacy as a fundamentally social. From the start Peirce was at pains to emphasize that "the very origin of the conception of reality shows that this conception essentially involves the notion of a COMMUNITY," that the real problem is "how to fix belief, not in the individual merely but in the community" ([1868] 1955: 247; [1877] 1955: 13). Similarly, Mead, while acknowledging that "each individual has a world that differs in some degree from that of any other member of the same community," stressed that the individual "slices the events" from the standpoint of community life, and that his very ability to "carve out" an object and to handle it rationally is "social to the very core" ([1924-25] 1964: 276; 1934: 141).

While certain tenets of pragmatism may seem problematic, the pragmatist imaginative take on the social dimension of human existence looms larger and larger as the time goes by. Pragmatists were not the first to recognize the importance of social dimension—Scottish moralists (Stryker 1980) and romantic philosophers (Shalin 1984) had done so way before them. Still, Morris (1970: 96) hardly exaggerates when he describes the analysis of the social conditions as "one of the most important achievements of the pragmatist movement." Without society, pragmatists realized, there would be no rational human beings, no world of meaning and structure, and the primordial chaos would never be tamed. Precisely because the world out there is not fully determinate, because it can be carved out in so many ways, there is a need for an organizing principle, a reference frame guiding disparate individuals engaged in the process of determination. The individual learns to do the "carving" against the background of meaningful objects shared with others. He grows in the environment "endowed with meaning in terms of the process of social activity" (Mead 1934: 130), in which he partakes with other human beings, and "this community of partaking is meaning" (Dewey [1929] 1958: 185). It is insofar as the individual perspective on reality is mediated by and rooted in society that it attains a quality of being private or public, objective or subjective: "The objectivity of the perspective of the individual lies in its being a phase of the larger act. It remains subjective in so far as it cannot fall into the larger social perspective..." (Mead 1938: 548). The objectivity of any perspective is thus not an arbitrary matter—it is a social, and therefore historical, matter, and as such it invites, nay, requires sociological treatment. Which brings us to the project social interactionism proper.

Stated in pragmatist terms, the project of interactionist sociology consists in a systematic examination of the process of the determination of indeterminacy, insofar as this process shapes society and, in turn, is shaped by it. Put differently, it is an inquiry into the pluralistic social universe brought into being by various collectivities, each one creating a separate environment of meaningful objects that distinguish its members from those inhabiting different social worlds. A social world is real for those participating in the same universe of discourse. It is "a distinct world, with its own ways of acting, talking, and thinking, its own vocabulary, its own activities and interests, its own conception of what is significant in life ... its own scheme of life" (Cressey 1932: 31). Such a world is not objective in the traditional sense—it has no being in itself. It is not "a world of independent realities such as might be known by some ideal absolute subject; it is a world of ... data given to concrete, historically determined subjects, and of actions which these human subjects actually perform upon these objects of their own experience" (Znaniecki 1927: 536). There is more than a fleeting resemblance between Thomas's theorem, "If men define situations as real, they are real in their consequences" (Thomas and Thomas 1928: 572), and James's dictum, "…We need only in cold blood ACT as if the thing in question were real, and keep acting as if it were real, and it will infallibly end by growing in such a connection with our life that it will become real" ([1890] 1950, II: 321). The definition of the situation is that unmistakably pragmatist "looking at," "listening to," "reaching for" which constitutes an early, hidden, attitudinal stage of an overt act and which transforms "the big, buzzing confusion" of everyday life (James, quoted in Park [1924] 1955: 265) into a clearly recognizable environment and gives a semblance of order to "the irrational chaos of the real world" (Znaniecki 1919: 147). "The definition of the situation is equivalent to the determination of the vague," wrote Thomas; before the definition sets in, "the situation is quite undetermined," but as the definition unfolds, "the situation becomes definite" (Thomas [1918-20] 1966: 240, 23-4). That is when the flow of reality begins to show a pattern and the situation reveals its structured character. The pattern in question is not inherent; it is not a "fact" in the positivist sense of the word. "The great and most usual illusion of the scientist is that he simply takes the facts as they are … and gets his explanation entirely a posteriori from pure experience. A fact by itself is already an abstraction; we isolate a certain limited aspect of the concrete process of becoming, rejecting, at least provisionally, all its indefinite complexity" (Thomas [1918-20] 1966: 271).

Interactionists' frequent allusions to James should not be taken to mean that they endorsed his subjectivism. It is of paramount importance from the interactionist standpoint that definitions of the situation vary not only from individual to individual, but also from one group to another, that "different tribes define the same situation and pattern the behavior in precisely opposite ways" (Thomas 1937: 8-9), that "things do not have the same meanings with different people, in different periods of time, in different parts of a country" (Park and Miller 1921: 265). Interactionists understood that the "terms" in which we terminate indeterminacy are not private, that they belong to a specific time and place, that humans define the situation as members of certain groups, armed with "models of situations" and "super-individual schemes" (Znaniecki 1919: 199, 284). The symbolic environment individuals inhabit is a shared environment, and the outlook they develop is a shared outlook, reflecting a larger social act of which group members find themselves a part.[1] As the individual matures, he can challenge this shared world, but one thing he can ill-afford to do, as long as he remains a rational member of society, is to ignore it. His actions always refer to the world that is already there, the pre-determined world, the intersubjective universe existing on the intersection of objectively established group perspectives. The interactionist must begin with the historically determined world of culture and meaning, but he must understand it dialectically, i.e., not as the "block-universe" (James) existing by itself and informing the individual's conduct without being informed by it, but as the world that is still in the making, the world that continuously produces individuals as conscious human beings and that is continuously produced by them as a meaningfully objective whole.

To sum up, pragmatism was a reaction to the overdetermined picture of reality painted by rationalist and mechanicist philosophers. Following the train of thought initiated by transcendental idealists, pragmatists replaced the static, predetermined, inherently structured universe with the dynamic, emergent, historical world-in-the-making. This shift in perspective resulted in the figure-background reversal, which illuminated anew the problem of order. Whereas the chief difficulty for rationalist thought was to explain apparent irregularities and incessant transformations in the overdetermined world of natural order, the problem for pragmatists was coming to grips with order and structure in the overemergent world of natural indeterminacy. How can one do justice to the orderly nature of reality without doing violence to its emergent characteristics—such was the challenging question confronting pragmatist thinkers. It is in response to this challenge that pragmatists turned to the collective conditions of human existence as a source of meaning, stability, and order. Social interactionism was an outgrowth of this ingenious attempt to find in society an anchorage for the determinate world of objective reality. Interactionists accepted the pragmatist thesis that the world is not inherently determinate, that it is open to multiple determinations, which led them to the pioneering view of society as the pluralistic universe continuously produced by the collective efforts of individuals. Society-in-itself gave way in their work to society-in-the-making, the study of structural givens to the study of the production of social reality as objective and meaningful. With this reorientation, interactionists had to find their own way of coming to grips with structural properties of social life without glossing over its emergent characteristics. They also had to provide a dialectical account of the individual as both the product and producer of society. The view of society as social interaction can be seen as an attempt at resolving these vexing problems placed on the agenda by pragmatist philosophy.

Structure as Emergent Process:
The Interactionist View of Society

"Interaction" was more than a technical term in the vocabulary of social interactionism; it was also a philosophical category of wide-ranging significance. "The idea of interaction," wrote Park and Burgess ([1921] 1969: 129) in their famous textbook, "represents the culmination of long-continued reflection by human beings in their ceaseless effort to resolve the ancient paradox of unity in diversity, of the 'one' and the 'many,' to find law and order in the apparent chaos of physical changes and social events; and thus to find explanations for the behavior of the universe, of society, and of man." Note the reference to the "one" and the "many"—code words for the problem of universals and particulars. The authors clearly thought that interactionism offers the best hope for resolving this ancient paradox. Their solution, insofar as it applied to the relationship between the individual and society, was itself quite paradoxical. Neither individual nor society, according to interactionist theory, can be accorded unqualified primacy—each one is an aspect in the ongoing process of social interaction, and both are mutually constitutive. "The individual is no thrall to society. He constitutes society as genuinely as society constitutes the individual" (Mead 1935-36: 70). "The individual and society are neither opposed to each other nor separated from each other. Society is a society of individuals and the individual is a social individual" (Dewey [1897] 1972: 55). "'Society' and 'individual' do not denote separable phenomena, but are simply collective and distributive aspects of the same thing" (Cooley [1909] 1962: 314). "The human personality is both a continuously producing factor and a continuously produced result of social evolution" (Thomas [1918-20] 1966: 11). "[H]abit and custom, personality and culture, the person and society, somehow are different aspects of the same thing.... Personality [is] the subjective and individual aspect of culture, and culture [is] the objective, generic or general aspect of personality" (Park [1929] 1952: 203-4).

This argument is circular insofar as it explains the individual in terms of society and society in terms of individuals.[2] The circle in question is a dialectical or hermeneutical: it demands as a matter of principle that the part be explained in terms of the whole and the whole in terms of its parts, i.e., that the individual be understood as a subject and object of the historical process and society as a continuously produced and a continuously producing factor in social interaction. The originality of this approach consists in the fact that it eschews both sociological real-ism with its reified view of social bodies as superhuman entities existing before and apart from individuals, and sociological nominalism with its flawed notion of society as a convention set up at will by individuals endowed by nature with minds. The fight interactionists had to wage, accordingly, was on the two fronts—against the realist concept of so-ciety as superorganic body and against the nominalist theory of society as convention.

First and foremost, interactionist criticism aimed at the classical view of social order as external, atemporal, determinate at any given mo-ment, and resistant to change—a super-organic entity hovering above individuals in the Platonic realm of everlasting beings. In response to this "hypostatization of society" (Dewey [1927] 1934: 70) interaction-ists advanced a series of claims that "society is merely the name for a number of individuals, connected by interaction" (Ellwood 1907: 307), "rather a phase of life than a thing by itself" (Cooley [1902] 1964: 135), that "the social group does not exist as a real entity" (Park [1904] 1972: 24), that "social science cannot remain on the surface of social becoming, where certain schools wish to have it float, but must reach the actual hu-man experiences and attitudes which constitute the full, live and active social reality beneath the formal organization of social institutions..." (Thomas [1918-20] 1966: 13-14). These and similar utterances widely scattered throughout interactionist literature convinced many a com-mentator that interactionists, just as their pragmatist mentors, had little use for enduring, patterned manifestations of social life. This conclusion is incorrect. The post-rationalist tradition, in which both pragmatists and interactionists were steeped, did not render the notion of structure irrelevant—it rendered it problematic. The whole point was how best to fuse the notions of structure and process and to account conceptually for the fact that "an actual entity is at once a process, and is atomic," that "the stone is a society of separate molecules in violent agitation" (Whitehead 1929: 121). "Structure," intoned Dewey ([1929]1958: 72), is "an evident order of changes. The isolation of structure from the changes whose stable ordering it is, renders it mysterious..." "You cannot have a process without some sort of a structure," averred Mead (1936: 164), "and yet the structure is simply something that expresses this process as it takes place..." Hughes (1955: 6) preserved for us a telling story about Robert Park, who used to invoke an image of the classroom table while discussing the nature of the social group and urge his students to see both not just as things, but as fields, a product of the ongoing

interaction of individual particle. Hughes's reaction to Park's invoca-
tion of the image of the table qua electronic field is emblematic of the
interactionist concern with social order: "I suddenly saw," he recalls,
"that, not change, but the dynamics of remaining the same, is the miracle
which social science must explain" (1955: 6). Similar statements can
be found in the works of Znaniecki (1939: 84), Thomas (1939: 84), and
especially Ellwood (1910: 598), who went to great lengths to make the
point that society is "a mass of interactions, not haphazard, but regular,
coordinated, and controlled, working for the most part, toward definite
ends, and making groups true functional unities, ruled by habit largely....
The significant thing for the sociologist ... is not that these interactions
between individuals exist, but that they are regular: not haphazard, but
coordinated and controlled."

The gist of the interactionist argument concerning the fluid nature
of social order and the emergent character of social universals is that
the particulars belonging to a given universal (group, class, collectivity) are not tied to it inexorably, that they function simultaneously as
instances of different kinds, and their behavior as elements in one class
is affected by their membership in other classes. Which of these memberships will prove decisive at any given moment is problematic, and so is
the status of the universal comprised by the particulars. This becomes
dramatically evident in the sociological domain where the situation is
exacerbated by the fact that social particulars are individuals marked
by multiple memberships and the capacity to take a conscious attitude
toward their multiple group affiliations. "The difficulty," Park ([1904]
1972: 24) pointed out, "lies in the fact that the same individuals appear
as members of different groups ... that the same physical base is shared
by two completely different social structures. At any given moment the
individual can defect from one universal to another by literally "taking the role of the other" (Mead 1934: 254). As the individual gives
up one role and puts on a new mask, he makes a quantum jump from
one universal to another, and thereby affects, however marginally,
the objective status of the universal. Every time he universalizes his
action with reference to a given group, he fortifies its objectivity and
universality. Conversely, when he abstains from framing his action in
predesignated terms and terminates the situation's indeterminacy by
recourse to an alternative reference frame, he deprives it of a quantum
of objectivity and a corresponding measure of universality. Any single
episode of the individual's symbolic entry into and withdrawal from a
given universal can be negligible from the standpoint of its objective

status, but the cumulative effect of such border-crossing incidents is not. It forces social bodies to oscillate, renders them fuzzy not only at the fringes but at the very core, and it makes social universals emergent. Social universals emerge as real or meaningfully objective when they are placed in the perspectives of conscious individuals who, drawing on the same terminological media (symbols, definitions, values), identify themselves as instances of familiar classes and act according to their habitual selves. When individuals fail to generalize the situation in the same perspective and to universalize their own selves in the same terms, that is, when they fail to take "the attitudes of the generalized other" (Mead 1934: 156), the universal becomes less real and more nominal. Whether social universals are real or nominal is therefore a matter of degree, an empirical matter. We are dealing not with natural constants but with social variables whose value cannot be established a priori but must be gauged in concrete situations.

If we accept the emergent universality of social universals, we have to be ready to take the next step and acknowledge that there is a degree of indeterminacy endemic to any social whole (system, institution, structure). With humans crossing group borderlines at will, the outcome of each social encounter becomes a matter of probability. High as this probability might be, one cannot assume the outcome will follow the familiar pattern over time simply because it happened this way the moment before. What this means is that social structure is not an atemporal, immovable being lurking behind the scenes and shaping individual conduct (a sociological equivalent of the Newtonian ether independent of the movement of particles), but an event continuously made to happen by individuals in concrete situations (a sociological analogue of the relativist spatio-temporal structure informed by the interaction of particles). That is to say, structure does compel the behavior of individuals in a given situation, but the conduct of individuals structures the situation, gives it a recognizable pattern. Structure is only a possibility, a "virtual" reality until it becomes an event, is "eventualized," made to happen in the here and now of the practical situational encounter. "Reality exists in a present," pointed out Mead (1932: 1, 32), the situation is the "seat" of reality; and so we can say that every structure to the extent that it has reality must have a locus in a specific situational present—must be temporalized. Situations are structured by individuals who, in the course of interaction, establish a joint sense of the present, develop a sense of shared past, open common horizons to the future, and shape their conduct with respect to this collectively established and situationally sustained time-frame.

The pragmatist perspective on structure as emergent process is amply documented in interactionist research. Thrasher's (1927: 75) study of the Chicago gangs highlighted "the ganging process [a]s a continuous flux and flow," the never-ending business of "coalescing and recoalescing," the peculiar mode of aggregating, consensus building, status display, and settling disputes in the course of which the gangs are dissolved and regenerated as interactional wholes. Zorbough (1929: 53) left us an account of "the social game" of climbing the ladder of prestige in Chicago's high society. This game requires "a continual planning, maneuvering, reciprocation of invitations, efforts to 'keep in the swim'" from all those aspiring to a coveted position in a high society, and it is this game that assures the continuity in the social structure of an elite social group. Anderson's pioneering study illuminated the world of homeless men whose life revolves around "the game of getting by," "faking it," "making it," the game that has its own ethical code, status system and hierarchy of authority, and that must be learned and practiced if one is to survive in the harsh environs of Hobohemia (1923: 55). Whyte ([1943] 1981: 318, 323) compared his study of an Italian slum to "taking a moving picture instead of a still photograph," the effect he was able to achieve through a long-term involvement with the local racketeers, policemen, politicians, and other inhabitants of the slum, whose personal transactions offered him a rare glimpse of "the social structure in action." These are the studies of structure across space and time, structure in action as it manifests itself in the thoughts and actions of individuals. The concern for the emergent properties of social reality is underscored by the gerundive mode of description—"ganging," "climbing," "getting by." This grammatical form favored by interactionists helps readers vicariously share a present in which the social world unfolds as a process continually recreated by individual participants. To facilitate the sense of presence and immersion interactionists supply the glossaries of local terms, the local lingos, which represent "different universes of discourse,—'little languages' whose meanings depend on past experiences peculiar to the groups, catchwords, jokes, and songs linked to group memories" (Thrasher 1927: 266). Encysted in these "little languages" are guidelines for making appropriate sense of different situations that the inhabitants of a given universe of discourse may encounter in their lives. Drawing on this common stock of meanings, metaphors and precepts, individuals can converse with each other, share the same sense of past and present, bring about an anticipated future, and in the process of doing so regenerate their world as an objectively meaningful whole. Because of all the incessant transmutations this world may appear chaotic to a casual observer, but it has a definite structure, and it has a structure precisely because it is continuously processed, acted out, communicated from one individual to another. This is what Dewey ([1916] 1966: 4) seems to have expressed in a passage quoted again and again by interactionist sociologists: "Society not only exists by transmission, by communication, but it may be fairly said to exist in transmission, in communication," and what Park ([1927] 1955: 15) was trying to say when he urged that "in a study of a social group ... the point of departure is, properly, not structure, but activity." The message here is not that structure is a fiction but that it should be grasped as an actual occasion or event (dis)continuously produced by conscious human beings in concrete situations.

Our discussion should not be taken to mean that structure makes an appearance in interactionist theory as a dependent variable only. There is a parallel and equally important for interactionists flow of determination from society to individual, from situation to definition (Kon and Shalin 1969) without which "the dynamics of remaining the same" (Hughes) would remain a mystery. Indeed, most interactions follow patterns fairly independent from individual whims. The question is why do individuals converge around certain perspectives and definitions rather than fly apart on separate tangents? This is primarily due to the fact that once defined and collectively established, interactions form what Dewey ([1929] 1958: 271-2) called "relatively closed fields" or "fields of interaction" which possess a measure of autonomy and a force of their own, felt by everyone drawn into these fields. The social world is comprised by interactional fields, strong and weak, that invoke in the minds of the participants certain meanings and suggest, with various degrees of urgency, appropriate action plans. Conduct does not unfold in a vacuum; it is guided and, in many cases, plainly coerced by the field, so that "anything changes according to the interacting field it enters" (Dewey [1929] 1938: 283). The coercive power of the field is most evident in the early years of our lives, when we are forced to make do with a world that is already there, predetermined by others, organized into enforceable networks of interactions. "The child," wrote Thomas (1923: 42), "is always born into a group of people among whom all the general types of situation which may arise have already been defined and corresponding rules of conduct developed. And where he has not the slightest chance of making his definitions and following his wishes without interference." What we see, think, and claim as our own at this stage of our development is determined by the situation, which clues us to the appropriate definitions and modes of conduct. Our mind at this point is little more than the functional ability to survey the larger social act in which we are imperatively implicated, and our self is a reflection of a part we are assigned to play in this act. In due course we acquire a measure of autonomy from our interactional fields and learn to take a critical attitude toward ourselves, yet our rationality remains commensurate with and will always be judged by our ability to act with reference to a larger social act. This ability to weave one's action into a collective act or to place oneself in the perspective of "the generalized other" is what interactionists called "mind." From the ontogenetic standpoint, the mind is primarily a way of grasping the world in the terms supplied by others, participating in the universe of discourse already in place, and acting as a member of a team. The locus of the mind is individual, but its content is not—it is social through and through, and as such, it assures mind's special role as an agent of social control: "...The mind that appears *in* individuals is not as such individual mind.... *Mind* as a concrete thing is precisely the power to understand things ... in terms of the use to which they are turned in joint or shared situations. And *mind in this sense is the method of social control*" (Dewey [1929] 1958: 219 and [1916] 1966: 33). "Mind is coterminal with the group" coming into existence when "the behavior of the group as a whole enters into the separate individual" (Mead 1982: 162 168). Acting rationally, with reference to one's self, the individual acts responsibly and with reference to society. He surely imposes on the world the categories of his mind and perceives the situation in terms of his self, but since his self and the categories of his mind, just as those of other individuals, have derived from kindred sources, the outcome turns out to be orderly rather than chaotic. And should the individual disregard the operative interactional field and choose the self uncalled for by the situation, he will be promptly, and more or less painfully, reminded of its gravitational force. A new girl quickly learns that the conventions of polite society are out of place in the taxi-dance hall (Cressey 1932: 38-9). A member of the youth gang has to forgo contacts with girls after the drubbing from the leader (Thrasher 1927: 292). And Dollard (1937: 49) is crassly reminded about the realities of caste in the Deep South as he seeks contacts with blacks. When the individual's definition of the situation comes into conflict with a collectively established one, the mechanisms of social control come into play. Interactionist theory, thus, clearly recognized the role of "the community as a defining agency" (Thomas 1923: 43-4), the fact that the matrices of meaning in terms of which we define our world are socially derived and publicly enforced.

To summarize, interactionist theory entails a dialectical circle—man is an author of his social world, but he is also a product of society. From the interactionist standpoint it is equally correct to say, "the self defines the situation" and "the situation provides the individual with a self." At any given moment the self is the expression of the entire situation or interactional field in which the individual is acting, while the situation is the reflection of the totality of selves engaged in an interactional encounter. The two are locked together in the process of mutual adjustment in the course of which both emerge as objective, determined realities. This mutual adjustment is not a mechanical process. Individuals are the ones who do the choosing, who identify or fail to identify with the self called for by the situation. As parts of different fields they can gear their actions to alternative selves. Still, the actions of individuals, like the actions of physical particles, are non-random though marked by a degree of indeterminacy; structured, though the underlying pattern may be illusive; predictable, though predictions must be couched in probabilistic terms.

It would be wrong to look for a full-fledged theory of social structure in early social interactionism. Many pertinent questions (e.g., why some transactions evolve into strong interactional fields whereas others remain weak, how the "little languages" are integrated into the general universe of discourse, what determines the choice of identity in the situation where interactional fields put conflicting claims on the individual) remained in it unanswered. And one can still feel skeptical as to whether interactionist theory explains satisfactorily "the dynamics of remaining the same," given the diversity of social fields and degrees of freedom assigned to the movement of individuals. Despite these weaknesses, original interactionist theory had important strengths that made it superior to contemporary formulations. Social interactionists diverged from the classical approaches in making the order appear simultaneously as the *explanandum* and the *explanans*, rather than as something that must be either taken for granted or treated as perennially problematic. They offered a new perspective on social structure as fluid and stable at the same time, an emergent process that functions simultaneously as an antecedent and an outcome of social interaction. Interactionist theory transcended the dichotomy of realism and nominalism by bringing man and society into one continuum and conceptualizing each as byproducts of the production of social reality as objective and meaningful. The individual appears in this theory as both the actor and the author of the social script, a constituent of many interactional fields, none of which can claim his undivided allegiance. A self-conscious being, he can refuse to act as his allegedly natural determinations dictate, cross the borderlines separating one class from another, and assert oneself as an "instance of a different kind." Society as a whole transpires here as a universe of inter-ferentially overlapping fields, coalescing around symbols and meanings and exerting cross-pressures on individuals caught in their gravitational pull. When the borderlines separating these interactional fields are strictly policed, they behave like "bodies," revealing their "corpuscular" prop-erties. On other occasions their "wave-like" properties are in evidence, as crisscrossing identifications whittle away at their thingness, turning the fields into fuzzy, gaseous, penetrable formations. But the important thing for social interactionists is that society is both a body and a field, a structure and a process, and that in order to understand it as a living reality researchers should get involved in situations where it is made to happen by self-conscious human beings.

Knowing as Participation:
The Methodology of Interactionist Research

Studying society-in-the-making meant more than describing it in scientific terms; it also meant understanding—better still—experiencing it, if possible by direct immersion in the mundane world of everyday life where it is routinely generated by the participants in social intercourse. To accomplish this feat, interactionists had to assume a role markedly different from that of a classical scientist—they had to become participant observers. Participant observation as a method of sociological research raised a host of methodological problems unknown to classical sociology. In dealing with these problems interactionists drew heavily on pragma-tist epistemology that did away with the notion of a "world complete in itself, to which thought comes as a passive mirror, adding nothing to fact" (James [1909] 1970: 80) and that postulated that "knowing is not the act of an outside spectator but of a participant inside the natural and social scene" (Dewey [1929] 1960: 196).

Rationalist epistemology failed, according to pragmatists who drew some of their inspiration from romantic idealism, and it failed on more than one count. First, it was built on the erroneous premise that "the processes of search, investigation, reflection, involved in knowledge must be outside of what is known, so as not to interact in any way with the object to be known" (Dewey [1929] 1960: 23). Second, rationalists were mistaken in their belief that the knower could approach his object without preconceptions and biases—every research endeavor is rooted in some "practical interests," "aesthetic" attitudes, and theoretical presuppositions which represent "irreducible ultimate factors in determining the way our knowledge grows" (James [1890] 1950 11: 343). Third, pragmatists rejected the rationalist view of "verification as a process of comparing ready-made ideas with ready-made facts," supplanting it with a notion that "both idea and 'facts' are flexible, and verification is the process of mutual adjustment, of organic interaction" (Dewey [1890] 1969: 87). Fourth, pragmatists decried the tendency of classical rationalism to "conceive a concrete situation by singling out some salient or important feature in it, and [then] reducing the originally rich phenomenon to the naked suggestions of that name abstractly taken, treating it as a case of 'nothing but' that concept" (James [1909] 1970: 249). Fifth, and finally, pragmatist epistemology diverged from the traditional one in its deliberate blurring of the borderline between scientific and common sense knowledge, that is, "theoretic knowledge, which is knowledge *about* things, as distinguished from living or sympathetic acquaintance with them" (James [1909] 1967: 249-50). This formulation, prompted by the special needs of human sciences, encouraged intimate familiarity with social reality and direct understanding of human conduct in terms of an individual's own experience.

Pragmatist epistemology had a direct impact on the methodology of interactionist research. It looms large in Park's renouncing the tendency "to substitute for the flux of events and the changing character of things a logical formula," as well as in his commitment to "personal and first-hand involvement with the world" ([1940] 1953: 74, 72). It is echoed in Znaniecki's attacks on the rationalist premise that "knowledge reproduces reality in its preexisting determination" (1919: 232). It is unmistakable in Cooley's critique of abstract and statistical reasoning and his desire to "illuminate the concrete object" (1927: 143-6). It is behind Thomas's argument that "we must put ourselves in the position of the subject [because] the environment by which he is influenced and to which he adopts himself, is his world, not the objective world of science—is nature and society as he sees them, not as the scientist sees them" ([1918-20] 1966: 23). And last, pragmatist epistemology is firmly entrenched in the research practice of the second generation of social interactionists who took for granted that "in order to get knowledge [of society], one must participate significantly in the collective life. This means that one must come into human contact with people and this in turn means intimacy, sharing, and mutual identification" (Dollard 1937: 29). The term "participant observation," it should be noted, was not in use by interactionists until the mid-1920s when Lindeman introduced it as a method of grasping social reality in terms of the meaning it has for the participants (1924: 177-200). However, the idea behind it had been in circulation for more than a decade, since at least the time when Cooley ([1909] 1962: 7) identified the manner in which the sociologist ought to proceed as "*sympathetic introspection*" or "putting himself into intimate contact with various sorts of persons and allowing them to awake in himself a life similar to their own, which he afterwards, to the best of his ability, recalls and describes." Participant observation shared with life history and documentary analysis—two other principal methods of interactionist research—the goal of recovering the meaning that social reality has for those participating in its production.[3] It carried this goal one step further, to the point of actually "observing human intelligence trying to make sense out of the experience" (Dollard 1937: 19). Observing human intelligence at work implied several things. It meant studying people *in situ*, in their natural habitat; it required the readiness on the part of the researcher to enter personal relations with the subjects, to share their problems, feelings and thoughts; most importantly, it implied that the research act may enter the course of events and affect the situation under study. The participant mode of observing reality violated the canons of classical methodology, in that it blurred the line between the knower and the known and thus risked contaminating the natural purity of things themselves. For the interactionist researcher the transaction between the knower and the known—and the resultant complementarity effect—was not only normal but also unavoidable. It fully accorded with the pragmatist thesis that empirical knowledge presupposes the "common system of the knowing and the known," and it was a direct realization of the pragmatist quest for "unfractured observation" (Dewey and Bentley 1949: 1041).

Criticism most often raised by the opponents of interactionist methodology concerns its logico-theoretical component. The charge is that interactionists immerse themselves in the research situation without spelling out in advance their theory and hypotheses, which makes systematic testing of their propositions impossible. The participatory nature of interactionist research, it is further argued, leaves too much room for subjectivism and error. The source of the problem, according to the critics (Huber 1973; Lewis and Smith 1980), is the pragmatists' nonchalant attitude toward formal logic and conceptual reasoning, as well as their undue preoccupation with the exceptional, colorful, and irregular. Whatever one can make of this criticism, we should flatly reject its implication that pragmatists and interactionists ignored the role of logic and theoretical reasoning. The hiatus between "the rational organization of reality and the irrational chaos of the real world taken in its historical concreteness" (Znaniecki 1919: 147) should not be taken to mean that the world of uncertainty cannot be dealt with rationally. What pragmatists and interactionists decried was the undisciplined use of abstract reasoning—the situation where, in the words of Rucker (1969: 166), "fixed logics and formal systems of any sort become strait-jackets instead of tools for inquiry." The gist of the argument was that formal logic fully applies to the Platonic domain of the ideal being where genera and species comprise mutually exclusive classes and abide by the laws of identity, noncontradiction, and excluded middle. As long as we stay within this domain of pure rationality we can rely on these laws, knowing that its objects (such as objects of mathematics) possess no other properties but those assigned to them by the researcher. Following closely in the steps of formal logic, classical research methodology sought to minimize things' multiple determinations and to maximize their consistency by neutralizing their alternative manifestations. This is what typically happens in the experimental situation where the scientist, through a system of controls, strips a thing of its multiple identities and forces it to behave according to the class to which it has been squarely reduced. But rationality and logical consistency achieved *in vitro* is purchased at the price of suppressing indeterminacy—the generic feature of life *in vivo*. The moment we reach out into the empirical world we face a different situation where "other factors" are never equal, where things refuse to behave according to their a priori established class memberships and obey the laws of logic. Actual particulars, especially those in the social world, are distinguished by their "capacity to be several things at once" (Mead 1932: 49), something the law of identity expressly forbids. No impregnable boundary can hedge off individuals of one denomination from those in the next taxon. By taking the role of the other individuals can instantly change their class identity, which makes class attribution a risky undertaking. The traditional definition of class as a totality of things satisfying the idea of a class therefore needs to be qualified by the following propositions: A thing in itself is indeterminate, its identity as a class member is emergent, and it has no logical status apart from the inquirer and the process of inquiry where it is transformed into a definite self-same object. Such was the message pragmatists were getting across when they criticized formal logic and sought to amend it with what they variously described as the "logic of inquiry," "logic in use, "the logic of situations"—the logic whose purpose was to account for "the transformation of an indeterminate unsettled situation into a determinate unified existential situation" (Dewey 1938: 296). This was a seminal attempt, inconclusive as it might be, to come to grips with the fact that the laws of formal logic, like the laws of Euclidean geometry, are not the properties of things themselves but useful idealizations, that whatever rationality and consistency one finds in the world is of our own making, and that no matter how successful we are in transforming—theoretically and practically—the world of indeterminacy into the world of law, the gap between the immaculate rationalities of reason and the empirical reality of obdurate things never disappears.

Now, if we take a look from this vantage point at the interactionists' ambivalence about formal theorizing, their unwillingness to spell out in advance all the hypotheses, and their desire to find things out in the situation, we can see a clear rationale for their position. Interactionists do not consider adjudication—a systematic reduction of things to logical categories—a technical problem, as classical scientists do, but see it as a substantive problem requiring direct and continuous examination. They do not abide by the principle of mutual exclusiveness which requires placing each thing in one taxon and disposing of the ambiguous objects by confining them to a residual box specially reserved for marginal cases. All social particulars, according to interactionists, are marginal and situationally emergent. Their identities inevitably spill over the classificatory borderlines. Attempts to reduce them squarely and irreversibly to preconceived categories are bound to backfire, particularly when we try to predict their behavior on the basis of such unambiguous class attributions. The way out of the predicament, interactionist methodology suggested, is to map things simultaneously into various taxa and treating their identities as probabilities to be ascertained by direct observation in concrete situation. The interactionist strategy enables the researcher to track the situational reincarnation of things themselves as objects with set properties, to observe *in vivo* their metamorphoses in space and time (or rather times). Abstractions, generalizations, conceptual reasoning all have their place in interactionist research, but used cautiously, with an eye to emergent transformations and situational inconsistencies that qualify the power and reach of theoretical abstractions and hypothetical propositions. Instead of forcing the individual to take an unambiguous stance, reducing him once and for all to a single category and glossing over its discrepant properties, interactionists encourage individuals to show their many faces and selves. Their strategy is designed to maximize validity, even where this requires a sacrifice of reliability. Taken in its most generic sense of reproducibility, reliability is secured by the neutralization of the multiple determinations that mark things at large—the more thoroughly the thing is stripped of its multiple identities, the more reliably the measuring device yields the same result on successive occasions. But the more reliable the data obtained in this way, the less valid it is; for if validity refers to things at large, it must square off with the objective indeterminacy of the situation, i.e., with all those "other factors" that have been factored out under the *ceteris paribus* clause and that immediately crowd in the moment we move from the experimental setting to the ecologically sound situation. ". . . The more precise and unambiguous the terms become, the less valuable they are" (Blumer 1939: 124)—this poorly understood precept expresses the interactionist intuition that validity is the price at which traditional researchers purchase the reliability of their data.

Potentially more damaging to interactionist methodology is the charge that sympathetic understanding with its focus on the fleeting and the irregular leaves too much room for subjectivism. Again, let us not forget that interactionists were acutely aware of the problem. "Perception of social events based on participation is difficult to standardize; yet," Dollard (1937: l9) hastened to add, "I believe that my experience can be repeated, that others can be trained to see what I have seen, and more, that the construct has predictive value." The key to this optimism is the pragmatist concept of meaning as a social, action-bound phenomenon. Participant observers are not hunting for obscure, hidden, idiosyncratic and endlessly reinvented meanings —first and foremost they are interested in well established and collectively sanctioned definitions of the situation, in routine transactions forming enduring structural patterns. Nor do they rely on any sort of inner vision to divine the definition of the situation. When Cressey, the author of the taxi-dance hall study, raises the question, "What does this life mean for these girls? .... What does this dance hall mean in the lives of young boys, the older men, the European immigrants, and the youthful Filipinos?" (1932: 15), he relies on the observation of their behavior as much as on the personal accounts they make of their actions. Interactionists are not prepared to take rationalizations and verbally expressed attitudes as ultimate causes of conduct. Attitudes and behavior are inextricably linked; one cannot be studied without the other; attitude-taking is itself a form of conduct that must be judged in context and compared to other forms of conduct. As participant observers, interactionists seek to establish "(1) What is the group doing? (2) What does the group think it is doing?" (Lindernan 1924: 190), and since the two things are not always consistent, inter-actionists remain on the alert for discrepancies, seek to diversify their local sources of information, and check their generalizations against the data from outside sources. The sociologist qua participant observer never submerges himself entirely in the community life he studies—he measures his involvement with detachment, sympathy with reflection, heart with reason, all of which makes the replication of interactionist research not nearly as outlandish as it may sound and assures a higher predictive value of interactionist findings than most formal measure-ments could offer.

One more objection to interactionist methodology concerns its fa-voring of qualitative over quantitative data. Early interactionists often raised their voice against the spirit of quantification and the wisdom of emulating the physical sciences (Cooley 1930: 315: Ellwood 1933: 13; Znaniecki [1934] 1968: viii; Thomas [1918-20] 1966: 14). The reason for this ambivalence was the familiar pragmatist reluctance to see a rich phenomenon reduced to a taxon. The act of measurement which "enables things qualitatively unlike and individual to be treated as if they were members of a comprehensive, homogeneous, or nonqualita-tive system" (Dewey [1929] 1960: 241), exacerbates the reductionist propensities of rationalism and breeds the "disdain for the particular, the personal, and the unwholesome" (James [1909] 1967: 309). However, pragmatists were not obscurantists. They understood the importance of measurement and quantification, as did interactionists. Opposing "the worship of statistical technique," interactionist sociologists repeatedly expressed their belief that "the method of statistics and of case study are not in conflict with each other: they are in fact mutually complementary" (Burgess1927: 120; see also Lindeman 1924: 97; Park [1929] 1952: 208; and Cooley 1930: 315). For interactionist researchers the value of quantification is chiefly heuristic—it shows the relations worthy of further thought and examination. Much of their interpretative work is done within the situation where they settle down to observe and think. Their research is literally a search for right questions to ask. "As I sat and listened," recalls Whyte ([1943] 1981: 303), "I learned the answers to questions that I would not even have had the sense to ask if I had been getting my information solely on an interviewing basis." In other words, interactionists avoid the premature closure of the theoretical process, remaining on the lookout for the unforeseen and serendipitous, ready to "discover[.] new categories as emergencies of the group's changing activities" (Lindeman 1924: 192). What they lose in quantitative precision and reproducibility, they make up for in the qualitative grasp of detail, in the breadth of theoretical possibilities, and above all in truthfulness to the objective indeterminacy of the situation.

Interactionist research posed a number of methodological problems that early interactionists could not solve, or even address, some of which still remain unresolved. The most fundamental of these is the problem of determination. Interactionists distinguished between "the situation as it exists in verifiable, objective terms, and as it has seemed to exist in terms of the interested persons" (Thomas and Thomas 1928: 572), but they gave few clues on how to navigate between these two forms of determinations, how the researcher's own explanatory terms are superadded to the native meanings, and vice versa, how native explanations are incorporated into the body of the researcher's theoretical propositions. Equally prone to confusion are the interactionists' philippics against overly precise concepts. Social reality is indeed too inconstant—at the core and on the fringes—to be readily subsumed under a neat label, but the solution is not fuzzy concepts and loose theorizing, as some interactionists seem to imply, but a judicious assigning of each individual case to several taxons, with conceptual categories kept sharply bounded and structural interconnections rendered explicit. The fact that social situations are uncertain and indeterminate does not mean that uncertainty cannot be patterned and indeterminacy described in structural terms. Also, interactionists underestimate what math and statistics could do for their cause. Perhaps traditional statistics (which is in effect the statistics of classical thermodynamics with its dubious assumption that every individual in the population, like a card in a deck, is a thing with a clear-cut and immutable identity) is of limited use from the interactionist standpoint, but if its general premises are any guide, the non-classical statistics of quantum mechanics and fuzzy sets may prove a valuable addition to the methodological arsenal of pragmatism inspired sociology. These drawbacks notwithstanding, interactionist methodology constituted an important advance in methodology or social research. Interactionists took seriously the objective indeterminacy of the social world to which they sought to adjust their research practice. This adjustment led to the recognition that no impregnable borders separate the knower from the known, that the research act inevitably leaves its mark on the object, and that the researcher must be prepared to become a participant in the social process he studies. Mindful of the emergent nature of social reality, interactionists avoided the irreversible reduction of individual identities to preconceived categories and encouraged the individual to manifest one's multiple selves, even when these are logically inconsistent and methodologically hard to glean. They eschewed the premature closure of theoretical deliberations, measuring their preconceptions against the unfolding realities of the situation and allowing their propositions to be revised in the course of inquiry. Interactionists also recognized that the relationship between validity and reliability is that of the Heisenbergian uncertainty—the two cannot be maximized simultaneously with arbitrary precision—and committed themselves to validity as their primary concern. This goal was best realized in the Chicago interactionists' ecological school of urban studies, where "ecological" meant not just describing cityscapes and local populations as they appear to an external observer, but maximizing the ecological validity of the findings by observing people across space and time, in their natural surroundings, making sense together of the world they inherited, continuously reproduce, and consciously and unconsciously transform.

Progress as Ongoing Reconstruction:
The Ideological Underpinning of Social Interactionism

Fledgling immigrants from Europe and high society socialites, residents of exclusive neighborhoods and denizens of the slum, remnants of the old Southern nobility and the descendants of slaves, itinerant workers and gadflies of the artistic demimonde, members of organized crime families and pursuers of religious orthodoxy—such were the objects of early interactionist research. Inhabitants of the pluralistic universe called the United States, these people managed to carve in it a niche, a symbolic world of their own, reflecting their unique cultural, ethnic, class, professional, and religious background. The interest interactionists took in these people was more than academic. Nor was it spurred exclusively by their fascination with the contrasting life-styles and manners of defining the situation. Theirs was an interest (concern may be a better word) informed by the progressive spirit of the time and rooted in the profoundly democratic values inherited from American pragmatists.

From the beginning pragmatists rejected the view of knowledge production as a purely intellectual endeavor propelled by man's desire to know things in general, *in abstracto*. The process of reasoning, according to Peirce (1931-58, VIII: 198-200), is largely a matter of acquiring beliefs on which humans can act. In Dewey's view, "ideas are worthless except as they pass into actions which rearrange and reconstruct in some way, be it little or large, the world in which we live" ([1929] 1960: 138). The whole project of pragmatism, with its emphasis on the indeterminate, the practical, the malleable, can be seen as a philosophical justification for social reconstruction in the age obsessed with reform. Pragmatism took shape at the dawning of the Progressive era, when rapid social change threatened to disrupt the fabric of the American social order. The decline of rural life, the massive population movement from country to city, the appalling conditions in urban slums, the influx of immigrants from Eastern Europe, the demise of entrepreneurial individualism, the rise of giant corporations—these all too familiar symptoms of modernity set afoot a movement for social reform that was supported by a wide spectrum of social classes. Oscillating between the enthusiasm for social change and the fear of its consequences, progressive thinkers desperately searched for a middle path between laissez faire capitalism and socialism, for a program that would undermine the appeal of political radicalism without taking steam out of the reform movement. Pragmatists were at the forefront of this struggle for "a more balanced, a more equal, even, and equitable system of human liberties" (Dewey 1946: 113). Dewey was a recognized leader of this movement, whose crusade for progressive education in America left an indelible mark on the spirit of the era (Goldman 1936; White 1937; Graham 1967; Marcell 1974). Mead's involvement with progressive causes, although mainly on the local scene, was equally strong, as his leading role in the Education Association of Chicago, the Immigrants' Protective League, and other progressive organizations demonstrates (Rucker 1969: 21). Peirce and James did not take active part in the progressive movement (in part because of their early deaths), but Peirce's pronouncements on social issues, although tinged with prejudices, were full of lofty idealism and vaguely progressive sentiments, while James stressed the connection between pragmatism and ameliorism and toward the end of his life came close to endorsing "the more or less socialistic future toward which mankind seems drifting" (James [1910] 1962: 488; Perry 1964: 242-32). As seen from the historical standpoint, the key issue of the time was social reconstruction that "takes into account the intimate and organic union of the two things: of authority and freedom, of stability and change" (Dewey 1946: 93), as opposed to the catastrophic, revolutionary reconstruction. "That is the problem of society, is not it?" queried Mead (1936: 361-2). "How can you present order and structure in society and yet bring about the changes that need to take place, are taking place? How can you bring those changes about in orderly fashion and yet preserve order? .... That is the problem, to incorporate the methods of change into the order of society itself." Institutionalizing social change was the goal to which pragmatists committed themselves. In their efforts to make social change more rational and humane they turned to science for guidance. Not that pragmatists believed in ready-made answers which science could furnish for the modern predicament. They turned to science as a best available model of democracy in action, the model of a community based on rational discourse, where every member is a free participant, each claim is open to experimental validation, and all solutions are subject to revision. Science clued pragmatists to their ideal of society as "'universal' discourse" (Mead 1934: 269) and individuals as "the constant makers of a continuously new society" (Dewey [1929] 1962: 143). The unity or scientific and social endeavors was endorsed by Peirce, who stressed that the very nature of science and logic "inexorably requires that our interests shall not be limited. They ... must embrace the whole community. The community, again, must not be limited, but must extend to all races of beings with whom we can come into immediate or mediate intellectual relation. It must reach, however vaguely, beyond the ideological epoch, beyond all bonds" ([1931-38] VII: 398). A community built on the principles of free rational discourse will be governed by the authority of the "public"—a body of individuals conscious of their interests and determined to have their voice heard (Dewey [1927] 1954). Such a community would do away with the traditional opposition of the individual and society—it would make the individual a master of his own destiny, a true subject of the social process, and at the same time, a responsible social being and an agent of social control. "[T]he idea of democracy as opposed to any conception of aristocracy is that every individual must be consulted in such a way, actively not passively, that he himself becomes a part of the process of authority" (Dewey 1946: 33). The scientist's role in social reconstruction was to educate people, to give them means for solving their problems, to alter their consciousness and thereby the very society that made this consciousness possible. Hence, the enormous emphasis on education and getting knowledge to the public endemic to the pragmatist movement.

It is not necessary to go over the long list of reform causes and associations with which interactionist sociologists identified themselves in the heyday of progressivism (see Faris 1970; Carey 1973; Coser 1978). What is to be stressed is the lesser known fact of the long-standing collaboration between pragmatists and interactionists on the issues of reform. When Dewey contemplated launching a socialist weekly he turned to Park, then his student and a journalist of some renown, for collaboration. As Park's unpublished notes show, he was very much aware of the philosophical and ideological connection between pragmatism and the social survey movement:

> There has grown up in this same period a school of philosophy which is intimately associated with this [social] survey movement. This is pragmatism.... I might call this larger movement the pragmatic movement. I think I will. In this sense pragmatic would mean that fact is never quite a fact merely because it is investigated and recorded. It only becomes a fact in the fullest sense of the term when it is delivered and delivered to the persons to whom it makes a difference. This is what the survey seeks to do. It seeks to get and deliver the fact; that is to publish them and publish them in such a way that they get results (Park papers, box 3, folder 1, c. 1918).

Pragmatist themes are also readily detectable in interactionist writers who recognized the necessity of social change and the role the science of society could play in "a production of new schemes of behavior and new institutions better adapted to the changed demands of the group; we call this production of new schemes and institutions ... *social reconstruction*" (Thomas [1918-20] 1966: 3-61). The pleas for change issued by interactionists were accompanied by the qualifications, echoing the agenda of romantic idealists:change should not be catastrophic, it should be guided by intelligent understanding. Hence, the typical distinction between "moderate change, which is usually wholesome, giving us the stimulus needed to keep our minds awake, and radical change, involving displacement" (Cooley [1918] 1966: 180; cf. Park [1927] 1933: 33; Thomas [1918-20] 1966: 230; Faris 1937: 4). Sociological knowledge can have an ameliorating effect on the course of social change if social scientists realize that they are a part of society they study and consciously use their skills and knowledge to further the cause of progress. The audience interactionists addressed was not exclusively made up of politicians and professional reformers; it also included the general public. The view of the public as a recipient of sociological knowledge reflected the democratic values of interactionist thinkers, their undivided commitment to a political system that "is based on the participation of every member and [that] assumes in all the wish and ability to participate; for in the last analysis we mean by democracy participation by all, both practically and imaginatively, in the common life of the community" (Thomas 1966: 196). With this ideal in mind interactionists set out to define their research objectives and to select subjects for their research. Poor, blacks, immigrants, delinquents, itinerary workers, bohemians—all those excluded from effective participation in the larger, national universe of discourse were disproportionately represented in interactionist studies. Locked in their parochial worlds, these groups and individuals could not share in the American democracy in a manner consistent with the participatory ideals of pragmatists and interactionists. The purpose of interactionist research was to sensitize these people at the fringes of American society to their role as participants in a larger discourse, to increase their input into the democratic process, and thus transform them into a public.

A variety of charges has been leveled against the ideological positions of interactionists, most of these revolving around their overly optimistic vision of American democracy and their failure to grapple with the harsh realities of power and inequality (Shaskolsky 1970; Lichtman 1970; Huber Rytina and Loomis 1970; Kanter 1972; Reynolds and Reynolds 1973; Smith 1973; Huber 1973; Ropers 1973). Some of this criticism, insofar as it applies to social interactionism, is correct. The problem, though, is not the interactionists' uncritical reliance on pragmatism as much as their failure to follow consistently the tenets of pragmatist philosophy. It is not true that the pragmatists' account of American democracy was a "utopia written in the present tense" (Shaskolsky 1970: 19), that the pragmatists' perception of reality was "untouched by alienation" (Lichtman 1970: 80) and effectively signified the endorsement of "the status quo" (Huber 1973: 273). Pragmatists recognized "the tragic breakdown of democracy" (Dewey 1946: 116), "the chasm that separates the theory and practice of our democracy" (Mead [1923] 1964: 263), and they spoke clearly about the multiple failures of the present political system ridden with "the inequality that arises and must arise under the operations of institutionally established and supported finance-capitalism" (Dewey 1946: 117). They were painfully aware of "the tragedy of industrial society" with its "routine and drudgery of countless uninterested hands" and "the blind production of goods, cut off from all the interpretation and aspiration of their common enjoyment" (Mead [1923-26] 1964: 293-6). Far from satisfied with the program of piecemeal reforms confined to welfare measures, pragmatists maintained that "in order to endure under present conditions, liberalism must become radical in the sense that, instead of using social power to ameliorate the evil consequences of the existing system, it shall use social power to change the system."[4] Dewey believed that "actual and concrete liberty of opportunity and action is dependent upon equalization of the political and economic conditions under which individuals are alone free *in fact, not in some abstract metaphysical way*" (Dewey 1946: 116). Dubious also seems the assertion (Huber Rytina and Loomis 1970; Huber 1973) that the pragmatist view of science as politically engaged renders it uniquely susceptible to the manipulation by extant powers.[5] To insure that scientific inquiry retains its integrity in the face of political pressures, according to pragmatists, one should seek not to rid science of ideological biases but to spell them out, turning preconceptions into acknowledged premises and letting the audience judge how these might have affected the inquiry.

Turning to interactionism, we have to admit that with all their debt to pragmatism, interactionist sociologists did not go far enough in heeding its values and fulfilling its political commitments. Interactionists realized that "our democracy is not working perfectly at present" (Park and Miller 1921: 261); they acknowledged the need of social reconstruction (Thomas [1918-20] 1966: 6) and aligned themselves with the underdogs against "middle-class conventional values" (Anderson 1973: xii). On occasion, they even took part in direct political action (Whyte [1943] 1981: 338). But interactionists failed to take on the American political system the way pragmatists did in the 1920s and 1930s. They did not attempt to link the local symbolic worlds and the miseries of their inhabitants to the larger political, social, and economic institutions. And they offered little systematic analysis of how the individual's class and status affect his participation in the production of social reality.

Besides these drawbacks stemming from the failure of interactionists to follow in the steps of pragmatists, there were others that could be laid at the door of pragmatism. Fisher and Strauss (1978: 1979) rightfully point out that pragmatists and interactionists relied too heavily on persuasion, education, and socialization as instruments of social reconstruction. The idea that people will see—and choose—a more rational and humane way if only they are provided with the knowledge of their conditions, reflects a benign view of human nature that may not withstand historical criticism. Also, in their desire to uphold the voluntaristic and participatory character of democracy, pragmatists and interactionists did not do justice to political organization and power politics as means of effecting meaningful social change. Their optimism about prospects for the peaceful transformation of American society into a politically and economically more equitable system might have reflected their underestimation of the power of vested interests and the inertia of political and social institutions. Finally, along with pragmatists, interactionist thinkers offered a rather vague rationale for the division of labor between scientific research and political activism.

All said and done, social interactionism was one of the more openly committed currents in the early twentieth century American sociology. The interactionist notion of sociological practice reflected the pragmatist view of truth as a practically accomplished unity of knowledge and reality. This view underscored the necessity of social reconstruction, the role of scientists as participants on the social scene, and the contribution sociological knowledge could make to directed social change. Knowledge is power and power must belong to people—from this pragmatist premise interactionists derived their commitment to disseminating knowledge and reaching the general public as goals of sociological practice. The very emphasis on structure and process can be seen as an outgrowth of the interactionists' progressivist leanings, of their yearning for stability and change, individual initiative and social responsibility. This dual commitment remains a trademark of contemporary interactionist thought which strives to understand society in the making—society as a process of ongoing social reconstruction.

Conclusion

"The social sciences, in particular, express what society is in itself, and not what it is subjectively to the person thinking about it." Fittingly, this creedal statement occurred in a series of lectures on pragmatism which Durkheim (1983: 88) gave in the academic year of 1913-14. Durkheim's critical attitude toward pragmatists might have changed had he lived long enough to see their sociologically relevant works, but his main thesis—sociology based on pragmatist epistemology is incompatible with studying society in itself—would surely stand. His brand of functionalism, which was fastened to the rationalist injunction of dealing with facts themselves, stood clearly in the tradition of classical science, and as such did not accord with the nonclassical ideas of pragmatism. Indeed, Dewey's *Quest for Certainty* was a philosophical response to the paradigmatic shift in physics, and specifically to Heisenberg's principle of uncertainty, just as Mead's latter work was a self-conscious effort to spell out the implications of the principle of relativity for the human sciences. It was on this meta-theoretical foundation furnished by pragmatists and their German counterparts that interactionists built a school of sociology which become a prototype of a non-classical social science.

Interactionist sociologists accepted the relativist premise that the sense people make of reality is part and parcel of its objective being, from which they inferred that sociologists must deal not only with society *in* itself but also with society *for* itself. Having rejected the notion that social facts should be treated as things, interactionists resolved to treat things as social facts carved out by the collective efforts of historically situated individuals. To the traditional preoccupation with the inherent order of society interactionists juxtaposed their concern for the objective indeterminacy of the situation and the emergent properties of social structure. The dialectical tenets of social interactionism opened the way for understanding not only how society produces the individual, but also how individuals produce society.

The dialectical tension in the interactionist premises made itself felt in the division within the interactionist movement between its more voluntaristically and less voluntaristically oriented branches. The proponents of the former focused their research on the breaks in the routine functioning of social structures, the inevitable gaps in the operation of formal orders, and other manifestations of indeterminacy responsible for novelty and serendipity in social life. In its more extreme form, this approach tends to exaggerate the freedom of the individual to claim a membership in social categories and to shift at will from one self to another, presenting what may be called an "overemergent view of social reality" as inescapably problematic. A different brand of interactionism emphasizes the normative constraints and the power of ascription in society. Those favaoring this approach point out that, more often than not, the world constructed in the course of symbolic interaction tends to be a replica of the familiar social order rather than something qualitatively new, and that individuals, despite all their autonomy and defining powers, typically end up defining their selves and the situation in a predictable, patterned manner, which reveals the power of social constraints. The strength of this approach is in its proponents' concerted efforts to make structure a focal concept in interactionist sociology. Its weakness, exacerbated in part by the greater reliance on laboratory and synchronic forms of research, is in its blurring the temporal dimension of structural processes, which by its nature is more amenable to participatory and diachronic modes of research. No hard and fast line separates the two branches of social interactionism, although pronouncements of some interactionists made it appear so.[6] Even though the term structure is not frequently mentioned by Shibutani, Strauss, Glazer, Stone or Denzin, this does not mean that they are oblivious to the fact of structural constraints.[7] By the same token, the emphasis of Stryker, Burke, Weinstein, McCall, and Simmons on the patterned nature of the identity selection process does not mean they disown the interactionist commitment to studying society in the making.[8] The worst thing that could happen to interactionists is yielding to a sectarian strife along the situation vs. frame, indeterminism vs. determinism, voluntarism vs. structuralism fault-lines. For the different emphases in contemporary interactionism represent the two sides of the whole story, and juxtaposing them could only undercut the raison d'être of interactionist sociology—its dialectical premise that society produces individuals qua human individuals at the same time that it is produced by them qua human society. The task now facing social interactionists is to join forces and incorporate various contributions into a unified interactionist theory of social structure. Another challenge before interactionist theory is to bridge the gap between the micro- and macro-level analyses of social phenomena.[9] In doing so, interactionists need to reexamine the origins of interactionist sociology, its meta-theoretical foundation—romantic idealism and pragmatist philosophy, and its master concept of the (in)determinacy of the situation. If interactionists are serious about tackling the issues of power, class, and inequality, they will also have to reclaim the political commitments of their pragmatist predecessors.

Notes

1.   In pragmatist terms, Joas (1983: 11) points out, it is appropriate to say that "we find our purposes or ends in the world, and we are practically embedded into the world prior to every intentional act." This statement needs to be qualified, for it does not take into account the dialectical nature of the relationship between intentionalities and situations, and specifically the fact that intentionalities can attain a degree of autonomy from the situation and serve as a source of innovations.

2.   It is this circular reasoning that is largely responsible for recent attempts to revise the history of social interactionism by reclassifying interactionists into sociological realists and nominalists (Lewis and Smith, 1980). The whole division appears to be an attempt to get around the fundamental paradox of interactionist thought, the paradox of man being simultaneously a product and producer of society. The pragmatist approach transcends the traditional dichotomy of nominalism and realism through its emphasis on the intercessory role of action, which has the power to universalize the particular and to particularize the universal. What this means is that universality is neither *universalia in intellectu* (the nominalist view), nor *universalia in rebus* (the realist view), but *universalia in actu* (the pragmatist view), or emergent universality, which is as objective as the action it affords and as universal as the community behind it.

3.   All three methods were often used by social interactionists in conjuncture, as parts of the case study approach, whose qualitative emphasis contrasted with more quantitatively oriented modes of research.

4.   Dewey (1946: 132). Hook (1969: 223) remarks that many radicals, without realizing this, rely on Dewey's arguments to denounce Dewey's liberalism.

5.   Those advancing this criticism are prone to draw far-reaching parallels between pragmatist and Marxist views of science. Although pragmatists and Marxists share some methodological and substantive concerns, they differ on one fundamental

point—for Marx, an ideal democracy of the future is a necessity and the task of science is to facilitate the inexorable march into the future; for Dewey, a more rational and humane society is only a possibility and the task of science is to alert people to the potential for social reconstruction.

6. In his 1978 address to the Society for the Study of Symbolic Interaction Blumer subjected to criticism the notion of social structure, leaving an impression, perhaps unintentionally, that he considers it useless for interactionist sociology.

7. An overview of the works of these authors can be found in Maines (1977).

8. The work of this group of interactionists is discussed in Stryker (1980).

9. On the importance of bridging the macro-macro divide see Shalin (1978).

References

Anderson, Nels. 1923. *The Hobo: The Sociology of the Homeless Man.* Chicago: University of Chicago Press.

_____. 1975. *The American Hobo: An Autobiography.* London: E. J. Brill.

Blumer, Herbert. 1939. *Critique of Research in the Social Sciences: An Appraisal of Thomas and Znaniecki's The Polish Peasant in Europe arid America.* Bulletin 44. New York: Social Science Research Council.

Burgess, Ernest W. 1927. "Statistics and Case Studies as Methods of Sociological Research." *Sociology and Social Research* 12: 103-20.

Carey, James T. 1975. *Sociology and Public Affairs: The Chicago School.* London: Sage Publications.

Cooley, Charles Horton. [1902]1964. *Human Nature and the Social Order.* New York: Schocken Books.

_____. [1909] 1962. *Social Organization.* New York: Schocken Books.

_____. 1927. *Life and the Student, Roadside Notes on Human Nature, Society, and Letters.* New York: Alfred A. Knopf.

_____. [1918] 1966. *Social Process.* Carbondale: Southern Illinois University Press.

_____1930. *Sociological Theory and Social Research.* New York: Henry Holt & Co.

Coser, Lewis. 1978. "American Trends," pp. 287-320 in *A History of Sociological Analysis,* edited by Tom Bottomore and Robert Nisbet. New York: Basic Books.

Cressey, Paul G. 1932. *The Taxi-Dance Hall: A Sociological Study in Commercialized Recreational City Life.* Chicago: University of Chicago Press.

Dewey, John [1888] 1969. "The Ethics of Democracy," pp. 227-49 in *John Dewey, The Early Works 1882-1889,* Vol. 1. Carbondale: Southern Illinois University Press.

_____. [1890] 1969. "The Logic of Verification," pp. 83-92 in *John Dewey, The Early Works,* Vol. 3, Carbondale: Southern Illinois University Press.

_____. [1897] 1972. "Ethical Principles Underlying Education," pp. 54-83 in *John Dewey, The Early Works 1882-1898,* Vol. 5. Carbondale: Southern Illinois University Press.

_____. [1916] 1966. *Democracy and Education.* New York: Free Press.

_____. [1927] 1954. *The Public and its Problems.* New York: Henry Holt & Co.

_____[1929] 1958. *Experience and Nature.* New York: Dover.

_____. [1929] 1960. *Quest For Certainty: A Study in the Relation of Knowledge and Action.* New York: Capricorn Books.

_____. [1929] 1962. *Individualism, Old and New.* New York: Capricorn Books.

_____. [1931] 1963. *Philosophy and Civilization.* New York: Capricorn Books.

_____. 1938. *Logic: The Theory of Inquiry.* New York: Henry Holt & Co.

_____. 1946. *Problems of Men.* New York: Philosophical Library.

Dewey, John and Arthur Fisher Bentley. 1949. *Knowing and the Known.* Boston: Beacon Press.

Dollard, John. 1937, *Caste and Class in a Southern Town*. New York: Yale University Press.

Durkheim, Emile. 1983. *Pragmatism and Sociology*. Cambridge: Cambridge University Press.

Ellwood, C. A. 1907, "Sociology: Its Problems and Its Relations," *American Journal of Sociology* 13: 300-48.

_____. 1910. "The Psychological View of Society." *American Journal of Sociology* 15: 596-610.

_____. 1933. *Method in Sociology: A Critical Study*. Durham, NC: Duke University Press.

Faris, Ellsworth. 1937, *The Nature of Human Nature and Other Essays in Social Psychology*. New York: McGraw Hill.

Faris, Robert E. 1970. *Chicago Sociology 1920 -1932*. Chicago: University of Chicago Press.

Fisher, Berenice M. and Anseim L. Strauss. 1978. "Introduction," pp. 457-98 in *A History of Sociological Analysis*, edited by Tom Pottomore and Lewis A. Coser. New York: Basic Books.

_____. 1979. "George Herbert Mead and the Chicago Tradition in Sociology." *Symbolic Interaction* 2: 9-26.

Goldman, Eric. 1956. *Rendezvous with Destiny: A History of Modern American Reform*. New York: Vintage.

Gouinlock, James. 1972. *John Dewey's Theory of Value*. New York: Humanities Press.

Graham, Otis L. 1967. *An Encore for Reform: The Old Progressives and the New Deal*. New York: Oxford University Press.

Hall, Peter M. 1972. "A Symbolic Interactionist Analysis of Politics."' *Sociological Inquiry* 42: 93-99.

Hook, Sidney. 1969. "John Dewey and the Crisis of American Liberalism." *Antioch Review* 29: 218-32.

Hughes, Everett Cherrington. 1955. "Preface," pp. 4-8 in *The Collected Papers of Robert Ezra Park*, edited by Everett Cherrington Hughes, Charles A. Johnson, Jitsuichi Masuoka, Robert Redfield, and Louis Wirth. Vol. III. New York: Free Press.

Huber, Joan. 1973 "Symbolic Interaction as a Pragmatic Perspective: The Bias of Emergent Theory." *American Sociological Review* 38: 278-84.

Huber Rytina, Joan and Charles P. Loomis. 1970. "Marxist Dialectics and Pragmatism: Power as Knowledge." *American Sociological Review* 35: 308-18.

James, William. [1890] 1950. *The Principles of Psychology*. Vols. I & II. New York: Dover.

_____. [1907] 1955. *Pragmatism*. Cambridge, MA: Harvard University Press.

_____. [1909] 1967. *The Meaning of Truth*. Ann Arbor: The University of Michigan Modern Library.

_____. [1909] 1970. "A Pluralistic Universe" in *Essay's in Radical Empiricism and Pluralistic Universe*. Gloucester: Peter Press.

_____. [1910] 1962. "The Moral Equivalent of War." pp. 480-91 in *The Progressive Years. The Spirit and Achievement of American Reform*, edited by Otis Pease. New York: George Braziller.

Joas, Hans. 1983. "In Defense of Earlier American Sociology." Paper presented at the 78th Annual Meeting of the ASA, Detroit.

Johnson, David G. and Peggy A. Shifflett. 1981. "George Herbert Who? A Critique of the Objectivist Reading of Mead," *Symbolic Interaction* 4: 143-55.

Kanter, Rosabeth M. 1972. "Symbolic Interactionism and Politics in Systematic Perspective." *Sociological Inquiry* 42: 77-92.

Kon, Igor S. and Dmitri N. Shalin. 1969. "D, G. Mid i Problema Chelovecheskogo 'Ia'" G. H, Mead and the Problem of the Human Self." *Voprosy Filosofii* 12: 85-95.

Kuhn, Thomas. 1970. *The Structure of Scientific Revolutions*, Chicago: University of Chicago Press.

Lewis, David J. 1976. "The Classic American Pragmatists as Forerunners to Symbolic Interactionism." *Sociological Quarterly* 17: 341-59.

Lewis, J. David and Richard L. Smith. 1980. *American Sociology and Pragmatism. Mead, Chicago Sociology arid Symbolic Interactionism.* Chicago: University of Chicago Press.

Lichtman, Richard. 1970. "Symbolic Interactionism and Social Reality: Some Marxist Queries." *Berkeley Journal of Sociology* 15: 75-94.

Lindeman, Eduard C. 1924. *Social Discovery, An Approach to the Study of Functional Groups.* New York: Republic Publishing Co.

Maines, David R. 1977. "Social Organization and Social Structure in Symbolic Interactionist Thought." *Annual Review of Sociology* 3: 235-59.

Marcell, David W. 1974. *Progress and Pragmatism.* Westport, CT: Greenwood Press.

McPhail, Clark and Cynthia Rexroat. 1979. "Mead vs. Blumer: The Divergent Methodological Perspectives of Social Behaviorism and Symbolic Interactionism."' *American Sociological Review* 44: 449-67.

Mead, George Herbert. [1908] 1964. "The Philosophical Basis of Ethics," pp. 82-93 in *Selected Writings, George Herbert Mead*, edited by Andrew J. Reck. New York: Bobbs-Merrill.

_____. [1924-1925] 1964. "The Genesis of the Self and Social Control," pp. 267-93 in *Selected Writings, George Herbert Mead*, edited by Andrew J. Reck. New York: Bobbs-Merrill.

_____. [1925-1926] 1964. "The Nature of Aesthelic Experience," pp. 294-305 in *Selected Writings, George Herbert Mead*, edited by Andrew J. Reck. New York: Bobbs-Merrill.

_____. 1929. "Bishop Berkeley and His Message." *Journal of Philosophy* 26: 421-30.

_____. 1932. *The Philosophy of the Present.* Chicago: University of Chicago Press.

_____. 1934. *Mind, Self and Society.* Chicago: University of Chicago Press.

_____. 1935-1936 "The Philosophy of John Dewey." *International Journal of Ethics* 46: 64-81.

_____. 1936. *Movements of Thought in the Nineteenth Century.* Chicago: University of Chicago Press.

_____1938. *The Pllilosophy of the Act.* Chicago: University of Chicago Press.

_____. 1982. *The Individual and the Social Self.* Unpublished Work of George Herbert Mead, edited by David L. Miller. Chicago: University of Chicago Press.

Mortis, Charles W. 1970. *The Pragmatic Movement in American Philosophy.* New York: Braziller.

Park, Robert E. [1904] 1972. "The Crowd and the Public," pp. 3-84 in Robert Park. *The Crowd and the Public and Other Essays*, edited by Henry Elsner, Jr. Chicago: University of Chicago Press.

_____. [1924] 1955. "Human Nature, Attitudes and Mores," pp. 267-92 in *The Collected Papers of Robert Ezra Park.* Vol. III. Society, edited by Everett Cherrington Hughes, Charles A. Johnson, Jitsuichi Masuoka, Robert Redlield, and Louis Wirth. Glencoe, IL: Free Press.

_____. [1927] 1955. "Human Nature and Collective Behavior," pp. 13-21 in *The Collected Papers of Robert Ezra Park.* Vol. III. Society, edited by Everett Cherrington Hughes. Charles A. Johnson, Jitsuichi Masuoka, Robert Redfield, and Louis Wirth. Glencoe, IL: Free Press.

_____. [1929] 1952. "Sociology. Community and Society," pp. 178-209 in *The Collected Papers of Robert Ezra Park*. Vol. II. Human Communities, edited by Everett Cherrington Hughes, Charles A. Johnson, Jitsuichi Masooka, Robert Redfield, and Louis Wirth. Glencoc, IL: Free Press.

_____. [1940]. "News as a Form of Knowledge," pp. 71-88 in *The Collected Papers of Robert Ezra Park*. Vol. III. Society, edited by Everett Cherrington Hughes. Charles A. Johnson, Jitsuichi Masuoka, Robert Redfield, and Louis Wirth. Glencoe. IL: Free Press.

Park Papers. n.d. *Robert E. Park Papers,* University of Chicago Archives.

Park, Robert E. and Herbert A. Miller. 1921. *Old World Traits Transplanted.* New York: Harper & Brothers Publishers.

Park, Robert E. and Ernest W. Burgess. [1921] 1969. Introduction to the Science of Sociology. Chicago: The University of Chicago Press.

Peirce, Charles. [1868] 1955. "Some Consequences of Four Incapacities," pp. 228-50 in *Philosophical Writings of Peirce*, edited by Justus Buehler. New York: Dover.

_____. [1877] 1953. "The Fixation of Belief," pp. 5-22 in *Philosophical Writings of Peirce*. edited by Justus Buchler. New York: Dover.

_____1931-1958.*Collected Papers of Charles Sanders Peirce*, 8 Vols. Cambridge, MA: Harvard University Press.

Perry, Ralph Barton. 1964. *The Thought and Character of William James*. New York: Harper & Row.

Reynolds, Jenice M. and Larry T. Reynolds. 1973. "Interactionism: Complicity and the Astructural Bias." *Catalyst* 7: 76-85.

Ropers, Richard. 1973. "Mead, Marx and Social Psychology." *Catalyst* 7: 42-61.

Rucker, Darnell. 1969. *The Chicago Pragmatists*. Minneapolis: University of Minnesota Press.

Shalin, Dmitri N. 1978. "The Genesis of Social Interactionism and Differentiation of Macro- and Micro-Sociological Paradigms." *Humboldt Journal of Social Relations* 6: 3-38.

_____. 1984. "The Romantic Antecedents of Meadian Social Psychology." *Symbolic Interaction* 7: 43-65.

_____. 1986. "Romanticism and the Rise of Sociological Hermeneutics." *Social Research* 53 (forthcoming).

Shaskolsky, Leon. 1970. "The Development of Sociological Theory in America: A Sociology of Knowledge Interpretation," pp. 6-30 in *The Sociology of Sociology*, edited by Larry T. Reynolds and Jenice M. Reynolds. New York: David McKay Co.

Smith, Dusky Lee. 1973. "Symbolic Interactionism: Definitions of the Situation From Becker to Lofland." *Catalyst* 7: 62-75.

Stone, Gregory, David Maines, Harvey Farberman, Cladys I. Stone, and Norman Denzin. 1974. "On Methodology and Craftsmanship in the Criticism of Sociological Perspectives." *American Sociological Review* 39: 456-63.

Stryker, Sheldon. 1980. *Symbolic Interactionism: A Social Structured Version.* Menlo Park, CA: Benjamin/Cummings Publishing Co.

Thayer, H. S. 1973. *Meaning and Action: A Study of American Pragmatism.* Indianapolis: Bobbs-Merrill.

Thomas, William I. [1918-1920] 1966. *The Polish Peasant in Europe and America*, with Florian Znaniecki, in W. I. *Thomas on Social Organization and Social Change. Selected Papers*, edited by Morris Janowjtz. Chicago: University of Chicago Press.

_____. 1923. *The Unadjusted Girl, With Cases and Standpoint for Behavioral Analysis.* Boston: Little Brown and Co.

_____. 1937. *Primitive Behavior. An Introduction to the Social Sciences*. New York: McGraw-Hill.

_____. 1939. "Comments by W. I. Thomas," pp. 82-87 in Herbert Blumer, *Critique of Research in the Social Sciences: An Appraisal of Thomas and Znaniecki's The Polish Peasant in Europe and America*, Bulletin 44. New York: Social Science Research Council.

_____. 1966. *W. I. Thomas on Social Organization and Social Change: Selected Papers*, edited by Morris Janowitz. Chicago: University of Chicago Press.

Thomas, William I. and Dorothy Swaine Thomas. *1928. The Child in America: Behavior Problems and Programs*. New York: Alfred A. Knopf.

Thrasher, Frederick M. 1927. *The Gang. A Study of 1,313 Gangs in Chicago*. Chicago: University of Chicago Press.

White, Morton C. 1937. *Social Thought in America: The Revolt Against Formalism*. Boston: Beacon Press.

Whitehead, Alfred North. [1929] 1937. *Process and Reality*. New York: Macmillan.

_____. 1938. *Science and the Modern World*. Middlesex: Penguin Books.

Whyte, William Foot. [1943] 1981. *Street Corner Society: The Social Structure of an Italian Slum*. Chicago: University of Chicago Press.

Znaniecki, Florian. 1919. *Cultural Reality*. Chicago: The University of Chicago Press.

_____. [1923] 1967. *The Law's of Social Philosophy*. New York: Russell & Russell.

_____. 1927. "The Object Matter of Sociology." *American Journal of Sociology* 22: 529-84.

_____. [1934] 1968. *The Method of Sociology*. New York: Octagon.

_____. 1939. "Comments by Florian Znaniecki," pp. 87-98 in Herbert Blumer, *Critique of Research in The Social Sciences: An Appraisal of Thomas and Znaniecki's The Polish Peasant in Europe and America*. Bulletin 44. New York: Social Research Council.

Zorbaugh, Harvey Warren. 1929. *The Gold Coast and a Slum: A Sociological Study of Chicago's Near North Side*. Chicago: University of Chicago Press.

4

Challenging Critical Theory: The Frankfurt School, Communicative Action, and the Pragmatist Revival

For much of the twentieth century, pragmatism was perceived in Europe as a crude expression of Anglo-Saxon utilitarianism. Even thinkers sympathetic to the new American current found it inferior to the continental philosophical tradition. Less charitable critics, notably the writers close to the critical theory circle, dismissed pragmatism as instrumental reason run amok, a technocratic decisionism severed from substantive-rational moorings. It was not until the 1960s that respectable European thinkers began to pay more favorable attention to pragmatism and its sociological counterpart, symbolic interactionism. A notable example is Jürgen Habermas who recently admitted, "I have for a long time identified myself with that radical democratic mentality which is present in the best American traditions and articulated in American pragmatism" (Habermas, 1985, p. 198). This statement is noteworthy not only because it holds fresh promise for a transatlantic dialogue, but also because it points to the renewed interest among critical thinkers in liberal democracy and its emancipatory potential.

While the search for common ground will be welcomed on this side of the Atlantic, it will also raise some eyebrows. There are important

An earlier version of this paper was presented in 1989 at the Annual Meeting of the American Sociological Association. It was later published as "Critical Theory and the Pragmatist Challenge" in *American Journal of Sociology*, 1992, Vol. 98, pp. 237-279. I wish to thank participants in the Sociology Department Seminar at Boston University for helpful comments on an earlier draft of this article. The critical feedback from Mitchell Aboulafia, Thomas Alexander, Bob Antonio, Thomas Burger, Lewis Coser, Bruce Mazlish, Gene Rochberg-Halton, and Lon Shelby is also gratefully appreciated.

points on which critical theorists and writers steeped in pragmatism part company. The former have a penchant for totalities, are conversant with rationality at large, and have profound reservations about bourgeois democracy, whereas the latter attend to the particular, revel in multiple rationalities, and place much stock in democratic institutions. So, when Habermas (1986, p. 193) describes pragmatism as "a missing branch of Young Hegelianism," he is sure to make some critics wonder if his European biases blinded him to pragmatism's native roots.

I see nothing objectionable in the efforts to trace pragmatism's European lineage. Nor do I agree with those who think Habermas has gotten pragmatism all wrong. A movement as diverse as this lends itself to more than one reading, and Habermas does an important service by illuminating its various facets, notably its political dimension, which American sociologists claiming the pragmatist legacy tend to undervalue. Still, I want to take issue with Habermas because something is amiss in his analysis—the pragmatist sensitivity to indeterminacy, contingency, and chaos. This sensitivity is in tune with trends in modern science, and it deserves closer attention from sociologists than it has been granted so far. It is my contention that taking objective indeterminacy seriously would require rethinking central conclusions in Habermas's theory of communicative action. In particular, I would like to show that Habermas elevated verbal intellect at the expense of noncognitive intelligence and thereby truncated the pragmatist notion of experience. I will also argue that incorporating the pragmatist perspective on democracy brings an important corrective to the emancipatory agenda championed by critical theorists.

Critical theory and Habermas have received a fair amount of attention (Jay, 1973; McCarthy, 1978; Held, 1980; Geuss, 1981; Thompson and Held, 1982; Antonio, 1983; Bernstein, Forester, 1985; Ferrara, 1985; Benhabib, 1986; Wolin, 1987). With the exception of the piece by Antonio (1989), however, few authors have explored in depth the interfaces between pragmatism, democracy, and Habermas's thought, and none, to my knowledge, has dealt with the pragmatist notion of experience and its bearings on Habermas's views. My discussion centers on the theory of communicative actions—a segment in Habermas's total corpus where he joins issues with pragmatism and makes a concerted effort to incorporate its democratic ethos into the European project of critical theory. I begin with the sources of critical theorist's ambivalence toward democracy. Next, I examine how Habermas merged the pragmatist and critical theory traditions. And finally, I subject his construction to criticism, using the pragmatist notions of experience, indeterminacy, and democracy as analytical tools.

From Critical Idealism to Critical Theory

It was not until Kant ([1781] 1966, p. xxiv) declared, "our age is, in every sense of the word, the age of criticism, and everything must submit to it," that the term "critical" entered the philosophical lexicon in its modern sense. Kant chose his nomenclature deliberately to highlight the difference between the age of reason and the age of criticism, between overconfident rationalism of *philosophes* and "my transcendental or, better, *critical* idealism" (Kant [1783] 1950, p. 41). According to Kant, reason could no longer derive its mandate from divine inspiration or natural law but must lay its own standards for judging the true, the good, and the beautiful. For reason is not an outside observer impartially stating the truth and legislating a better future but a participant observer whose rational activity gives the world its meaning and whose very unreflexivity breeds oppression. The objective structures of our world, physical or social, are grounded in the a priori structures of the mind itself. To change the former, the subject has to grapple with the latter. Which is to say, emancipation starts with self-reflection; only after reason has exposed its own prejudices and learned its limits can it proceed with its appointed task. Hence, the endless exhortations by Kant's successors to do away with "the dogmatic tendency in man" (Fichte [1794] 1970, p. 161), "dogmatism as a way of thinking" (Hegel [1807] 1967, p. 99) and get on with "a strenuous reacquisition of everything which has once been acquired" (Schelling [1800], 1978, p. 1).

These utterings sound vaguely subversive, but in the post-revolutionary climate of early nineteenth century Europe they had a distinctly conservative ring to them. Anxious to avoid the bloody excesses of the French Revolution, critical idealists hastened to assure the world that the project of modernity they inherited from the Enlightenment would be carried out by peaceful means. The only force they were willing to tolerate was the force of reason—the mind grounded in principles, conscious of its moral moorings, and committed to the public good. This is what post-Kantian idealists called *Vernunft* and juxtaposed to *Verstand* or everyday understanding that, unbeknownst to itself, weaves the familiar world from its biases, preconceptions, and particularistic interests. Viewed at from this angle, the battle for emancipation is "the battle of reason ... to break the rigidity to which understanding has reduced everything" (Hegel [1817] 1975, p. 53).

Vernunft is bound to strike some readers as an oversoul or a super-human agency, but there is nothing especially mysterious about it. While the telos of reason is humanity as a whole, its *locus operandi* is the individual speaking on behalf of reason. Society is fully rational when its members heed the claims of reason they have raised, when they act their conscience and submit to a tribunal within which one is simultaneously a defendant and a judge: "The consciousness of an *inner tribunal* in man ... is conscience.... This original intellectual and ... moral capacity, called conscience, has this peculiarity, that although its business is a business of a man with himself, he is obliged by his reason to look upon it as carried on at the command of another person. For the transaction is here the conduct of a law-case ... before a judge" (Kant [1803] 1904, p. 289).

The spirit of this statement is remarkably modern and democratic. It implies that every individual, regardless of the origin and status, is a rational being and a potential agent of emancipation, whose dormant capacity for criticism can be roused by the critical idealist's path-breaking intellections. Emancipation through reason transpires here as a project that humans qua rational beings accomplish by subjecting to critical analysis the a priori grounds for their conduct, freeing themselves from prejudices, and unswervingly following standards they have justified to themselves as universal, equitable, and humane.

The project of emancipation through reason came under attack during the reaction that followed the French Revolution, but its bourgeois democratic ethos continued to nourish the moral imagination well into the nineteenth century. This ethos was still palpable in the young Marx who called for "*a ruthless criticism of everything existing*" and urged the "reform of consciousness [which] consists solely in letting the world perceive its own consciousness by awakening it from dreaming about itself, in explaining to it its own actions" ([1843] 1972, p. 8; [1843] 1971, p. 82). Marx's commitment to emancipation through criticism, wore thin in the revolutionary climate of the time. By the mid-1840s, he began to doubt the peaceable route to emancipation, and along with other young Hegelians, set out to investigate what keeps reason from exercising its curative powers. The main impediment, Marx concluded, was the class domination and institutions it span—law, morality, and philosophy, through which the capitalist state obfuscates the oppression and perpetuates false consciousness among the toiling masses. The ruling class has the power to protect its particularistic interests, and it is naive to believe that it would bow to the voice of universal reason and agree to yield its power peacefully. Bourgeois democracy is a sham; its much touted freedoms stand in the path of emancipation, insofar as they legitimize the exploitation and prevent workers from understanding their role as a driving force in history. The real hope for emancipation lies with the concrete historical agent, the proletariat, a universal class for which criticism is not just a theoretical exercise but a practical revolutionary endeavor and which can bring about communism—a society based on genuinely free discourse. Such a society frees consciousness from systematic ideological distortions, brings every rational individual into critical discourse, and thus for the first time makes reason truly universal and society fully rational.

The dilemma Marx bequeathed to his successors—must reason rely on democratic procedures or class violence to achieve its emancipatory objectives?—informs much of the debates about critical theory in the twentieth century. Few participants in these debates failed to acknowledge that "the critical theory is the heir of ... German idealism" (Horkheimer [1937] 1976, p. 223). All agreed that it aims at "the transformation of society [which] eliminates the original relationship between substructure and superstructure" (Marcuse [1937] 1968, p. 144) and has as its ultimate goal "a society in which the 'people' have become autonomous individuals [freely] choosing their government and determining their life" (Adorno 1965, p. 105). How exactly these goals were to be accomplished remained a contentious issue. The fact that bourgeois democracy failed to forestall fascism had seriously undermined the trust in liberalism's emancipatory potential. The disillusionment ran especially deep among the writers gathered around Horkheimer and the Frankfurt School, who sought to forge a historical and conceptual link between totalitarianism and liberal rationalism. The impotence of bourgeois democracy is transparent in its surrender to totalitarianism, the kind that the Third Reich exemplifies most vividly. Indeed, "we can say that liberalism 'produces' the total authoritarian state out of itself, as its own consummation at a more advanced stage of development" (Marcuse 1968a, p. 19). "The pattern of all administration and 'personnel policy'," according to Adorno ([1951] 1978, p. 131), "tends of its own accord—towards Fascism." Horkheimer (1978, p. 219) made a similar diagnosis, charging that left to its own devices, "democracy leads to its opposite—tyranny."

Critical theorists were aware that the United States did not fit neatly into this scenario, yet they convinced themselves that America was rapidly moving toward the "administered state" whose more subtle forms of domination bore equally ill tidings. The media-based domination they found in capitalist America looked every bit as pervasive, even if somewhat more benign, as the one undergirding a totalitarian state. The culture industry of capitalism works over time to produce mass consciousness suitable for the market economy and amenable to social control. Marcuse's *One-Dimensional Man* (1964) is the best known account of the bondage in which reason finds itself in a capitalist society, though basic insights articulated in this book had been familiar to critical theorists for decades (Horkheimer and Adorno [1944] 1989, p. 222).

While critical thinkers had few reasons to cheer European liberalism, they could not find much solace in the Marxist scenario either. For one thing, the proletarian masses failed to act as the agents of historical emancipation Marx hailed them to be, revealing instead unmistakably conservative leanings, and then, precisely in the countries where "late capitalism" seemed to have reached its final stage. As the century waxed on, critical theorists became painfully aware that the states claiming Marx's legacy had evolved a totalitarianism all their own, equally inimical to critical theory's lofty ideals. Already in the 1920s critical thinkers questioned Marx's thesis about "the universal class" and spurned Lukács' apology for Communist Party domination. After World War II, their disaffection for Marxist states and left totalitarianism grew stronger (Neumann 1953, pp. 15-19; Marcuse 1958; Adorno [1966] 1973, p. 367; Horkheimer 1978, p. 230). Horkheimer expressed this indignation with particular force, sparing neither "the tendency toward fascism in capitalist states" nor "a sudden turn of left-radical opposition into terrorist totalitarianism" (Horkheimer 1978, pp. 230, 233).

Marcuse was perhaps the only original Frankfurt School member willing to sanctify violence as "a 'natural right' of resistance for oppressed and overpowered minorities to use extralegal means" (1965, p. 116). But his views did not sit well with the old generation critical thinkers, who refused to endorse left-wing terrorism and student militancy. This refusal precipitated the split within the New Left, with the younger generation opting for radical action and the older one left wallowing in the doubts about critical theory's practical import. "There certainly can be no true criticism without an intellectually grounded hope which derives its legitimacy from realistic possibilities," urged Horkheimer (1978, p. 138). Yet with the liberal path toward emancipation blocked by the market-driven media and class warfare discarded as a viable alternative, it was precisely "an intellectually grounded hope" that critical thinkers found in short supply. After the Second World War it became obvious to many observers that "Critical Theory was now incapable of suggesting critical praxis" (Jay, 1973, p. 279). It is in this climate of uncertainty about the prospects for emancipation that critical theorists proclaimed the eclipse of reason and embraced Weber's prophesies about the rationalization's crippling effect on democracy.

What attracted Frankfurt School theorists to Weber was his dower view of reason as an agency whose power to control the world subverts human longing for meaningful existence. This ironic capacity to render the world manageable and meaningless at the same time has been a central theme in emancipatory scholarship from the start. Already in his prize winning *Discourse on the Science and the Arts* Rousseau articulated the paradox of industry begetting poverty and culture breeding oppression. Critical idealists developed it further in their metaphysics of reason that remains estranged from itself and its products until it realizes its own responsibility for the world out there. Marx's theory, which blends the French Enlightenment and German idealism, offered another variation on this theme—history is the ongoing struggle of humanity to free itself from the dehumanizing consequences of its relentless drive to perfect the production forces, the drive that multiplies goods and miseries alike. These insights, minus the attendant optimism about reason's ultimate triumph, found their way into Weber's theory of global rationalization.

Reason's power to assert control, to increase efficiency, to calculate the future—to achieve a proximate goal, is designated by Weber as "instrumental" or "formal rationality." The capacity to judge value, to realize a higher purpose, to pursue a just cause—to lead a meaningful life, is termed "value" or "substantive rationality" (Weber, 1964, pp. 184-186, 211-212). The relationship between the two is antinomian—the greater mastery reason achieves over the world of things, the less room left for the questions of meaning and value; the more organized reason becomes internally, the narrower the scope for personal choice; the farther the state extends its bureaucratic procedures, the heavier its domination over the individual. A telling example is representative democracy, which purports to express people's will but in fact subverts its professed goal by virtue of its complexity, pervasive legalism, and growing dependence on the party apparatus, which inexorably comes to dominate politics. Democracy, Weber (1964, pp. 407-423) concluded, is the most efficient form of domination, all the more pernicious that it conceals its totalitarian proclivities under the veneer of bureaucratic rationality and popular rhetoric. The future of modernity is the "iron cage" that reason unwittingly forged for itself and where it is destined to dwell—unfree, disenchanted, longing for meaning, unsure of its higher purpose (Weber [1904-1905] 1958, p. 182).[1]

It is easy to see how much *Critique of Instrumental Reason, One Dimensional Man,* or *Negative Dialectics* owe to this dark vision. Weber's insights into the rationalization process and its unintended systemic consequences have been absorbed into such critical-theoretic concepts as "administered state," "totalitarian democracy," "expert cultures," "isolation through communication," "media-distorted discourse." His disdain for formal democracy seems to have been borne out by historical developments in the capitalist West and the communist East. And his skepticism about the prospects for substantive democracy neatly rationalized the Frankfurt School's failure to tie its theory to political practice. There was a penalty, of course, that critical theorists had to pay for embracing Weber—surrendering rational hope for emancipation. This is what "melancholy science," as Adorno dabbed critical theory, was coming to. And this is why Jürgen Habermas found the Frankfurt School's confines too narrow and moved beyond its fold. He did it to take a fresh look at the question that the old generation critical thinkers left unanswered: Is emancipation through reason a rational hope? Habermas's *Theory of Communicative Action* can be seen as an attempt to invigorate critical theory by merging the continental and Anglo-Saxon traditions and bringing the pragmatist perspective to bear on the project of emancipation through reason.

From Critical Theory to Communicative Action

"It is only in Western nations that the precarious and continually threatened achievements of bourgeois emancipation and the worker's movement are guaranteed to any extent worth mentioning.... And we know just how important bourgeois freedoms are. For when things go wrong it is those on the Left who become the first victims" (Habermas 1986, p. 42). This programmatic observation illuminates a paradox: the very fact that the Institute for Social Research, the hotbed of critical thinking, has been thriving in a capitalist society seems to suggest that it serves the existing order. This contradiction has not been lost on the right- and left-wing critics, who alternatively charged the Frankfurt School leaders with ingratitude toward the existing order or betraying the working class interests. In their defense, critical theorists pointed to the marginal position they occupy in the academe, the media's power to blunt the critical message, and the false consciousness pervading capitalist society, yet these explanations are rather half-hearted, given the prominent positions that critical theorists acquired in German academia after World War II, and they certainly do not go to the heart of the matter. The real problem is that "the old Frankfurt School never took bourgeois democracy very seriously" (Habermas 1986, p. 98). By contrast, Habermas takes pain to emphasize that academic freedom is for real, that bourgeois democracy is a major historical accomplishment, and that its liberal institutions are indispensable for genuine criticism. All this by no means obviates the fundamental criticism that critical theorists have leveled against the capitalist order, most signally against "the pervasive inequality of freedom [and] unequal opportunity of access to the means of democratic persuasion" (Marcuse [1968] 1976, p. 326). Habermas accepts the premise that the rationalization process has produced systemic consequences highly injurious to the democratic process: modern systems are unmanageably complex; consumerist economy manufactures false needs; mass media manipulates public opinion; expert cultures obfuscate the public's stakes in technical issues; and the relentless bureaucratization robs humans of their autonomy, dignity, and solidarity (Habermas [1962] 1989, pp. 141-222; [1981] 1987, pp. 332-73). These are the familiar ills of late capitalism. Formidable though they are, they do not spell democracy's impending doom. The old school critical theorists have grown unreasonably pessimistic about the project of modernity. Their pessimism is historically unfounded and theoretically fallacious—the prospects for emancipation through reason "can today no longer be disqualified as simply utopian" (Habermas [1962] 1989, pp. 235). The agenda for the day is "the reconciliation of a modernity which has fallen apart," the rededication to the idea "that without surrendering the differentiation that modernity has made possible in the cultural and economic spheres, one can find forms of living together in which autonomy and dependency can truly enter into a non-antagonistic relation, that one can walk tall in a collectivity that does not have the dubious quality of backward-looking substantial forms of community" (Habermas 1986, pp. 125). To salvage the project of modernity, critical theory must cure the democratic process of distortions it suffers in a capitalist society. How can this be done? Habermas answers with a prescription borrowed from American pragmatism: by mobilizing the public, revitalizing public discourse, getting personally involved in politics.

Habermas's willingness to join issues with pragmatism is very much at odds with the German tradition, in which the intellectual was "bred in the veneration of theory and history, and contempt for empiricism and pragmatism" (Neumann 1953, pp. 19). Frankfurt School thinkers were

solidly embedded in this tradition, their writings evincing little appreciation for pragmatism's emancipatory potential (Marcuse 1939/1940;
Horkheimer 1937, 1947). They dismissed pragmatism in a wholesale
fashion as "the abasement of reason" and "a genuine expression of the
positivistic approach," a philosophy which advocates the "reduction of
reason to a mere instrument" and serves as a "counter part of modern
industrialism, for which the factory is the prototype of human existence, and which models all branches of culture after production on the
conveyor belt, or after the rationalized front office" (Horkheimer 1947,
pp. 45-54). Habermas's break with this tradition was not instantaneous.
According to his own account (Habermas 1986, pp. 104, 151, 193), his
interest in pragmatism goes back to the early 1960s, when Karl Otto
Apel encouraged him to read Peirce and other pragmatists. *Knowledge
and Interest*, published in Germany in 1968, is the first work in which
Habermas treats pragmatism systematically. There is no mention of
Mead in this volume, Dewey is cited once or twice, but Peirce is treated
at length as a representative pragmatist thinker. The treatment is more
sympathetic than the one accorded by Marcuse and Horkheimer, but it
does not break completely with the thesis, first advanced by Max Scheler
([1926] 1977), that pragmatism exemplifies a formal-rational preoccupation with nature that undermines the normative discourse embedded in
substantive rationality. What Habermas (1986, p. 193) finds appealing
in Peirce is the "logical socialism" implicit in the latter's exalted view
of a community of rational thinkers engaged in critical inquiry and
ceaselessly advancing toward the truth through uncoerced discourse,
rational argumentation, and consensus building. It was not until Habermas encountered Dewey and Mead, however, that he fully realized the
momentous implications that Peirce's ideas had for critical theory.

"The radical-democratic branch of Young Hegelianism" is a cognomen
Habermas (1986, p. 151) coins to frame the pragmatism espoused by
Dewey and Mead. This apt description highlights the often overlooked
debt that pragmatist thinkers owe to German idealism, the ingenuous
manner in which Peirce, Dewey, Mead, and to a lesser extent, James
developed a Hegelian concern with language, communication, and
intersubjectivity—the social dimension of reason. Dewey's writings
were particularly instrumental in sensitizing Habermas to the continuity between scientific inquiry and democratic discourse, to the fact that
"freedom of inquiry, toleration of diverse views, freedom of communication, the distribution of what is found out to every individual as the
ultimate intellectual consumer, are involved in the democratic as in the

scientific method" (Dewey 1939, p. 102). From the same source comes his appreciation for the public and its role in sustaining inquiry into communal affairs. The prospect for democracy, Dewey contended and Habermas agreed, "rests upon persuasion, upon ability to convince and be convinced," upon "the improvement of the methods and conditions of debate, discussion and persuasion. That is *the* problem of the public" (Dewey 1916, p. 134; 1939, p. 102). Taking one step further, Dewey (1946, p. 132) comes up with an appeal that critical theorists would have appreciated, if not fully endorsed: "Humane liberalism in order to save itself must cease to deal with symptoms and go to the causes of which inequalities and oppressions are but the symptoms. In order to endure under present conditions, liberalism must become radical in the sense that, instead of using social power to ameliorate the evil consequences of the existing system, it shall use social power to change the system."

Mead caught Habermas's attention for some of the same reasons that Dewey did, but in addition to his progressive democratic agenda, Habermas found in Mead's writings a theory that "elevated symbolically mediated interaction to the new paradigm of reason" and that signified a major advance beyond the old "paradigm of the philosophy of consciousness" (Habermas 1984, p. 390). This point, crucial to Habermas's own project, deserves some elaboration. We can recall that critical idealists placed much stock in the historical process which elevates biased, unreflexive, everyday understanding (*Verstand*) to the loftier status of self-conscious reason that spearheads criticism and attends to higher truths (*Vernunft*). Habermas traces this trust in the noble faculties of reason to the tradition that stretches from Descartes, through German idealism, to critical theorists. The problem with this tradition is that it does not incorporate the sociological perspective on reason as a communicative affair; instead, it treats reason as a unitary phenomenon modeled after instrumental labor activity, as a process bound to the subject who confronts the world on its own and singlehandedly transforms it into a rational objective whole. Hegel's objective idealism did entail some tantalizing insights into the role that language and community play in the genesis of self-consciousness, but much of his work followed the old paradigm, and whatever sociologically relevant ideas he had presaged failed to take root on German soil.[2] By contrast, American pragmatists seized this neglected aspect of German idealism, expanding it into a new paradigm of reason as social through and through. Sidestepping the familiar pair of *Verstand* and *Vernunft*, the new paradigm gives prominence to *Verstandigung*, the interactive process of reaching understanding. "The change in perspective from solitary rational purposiveness to social interaction," writes Habermas (1987a, p. 149), "does promise to illuminate the very process of mutual understanding [*Verstandigung*]—and not merely of understanding [*Verstehen*]." Mead, Habermas continues, resolutely renounced the paradigm of reason as solitary consciousness and went farther than other contemporary scholars to lay out the paradigm of reason as communicative action and spell out its implications for the emancipatory agenda, which is why his ideas must be included in any theory that assigns to self-consciousness and critique a role in social reconstruction.

Indeed, Mead not only joins in the classical discourse on rationality and emancipation through reason but also pushes it in a new direction. His discussion owes much to German idealism, which Mead studied as a student at Harvard and in Berlin and then taught for many years at the University of Chicago.[3] His views on evolution as a process that brings nature to self-consciousness and assures humans "some degree of control of the process of evolution out of which they arose" (Mead 1938, p. 511) bring to mind Hegel's phenomenology, with its dialectics of reason objectifying itself in nature, finding itself estranged from its own products, and then gradually rediscovering its authorship over the way things are. But Mead's approach is also thoroughly informed by the evolutionary perspective and the pragmatist determination to tie thinking to conduct. "What I have attempted to do," explains Mead (1934, p. 334), "is to bring rationality back to a certain type of conduct, the type of conduct in which the individual puts himself in the attitude of the whole community to which he belongs. This implies that the whole group is involved in some organized activity and that in this organized activity the action of one calls for the action of the other organisms involved. What we term 'reason' arises when one of the organisms takes into its own response the attitude of the other organisms involved.... When it does so, it is what we term 'a rational being.'" Reason is historically embedded in communal existence; once brought into being, it transforms community life itself, for "when the process of evolution has passed under the control of social reason," it "becomes not only self-conscious but also self-critical" (1938, p. 508, 1934, p. 255). From a central preoccupation with the mastery over things, reason now turns toward the questions of value. To use Weberian terminology, reason becomes substantive, it reevaluates values, rationally resolves social conflicts, and endeavors to revamp the entire social order from which it sprang:

The rational solution of the conflict, however, calls for the reconstruction of both habits and values, and this involves transcending the order of the community. A hypothetically different order suggests itself and becomes the end in conduct.... In logical terms there is established a universe of discourse which transcends the specific order within which the members of the community may, in a specific conflict, place themselves outside of the community order as it exists, and agree upon changed habits of action and a restatement of values. Rational procedure, therefore, sets up an order within which thought operates.... Its claims are the claims of reason. It is a social order that includes any rational being who is or may be in any way implicated in the situation. (Mead [1930] 1964, p. 404)

A close look at Habermas's theory reveals the full measure of his debt to pragmatism. We find in his work the same mixture of historical optimism that harks back to critical idealism and tough-minded realism found in progressive era pragmatism. The belief in "a noncoercively unifying, consensus building force of a discourse in which the participants overcome their at first subjectively biased views in favor of a rationally motivated agreement" is combined here with a keen awareness that communications remain "systematically distorted" in a "money-bound," "media-steered" society which keeps public discourse from realizing its full critical potential (Habermas 1987, p. 315; [1981] 1987, pp. 256-82). In spite of these instructive continuities, there are several issues on which Habermas and pragmatists part company. I shall come back to the pragmatist critique of Habermas in the next section, but first, here are the points over which Habermas takes issue with pragmatists.

From the sociological perspective, the pragmatism's central contribution is to an "action-theoretic" framework. Symbolic interactionists have explored at length the linguistically mediated interactions in which human identities are formed, and thereby expanded our understanding of the communicative foundations of lifeworlds. At the same time, the pragmatism-inspired social theory has little to offer to "system-theoretic" approaches, Habermas insists. It ignores the normative underpinnings of society, its functional needs as a system, and cannot satisfactorily explain how communicative distortions and social oppression are generated and reproduced. Thus, Mead assumes the normative status for his notion of the "generalized other" without explaining where its power to control behavior comes from. Similarly, Dewey is too sanguine about democratization's byproducts—expert cultures and administrative procedures, which are as endemic to modern democracy as they are subversive of its substance. "[W]e want democratization," Habermas (1986, p. 67) intones, "not so much in order to improve the efficiency of the economy as to change the *structures* of power: and in the second place to set in motion ways of defining collective goals that merely administrative procedures or power-oriented decisions would lead astray or cripple."

It is arguable whether pragmatism has no normative dimension, let alone is inherently incapable of dealing with structural phenomena, but it is fair to say that system-theoretic issues have not been central to pragmatist analysis and interactionist sociology in the past. To offset this limitation of classical pragmatism, Habermas seeks to complement it with ideas from several other sources. From Weber, he borrows his insight into the differentiation of value spheres; from Durkheim—the notion of normative constraint; from Parsons and Luhmann—a version of system theory; from Austin, Wittgenstein, and Searle—the theory of speech acts; and from Kohlberg and Piaget—the genetic theory of moral growth. Combining these ideas with the Meadian theory of symbolic interaction, Habermas formulates his theory of communicative action (TCA), with its conceptual core—"universal pragmatics." Habermas uses the term "pragmatics" in a different sense than Peirce, who saw in it a branch of cosmology dealing with signs in their natural settings, or Morris, who used the term to designate a part of semiotics explicating the relations between symbols and their users. The pragmatics that Habermas has in mind is "universal"—it purports to unveil most general standards that govern rational communications in human discourse. Drawing on Weber's theory, he isolates three basic forms of discourse or value spheres which become progressively autonomous in the course of historical rationalization: theoretic/scientific, moral/practical, and expressive/aesthetic. Communications within each of these domains revolve around a peculiar validity claim: theoretic discourse concerns the truth of our propositions; practical discourse bears on the justice of our actions; and aesthetic discourse highlights the sincerity of our feelings. Although these validity claims are intertwined with scientific, moral, and artistic discourses, they are not bound exclusively to these specialized value spheres. In our everyday life, we routinely assert facts, appeal to norms, and claim to be sincere, that is, raise and settle validity claims concerning truth, justice, and authenticity, and by doing so, we continuously reproduce our normative, cultural, and private worlds. In the language of speech act theory, we "do things with words" via "performative actions" which are linguistic facts just as they are social facts. Now, the crucial point Habermas makes is that the validity claims remain largely unthematized in everyday transactions, where they are redeemed not so much by recourse to reasons and arguments as through strategic action and appeal to custom. It is the task of universal pragmatics to render these unreflexive validity claims problematic, help settle them by rational means. Universal pragmatics articulates "a procedural concept of rationality," "a pragmatic logic of argumentation," and promises to certify "the rationality of process of reaching understanding" (Habermas [1985] 1987; 1985, p. 196). Its main premise is that any communicative act aimed at reaching understanding contains implicit, context-free, and imminently social standards that must be met if its outcome is to be judged rational. The situation where such standards are fully met is called "ideal speech situation."

Habermas does not provide a glossary of rules underlying the ideal speech situation, nor does he offer any final formulation, as he continues to revise his theory ever since he had first outlined it in the late 1960s (Habermas [1968] 1970; [1976] 1979). Still, I think these procedural rules or guidelines for achieving communicative rationality can be codified as follows:

1. An ideal speech situation provides every interested individual a chance to participate in discourse and argue one's viewpoint.
2. It is free from coercion, domination, and power play—all purely instrumental and strategic motifs.
3. It differentiates cognitive, normative, and expressive validity claims implicit in our assertions and redeems them through arguments alone.
4. It makes a freely reached consensus the sole foundation for democratic will-formation and policy articulation.
5. It leaves a rationally motivated agreement open to revision in light of further deliberations.

The thing that strikes one immediately is how well these stipulations jibe with the critical idealist's belief in *Vernunft* as "the true tribunal for all disputes of reason [which] secures to us the peace of a legal status, in which disputes are not to be carried on except in the proper form of a *lawsuit*" (Kant [1781] 1966, p. 486). The continuity does not escape Habermas, who grounds his theory on the "principle, that—expressed in the Kantian manner—only reason should have force" (Habermas [1968] 1970, p. 7). At the same time, Habermas is quick to point out that his theory is not to be confused with transcendental idealism. Universal pragmatics presupposes certain standards for rationality and serves as a measuring rod for judging concrete communicative practices, yet its validity is not entirely a priori. Procedural standards for rationality encysted in universal pragmatics are counter-factual: "One should not imagine the ideal speech situation as a utopian model of an emancipated society" (Habermas, 1986, p. 90). Nor should an ideal speech situation be confused with an ideal type, for the latter professes ethical neutrality whereas the former is self-consciously normative and prescriptive. Universal pragmatics is the case of "reconstructive theory" (Habermas [1976] 1979, pp. 8-9, 178-9)—a theory whose normative thrust does not preclude empirical validation, even if it can be achieved only indirectly. Taking his clues from Durkheim's writings on the sacred and Piaget-Kohlberg's research on moral growth, Habermas infers that the movement toward communicative rationality is both an evolutionary trend, evident in the shift from sacred to discursive practices, and an ontogenetic current, manifest in the gradual increase in the individual's capacity for moral reasoning. At the heart of modernity is the empirically observable drive toward rationalization which gradually replaces "the weight of tradition with the weight of arguments," "an attitude of faith based on the authority of a doctrine with a theoretical attitude," and it is this relentless drive that pulls society away "from the sacred foundations of legitimation to foundation on a common will, communicatively shaped and discursively clarified in the political public sphere" (Habermas [1976] 1979, p. 113; [1981] 1987, p. 81). This shift, most apparent in the history of the Occident, can be gleaned from the gradual gain in human rights, the emergence of the independent judiciary, the separation of cognitive and power claims, the strengthening of voluntary associations, and similar developments that mark the movement, however contradictory, toward communicatively-rational forms of legitimation.

Bureaucratization, juridification, mediatization, and such like systemic dysfunctions point to another, less benign facet of rationalization. Subjected to the capitalist market imperatives, these developments produce distortions that undermine communicative rationality and weaken public discourse. As each value sphere evolves according to its own logic, it becomes insular, impregnable to considerations from other value spheres. Technical issues are separated from moral concerns, ethical demands are severed from expressive needs, personal agendas come into conflict with public ones. The mass media further exacerbates these trends by making a spectacle out of public discourse, turning it into an entertainment: "Discussion, now a 'business,' becomes formalized; the presentation of positions and counterpositions is bound to certain prearranged rules of the game; consensus about the public matter is made largely superfluous.... Critical debate arranged in this manner fulfills important social-psychological functions, especially that of a tranquilizing substitute for action" (Habermas [1962] 1989, p. 164). It needs to be stressed that the problem for Habermas is not modernity and rationalization as such, but fractured modernity and one-sided rationalization, and the cure is breaking the walls separating value spheres without destroying the autonomy and an insight peculiar to each. The question, in other words, is how to "bring viewpoints of moral and aesthetic critique to bear—without threatening the primacy of questions of truth" (Habermas [1981] 1987, p. 398). If this can be done at all, it is through public discourse, by painstakingly redeeming the validity claims implicit in our communications and following the rules of procedural rationality elucidated in the universal pragmatics. One hundred percent procedurally rational communications may be impossible to achieve, but by opening up the legitimation process to all members of society and linguistifying norms previously immune to rational adjudication, we, at the very least, assure movement in the right direction. Take the ideal speech situation seriously, Habermas advises, rid yourself of hidden agendas and avail yourself to procedurally rational discourse, and you help bring about an emancipated society, a democracy that is substantively rational. "[T]he false alternative set up by Max Weber, with his opposition between substantive and formal rationality, is overcome" (Habermas [1985] 1987, p. 315).

Commentators agree that TCA constitutes an advance, or certainly a new beginning, for critical theory. This advance has not come cheaply. In some respects, Habermas's theory was a step backward (e.g., TCA does not show Adorno's sensitivity to the indeterminate and the irrational). Settling old issues, Habermas has raised new, sometimes even more vexing ones. Is reason genderless and classless? Does it have to shed its ethnic, racial, religious, cultural, and personal colors before it can do its critical job? How can theoretical, practical, and aesthetic discourses inform each other without losing their vital autonomy? What about contingency and indeterminacy thwarting our best plans and good-faith efforts? Is the lack of rational consensus a sign that communicative action has failed? These are some of the questions that TCA has stirred up and that have generated a voluminous literature.[4] I shall try not to repeat the more obvious criticisms voiced in the past, and, in keeping with my objectives, confine my comments to the issues on the interfaces of pragmatism, democracy, and critical theory.

From Communicative Action to Pragmatic Politics

The ideal speech situation outlined in Habermas's universal pragmatics is more than a prescription for successful communication. Enciphered in its principles is a blueprint for rational society—a society whose members make good sense, offer rationales for their action, mean what they say, and practice what they preach. This lofty image, which brings to mind the ancient quest for a way of life combining truth, justice, and happiness, has undeniable appeal. It is also flawed in several respects. The critique that follows is sympathetic, for I share Habermas's humanistic agenda, yet it is principled because I question some of his key premises. My discussion draws on the pragmatist ideas left out in Habermas's analysis, and it is organized around the following themes: (1) disembodied reason vs. embodied reasonableness; (2) determinate being vs. indeterminate reality; (3) discursive validity vs. pragmatic certainty; (4) rational consensus vs. reasonable dissent; (5) transcendental democracy vs. democratic transcendence; and (6) rational society vs. sane community. It should be noted that I do not picture pragmatism as a monolithic movement free from internal contradictions and inconsistencies. However, the present reconstruction centers on pragmatists' shared concerns, and especially on their common stance against rationalism with its overdetermined view of reality, the vestiges of which can be found in Habermas's thought.[5]

1. Disembodied Reason vs. Embodied Reasonableness

My first objection concerns the place Habermas assigns to reason in relation to nature and human body. Reason appears in TCA primarily as thinking (consciousness, understanding, cognition). It has no obvious relation to the human body and noncognitive processes (emotions, feelings, sentiments). What pragmatists call "experience" has shriveled into verbal intellect, which assumes in TCA a privileged position as a locus of rationality. Communicative competence is predicated on reason's capacity to be "relieved of the pressure of action and experience," to "transcend all limitations of space and time, all the provincial limitations of the given context" (Habermas [1981] 1984, p. 25; [1981] 1987, p. 399). Rational discourse, correlatively, deals in ideas, concepts, and reasons, rather than in sentiments. The latter represent an inferior species of intelligence, in that they have limited generalizability, cannot be readily communicated, are inimical to rational criticism and hostile to intellect. To the extent that noncognitive elements enter discourse, they have to be measured by theoretically grounded standards, a process that certifies our emotive life as authentic and sincere. Affects that do not pass the test set up by reason are deemed "irrational" and subjected to "therapeutic critique," which helps the individual "to free himself from illusions, and indeed from illusions that are based not on errors (about facts) but on self-deceptions (about one's own subjective experiences)" (Habermas [1981] 1984, p. 21).

By contrast, pragmatists caution against the "hypostatization of cognitive behavior" (Rorty, 1982, p. 201) and warn that consciousness "is only a very small and shifting portion of experience" (Dewey, 1916a, p. 6). "Reason, anyway, is a faculty of secondary rank," Peirce (1976, p. xxi) remarks, "Cognition is but the superficial film of the soul, while sentiment penetrates its substance." What is important for the pragmatist is that cognitive behavior belongs to a larger context of material practice, which philogenetically and ontogenetically antedates mind's conceptual faculty. Communication is contingent on minding something together, carrying out a larger act in which participants are engaged bodily as well as mentally. "Mental processes imply not only mind but that somebody is minding" (Mead 1938, p. 69). "The mother minds her baby; she cares for it with affection. Mind is care in the sense of solicitude, anxiety, as well as of active looking after things that need to be tended" (Dewey [1934] 1958, p. 263). Pragmatists refuse to isolate communicative actions from this larger context, from "the universe of nonreflectional experience of our doings, sufferings, enjoyments of the world and of one another" (Dewey 1916a, p. 9). Notice that the pragmatist maxim—knowing is doing—brooks no anti-intellectualism. Pragmatists do not deny the key role abstraction and generalization play in theoretical discourse, nor do they dispute that private interests and crude emotions can distort reasoning. Nevertheless, pragmatists argue, the "conclusion is not that the emotional, passionate phase of action can be or should be eliminated in behalf of a bloodless reason. More 'passions,' not fewer, is the answer.... Rationality, once more is not a force to evoke against impulse and habit. It is the attainment of a working harmony among diverse desires" (Dewey [1922] 1950, p. 195-6). Pragmatists are quick to point out that "reasoning has no monopoly of the process of generalization," that "[s]entiment also generalizes itself" (Peirce 1976, p. xxi). Feelings can be universalized and communicated even more readily than ideas. We share attitudes before we share thoughts (Mead 1934), sympathize before we understand (Benhabib 1987), feel other people's pain before we know its source (Rorty 1989). Habermas shows little appreciation for such nondiscursive communication, or at least does not carve for it adequate conceptual space. He elevates the cognitive form of universality above all others and in the process inadvertently devalues human experience as merely private and intellectually mute.

This indifference to the nondiscursive element in discourse, to the fact that just "[a]s the body becomes 'encultured' ... so culture becomes 'embodied'" (Alexander, 1987, p. xix), is a vestige of rationalism and its notorious tendency to think in dichotomies, such as subject and object, reason and nature, sentiment and intellect, and so on. Pragmatists, on the other hand, are convinced that noncognitive prehensions have an intelligence all their own, which a radically theoretical attitude tends to ignore or, worse, suppress. Contrary to the rationalist view, reason has a lot to learn from noncognitive functions. Feelings point to a crisis in experience, sentiments signal when general principles take a beating from obdurate reality, and emotions provide a running commentary on the success of our plans. To divest reason from living experience is to disembody it, to leave it helpless in the face of perennial indeterminacy and contingency with which humans have to struggle in their everyday existence. When thinking leaves experience far behind and escapes into *theoria*, it is likely to lead practical action astray.

I am not trying to ascribe to Habermas a view that feelings and emotions are inherently irrational and need to be suppressed in favor of pure reason. He is also right when he says that some of our sentiments are systematically distorted and have to be subjected to therapeutic critique. My point is rather that TCA leaves out from its purview the noncognitive forms of intelligence irreducible to verbal intellect, what pragmatists call "embodied" or "concrete reasonableness" (Rochberg-Halton, 1986; Alexander, 1987). Reasonableness is minding embedded in practical activity and embodied in emotionally charged situations. It does not scoff at common sense or *Verstand*, and it resists *Vernunft*'s imperious tendency to subordinate other faculties to its dictate. Knowledge uninformed by feelings and stripped of emotive elements can be rational without being reasonable, and it achieves certainty by discarding insight from the senses in favor of the rationales laid out by the intellect. Yet, even though both noncognitive experience and speculative thought partake in the world, the former is embedded in nature more immediately, yielding instant information about the changing situation through its affective states vital to the organism: "[E]xperience is *of* as well as *in* nature. [It] reaches down into nature; it has depth. It also has breath and to an indefinitely elastic extent. It stretches. That stretch constitutes inference" (Dewey [1929] 1958, p. 4a). "The continuum which [sentiment] forms instead of being like that of reason merely cognitive, superficial, or subjective ... penetrates through the whole being of the soul, and is objective or to use a better word extant, and more than that is existent" (Peirce, 1976, p.

xxi). Reason's access to the world is mediated by a feeling body, whose action will ultimately certify our validity claims. It is in the Platonic domain that reason reigns supreme, the domain where objects are not contaminated by impurities besetting the mundane realm and obey laws prescribed by pure reason. As long as reason stays within this rarified chamber, it can abstract from concrete situation and take a profitable leave of one's emotional investments, but as soon as knowers step into the world of uncertainty, they fall back on an auxiliary intelligence about things themselves that only noncognitive faculties can supply. Human intelligence is emotional just as emotions are intelligent, and this is so because we live in the world of indeterminacy which no rational faculty and theoretical rigor can expunge.

2. Determinate Being vs. Indeterminate Reality

The residual place Habermas assigns to body and noncognitive experience is consistent with a rationalist ontology. This ontology paints an overdeterminate picture of the universe as factual, internally structured, determined prior to the knower's engagement in it, and marked by "the categorical distinctions between the objective, social, and subjective worlds" (Habermas [1981] 1987, p. 159). The early and relatively undifferentiated worldviews (those centered about mythology or religion) tend to blur the distinctions between these three worlds and the validity claims peculiar to each. Knowledge appears in such worldviews as a mixture of the objective and the subjective, the particular and the general, the cognitive and the emotional, with no sharp line drawn between verifiable facts, culturally sanctioned dogma, and patently idiosyncratic claims. The modern—scientific—outlook allows to separate verifiable facts from commonly held illusions and makes possible, at least in principle, the rational adjudication of conflicts in the normative sphere. Purified by proper method from unwarranted preconceptions, ideological obfuscations, and personal biases, Habermas concludes, public discourse ought to yield a rationally motivated consensus about facts in a shared universe and suggest the most rational course of action.

Twentieth-century pragmatist ontology has come to us bearing different labels—"pluralism," "perspectivism," "objective relativism," and more recently "new fuzziness" (Rorty 1989, p. 51), yet its basic insight is essentially the same: "Uncertainty does not belong simply to the values, it belongs to the facts as well" (Mead, MP, b8, f1).[6] "Any view which holds that man is a part of nature, not outside it," writes Dewey (1946,

p. 351), "will certainly hold that indeterminacy in human experience, once experience is taken in the objective sense of interacting behavior and not as a private conceit added on to something totally alien to it, is evidence of some corresponding indeterminateness in the process of nature within which man exists (acts) and out of which he arose." The pragmatist ontology pictures a universe vastly different from the one envisioned by classical rationalism, "a universe which is not all closed and settled, which is still in some respects indeterminate and in the making ... an open universe in which uncertainty, choice, hypotheses, novelties and possibilities are naturalized" (Dewey [1927] 1950, p. 52). Such a universe is full of uncertain outcomes defying our best efforts to reduce chaotic processes to a theoretical schema in which all effects have identifiable causes and our destiny submits to rational manipulation. Pragmatist philosophy "gives us a pluralistic, restless universe, in which no single point of view can ever take in the whole scene" (James [1897] 1956, p. 177). "Man lives in a world of surmise, of mystery, of uncertainties," admonishes Dewey ([1934] 1958, p. 198), "'Reasoning' must fail man..." Again, it is easy to misconstrue these musings as a sign of anti-intellectualism, but the point is not that rational knowledge is futile, but that rationalists underestimate the contingency endemic to the world and vastly exaggerate reason's capacity to marshal it as an orderly flow of objective reality.

What is to be stressed here is that we are dealing not with residual indeterminacy reflecting the limits of our current knowledge but with "objective uncertainty" and "indeterminate reality," the emergent universe in which "deliberation and choice are determining factors" (Dewey [1922] 1950, p. 310). It is up to concrete reasoning—always an interest-bound, socially anchored, situationally specific undertaking—to lift the world from its natural state of indeterminacy and turn it into a meaningful, manageable, semi-orderly whole. This objective whole maintains its predictable properties insofar as we sustain our interest in it, as long as our determined collective efforts last. Each time we pass a judgment on the situation at hand—literally terminate indeterminacy—we bring out some of its potentialities and render obscure its other possible determinations. An act of doing justice which a theoretical, normative, or aesthetic judgment aspires to be is thus inevitably an act of doing violence. Just as it opens one horizon of meaning it closes an indefinite number of alternative determinations (fittingly, "to terminate" means "to extinguish," "to put an end to," as well as "to bring into focus" and "frame in definite terms"). Whatever determinacy we encounter in the world is, consequently, of our own making. We terminate indeterminacy in deed and *in situ*, using terms supplied by a community, and we do so as participant observers who are part and parcel of the situation we seek to comprehend. "If there were no human beings (or comparable sentient creatures) there would be no situations in nature" (Gouinlock, 1972, p. 8). The knower's embeddedness in the world as a participant observer has far-reaching epistemological implications, none more important than this: redeeming validity claims about the world of uncertainty is not a matter settled through argument in the propositional discourse but a pragmatic endeavor accomplished via social intercourse.

3. Discursive Validity vs. Pragmatic Certainty

One of the pillars on which Habermas founded TCA is his "consensus theory of truth" (Habermas [1971] 1973, p. 19; [1981] 1984, p. 8-42). We can speak more broadly about the discursive theory of validation, for all validity claims, including rightness and sincerity, are at issue. This theory stipulates that validity claims must be redeemed through arguments and that "communicative actors can achieve an understanding only by way of taking yes/no positions on criticizable validity claims" (Habermas [1981] 1984, p. 70). If "reasons that force us to take a rationally motivated position of yes/no" (Habermas 1985, pp. 194-5) failed to produce a consensus, a communicative action has missed its stated end. Such failure signifies that the participants lacked candor to carry out communicative action to its rational conclusion. One notable exception allowed by discursive theory of validation involves aesthetic discourse: "[T]he claims to sincerity connected with expressive utterances is [*sic*] not such that it could be directly redeemed through argument as can truth or rightness claims.... The sincerity of expressions cannot be *grounded* but only *shown*; insincerity can be *revealed* by the lack of consistency between an utterance and the past or future actions internally connected with it" (Habermas [1981] 1984, p. 41). No extradiscursive effects are allowed into theoretical and normative discourses, where participants are compelled toward a rational consensus by methodically advancing well-formed propositions, following the internal logic of the argument, and adjudicating conflicts by strictly theoretical means.

While TCA attends to discursive validity vouchsafed through propositional formal logic, pragmatist theory focuses on "pragmatic certainty" (Rosenthal 1986, p. 59) that requires joined action and logistical reasoning as much as argumentative skills. Discursive validation is part of a larger human practice where all ideational objects have their roots. There are no objects to perceive, to value, to abstract from, according to pragmatists, until there has been the "full completion of the act" or "consummation" (Mead 1938, p. 23). The world that lends itself to objective judgment is already an objectified world, reality transformed by our perception, cognition, and collective action, and to say that our thought is true to this world makes as much sense as to say that this world is true to our preconceptions about it. Either way, to be certain about our claims, we have to engage in collective transformative action. Pragmatists are at one with Marx on this: "The question whether objective truth is an attribute of human thought—is not a theoretical but a *practical* question" ([1846] 1963, p. 197). That is to say, there is more to redeeming truth claims than finding good reasons and building consensus about them. We need to be certain that the predicated identity between knowledge and reality can be practically redeemed, which means immersing oneself in the situation, joining in a collective act, and carrying it to a completion.

A word of caution against setting up a false dichotomy between practically reached certainty and communicatively established consensus is called for—one is meaningless without the other. What pragmatist critique presented here aims at is redressing the imbalance. Rational arguments have been advanced in favor of letting out mentally ill patients who pose no immediate threat to themselves and to the public, and a good deal of public consensus was built around this issue in the 1960s, yet this rational policy turned out to be a failure, as the logistics of providing for the ex-patient's needs via neighborly communities proved to be much too formidable. The morale here is that we cannot always redeem substantive claims—to be certain about their pragmatic merit—in advance of staking our action on their truthfulness or, for that matter, justness and sincerity (the premise equally applies to theoretical, normative, and aesthetic discourses). The pertinent question for pragmatists is not whether a proposition is true according to some intrinsic rationality, but whether the real situation allows itself to be shaped according to a stated rationale. To find out how consensually validated terms mesh with reality, we have to move beyond symbolic and performative action and try to terminate extant indeterminacy (or re-terminate established determinacy) through practical social intercourse. Truth is no longer grasped here in the rationalist manner as *adequatio intellectus et rei* but is pragmatically conceived as a practically accomplished unity of knowledge and reality. In this reckoning, to inquire whether an action-transformed situation is true to our concepts is synonymous with asking whether our propositions correspond to objective reality. To accomplish pragmatically the predicated unity of knowledge and reality, the knower has to engage in what interactionists call "joint action" (Blumer 1969, p. 17). Situated on the intersection between labor and discourse, this domain has little conceptual footing in TCA. Yet, this is a domain of the utmost importance, the realm of everyday living and minding together where theoretical, normative, and aesthetic discourses merge into one, where humans feel, think, and transact at the same time, and where a different logic is called upon to help us master everyday contingencies.[7] The pragmatist logic is the logic in use; it stipulates that reality does not always lend itself squarely to yes/no judgments and allows practical knowers to say "perhaps," "it depends," "who knows," and use other indeterminate truth values to break situational indeterminacy. The dilemma with which James ([1909] 1967, pp. 208, 207) found himself confronted in the pluralistic universe—"either give up my intellectualistic logic, the logic of identity ... or, finally, face the fact that life is logically irrational"—is familiar to every practical knower who had to contend with everyday indeterminacy and who could conclude with James that "Logic being the lesser thing, the static incomplete abstraction, must succumb to reality, not reality to logic." Binary logic favored by rationalist thought is replaced in pragmatism by the logic in use, also known as the logic of inquiry or the logic of situation. This pragmatist logic signals a break with "the rationalism's disdain for the particular, the personal, and the unwholesome" (James [1909] 1967, p. 309). It stipulates that judgment is "in" this world as much as it is "about" it, that "the proposition is itself a factor in the completion of the situation," and it traces "the transformation of an indeterminate unsettled situation into a determinate unified existential situation" (Dewey, 1916a, p. 338; 1938, p. 296). The quest for rational truth and moral rightness is supplanted here by the quest for warranted assertability and practical certainty. Whereas the former depends on discursive validation and "comparing ready-made ideas with ready-made facts," the latter requires pragmatic inquiry and presumes that "both idea and 'facts' are flexible, and verification is the process of mutual adjustment, of organic interaction" (Dewey [1890] 1969, p. 87). The quest for pragmatic certainty sensitizes the knower to fuzzy things, multiple realities, semi-chaotic systems, and it favors participant observation as a practical way to fathom objective uncertainty. The radically pragmatic epistemological stance also entails clear ethical and political implications, in that it counsels tolerance to ambiguity, calls for personal responsibility, and encourages rationally motivated dissent.

4. Rational Consensus vs. Reasonable Dissent

My next criticism concerns TCA's emphasis on consensus and its disregard for the constructive properties of dissent. On several occasions, Habermas ([1976] 1979, pp. 92, 1) qualifies as "normal" situations and communications that are "largely conflict-free." Consensus is communication's raison d'être, certainly in an ideal speech situation where "all participants pursue illocutionary aims without reservation in order to arrive at an agreement that will provide the basis for a consensual coordination of individually pursued plans of action" (Habermas [1981] 1984, pp. 295-6). The broader the consensus, the greater the rationality. Anything that falls short of universal consensus is, on this premise, less than fully rational. Discourse ethics demands that those partaking in rational discourse should be motivated by "intention of convincing a *universal audience* and gaining general ascent for an utterance" (Habermas [1981] 1984, p. 26). Anybody who refuses to join in an emerging rational consensus, spurns communicatively certified reasons, or stops short of trying to convince all other participants about the merit of one's proposition, violates the norms of discourse ethics. The spirit of communicative action militates against accepting conflict as a normal part of the communication process and dissensus as a rational product of action aimed at reaching understanding. "To be sure," Habermas (1985, p. 194) admits, "it is also a characteristic of modernity that we have grown accustomed to living with dissent in the realm of questions that admit of 'truth'; we simply put controversial validity claims to one side 'for the time being.'" Dissent about truth claims, in other words, is more an expediency than a principled stance in a communicatively shaped situation. In the long enough run, it must yield to rational consensus.

Pragmatist ontology and epistemology suggest a different approach, which accentuates the limits of theoretically grounded consensus and highlights the productive properties of dissent. "Real possibilities, real indeterminations, real beginnings, real ends, real evil, real crises, catastrophes, and escapes, a real God and a real moral life, just as common sense conceives these things, may remain in [a radically pragmatic] empiricism which that philosophy gives up an attempt either to 'overcome' or to reinterpret in monistic form" (James [1897] 1956, p. ix). The universe so conceived belies TCA's consensual bias. The inexhaustible possibilities of being hidden in its depths can hardly be fathomed through a thin-gruel theoretical consensus. It is as if we choose to understand Bach by reading the music sheets rather than by listening to his fugues.

Communication at the level of formal notation is what Habermas seems to propose in order to ferret out the communication's rational content. Yet score is not the only thing that counts in music; each recital offers a dissenting yet valid interpretation or rather improvisation (just think about the vastly different communication that takes place when Horowitz, Gould, Davidovich, or the Modern Jazz Quartet interpret Bach). The pluralistic universe envisioned by pragmatists encourages dissent, warrants a wide margin of uncertainty, and invites caution toward policies based on purely theoretical calculations.

Habermas's universal pragmatics leaves hardly any room for the honest difference of opinion. A disagreement that refuses to go away is taken here as a sign of a failure, and a moral one at that, hinting at a strategic motif at work and/or betraying a week communicative resolve. By grounding a rational consensus in sound reasons, Habermas also finds himself saddled by an awkward implication that whosoever refuses to abide by the communicatively established consensus is by definition less than fully rational. In the pragmatist reckoning, there is no necessary relationship between procedural rationality and substantive consensus. Public discourse is as much about consensus building as it is about fostering dissent. This is not to say that Habermas would deny the role that dissent plays in public life, only that he does not explore conceptual implications of genuine, productive, rationally motivated dissensus. In pragmatist theory, by contrast, dissensus and consensus are accorded an equally prominent theoretical status. The proper function of communicatively achieved consensus is to designate reasons sound enough to merit pragmatic validation. A freely achieved consensus is usually partial, imperfect, provisional; it does not obviate the need for conflict but legitimizes it as an inalienable part of rational discourse. Nor does communicative action merely tolerate dissent—it encourages it as vital to community's well-being. Dissent is the first sign that communication was uncoerced and participants expressed themselves freely. It is in the countries where the speech situation is far from ideal that consensus is forged, disagreement is discouraged, and dissent is punished by the parties in power. What makes the dissenting attitude rational is the realization that various lines of argumentation can be meritorious, that the situation lends itself to more than one adjudication, that the attendant risks and uncertainties are great, and that the widest possible consensus is bound to break down the moment we set out to implement it.

All this should not be taken to mean that discursive consensus has no practical value, nor do I mean to suggest that Habermas is intolerable to dissent. He is correct in saying that basic ground rules must be agreed upon before we can dissent in a meaningful and productive manner. Still, I feel that Habermas does not make nearly enough of rationally motivated dissensus, nor does he explore the practical consequences of dissent with which we must square off once we have agreed to disagree. Rational consensus, like a generally accepted moral rule, is but "a tool for analyzing a specific situation, the right or wrong being determined by the situation in its entirety, and not by the rule as such" (Dewey and Tufts [1908] 1976, p. 302). We cannot play chess without agreeing on rules, drive a car without knowing traffic signs, or live in a community without following social conventions, yet we routinely disagree about the best chess move, the safest response to an emergency, or a just solution to a social problem, and the more complicated the situation, the more room it leaves and requires for the honest difference of opinion. This goes not only for common folks unschooled in hermeneutics but also for well-seasoned experts, such the U.S. Supreme Court Justices, who, for all their schooling in constitutional law, rules of evidenced, and legal procedures, routinely disagree about the right holdings. Being at odds with oneself, being of two (or more) minds on a given issue, is a distinctly human and imminently rational sentiment. We call it "ambivalence," and we find it handy in dealing with muddled situations surrounding us in all fronts, most signally moral situations, which rarely submit to general principles. "[E]very moral situation is a unique situation," pragmatists contend (Dewey [1920] 1950, pp. 132-3), "the primary significance of the unique and morally ultimate character of the concrete situation is to transfer the weight and burden of morality to intelligence." The key word here is "intelligence"—the pragmatist name for reason firmly embedded in concrete situation, fully in touch with its feelings, mindful of uncertainties and risks involved. Such embodied reason has a modern temper befitting democracy, and the "gospel of uncertainty" (Kloppenberg 1986, p. 413) it brings into the project of modernity offers an important corrective to the emancipatory agenda championed by classical and contemporary critical theory.

5. Transcendental Democracy vs. Democratic Transcendence

Although the index for Habermas's monumental study does not mention the term, TCA is very much a treatise on democracy, or rather its perversion in modern society. According to Habermas, whose views on the subject go back to his *Habilitationsschrift* ([1962] 1989), the capitalist welfare state subverts the substance of the democratic process through bureaucratic procedures and mediatized communications which, on the one hand, bring more people into the public sphere than any other political system, but on the other, emasculate it by whittling down its participatory substance. Late capitalist society stifles "the possibilities for spontaneous opinion formation and discursive will-formation through a segmentation of the voter's role, through the competition of leadership elites, through vertical opinion formation in bureaucratically encrusted party apparatuses, through autonomized parliamentary bodies, through powerful communication networks, and the like'" (Habermas [1981] 1987, p. 365). Communicative action is bound to be distorted under these quasi-democratic conditions, and a manufactured consensus is likely to be false as long as capitalist market imperatives are allowed to influence various social strata's access to and participation in public affairs. Nor does he cite the incurably formalistic logic of rational administration that critical theorists singled out as the culprit. The gist of the problem, for Habermas, is the disuse, misuse, and abuse that the public sphere falls into under certain historical conditions—the conditions that can be rectified and ameliorated through critical inquiry into our communicative practices. Such inquiry falls within the domain of "'transcendental hermeneutics" or "transcendental pragmatics" which offer "a reconstructive analysis oriented to general and unavoidable presuppositions" and reveal "structures of mutual understanding that are found in the intuitive knowledge of competent members of modern societies" (Habermas [1976] 1979, p. 23; [1981] 1987, p. 383). The crucial point in the whole argument is that the a priori conditions for reaching understanding explicated by transcendental (or universal, as Habermas prefers to call it) pragmatics are fundamentally the same as the conditions for achieving a democratic society. This is already evident in the rational procedures guiding communicative action. These procedures, encoded in the ideal speech situation, can be read as prescriptions for substantive democracy[8] or "*democratic form* of decision-making, namely: rationalizing decisions in such a way that they can be made dependent on a consensus arrived at through discussions free from domination" (Habermas [1968] 1970). Notice that substantively rational decisions cannot depend on opinion polling, electioneering, and vote-counting because such mechanisms of formal representation transfer individual's discursive rights to others and succeed chiefly in "a cleansing of political participation from any participatory content" (Habermas [1981] 1987, p. 350). Formally democratic decisions and collective actions based on them are marred by nondiscursiveness and thus are communicatively flawed, which is why "majority decisions are held [in TCA] to be only a substitute for the uncompelled consensus that would finally result if discussion did not always have to be broken off owing to the need of a decision" (Habermas [1968] 1970, p. 7). A communicatively sound social order must be based on a rationally motivated, freely achieved, universal consensus, which simultaneously satisfies the transcendental conditions for successful communicative action and for genuinely democratic society.

There is much in the above argument that dovetails with, if not derives from, pragmatism. Pragmatists acknowledge that modern societies produce systemic consequences and have functional implications detrimental to the participatory ideal. Long before Habermas they thought that "discontent with democracy as it operates under conditions of exploitation by special interests has justification" and warned that "the functional aspect is contradictory to the ends of democracy" as long as "there is the opportunity for exploitation of the individual" (Dewey 1948, p. 133; Mead, 1934, pp. 288-9). Since the onset of the Progressive era pragmatists stressed that "No government by experts in which the masses do not have the chance to inform the experts as to their needs can be anything but an oligarchy managed in the interests of the few" (Dewey [1927] 1954, p. 208). Habermas's vision of a communicatively sound social order is also adumbrated in pragmatism which treats democracy as a form of communication, "a name for a free and enriching communion" (Dewey [1927] 1954, p. 184), and trusts humans to resolve their differences by discovering common goods. "Reason is then a medium within which values may be brought into comparisons with each other, in abstraction from the situations," reads a particularly Habermasian passage in Mead ([1930] 1964, p. 406), "and within this impartial medium it becomes possible to reconstruct values and our conduct growing out of them." In spite of these instructive continuities, there are several points on which Habermas and pragmatists diverge.

Pragmatists are not satisfied with discursive elucidation of common values and universal principles. "[T]he universe of discourse," they are likely to stress (MP, b8, f8), "is rather the universe of intercourse"—the latter brings to a test the precepts furnished by the former. "The ethical problem is always a specific one," says Mead ([1930] 1964, p. 405); "the problem itself defines the values." "Especially does the pragmatist deny that the solution of our problems can be found in any vision given in the mount or prearranged order of society" (MP, Addenda, b3, f7). Universal pragmatics does not exactly offer us a prearranged order, but its procedural strictures are too general, too far removed from messy things out there to help us navigate in the world of uncertainty. TCA goads us towards consensus and demands the unequivocal commitment to certain policies even before we had a chance to find out whether they pass muster in life. Only immersion into the practical world, with all its hazards, confusions, and unforeseen developments, can clarify what a given consensus means, which reality it engenders. Habermas ([1971] 1973, p. 19) misses this point when he disparages the pragmatist rush to action and praises the virtues of discursive situations "which transcend the compulsions of action." Pragmatists do not deny reason its proper rights—they want to subject its pronouncements to pragmatic test. Truth is a practically accomplished unity of knowledge and reality, and that means tinkering with things and events to make sure they match our theoretical calculations. In the process, we are certain to run into unforseen circumstances, unanticipated consequences, unyielding particulars, which need to be transcended *in situ* and not just *in theoria*. As chaos theory tells us, minor changes in one variable can have vast ramifications for a system as a whole. This applies to human societies as well, which evolve patterned ways of handling indeterminacy.

If society is a semi-ordered chaos routinely generating unanticipated consequences, as pragmatism implies, then democracy is a historically specific mode of managing uncertainty. "Democracy expects the unexpected" (Betz 1974, p. 216) and "recognizes that uncertainty is inevitable and then turns it to positive account" (Dewey and Child 1933, p. 309; see also Przeworski 1986). Democratic systems thrive on uncertainty. They rely on market, competition, ad hocing, and muddling through as necessary, even if distortion-prone, mechanisms for handling a large number of incalculable variables. By the same token, they promote conflicting life-forms, open up public discourse for an ever-widening range of participants, and maximize the public's role in defining the terms in which indeterminacy can be legitimately terminated. Contrariwise, non-democratic polities seek to expunge uncertainty through exhaustive planning, centralized control over terminological practices, and punitive actions against dissenters favoring alternative terminologies. The less democratic the system, the more it fears discord and values consensus, and the more likely it is to favor a monopoly on the terminological means of production of social reality as objective and meaningful. This is the reason why pragmatists do not accept consensus, however discursively sound, as the highest democratic value. The pluralistic universe presupposed by pragmatist thought precludes any one standpoint from being anointed as unassailably true, good, and authentic. If any claim merits such honorific title, it is the agreement to disagree, without which a democratic process is indeed unthinkable. Democratic institutions make extra room for the honest difference opinion, not narrow it; maximize opportunities for dissent, not just for consensus; and protect minorities from aspersions the majority is apt to cast on their rationality. Dissenting insights may be rejected by the community, and for good reasons, yet they are to be safeguarded because they hint at the unrealized potentialities of being.

To be sure, democratic societies fall short of their professed ideal of the unlimited access to public discourse and allow assorted elites an undue influence over public affairs, but this is a poor reason to discount nondiscursive means in politics. When we vote, select representatives, delegate authority to experts, and empower the executive branch, we admittedly move away from democratic discursiveness and thereby open the door for the kind of distortions Habermas so eloquently decries. But without these formal means we could not break the discursive impasse or react efficiently to situations that require prompt action. If we take discourse ethics seriously, we should keep on arguing until a universal consensus has emerged, lest our good faith efforts are put into question. Such demands are unrealistic; they are certain to run afoul the hung jury predicament and founder on the kind of problems Rousseau faced when he tried to reconcile *volonte general* and *volonte de tous* in his proposal for direct democracy (See Schumpeter 1950, pp. 235-268; van den Berg 1990, p. 163). From the pragmatist standpoint, the fact that participants resort to a show of hands and settle for a less than universal consensus is no affront to reason. Majority decision serves as a democratic, if formal, device for reaching a working consensus about conflicting rationalities vying for practical validation. To test a rationality means not only going beyond communication but also assuming responsibility for our action—not just discursive action but also joint act that has practical consequences and that presupposes a different type ethics than the ethics of discourse.

The pragmatic ethics—I call it the "ethics of uncertainty"—urges close attention to the "correlation between the means used and the consequences that follow" (Dewey, 1948, p. 138). Attention to consequences produced by our conduct is mandatory because different lines of action incur varied risks and beget unpredictable, irreversible outcomes. Rational people disagreed whether or not we should have relied on economic sanctions to force Saddam Hussein from Kuwait, but once the decision was made to forge ahead with the military option, consequences befell on the innocent and the guilty alike. The Lithuanian government's bid for independence was well grounded in reasons, yet it produced a bloody backlash few people were able to foresee. No matter how discursively validated a policy is, responsibility for the consequences are to be borne by the individual. The ethics of democracy is the ethics of responsibility, and as such, it contrasts with the ethics of good faith and ultimate ends, which seeks to suppress uncertainty and narrow the scope for individual judgment.

To be sure, Habermas did not endorse the ethics of ultimate ends. His writings on German politics belie any such accusation. Nor does he subscribe to the utopian vision of Jacobin democracy that imposes its will on the unwilling subjects. And yet in its implications, discourse ethics is not free from some of the difficulties faced by the moral systems based on good faith and end-rational grounding. Discursive morality pleads for a domination-free life, forswears force other than the force of reason, and aims at substantive democracy, yet its results prove ironic. Reason cannot escape domination as long as it seeks to impose on the world an overarching rationality in the face of the ample evidence that things themselves do not suffer theory gladly and are sure to spoil our best faith efforts. A consensus compelled by no other force than that of good reasons is still a forced consensus if it chains the individual to a predetermined rationale, situational contingencies notwithstanding. And transcendental democracy is likely to remain a utopian trap if it does not make room for personal responsibility. By digging the communicative foundations of a rational social order, Habermas gave the critical-theoretic program a much needed lift, yet his communicatively grounded reason still needs to be enlightened to fulfill its emancipatory promise. It is not free from intolerance and maximalism. It can use ambivalence, common sense, compassion—the virtues of intelligence which pragmatists consider central to democratic transcendence and sane existence in the world of uncertainty.

6. Rational Society vs. Sane Community

Habermas shares with classical critical theory its predilection for "democratization, decentralization and socialist positions," yet his agenda differs from the one implicit in the Frankfurt School, in that he respects liberalism, appeals directly to the public, and "demands a *remoralization* of politics" (Habermas 1986, p. 71). All systemic distortions, according to TCA, are prefigured in the communicative domain. If social organization has turned oppressive and politics collapsed into administration, it is because our transactions have grown communicatively irrational. With the community as a whole losing control over society's steering mechanisms, special interests seize the opportunity to assert their particularistic rationalities under various ideological covers. Repackaged for mass consumption, these (ir)rationalities are translated back onto the individual plane. Here, through the mechanisms of consumption and socialization, they are bred into actor's bones, producing distorted needs and mentalities which help reproduce impersonal bureaucracies and oppressive institutions. System has uncoupled itself from the private sphere. It has stripped humans of their dignity, usurped their autonomy, perverted their needs—it has colonized the life world. To reclaim control over the system, the community must cut bureaucracy down to size, symbolically as well as literally, and recreate the conditions akin to the intellectual salons of the Enlightenment, where men and women gathered to make sense together and furnish intellectual insights that would later be felt throughout society. The task for our time is to open the political forum to the public at large, refocus attention on communicative action, and radically upgrade the quality of the processes aimed at reaching understanding: "The reevaluation of the particular, the natural, the provincial, of social spaces that are small enough to be familiar, of decentralized forms of commerce and differentiated public sphere—all this is meant to foster the revitalization of possibilities for expression and communication that have been buried alive" (Habermas [1981] 1987, p. 395). The communicative sphere must be freed from distortions, and that means taking seriously our assertions about facts, becoming reflexive about normative bonds we forge through our performative actions, making a personal commitment to be sincere. We have to learn to speak to ourselves and others in the voice of reason. Herein lies hope for "the possibility of settling our disagreements by adducing reasons," of releasing the "emancipatory potential built into communication structures themselves" and achieving a communicatively "rational society" (Habermas [1981] 1987, pp. 74, 390).

Once again, we can see how well Habermas's "communicative socialism" (O'Neill 1985, p. 59) fits in with the pragmatist agenda and how much his specific program veers away from it. Pragmatists agree with Habermas that bureaucratized social systems should be scaled down and made accountable to the public. "Democracy must begin at home, and its home is the neighborly community" (Dewey [1927] 1954, p. 213). Like Habermas, they believe in the "passing of functions which are supposed to inhere in the government into activities that belong to the community" (Mead, 1899, p. 369). "[T]he most concrete and fully realized society is not that which is presented in institutions as such," contends Mead ([1915] 1964, pp. 166-7), "but [in] the readjustments of personal interests that have come into conflict and which take place outside of court, in the change of social attitude that is not dependent upon an act of legislature." But look at the values pragmatists praise in the communicatively shaped order—"the community values of friendship, of passion, of parenthood, of amusement, of beauty, of social solidarity in its unnumbered forms" (Mead [1927] 1964, p. 311)—this is not the list you find in TCA. The two perspectives share broad objectives but differ in significant details and practical means.

Habermas wants to clear communications from inarticulate sentiments, private interests, logical inconsistencies, and similar distortions as inimical to reason. Pragmatists find these essential to keeping one's sanity amidst the semi-chaotic order surrounding us in everyday life. Pure reason has always looked with suspicion at passion and sentiment, but it has never succeeded in purging itself from their invidious touch. Reason has shown itself to be intolerant of ambiguity, contemptuous of common sense, disdainful of compromise, proud of its intellectual machismo in dealing with particulars, and arrogantly dismissive of its own blunderings in the practical domain. History is filled with records of human enterprises bearing reason's seal of approval and stoking nothing but bitter ironies—revolutions that abuse human rights in the name of humanity; laissez faire liberalism that spawns monopolies under the banner of free trade; centralized economies that excel in producing shortages under the aegis of the plan; welfare programs perpetuating an underclass camouflaged by the rhetoric of fair chance—the list goes on and on. Habermas ([1985] 1987, p. 310) has a point when he sees the problem "not as an excess but as a deficit of rationality," but then he may be too kind to pure reason. He does not go far enough in his critique of "Western 'logocentrism,'" which is hard to do without acknowledging intelligence native to instinct and safeguards inherent in common sense. Deracinated affect is a dangerous thing, but so is the reason that plugs its ears to elude the siren voices of sentiment. Cultures that have mindlessly entrusted themselves to the guidance of pure reason and "undercut instinct, common sense, and the reasonableness of sentiment" have insured their own "imminent extinction at the hands of unhinged reason" (Rockberg-Halton, 1986, p. 144). "[M]otivation through 'good reason's" (Habermas [1976] 1979) does not forestall the emergence of the bureaucratic "megamachine" devouring its creators (Mumford, 1967). Pushing body, instinct, and sentiment to the life world's periphery does not make culture more humane (Alexander, 1986). And as Dewey acutely sensed, abstract thought that shuns senses and spurns the ordinary reveals its insensitivity in practical affairs ([1922] 1950, pp. 198, 196):

> Men who devote themselves to thinking are likely to be unusually unthinking in some respects, as for example in immediate personal relationships. A man to whom exact scholarship is an absorbing pursuit may be more than ordinarily vague in ordinary matters. Humility and impartiality may be shown in a specialized field, and pettiness and arrogance in dealing with other persons.... 'Reason' as a noun signifies a happy cooperation of a multitude of dispositions, such as sympathy, curiosity, cooperation, exploration, experimentation, frankness, pursuit—to follow things through—circumspection, to look about at the context, etc., etc.

To guard against its own excesses, reason must be enlightened by feeling, edified by emotions, ennobled by desire. Above all, it must be sensitized to objective uncertainty. Coming to grips with the nondiscursive element in our experience not only helps safeguard reason from overindulging in abstractions but also opens the door to creativity and social reconstruction. Habermas appears to overlook this point when he commits himself to "the cognitivist position" that social problems can be solved within the domain of *Verstandigung*, strictly "by way of argumentation" (Habermas [1981] 1985, p. 19). For their part, pragmatists accentuate the role of intuitive impulses and appeal to artistic imagination as powerful tools for breaking the routines of experience, smashing barriers separating groups, generating fresh insights into troublesome social issues (Dewey [1934] 1958). "To the degree that we make the community in which we live different we all have what is essential to genius," explains Mead (1934, pp. 218, 214). "[Social creativity involves] those values which are found in the immediate attitude of the artist, the inventor, the scientist in his discovery, in general in the action of the 'I' which cannot be calculated and which involves a reconstruction of society, and so of the 'me' which belongs to this society." Social change is predicated here not just on the linguistically mediated "me" as it makes an appearance in discursive communication but on the instinctive, aesthetic, unpremeditated "I" that bursts forth on the social scene and makes individual experience valuable to the community as a whole.

From this pragmatist angle values appear inseparable from habit, instinct, behavior—they are "valuations, habitualized acts of judgment rather than simply inert norms" (Rochberg-Halton 1986, p. 16). To be effective, social norms have to find their way into mind's noncognitive recesses and become suffused with emotions, transformed into habits, translated into routine judgments: "No social modification, slight or revolutionary can endure except as it enters into the action of a people through their desires and purposes" (Dewey 1933, p. 318). Humane community is first and foremost an attitude shared by its members, a feeling like empathy or solidarity generalized to a point where it can inform social routines. Such nondiscursive communications instrumental to communal being by no means imply diminished rationality. "Another meaning of 'rational' is, in fact, available. In this sense, the word means something like 'sane' or 'reasonable' rather than 'methodical.' It names a set of moral virtues: tolerance, respect for the opinion of those around one, willingness to listen, reliance on persuasion rather than force" (Rorty 1987, p. 40). The last point hints at broadening communicative action to include rhetoric and suasion. Communicative, or rather communal, actions need not be a zero-sum game where my being in the right means you're in the wrong. Communal living requires tolerance to contradictions which TCA proscribes as "a sign of a more irrational conduct of life" (Habermas [1981] 1985, p. 61). Inconstancy and paradoxicality are endemic to the pluralistic universe, to the "big, buzzing confusion" that James founded at the core of our being. This universe is composed of many verses and is shot through with competing perspectives. It allows reason to be scattered across disparate social niches; it makes it appear under jarring sexual, racial, ethnic, religious, cultural, and social guises; it does not demand that various life forms be brought to a common denominator other than their proponent's commitment to coexist peacefully, respect each other's uniqueness, and where possible, draw on experience accumulated by others. As such, the pluralistic universe serves as the epitome of modernity pragmatically understood.

The pragmatist outlook on modernity is closer to Simmel than to Weber in that pragmatists find modernity distinguished by the expansion of the meaningful domain rather than its contraction, the unfettering of reason rather than its encagement, the revitalization of the lifeworld rather than its disenchantment. The pluralistic universe does present the modern individual with the mind-boggling question how to wade through jangling possibilities and keep one's sanity intact, yet pragmatists see this situation less as a threat than a promise, insofar as it makes for a more meaningful life—as in *life full of meaning* (James [1897] 1956,

p. 184-215). Today's pragmatists feel no compulsion to transform this semi-rational/semi-absurd world into a unified, logical, communicatively purified, perfectly transparent block universe. To deal with modern life's chaotic cross-currents, they cultivate "irony," aim for "a de-theoreticized sense of community," and "take seriously Dewey's suggestion that the way to reenchant the world, to bring back what religion gave our fore-fathers, is to stick to the concrete" (Rorty 1985, p. 173).

This modest program has several practical implications. For one thing, it suggests that not every evil and irrationality can be communicatively exorcised—some are endemic to human conditions and are best dealt with through joint narrative, communal grieving, shared muteness, glossing over, and bracketing. The pragmatist stance calls for affec-tive sanity; it implies that universalizing the feeling of empathy and compassion is at least as important for sane existence as staking and redeeming validity claims. It calls for irony, humor, and ambivalence in handling many an absurdity of everyday life. (Rorty [1989:61] has a point when he calls Habermas a liberal without irony, for just as any other virtue, earnestness can be carried too far). Pragmatism also has a clear political dimension. It has been historically aligned with progressive reforms aimed at systemic distortions that limit access to public discourse, the most insidious among these distortions being economic deprivation (Faris 1970; Deegan and Burger 1978; Diner 1980; Shalin 1988). At the same time, politics in the pragmatist key is rather ideologically atonal. Laissez faire market, socialized medi-cal services, industrial growth, entitlement programs—these are but means to make our communal being more reasonable and sane, and if the results prove to be other than expected, pragmatists do not hesitate to acknowledge so much and try other means. Critics have variously spurned this stance as conservative, radical, or opportunistic, but it de-fies any partisan label.

Above all, pragmatists call for personal efforts in one's immediate community. In this respect, they follow Anton Chekhov's counsel to avoid grandstanding and take up small deeds. That is to say, pragmatism challenges us to start with ourselves, become reasonable with those closest to us, get out to a town meeting, PTA gathering, neighborhood association, and try to body forth a better community by talking, humor-ing, cajoling its members into more reasonable ways. Once our efforts are met with success in our own abode, they are likely to be noticed and fire up action elsewhere. As the progressive era pragmatist reformers had learned, social reconstruction starts in one community, envelops the city, moves to the state level, and then comes to the national legislature. The scheme does not fit each case and every country, but it suggests the kind of pragmatic grass-root politics without which democratic reconstruction could not become an ongoing concern. As long as we are willing to exert ourselves on behalf of our own community, pragmatists urge, we make the burden of living more bearable for all and keep alive the hope for emancipation through reason that critical theory has clung to since Rousseau.

Conclusion

In fairness to Habermas, he foresees some of the objections raised in this essay. On several occasions, most copiously in his interviews, he intimated that he personally feels no urge to "bring a satisfying order to chaos," that "[t]here is nothing at all to which I have an unambivalent attitude," that rational society must be "as fallibilist and as open to self-correction as possible," that "every intervention in complex social structures has such unforeseeable consequences that processes of reform can only be defended as scrupulous processes of trial and error, under the careful control of those who have to bear their consequences" (Habermas 1986, pp. 126, 144, 187). Such statements qualify only as disclaimers, however, unless they are translated into theoretical terms. In its present form, TCA provides no conceptual room for indeterminacy, has little use for nondiscursiveness, fails to appreciate the critical potential of sentiment, and does not square off discursive ethics with the need for personal responsibility. This is exactly why it is so important for Habermas and pragmatists to continue searching for common ground. The crossfertilization will benefit both sides.

Pragmatists can learn from Habermas how to grasp in communication-theoretic terms systemic distortions delimiting access to public discourse. TCA offers valuable insights into the discursive bottlenecks that are created in an overloaded market system and that are prone to be exploited by particularistic interests. Habermas has put his finger on an issue that is (or should be) central to the pragmatism-inspired social inquiry—the need to bridge the gap between action-theoretic and system-theoretic languages, between micro- and macroscopic analyses of social processes. TCA also provides fresh food for thought on how the movement toward formal representation in democratic systems affects discursive will formation and what can be done to safeguard substantive democracy from the distortions it suffers when responsibility for public affairs is delegated to experts. Finally, Habermas's analysis should help contemporary interactionists to reclaim the critical dimension of early pragmatism and refocus their inquiry on the structural conditions that hamper access to public discourse and undermine the conditions for fruitful dissent.

Habermas and Continental critical theorists have something to learn from pragmatists as well. They are yet to acknowledge that reason uncaged is reason enlightened by sentiment, sensitized to uncertainty, steeped in ambivalence, willing to come to terms with common sense, humbled by the limits that nature sets to its ambitions. Liberated from its bias against indeterminacy, reason is likely to concede that a consensus based on good reasons alone is a poor guide for action and that the ideal speech situation must include among its provisions an agreement to disagree. In sum, critical theory could benefit from the pragmatist insights into embodied experience and objective uncertainty.

These concerns are consistent with the broadly based trends in modern science, which is increasingly turning its attention towards chaos, uncertainty, fuzzy logic, emergent processes, dissipative structures, and other patently nonclassical subjects. The time has come to reconsider pragmatist philosophy and interactionist sociology (which derived its inspiration from, though has not always been faithful to, pragmatism) with an eye to determining how both had presaged the developments in nonclassical science. The future agenda includes a sociology in the pragmatist key, the one that eschews both the irrationalism of *Lebensphilosophie* and the nihilistic proclivities of postmodernism—a critical social science of uncertainty that combines the commitment to emancipation with the readiness to meet head-on objective uncertainty.

Notes

1. For further discussion of Weber's views on formal and substantive democracy see Giddens (1972), Mommsen (1974), and Cohen (1985).
2. Habermas may be underestimating the extent to which the social dimension of reason was elaborated in the German tradition in general and transcendental idealism in particular. For an alternative view, see Royce (1919:65), Mead (1936:147), and Shalin (1986).
3. See Joas (1985) and Shalin (1984) on the Mead-idealism connection.
4. A wide range of critical comments on Habermas's corpus can be found in two representative collections: *Habermas: Critical Debates*, edited by Thompson and Held (1982), and *Habermas and Modernity*, edited by Bernstein (1985). For a more detailed discussion of Habermass' theory of communicative action see McCarthy (1978), Ferrara (1985), Benhabib (1985, 1987), and Antonio (1989).
5. Among contemporary writers on pragmatism, I found particularly useful the following: Alexander (1987), Bernstein (1983), Coughlan (1975), Joas, (1985),

Kloppenberg (1986), Rockberg-Halton (1987), Rorty (1979, 1982), and Rosenthal (1986).

6. The letters "MP" stand here and below for the George H. Mead papers gathered in the Special Collections Department of the Joseph Regenstein Library, University of Chicago. The letters "b" and "f" followed by a number indicate box number and folder number where a particular document is located.

7. Various attempts have been made to conceptualize this intermediate space. Durkheim searched for it in the intraprofessional type of interactions, as did Parsons, and Peter Berger detected it in the realm of communal, familial space. See David Sciulli (1988, 1992) for an overview of the issues involved.

8. The term *substantive democracy* is used here in a broad sense consistent with Habermas's vision of a communicatively-sound democratic system that is rich in participatory contnet, and as such, it contrasts to the notion of formal democracy where individuals are deprived of a meaningful opportunity to engage in communicative action.

References

Adorno, Theodor W. 1951. *Prisms*. London: Neville Spearman.

_____. [1966] 1973. *Negative Dialectics*. New York: Seabury Press.

_____. 1965. "Repressive Tolerance," pp. 81-118 in *Critique of Pure Tolerance*. Robert Paul Wolf, Barrington Moore, Jr. and Herbert Marcuse. Boston: Beacon Press.

_____. 1973. *The Jargon of Authenticity*. Evanston, IL: Northwestern University Press.

Alexander, Thomas M. 1987. *John Dewey's Theory of Art, Experience & Nature: The Horizons of Feeling*. Albany: State University of New York Press.

Antonio, Robert J. 1983. "The Origin, Development, and Contemporary Status of Critical Theory." *Sociological Quarterly* 24:325-51.

_____. 1989. "The Normative Foundations of Emancipatory Theory: Evolutionary versus Pragmatic Perspectives." *American Journal of Sociology* 94:721-48.

Benhabib, Seyla. 1987. "The Generalized and the Concrete Other: The Kolberg-Gilligan Controversy and Feminist Theory," pp. 77-95 in *Feminism as Critique: On the Politics of Gender*, edited by Seyla Benhabib. Minneapolis: University of Minnesota Press.

Benjamin, Walter. [1936] 1970. *Illuminations*. Cape.

Bernstein, Richard J. 1983. *Beyond Objectivism and Relativism: Science, Hermeneutics, Praxis*. Philadelphia: University of Pennsylvania Press.

_____. Editor. 1985. *Habermas and Modernity*. Cambridge, MA: MIT Press.

Betz, J. 1974. "George Herbert Mead on Human Rights." *Transactions of the Charles S. Peirce Society* 10:199-223.

Blumer, Herbert. 1969. *Symbolic Interactionism. Perspective and Method*. Englewood Cliffs, NJ: Prentice-Hall.

Cohen, Ira J. 1985. "The Underemphasis on Democracy in Marx and Weber," pp. 274-99 in *A Weber-Marx Dialogue*, edited by Robert J. Antonio and Ronald M. Glassman. Lawrence: University Press of Kansas.

Coughlan, Neil. 1975. *Young John Dewey*. Chicago: University of Chicago Press.

Dewey, John. [1890] 1969. "The Logic of Verification," pp. 83-92 in John *Dewey, The Early Works*. Volume III. Carbondale: Southern Illinois University Press.

_____. 1916. "Organization in American Education." *Teachers College Record* 17:127-41.

_____. 1916a. *Essays in Experimental Logic*. New York: Dover.

_____. [1916] 1966. *Democracy and Education*. New York: Macmillan.
_____. [1920] 1950. *Reconstruction in Philosophy*. New York: Mentor Books.
_____. [1927] 1954. *The Public and Its Problems*. New York: Henry Holt & Co.
_____. [1922] 1950. *Human Nature and Conduct*. New York: The Modern Library.
_____. [1927] 1950. "Pragmatic Acquiescence," pp. 49-43 in Gail Kennedy, ed. *Pragmatism and American Culture*. Boston: D. C. Heath and Co.
_____. [1929] 1958. *Experience and Nature*. New York: Dover.
_____. [1929] 1962. *Individualism, Old and New*. New York: Capricorn Books.
_____. [1934] 1958. *Art and Experience*. New York: G. P. Putnam's Sons.
_____. 1938. *Logic: The Theory of Inquiry*. New York: Henry Holt & Co.
_____. [1938] 1950. "The Pragmatic Acquiescence," pp. 49-53 in *Pragmatism and American Culture*, edited by Gail Kennedy. Boston: D. C. Heath & Co.
_____. 1939. *Freedom and Culture*. New York: Capricorn Books.
_____. 1946. *The Problems of Men*. New York: Philosophical Library.
Dewey, John and James H. Tufts. [1908] 1976. *Ethics*. In *John Dewey.*
The Middle Works, 1899-1924. Carbondale: Southern Illinois University Press.
Dewey, John and Childs, John L. 1933. "The Underlying Philosophy of Education," pp. 287-319 in *The Educational Frontier*, edited by W. H. Kilpatrick. New York: D. Appleton-Century.
Deegan, M. J. and J. S. Burger. 1978. "George Herbert Mead and Social Reform: His Work and Writings." *Journal of the History of the Behavioral Sciences* 14:362-73.
Diner, S. J. 1980. *A City and Its Universities, Public Policy in Chicago, 1892-1919*. Chapel Hill: University of North Carolina Press.
Faris, Robert E. 1970. *Chicago Sociology 1920-1932*. Chicago: University of Chicago Press.
Ferrara, Allesandro. 1985. "A Critique of Haberma's *Diskursetik*." *Telos* 64:45-74.
Fichte, J. G. [1794] 1970. *Science of Knowledge*. New York: Appleton-Century-Crofts.
Gadamer, Hans-Georg. [1967] 1977. "On the Scope and Function of Hermeneutical Reflection." Pp. 18-58 in Hans-Georg Gadamer, *Philosophical Hermeneutics*. Berkeley: University of California Press.
Giddens, Anthony. 1972. *Politics and Sociology in the Works of Max Weber*. London: Macmillan.
Geuss, Raymond. 1981. *The Idea of a Critical Theory*. New York: Cambridge University Press.
Gouinlock, James. 1972. *John Dewey's Theory of Value*. New York: Humanities Press.
Habermas, Jürgen. [1962] 1989. *The Structural Transformation of the Public Sphere. An Inquiry Into a Category of Bourgeois Society*. Cambridge, MA: MIT Press.
_____. [1968] 1970. *Toward a Rational Society*. Boston: Beacon.
_____. [1968] 1971. *Knowledge and Human Interest*. Boston: Beacon Press.
_____. [1971] 1973. *Theory and Practice*. Boston: Beacon.
_____. [1973] 1975. *Legitimation Crisis*. Boston: Beacon Press.
_____. [1976] 1979. *Communication and Evolution of Society*. Boston: Beacon.
_____. [1981] 1984. *The Theory of Communicative Action, Volume I. Reason the Realization of Society*. Boston: Beacon Press.
_____. [1981] 1987. *The Theory of Communicative Action, Volume II. Life World and System: A Critique of Functionalist Reason*. Boston: Beacon Press.
_____. 1985. "Questions and Counter Questions," pp. 192-216 in Richard J. Bernstein, editor, *Habermas and Modernity*. Cambridge, MA: MIT Press.
_____. 1986. *Autonomy and Solidarity. Interviews*, edited by Peter Dews. Verso: The Imprint of New Left Books.

_____. [1985] 1987. *The Philosophical Discourse of Modernity*. Cambridge, MA: MIT Press.

Hegel, G.W F. [1807] 1967. *The Phenomenology of Mind*. New York: Harper and Row.

_____. [1817] 1975. *Hegel's Logic. Being Part of the Encyclopedia of the Philosophical Sciences*. London: Oxford University Press.

Held, David. 1980. *Introduction to Critical Theory*. Berkeley: University of California Press.

Horkheimer, Max. 1937. "Der Neusten Angriff auf die Metaphysik." *Zeitschriftfur Sozialforschung* 6:4-53.

_____. [1937] 1976. "Traditional and Critical Theory," pp. 206-24 in *Critical Sociology*, edited by Paul Connerton. New York: Penguin Books.

_____. 1947. *Eclipse of Reason*. New York: Oxford University Press.

_____. 1974. Critique of Instrumental Reason. Lectures and Essays Since the End of World War II. New York: Seabury Press.

_____. 1978. *Dawn and Decline. Notes 1926-1931 & 1950-1969*. New York: Seabury Press.

Horkheimer, Max and Theodor W. Adorno. [1944] 1989. *The Dialectics of Enlightenment*. New York: Continuum.

James, William. [1890] 1950. *Principles of Psychology*, Vol 1 & II. New York: Dover.

_____. [1897] 1956. *The Will to Believe*. New York: Dover.

_____. [1909] 1967. *Pluralistic Universe*, in *Essays in Radical Empiricism and Pluralistic Universe*. Gloucester: David McKay Co.

Jay, Martin. 1973. *The Dialectical Imagination*. Boston: Little, Brown.

Joas, Hans. 1985. *G. H. Mead. A Contemporary Reexamination of His Thought*. Cambridge, MA: Polity Press.

Kant, Immanuel. [1781] 1966. *Critique of Pure Reason*. New York: Anchor Books.

_____. [1783] 1950. *Prolegomena to Any Future Metaphysics*. Indianapolis, IN: The Bobbs-Merrill Co.

_____. [1803] 1904. "Lecture Notes on Pedagogy." Pp. 101-222 in *The Educational Theory of Immanuel Kant*, edited by E. F. Buchner. Philadelphia: J. B. Lippincott Co.

Kellner, Douglas. 1985. "Critical Theory, Max Weber, and the Dialectics of Domination," pp. 89-116 in *A Weber-Marx Dialogue*, edited by Robert J. Antonio and Ronald M. Glassman. Lawrence: University Press of Kansas.

Kloppenberg, James T. *Uncertain Victory: Social Democracy and Progressivism in European and American Thought, 1870-1920*. New York: Oxford University Press.

McCarthy, Thomas. 1978. *The Critical Theory of Jürgen Habermas*. Cambridge: MIT Press.

Marx, Karl. [1843] 1971. "A Correspondence of 1843," pp. 79-82 in *Karl Marx, Early Texts*. New York: Harper & Row.

_____. [1843] 1972. "Letter to Arnold Ruge, September 1843," pp. 7-10 in *The Marx-Engels Reader*, edited by Robert C. Tucker. New York: W. W. Norton & Co.

_____. (1844) 1964. *The Economic & Philosophic Manuscripts of 1844*. New York: International Publishers.

_____. (1846) 1963. *The German Ideology*, Parts I & III. New York: International Publishers.

Marcuse, Herbert. [1934] 1968. "The Struggle Against Liberalism in the Totalitarian View of the State," pp. 3-42 in *Negations. Essays in Critical Theory*. Boston: Beacon Press.

_____. [1937] 1968. "Philosophy and Critical Theory," pp. 134-58 in *Negations: Essays in Critical Theory*. Boston: Beacon Press.

_____. 1939/1940. "Review of John Dewey's *Logic: The Theory of Inquiry.*" *Zeitschrift fur Sozialforshcung* 9:144-8.

_____. 1960. *Reason and Revolution: Hegel and the Rise of Social Theory* Boston: Beacon.

_____. 1964. *One-Dimensional Man.* Boston: Beacon.

_____. 1965. "Repressive Tolerance," pp. 81-118 in Robert Paul Wolff, Barrington Moore, Jr., and Herbert Marcuse, editors. *A Critique of Pure Tolerance.* Boston: Beacon Press.

_____. [1968] 1976. "Postscript 1968," pp. 325-9 in *Critical Sociology,* edited by Paul Connerton. Harmondsworth, Middlsex: Penguin Books.

Mead, George H. (n.d.) George Herbert Mead Papers. University of Chicago Archives.

_____. [1927] 1964. "The Objective Reality of Perspectives," pp. 306-19 in *Selected Writings: George Herbert Mead,* edited by A. J. Reck. New York: Bobbs-Merrill Co.

_____. [1930] 1964. "Philanthropy From the Point of View of Ethics," pp. 392-407 in *Selected Writings. George Herbert Mead,* edited by A. J. Reck. New York: Bobbs-Merrill Co.

_____. 1934. *Mind, Self and Society.* Chicago: University of Chicago Press.

_____. 1936. *Movements of Thought in the Nineteenth Century.* Chicago: University of Chicago Press.

_____. 1938. *The Philosophy of the Act.* Chicago: University of Chicago Press.

Kierkegaard, Søren. [1846] 1941. *Concluding Unscientific Postscript.* Princeton, NJ: Princeton University Press.

Mommsen, Wolfgang J. 1974. *The Age of Bureaucracy: Perspectives on the Political Sociology of Max Weber.* New York: Harper.

Mumford, Lewis. 1967. *The Myth of the Machine: Techniques and Human Development.* New York: Harcourt, Brace, Jovanovich.

Neumann, Franz. L. 1953. *The Cultural Migration. The European Scholar in America.* Crawford: University of Pennsylvania Press.

O'Neill, J. 1985. "Decolonization and the Ideal Speech Community," pp. 57-76 in John Forester, ed. *Critical Theory and Public Life.* Cambridge, MA: MIT Press.

Peirce, Charles S. 1976. *The New Elements of Mathematics.* Atlantic Highlands, NJ: Humanities Press.

Przeworski, Adam. 1986. *Capitalism and Social Democracy. Studies in Marxist Social Theory.* Cambridge, MA: Cambridge University Press.

Rochberg-Halton, Eugine. 1986. *Meaning and Modernity: Social Theory in the Pragmatic Attitude.* Chicago: University of Chicago Press.

Rorty, Richard. 1979. *Philosophy and the Mirror of Nature.* Princeton, NJ: Princeton University Press.

_____. 1982. *Consequences of Pragmatism.* Minneapolis: University of Minnesota Press.

_____. 1987. "Science as Solidarity," pp. 38-52 in *The Rhetoric of the Human Sciences,* edited by John S. Nelson, Allan Megill, and Donald N. McClosckey. Madison: The University of Wisconsin Press.

_____. 1989. *Contingency, Irony, and Solidarity.* Cambridge, MA: Cambridge University Press.

Rose, Gillian. 1978. *The Melancholy Science: An Introduction to the Thought of Theodore W. Adorno.* New York: Columbia University Press.

Rosenthal, Sandra. 1986. *Speculative Pragmatism.* Amherst, MA: MIT Press.

Royce, Josiah. 1919. *Lectures on Modern Idealism.* New Haven, CT: Yale University Press.

Schelling, F. W. J. [1800] 1978. *System of Transcendental Idealism.* Charlottesville: University of Virginia Press.

Shalin, D. N. 1984. "The Romantic Antecedents of Meadian Social Psychology." *Symbolic Interaction* 7:43-65.

_____. 1986. "Romanticism and the Rise of Sociological Hermeneutics." *Social Research* 53:77-123.

_____. 1986a. "Pragmatism and Social Interactionism." *American Sociological Review* 51:9-29.

_____. 1988. "G.H. Mead, Socialism, and the Progressive Agenda." *American Journal of Sociology* 93:913-51.

_____. 1991. "The Pragmatic Origins of Symbolic Interactionism and the Crisis of Classical Science." *Studies in Symbolic Interaction* 12:223-51.

Scheler, Max. [1926] 1977. *Erkentnis und Arbeit: Eine Studie uber Wert und Grenzen des pragmatischen Motivs in der Erkentnis der Welt.* Frankfurt.

Schumpeter, J. A. 1950. *Capitalism, Socialism and Democracy.* New York: Harper & Row.

Sciully, David. 1988. "Foundations of Societal Constitutionalism: Principles from the Concepts of Communicative Action and Procedural Legality." *British Journal of Sociology* 39:377-407.

_____. 1992. "Habermas, Critical Theory, and the Relativistic Predicament." *Symbolic Interaction* (forthcoming).

Van den Berg, Axel. 1990. "Habermas and Modernity: A Critique of the Theory of Communicative Action." *Current Perspectives in Social Theory* 10:161-94.

Weber, Max. 1964. *The Theory of Social and Economic Organization.* New York: The Free Press.

_____. [1904-1905] 1958. *The Protestant Ethics and the Spirit of Capitalism.* New York: Charles Scribner's Sons.

Wolin, Richard. 1987. "Critical Theory and the Dialectics of Rationalism." *New German Critique* 41:23-52.

5

Reading Text Pragmatically: Modernity, Postmodernism, and Pragmatist Inquiry

Postmodernism has been around for some decades now, but it was not until the 1980s that social scientists started paying this intellectual current close attention. Reasons for such a tardy response are several, starting with the fact that postmodernists do not look kindly at the social sciences and question the very possibility of theoretical knowledge. It is all the more interesting that symbolic interactionists were among the first in the social science community to join issue with postmodernism (e.g., Farberman 1980 1991; Denzin 1986 1989 1991 1990a 1990b 1990c 1992; Clough 1989 1992a; 1992b; Grug and Laurel 1989; Katovich and MacMurray 1990; Manning 1990,1993; Fontana and Preston 1990; Shalin 1991; Young 1991; Fee 1992). The interactionists' somewhat marginal position in academia may have something to do with the welcome reception they gave to postmodernism. The issues that symbolic interactionism has championed since its inception and that assured its maverick status in American sociology bear instructive resemblance to the themes championed by postmodernist thinkers. The same can be said about pragmatism, which fed the interactionists' animosity toward the spectator's theory of knowledge and fueled their preference for the perspectival approach to truth. The postmodernist critique of formal

A longer version of this chapter was published as "Modernity, Postmodernism, and Pragmatist Inquiry: An Introduction" in a special issue on "Self in Crisis: Identity and Postmodern Condition," *Symbolic Interaction* 1993, Vol. 15, pp. 303-332. The opening section introducing the special issue of the journal is omitted. I wish to thank David Dickens for his comments on an earlier draft of this paper.

logic, positivism, and scientism also strikes a responsive chord with pragmatism-inspired sociology, as is the emphasis on the marginal, everyday, and indeterminate. One more point on which interactionist and postmodern perspectives converge is self-identity, seen as plural and socially constructed.

Unmistakable though it is, the affinity between interactionism and postmodernism is highly selective. The pragmatist heritage that accounts for this affinity also points to fissures separating interactionist and postmodernist projects. Not surprisingly, the interactionists' response to postmodernism has not been unanimous. According to Denzin (1990a), the time has come for interactionists to embrace fully postmodernism and jettison that portion of their own heritage which does not square with the radically postmodern stance. Farberman (1990) disagrees with this assessment, welcoming certain postmodernist insights but rejecting its fixation on disembodied communication as inimical to pragmatism and its political sensibilities. The present essay examines the (dis)continuity between theoretical, methodological, and substantive tenets of postmodernism and pragmatist sociology. This undertaking is prompted by the sense that symbolic interactionism is at a crossroads, that in years to come we may witness deepening divisions within the ranks of interactionists. It is my hope that the Society for the Study of Symbolic Interaction will be able to learn from other perspectives, accommodate divergent views, and stand its ground where need be.

The Postmodernist Project

"[The] organ of knowledge must be turned around from the world of becoming," urged Plato ([430-355 B.C.] 1963, pp. 751-2, 753), "until the soul is able to endure the contemplation of essence and the brightest region of being." This celebrated maxim is at the heart of a philosophical tradition that equates knowledge with the firmest possible grasp the knower can lay on essence or being. Although it would eventually turn mainstream in the Occidental world, this tradition never silenced the doubters who spurned attempts to "draw soul away from the world of becoming to the world of being" (Plato [430-355 B.C.] 1963, p. 753) and kept searching for ways to reckon with the fact that "Everything flows and nothing abides; everything gives way and nothing stays fixed" (Heraclitus [c. 500 B.C.] 1969, pp. 70-1). It was Heraclitus who taught us that you could not enter the same river twice. Cratylus corrected him that you could not do it even once. Protagoras, Pyrrho, Diogenes, and other skeptics downplayed rational discourse and experimented with cynicism. The breakdown of the medieval order led to the resurgence of skeptical thinking, which formed an influential current in the Renaissance (Estienne, Erasmus). At the dawn of the modern era, the doubters gained prominence once again, with Gassendi, Bayle, and Hume paying skepticism their homage. As modernity's distempers and discontents grew more obvious, its critics recycled the old themes. Nietzsche famously proclaimed himself "contemptuous of every culture" (1968, p. 80), and so did Baudrillard: "I don't want culture, I spit on it" (1987, p. 81).

The conflict between the two schools has persisted throughout Western history, the modern/postmodern controversy being its latest incarnation. Postmodernists took up the old philosophical problem of how to capture the world of becoming in the language of being and gave it a resolute answer—we cannot. Geared to essence and sameness, our language is utterly inadequate for dealing with the fleeting and inchoate. As we fix our gaze on enduring properties, we could not help glossing over the continuous metamorphoses the world undergoes right before our eyes. We lump together as "the same" things heterogenous and unique; we spot "identity" in the dizzying transformations the self undergoes in its daily life; we boast our theories as "true representations" of a reality which keeps on turning into something else just as we squeeze it into our theoretical schema.

There must be something in reason that accounts for this mania for sameness and aversion to difference. This something, postmodernists conclude with Nietzsche, is the will to power, the unconscious desire that compels one to overlook the apparently accidental and fasten onto the fraudulently substantial: "The world with which we are concerned is false, i.e., is not a fact but a fable and approximation on the basis of a meager sum of observations; it is 'in flux,' as something in the state of becoming, as a falsehood always changing but never getting near the truth: for—there is no 'truth'…. To impose upon becoming the character of being—that is the supreme will to power" (Nietzsche 1968, p. 330). And again, "There exists neither 'spirit,' nor reason, nor thinking, nor consciousness, nor soul, nor will, nor truth: all are fictions that are of no use…. Knowledge works as a tool of power. Hence it is plain that it increases with every increase of power" (Nietzsche 1968, p. 266). The genealogy of knowledge, as Nietzsche conceived his enterprise, is an inquiry into the monumental self-deception Western reason has succumbed to in its quest for domination. According to postmodernists, this quest reached its apex in the modem era. The Age of Reason spawned an elaborate discourse about humanism, emancipation, freedom, and public good, but all this narrative profusion masks the primordial hunger for power and hegemony which relies on science in general and the human/social sciences in particular to secure control over the populace. "The exercise of power perpetually creates knowledge, and, conversely, knowledge constantly induces effects of power," writes Foucault (1980a, p. 52) in one of his Nietzschean passages, and "there is no point of dreaming of a time when knowledge will cease to depend on power; this is just the way of reviving humanism in a utopian guise." The will to power cum will to know produces social technologies designed to keep body and mind under control by infusing the two with programmed desires. Compulsory education, prison reforms, psychiatric wards, general hospitals, military schools, and similar social innovations that sprung to life in the Age of Reason played a key part in creating "man"—a thoroughly modern creature brought up to satisfy the needs of mass production in a capitalist society. To be a self, a subject, or a universal human being means to be constituted by social technologies and normalizing discourses in accordance with the system's hegemonic requirements. "Confronted by a power that is law, the subject who is constituted as subject—who is 'subjected'—is he who obeys" (Foucault 1980b, p. 85). As for the concern for civil rights on which modernity prides itself, one should not take it at face value, for such avowed humanitarianism is but auxiliary tool in the relentless struggle for supremacy:

> We have entered a phase of juridical regression in comparison with the pre-seventeenth-century societies we are acquainted with; we should not be deceived by all the Constitutions framed throughout the world since the French Revolution, the Codes written and revised, a whole continuous and clamorous legislative activity: these were the forms that made an essentially normalizing power acceptable. (Foucault 1980b, p. 144)

Derrida takes a different tack in his bid to unmask modernity's hidden agenda, but his writings reflect the familiar postmodernist themes. Objectivity, representation, truth—all the abstractions spawned by Occidental culture—are fictions masking reason's repressed desires, its spurious longing for an authentic moment in which being is revealed to the subject in its original purity and logical perfection. So strong is the West's need for presence that its intellectuals readily sacrifice the heterogeneous to the unitary, the inconstant to the stable, the uncertain to the determinate. Yet this one-sided focus on being only defers attention to its other—the non-being, which betrays itself in the binary categories: subject/object, mind/matter, truth/falsehood, nature/culture, and such like dichotomies inherent in our language. "We could thus take up all the coupled oppositions on which philosophy is constructed, and from which our language lives," writes Derrida (1973, p. 148), "not in order to see opposition vanish but to see the emergence of the other, the other as 'differed' within the systemic ordering of the same (e.g., the intelligible as differing from the sensible, as sensible deferred; the concept as differed-differing intuition, life as differing-differed matter; mind as differed-differing life; culture as differed-differing nature; and [so on]..." Derrida's deconstructive method aims at exposing the strategies of deception used by the writers to defer coming to grips with the impossibility of getting through to things themselves and apprehending a genuine presence presupposed by our knowledge. Deconstruction can be seen as dialectics in reverse: Whereas the latter seeks a higher synthesis in which the thesis and antithesis unite in a harmonious bliss, the former takes apart a proposition in order to show that it conceals within itself an unresolved contradiction, that it suppresses some unrecognized alterity screaming to get out from under the rhetorical rubble.

While Foucault styles his approach after Nietzsche's genealogy, Derrida owes much to Freud and Saussure. The unconscious is conceptualized in his work not so much as a psychological phenomenon (although it remains deeply rooted in desire) but as a sort of linguistic a priori governed by the logic of the sign. From Saussure's semiotics Derrida borrows the notion that the linguistic sign is binary in nature, comprising the signifier and the signified, its meaning ascertainable in and through the relationship to other signs. By analyzing which signs are invoked to elucidate a particular point and which ones are absent from the text (or present only as invisible traces and inaudible meanings), the deconstructive reading grasps the unconscious linguistic structure governing the writing without recourse to—indeed in spite of—the author's intentions: "Reading must always aim at a certain relationship, unperceived by the writer, between what he commands and what he does not command of the schemata of the language that he uses" (Derrida, 1976:158). A good example is Derrida's reading of Rousseau (Derrida 1976, pp. 95-268), which purports to show how the same structure of desire, manifest in the author's persistent recourse to certain linguistic props, informs Rousseau's writings on language and his confessions about his autoerotic practices. Whatever reason speaks about, it cannot conceal the traces of unreason buried in its unconscious and waiting to be disclosed through a skillful deconstruction.

Baudrillard pushes postmodernist thinking in the area more familiar to interactionists. Taking his cue from Thorstein Veblen and amplifying it with his own insights into the age of mass media, mass production, and mass consumption, Baudrillard (1981, p. 63) reaches this conclusion: "The empirical "object," given in its contingency of form, color, material, function and discourse (or, if it is a cultural object, in its aesthetic finality) is a myth. How often it has been wished away! But the object is *nothing*. It is nothing but the different types of relations and significations that converge, contradict themselves, and twist around it, as such—the hidden logic that not only arranges this bundle of relations, but directs the manifest discourse that overlays and occludes it." As modernity has reached its late stage, the signifier began to sever its relationship with the signified, performing the function of a substitute for and a simulation of reality. Sometime in the medieval world, Baudrillard (1975, p. 83) contends, symbols had an unbroken bond with reality, fashion and counterfeit were unknown, and the individual's identity was brutally stamped by the rigid estate system. Everyone was then exactly what one appeared to be. This stage was superseded first by the age of production which introduced fashion, counterfeit strategies, and multiple selves, and then by the age of simulation which has dispensed completely with any similitude between appearance and reality. "The object-become-sign no longer gathers its meaning in the concrete relationship between two people. It assumes its meaning in its differential relationship to other signs.... [Today] it is no longer a question of a false representation of reality (ideology), but of concealing the fact that the real is no longer real, and thus of saving the reality principle.... *The very definition of the real becomes: that of which it is possible to give an equivalent reproduction*" (Baudrillard 1981, p. 66; 1983, pp. 25 146).

We live in a hyperreal world where signs have acquired a life of their own, referring to nothing beside themselves and serving no other purpose than that of symbolic exchange. Individuals caught in this exchange are convinced that the objects they consume have an intrinsic use value, that consumers are real selves doing real choosing. But, Baudrillard contends, "use value is fundamentally an alibi for sign exchange value," "the system can only produce and reproduce individuals as elements of the system [which] cannot tolerate exceptions," and it is the individuals who are reproduced by the symbolic exchange system with all their selves and wants under "*the total constraint of the code*" (Baudrillard 1981, pp. 55, 86, 66). In its postmodern incarnation, power no longer forces individuals to comply: "power *seduces*," it rules by luring and ceaselessly renewing a "cycle of seduction, challenge and ruse" (Baudrillard 1987, pp. 43, 46). Hypermodern dupes inhabiting the hyperreal world, today's humans are busy assuring each other that they crave things they purchase and consume for their intrinsic qualities, but the sole (un)conspicuous object of each consumptive exercise is its power to certify the user's social worth. Postmodern society is a masquerade where participants don the masks of success to conceal the fact that they have no faces, no meaning, and no value. The mass media's unmasking zeal perversely contributes to this charade by threatening to expose the reality supposedly hidden under the official and unofficial disguises. This is a dodge—Watergate was no 'scandal,' Baudrillard tells us. Social science purports to be a critical endeavor but in fact it aids the hyper-modern subterfuge: "[S]ociology is most of the time both a dupe and an accomplice: it takes the ideology of consumption for consumption itself" (Baudrillard 1981, p. 61). Ours is "the age of simulacrum and simula-tion," the abode of "a hyperreal sociality, where the real is confused with the model," "referential reason disappears," and "any liberated form of speech constitutes one more turn in the spiral of power" (Baudrillard 1983, pp. 12, 53,102; 1987, p. 26).

One more figure central to the postmodern movement should be men-tioned here, Jean-François Lyotard. His slim volume, *The Postmodern Condition: A Report on Knowledge*, drew attention to the quiet revolu-tion within the hard sciences abandoning the old positivist fables about certainty, causality, determinacy, and other paragons of scientific thought. Today's scholars increasingly occupy themselves with postmodern mind twisters like "singularities," "discontinuities," "incommensurability," "paralogy," "chaos," "indeterminacy," "fracta," "catastrophes," and their willingness to thematize these phenomena as strategic properties marks a break with classical modern science (Lyotard 1984, pp. 58-61). Similar awareness, Lyotard urges, needs to be cultivated among the practitioners of the human and social sciences. Notions like "progress," "emancipa-tion," and "rationality" abounding in these disciplines are meaningless, self-referential, and unreflexive at the same time. Their users offer theoretical descriptions of facts, yet facts they purport to describe are discernible only if we presuppose a given theory to be true. A grand narrative legitimizing this circular reasoning and escaping scrutiny is at the heart of modernity:

> I will use the term *modern* to designate any science that legitimates itself with refer-ence to a metadiscourse of this kind making an explicit appeal to some grand narrative, such as the dialectics of Spirit, the hermeneutics of meaning, the emancipation of the rational or working subject, or the creation of wealth.... I define postmodern as incredulity toward metanarratives.... The narrative function loses its functors, its great hero, its great dangers, its great voyagers, its great goal. (Lyotard 1984, p. xxiv)

Along with Foucault, Lyotard zeroes in on the link between the scientific discourse of truth and the political discourse of power. The two are interchangeable, and both rely on each other's language games to legitimize their enterprises. "From this point of view, the right to decide what is true is not independent of the right to decide what is just, even if the statements confined to the two authorities differ in nature. The point is that there is strict interlinkage between the kind of language called science and the kind called ethics and politics: they both stem from the same perspective, the same 'choice' if you will—the choice called the Occident" (Lyotard 1984, p. 8). This intermingling of narratives is behind the horrors that the Age of Reason visited on its victims. "The nineteenth and twentieth centuries have given us as much terror as we can take. We have paid a high enough price for the nostalgia of the whole and the one, for the reconciliation of the concept and the sensible, of the transparent and the communicable experience" (Lyotard 1984, p. 81-2).

It is easier to say what postmodernists are against—modernity, rationality, positivism, domination, grand narrative—than to articulate what they are for. "Let us wage war on totality; let us be witnesses to the unpresentable; let us activate the differences and save the honor of the name," intones Lyotard (1984, p. 82). Such invectives are meant to rouse, but they are not especially instructive as research programs or guides for political action. Those fed up with the modern may take their cue from Nietzsche's call to look behind the mask, to find an unconscious interest working behind the scenes: "Every philosophy also *conceals* philosophy; every opinion is also a hideout, every word also a mask" (Nietzsche [1886] 1966, p. 229). Just as their illustrious predecessor, postmodernists show a fascination with reason's hidden agenda, with the irrational, and they favor aesthetically tinged methods for recovering the logical discontinuity that scientific gaze tends to occlude. Postmodern politics owes something to Nietzsche's ethical nihilism and disdain for democratic institutions: "Making men smaller and more governable is desired as 'progress'!... democratic institutions: they enhance weakness of the will ... . Means of *enduring* it: the reevaluation of all values. No longer joy in certainty but in uncertainty; no longer 'cause and effect' but the continuously creative; no longer will to preservation but to power" (Nietzsche 1968, pp. 79-80, 545). The postmodernists' revulsion of authority and contempt for collective action gives their pronouncements an anarchistic flavor, a cynical touch.

Foucault's genealogical approach is designed to expose "epistemes," "regimes of truth," and "forms of discourse" that generate specific modes of control over body and bring into existence "modern man," whose demise Foucault seeks to hasten. "It is comforting, however, and a source of profound relief to think that man is only a recent invention, a figure not yet two centuries old, a new wrinkle in our knowledge, and that he will disappear again as soon as that knowledge has discovered a new form" (Foucault 1973, p. xxiii). Knowledge in a postmodern key will have no need to invoke an authorial figure, for "the 'author' is a function of discourse" (Foucault 1980c, p. 124; cf. Barthes 1977, pp 142-48). Human self is but a fiction conjured up with the aid of anonymous economies of power, technologies of domination, and regimes of truth colonizing the human body and numbing the mind to make it fit production requirements. Foucault's utterings about "confounding domination," "liberating local discourses," and "the possibility of constituting a new politics of truth" (Foucault 1980a, p. 133 and in passim) hint at a political agenda, although its precise contours are unclear. Since power equals knowledge for Foucault, one surmises that new knowledge may be needed to challenge old powers, but the propensity of all knowledge to breed oppression undermines the quest for liberating knowledge. The ambiguous status of truth further complicates the matter, although last period of his intellectual career Foucault sounded optimistic about the prospect for unraveling the knowledge/power/ truth knot. "It is not a matter of emancipating truth from every system of power (which would be a chimera, for truth is already power) but of detaching the power of truth from the forms of hegemony, social, economic, and cultural, within which it operates at the present time" (Foucault 1980a, p. 132).

Baudrillard's program is largely negative. "You know that my way is to make ideas appear, but as soon as they appear immediately try to make them disappear," Baudrillard (1987, p. 128) confides to an interviewer. "Strictly speaking nothing remains but a sense of dizziness, with which you cannot do anything." Unlike Foucault, Baudrillard rejects the very possibility of theoretical knowledge: "It is impossible to think that theory can be nothing more than fiction. Otherwise no one would bother producing theory any more" (Baudrillard 1987, p. 108). Nor is he sympathetic to sociological research, for sociology pretends to study society as real while busily partaking in the general mystification. "I am a metaphysician, perhaps a moralist, but certainly not a sociologist," inveighs Baudrillard (1987, p. 84). "The only 'sociological' work I can claim is my effort to put an end to the social." Baudrillard's political hopes are pinned on a spontaneous revolt in the form of conning the con man and laughing off the powers:

For in terms of force relations, power always wins, even if it changes hands as revolutions come and go. [One cannot] exorcise power by force. Rather, each person knows deep down that any form of power is a personal challenge, a challenge to the death, and one that can only be answered by a counterchallenge to break the logic of power or, even better to enclose it in a circular logic. Such is the nature of this counterchallenge—nonpolitical, nondialectal, and nonstrategic .... [W]e need a symbolic violence more powerful than any political violence .... This is why *parody*, the reversal of signs or their hyperextension, can touch power more deeply than any force relation (Baudrillard 1987, p. 58-9).

Derrida's ethical sensibilities owe something to Nietzsche as well: "[Deconstruction] amounts to annulling the ethical qualification and to thinking of writing beyond good and evil" (Derrida 1976, p. 314). Spurning the race to reach the bottom of things, pass a moral judgment, or extract a political lesson from the deconstructed text, Derrida is determined to undermine the very idea of an "author" as an autonomous, moral, politically committed agent. The text itself is produced not so much by the author as by the linguistic code which, through incessant intertextual borrowing, cross-signification, and metonymy, spurs writing and begets more texts. Derrida's project promises to lay out ground rules for deciphering the linguistic unconscious, tracking the faint traces of the other suppressed in the textual structures. The liberating effect, if such is to be found in deconstruction, comes from the resistance to all authority and truth claims that pretend to ground its pronouncements in the knowledge of reality.

Lyotard's program calls for a warfare against the monopoly on truth enjoyed by assorted orthodoxies. Anyone who helps local forms of knowledge get off the ground and challenges the wisdom delivered from on high serves the cause of liberation—provided one acts alone and claims no authority beyond oneself. Taking issue with Habermas's theory of communicative action, Lyotard rejects efforts at consensus building via rational discourse. "Such consensus does violence to the heterogeneity of language games. And invention is always born of dissension. Postmodern knowledge is not simply a tool of the authorities; it refines our sensitivity to differences and reinforces our ability to tolerate the incommensurable. Its principle is not the expert's homology, but inventor's paralogy" (Lyotard 1984, p. xxv). Spurn the authority, spin the language game of your own, and you will advance the postmodern agenda, political or otherwise.

Postmodern Epistemology and Pragmatism

There are things about postmodernism that make a dialogue with its proponents difficult and give unsympathetic critics an excuse to dismiss it out of hand. Small or humble the postmodernist narrative is not—it is as grand in its design, sweeping in its generalizations, and dismissive of the opponents as any narrative could be. If every narrative is a self-referential fiction to be met with incredulity, there is no reason to exempt the postmodern philippics from this verdict. A dialogue across theoretical divides will grow stale when the references to reality, evidence, and truth are abolished and the very possibility of theoretical knowledge is questioned. Such problems baffled many critics grappling with radical postmodernism (Benhabib 1984; Habermas 1987; Bauman 1988 1990; Featherstone 1988; Heller and Feher 1989; Kellner 1989; Ellis 1989; Wellmer 1990; Agger 1990; Gergen 1991; Rosenau 1992; Dickens and Fontana 1994). Still, there is much in the postmodernist narrative that is thought provoking and challenging, that interactionists could relate to, and that brings to mind pragmatist philosophy.

About a century ago pragmatists revolted against the metaphysics of being and threw their lot with "the philosophies of flux" (Dewey [1929] 1958:50). In his article "Does Consciousness Exist?" James ([1904] 1970, p. 4) denied that mind "stands for an entity," an "aboriginal staff," casting it instead as "a function in experience which thoughts perform." He opposed "the logic of identity" and embraced "a pluralistic and incompletely integrated universe" that *"may exist in distributive form, in the shape not of all but of a set of eaches."* Pursuing their critique of rantirationalism, Mead and Dewey rejected the correspondence theory of truth because it failed to acknowledge that "what a thing is in nature depends not simply on what it is in itself but also on the observer" (Mead 1929:428). Pragmatists opposed the then common view that "the process of search, investigation, reflection, involved in knowledge ... *must* be outside of what is known." It was an article of faith for pragmatists that we live in "a universe which is not all closed and settled, which is still in some respects indeterminate and in the making an open universe in which uncertainty, choice, hypotheses novelties and possibilities are naturalized" (Dewey [1927] 1950, p. 52), that "Uncertainty does not belong simply to values, it belongs to the facts as well" (Mead Papers, University of Chicago Archives, b8, f1), that "communication is a condition of consciousness" (Dewey [1929] 1958, p. 180-1), that mind "is social to the very core" (Mead 1934, p. 141). Reason, according to pragmatists, is not a substance privileged in its access to things at large but a biosocial semiotic process embedded in nature and distinguished by its capacity to grasp the world perspectively, in its endless possibilities and permutations.

The continuity between postmodern and pragmatist epistemologies breaks, however, at a point where postmodernists mount their attack on human agency. Postmodernists paint a topsy-turvy universe in which objects possess their owner, languages speak the speaker, texts inscribe their authors, discourses turn participants into their mouthpieces, powers invade the body and imbue it with desires, and epistemes send individuals marching in class formations to replicate the existing order of things. Such is the Kafkaesque world we are supposed to inhabit, according to postmodernist writers. It all starts with a seminal metaphor: The self (subject, consciousness, society) can be analyzed as a text; the stakes are raised when somebody claims that everything is the text; and soon we are asked to believe that *"There is nothing outside the text"* (Derrida 1976, p. 158, italics in the original).[1] Even at this point one should not lose sight of what is instructive in postmodernist ruminations, namely that reality is chaotic, evolving, elusive, that grasping it the language based on binary oppositions presents a challenge, that one thing can function as many different objects and one object can be impersonated by different things, that something is invariably lost and distorted as we try to present our experience to ourselves and to others. But all this is a far cry from saying that reality is a fiction and truth is a sinister lie.

Derrida (1976, pp. 48-50), who sees Peirce as a precursor to his grammatology, quotes him to the effect that each sign must be explicated through other signs in a never-ending chain of successive interpretations. Nevertheless, he reads Peirce selectively, taking from his semeiotics only what accords with the Saussurian semiology and ignoring the key role that Peirce assigned to action and feeling in the signification process. Saussurian linguistics on which Derrida builds his theory is binary; the world in it exists as the relationship between the signifier and the signified, the meaning is predicated on the bond one sign forms to another, and interpretation is compelled by the rules encoded in the grammar. Peirce's semiotics, by contrast, is built around the triangulation process that juxtaposes qualitatively different interpretants such as emotions, physiological reactions, conceptual representations, and collective habits. "We must therefore conclude," writes Peirce (1931-58, p.7), "that the ultimate meaning of any sign consists either of an idea predominantly of feeling or of acting or being acted on." Which is his way of saying that interpretation does not remain enclosed within the syntactic/semantic field where one intellectual sign begets another but is broken off for the sake of feeling and action which test conceptual signs, validate their meaning, and correct abstractions that do not mesh with things. The meaning of the red light at a street intersection extends beyond its relation to the yellow and green lights—it is interpreted, and thereby constituted, by motorists' action. If drivers come to a standstill when they see the red light, the sign means "stop," "cease moving," "wait for further notice." If they keep crossing the intersection on red light, the sign means something else or nothing at all. The signifying process is not short-circuited upon itself. It goads us to move beyond the symbolic domain into the world of practice where our thought has a chance to prove itself. Hence, the maxim, "thought is essentially an action" (Peirce [1877] 1955:29) and its generalization, "the unit of existence is the act" (Mead 1938:65).

Does this mean that there is nothing outside action, that reality is a fiction? Not so, pragmatists contend. Reality as a self-enclosed, immobile being independent from us does not interest pragmatists, but objective reality—reality insofar as it becomes an object of our collective signifying practices—does. Such a reality has our thought, action, and symbols already embedded in it. It is always already constituted reality, whose obduracy is due not just to things themselves but to our ingenuity and collective efforts which neutralize some connections, bring to the fore others, mix things together in a novel way, making them more enduring, dependable, and predictable than they would be otherwise. Extratextual reality is comprised by things and events bound together into a semi-chaotic whole by our emotions, actions, and beliefs. Objective reality is contingent on transformative action which starts with an "impulse" that sparks "perception" that provokes "manipulation," that in turn results in the "consummation" of a project at hand (Mead 1938, pp. 23-25). As a meaningful object, the thing is subsequent to an action, "The physical thing arises in manipulation" (Mead 1938, pp. 197-8). There is no objective reality without physical manipulation that brings human bodies in contact with other physical bodies and tests our hypothetical constructs. Through this testing, which is fundamentally social, the individual acquires subjectivity and the thing becomes an object. If there is a subject, there must be an object, and vice versa, and both are contingent on social practice.

The only element in this progression left in the postmodernist analysis is consummation, understood chiefly as a passive symbolic consumption, imposed on us by some exchange system and requiring little probing. An epitome of subjectivity as subjugation, the postmodernist notion of consumption is a curious vestige of Cartesian dualism, with its ghost-in-the machine imagery and the subject qua receptacle for divinely inspired codes. Humans appear to be in a permanent state of receivership, never becoming actors able to produce (as opposed to re-produce) the existing codes and conditions. That is not what pragmatists have in mind when they talk about human subjectivity and agency. Being a self-conscious, active subject is to be a thing among things, to have a body wedged among other bodies, to feel pain just like any other sentient creature, to transact with all the actively embodied beings, to duplicate oneself in a linguistic code, and more than that—to forge new codes and meanings. That is how postmodernists see themselves; everybody else is a dupe, a TV freak who "indulges in systematic, nonselective viewing," "the individual is non-existent," "the constitutive social structure of the individual, and even his lived perception of himself [is a mirage]" (Baudrillard 1981, p. 55; 1981, pp. 75, 86). This sweeping gesture has rendered a fruitful metaphor extravagantly farfetched.

Emergent Self and Its Objective Reality

That self-identity is discontinuous and emergent is a stock idea of pragmatist sociology. The self is conceptualized here as a nonclassically propertied object that takes the role of the other and makes a quantum leap, revealing a different face on a moment's notice. To say that the self is a social process, however, is not to deny its objective reality or to dismiss the problem of self-identity. The self has emotional substance and active presence that cannot be wished away—not if you deal with a Bosnian woman ravaged by marauding soldiers, a child told that mommy and daddy are going their separate ways, or a worker with a pink slip in hand, wondering how to make the next rent payment. If you preach environmentalism but refuse to recycle your garbage, declare support for trade unions but decline to donate them your time, pronominalize the word "individual" in a gender-inclusive fashion but let your spouse spend the night with a sick child—your identity is a failed project. Whatever continuity you find in the self's emergent transformations is valid until further notice. Self-identity is an ongoing accomplishment; some have more of it than others; it is a moral project we chose to undertake, with the outcome open to contention and subject to revisions. You will fumble on occasion, break yourself into pieces, then try to put them back together, always wondering if you are what you seem or would like to be.

I take issue with Gergen (1991, p. 7) who asserts that in the hypermodern world "selves as possessors of real and identifiable characteristics—such as rationality, emotions, inspiration, and will—are dismantled." Even though our selves increasingly come under assault—are "wired to the media"—we have not been turned into cultural dupes and adjuncts to power. The hypermedia carries within itself the seeds of its undoing. If the *"central problematic of the postmodern period ... is who owns the data bank"* (Denzin 1986, p. 200), then power in the supermedia age can be more dispersed than ever, for there is a continuous proliferation of data bases and their owners competing with each other for waning public attention. One can argue that the current problems have more to do with the unprecedented power-fragmentation that undercuts democratic policy making and execution. If "power consists in the monopoly of the spoken word" (Baudrillard 1975, p. 145), then the present conditions make power more porous and ineffective. There could be no "monopoly of the code" (Baudrillard 1975, p. 127) where everyone is potentially a code-maker, codes breed like crazy, and community standards are challenged right and left. Today's media does not speak in one voice; it routinely contradicts itself, fosters cynicism in its audiences, and frequently fails to sway public opinion to one side or the other. Not to be ignored are counter-advertising practices, public service messages, televised exchanges where politicians do their darndest to expose each other's hidden agendas. It is debatable how effective these practices are, but they make it unlikely we would confuse Disneyland with reality. Most consumers know the real thing when they see it, be this cold beer, safe car, honest effort, or genuine affection. Nor is the distinction between truth and falsehood as obsolete as some postmodernists would let us believe.

Knowledge, Truth, and Power

Postmodernists are far too hasty giving up on truth. Just because truth as correspondence does not hold water and truth claims are susceptible to abuse, we should not judge it useless or worse. Those steeped in the pragmatist ethos see truth as a historically specific, socially sanctified, practically accomplished, radically incomplete, and subject to revision unity of knowledge and reality (subject and object, theory and practice). We mold things into objects to make them fit our theoretical constructs just as we revamp our rationalities in light of our practices. This pragmatist approach goes back to Peirce who was the first to conceive truth as provisional, grounded in inquiry, and certified by the community of inquirers. Peirce's successors understood that truth is socially constructed, that it can be used as an adjunct to a power and sacrificed to political expediency, but they would reject as spurious attempts to model scientific truth on forced confession, to equate "the production of truth according to the old juridico-religious model of confession, and the extortion of confidential evidence according to the rules of scientific discourse" (Foucault's 1980b, p. 64). The medieval inquisition procedures that Foucault uses as a paradigm for truth production secured their verities in private by inflicting pain on the victims and submitting confessions as the ultimate proof. Scientific truth requires replicable experiments, collective review, and continuous revision. No one can claim a monopoly on terminologies, let alone truth claims, in a scientific community, where we find conflicting theories vying for attention and a great premium placed on new instrumentalities. Any truth claim is potentially open to challenge here. Power and truth are interlocked but they are not interchangeable. Politics impacts science but the traffic is a two-way street here, with scientists standing ready to challenge political claims and programs.

Pragmatists are known to cross-reference scientific and democratic procedures, and they do so because they see in the operations of scientific community a model for "detaching the power of truth from the forms of hegemony, social, economic and cultural" (Foucault 1980a, p. 132). Warts and all, science is the best available model of democracy in action—it stands for a community whose members take pains to inquire, examine the evidence, debate their positions publicly, form conflicting research programs and shifting coalitions. Normal science is known to produce power plays, even outright falsifications, but it is far from the caricature that postmodernists paint when they talk about the rigid, hegemonic, positivistic scientific establishment. When science and democracy part company, both pay a heavy price. Democracy is a historically specific mode of managing uncertainty that breaks the (state, party, class) monopoly on the means of production of reality as objective and meaningful, limits experts' control over terminological frames, expands the circle of people who could raise truth claims, and maximizes opportunities for everybody to participate in public discourse (Shalin 1992a, p. 266-7).

Having dispensed with things themselves, postmodernists put in their place a new entity—power in itself. It grows especially cunning in the modem era, we are told. There it is, entering our bodies, activating our desires, giving us selves, lurking behind cruel social technologies, punishing rebels and dissenters alike. As wheels of power keep on turning, new strengths are added to the old ones. Modern medical care and hygienic practices help power establish control over body; the institutionalization of psychiatry sorts out the recalcitrant individuals from the pliable ones; universal education lets power shape its future servants' minds; the abolition of torture and capital punishment spares the body for machine labor; organized philanthropy helps earmark and contain deviance; human rights and legal reforms serve to normalize official discourses and preserve the hegemony, and so on and on. This is a curiously functionalist vision which bids us to believe that everything happens for a reason and serves to maintain the existing order of things. One is reminded of Durkheim ([1915] 1965) who insisted that "it is society alone which is the author" and who endlessly elucidated functions, all ultimately reducible to one—to affirm solidarity and preserve order.

Too honest and perceptive an observer, Foucault (1980a, p. 70) realizes he has a problem. After reviewing his work done in the 1960s and early 1970s, he concedes, "None of it does more than mark time. Repetitive and disconnected, it advances nowhere. Since indeed it never ceases to say the same thing, it perhaps says nothing." Ever since Foucault (1980a, pp. 82-108) would emphasize "resistance," "local criticism," "*insurrection of subjugated knowledges*," "the efficacy of dispersed and discontinuous offensives." His new language signals the movement away from power as repression to power as management of desire. What Foucault never fully acknowledges is that resistance, rebellion, and opposition imply stance-taking and, therefore, subjectivity and critical agency. Nor does he fully come to grips with the fact that the drive to know is not synonymous with the desire to dominate, that there is power as domination and power as empowerment, power as control over others and power as self-mastery. Power does not always rely on truth to get its way, and truth can make itself felt without recourse to power. What could be more grounded in hegemony than the relationship between parent and child—surveillance, toilet training, rote learning, moral nudging—ample opportunity to squelch any traces of independence in the poor devil. Yet more often than not, this domination yields human beings capable to act autonomously and raise their own truth claims against the very society that disciplined and punished.

It is a lame "promise that truth can be spoken to power, as if truth is outside power" asserts an interactionist with fine-honed postmodern sensibilities (Clough 1992, p. 360). "We, like the Chicago sociologists of old, have contributed to an opiate of the masses; the opiate that says sociological knowledge will protect this democratic society from itself," admits another interactionist-cum-postmodernist (Denzin 1992, p. 144). These statements strike me as too sweeping. Sociology might not save democracy from itself, but the two stand to learn from each other. The Chicago sociologists' commitment to democracy and its institutions should not be trivialized. Jane Addams gathered the poor, the homeless, the unemployed and tried to help them at Hull House. John Dewey spent his free time working in an experimental grade school, honing a curriculum for progressive education. George Mead surveyed the immigrants' homes in Chicago and helped hammer out agreements between garment union strikers and their employers. William Thomas marched with demonstrators demanding suffrage for women. Were our precursors cultural dupes unwittingly doing the power's bidding? I beg to differ. The old-guard pragmatist intellectuals did not hesitate to challenge the power. Workmen's compensation, minimum wages, the prohibition of child labor, the food and drug laws, antitrust measures, women suffrage, electoral reforms, and many other legislative initiatives from this era owe their passage to progressive pragmatists like Dewey and Mead. These reforms were no victories for the powerful. To be sure, some of the progressives' hopes for a humane society might seem naive today, but this is no reason to deny them the courage of their conviction or dismiss them as capitalist stooges brewing opiate for the people. These were fighters who believed in radical democracy where "actual and concrete liberty of opportunity and action is dependent upon equalization of the political and economic conditions under which individuals are alone free *in fact, not in some abstract metaphysical way*" (Dewey 1946, p. 116), and who were willing to put their own time and resources into politics. Judged from their experience, one can challenge power on behalf of truth—not an absolute truth that is free from value judgment but a heartfelt, painful truth that is rooted in alternative theories and facts and is carried out by committed communities of inquirers whose subversive criticism democracies have to tolerate if not encourage. The best way to challenge power is to protect democratic institutions and let public inquiry, with its internal safeguards and dissensions, to run its course. This approach suggests a different political and ethical agenda than the one we find in Nietzsche and his followers.

Politics in the Postmodern and Pragmatist Key

Postmodernists who model their stance on Nietzsche's frequently invoke the realm beyond good and evil. "We wish to attack an institution at the point where it culminates and reveals itself in a simple and basic ideology, in the notions of good and evil, innocence and guilt," declares Foucault (1980, p. 228). Baudrillard (1987, p. 71) expresses a similar sentiment, "We cannot avoid going a long way with negativity, with nihilism and all. But then don't you think a more exciting order opens up? Not a more reassuring world, but certainly more thrilling, a world where the name of the game remains secret. A world ruled by reversibility and indetermination..." Derrida (1976, p. 314) hails his method as "annulling the ethical qualification and to thinking of writing beyond good and evil." All right, but what would a radical postmodernist unaided by moral labels tell a child who tortures a pet or uses a racial slur? It would be hard to explain that this is not the right thing to do without committing a moral judgment. If text writes itself and an author is but a vehicle for a linguistic code, then crime commits itself and no responsibility should be pinned on the perpetrator. Notions of justice, fairness, and decency are pointless unless there are moral subjects ready to answer for their deeds.

It behooves us to remember how power and desire were fused in Nazi Germany, in Bosnia, Somali, Nagorno-Karabakh, and like places where Dionysian rage ruled the day, state power was radically decentered, moral judgments were swept aside, and "objective chance" and "pure events" (Baudrillard 1987, p. 88-9) reigned supreme. Is this what life beyond good and evil is like? Nietzsche might have welcomed with this turn of events:

> *I do not account the evil and painful character of existence a reproach to [power], but hope it will one day be more evil and painful then hitherto.* We new philosophers ... desire precisely the opposite of an assimilation, an equalization: we teach estrangement in every sense, we open up gulfs such as never existed before, we desire that man should become more evil than he has ever been before. (Nietzsche 1968, pp. 206, 516)

If knowledge is a power trip, the question arises how postmodernists intend to use their postmodern wisdom. We know that Heidegger and Paul De Man, two admirers of Nietzsche and key figures in the development of the postmodern movement, were involved with fascism. Did their political engagement have anything to do with their philosophical stance? Not necessarily, as I have argued elsewhere (Shalin 1992b), but there seems to be few safeguards in the postmodernist corpus to preclude such affiliations. Because of their messy encounters with politics in the past, postmodernists prefer to shun it altogether. Having dismissed the possibility of constructive political engagement, radical postmodernists have embraced deconstructive engagement as their favorite tool. In the process, they have obliterated the line between playfulness and self-indulgence, irreverence and rudeness, iconoclasm and desecration, skepticism and obscurantism. Their hypercritical gesture turns hypocritical when they choose to do nothing about inane society they profess to despise. The talk about texts, difference, meaningful absences, and forgetfulness of being can serve as a convenient excuse for evading personal responsibility and practical action. Aside from Michael Foucault, who took part in the prisoners' self-help and gay rights movements, postmodernists are slow to take a stance, and when they do, their actions do not square with their philosophical pronouncements.

Modernity and Postmodernism

Postmodernists paint modernity in gloomy colors, discerning in it the totalitarian desire to control bodies and minds. The Age of Reason is a particularly dark chapter in human history that unleashed the unprecedented reign of terror. Late modernity, variously referred to as hypermodernity or postmodernity, has sprung new indignities on its victims with its stultifying megamedia, jarring electronic communications, proliferating virtual realities, sign exchange systems, unbridled consumerism, and so forth. There is an apocalyptic feeling in the air about "this terrifying postmodern world that threatens to destroy all of us at any moment" (Denzin 1990a, p. 146). Such statements should not be taken lightly; they speak volumes about the feelings of those who live them through; and they appear to be born out, at least in part, by the horrors of the two world wars, the Holocaust, the Gulag, the Khmer Rouge massacres, and other grim legacies of our time. Still, such verdicts should not go unchallenged.

Postmodernists' animus toward modernity reflects their belief that oppression has been expanding exponentially since the onset of the modern age, that the low-tech power binges of bygone eras pale in comparison with the high-tech domination of today. In this reckoning, a boss sexually harassing a subordinate in a corporate boardroom is a more sinister creature than a feudal lord claiming the right to bed every bride in his principality on her wedding night. At least today's victims have legal recourse, which postmodernists single out for scorn. Modern legal instrumentalities spare the dissidents' lives and protect alternative life styles once buried in the dungeons and closets of premodern societies. I do not think postmodernists have made the case that the lifeworlds were less colonized before the Age of Reason when the state, the master of the manor, and the *padre familia* had a monopoly over truth claims. And while it is true that scientists helped engineer weapons of mass destruction, they also stood for nuclear disarmament, saved lives through medical research, brought relief from disastrous famines, and did much to improve quality of life for everyone.

The postmodern optic makes a caricature of historical modernity. It fails to take into account modernity's capacity for self-criticism and self-renewal. You would never know by reading Foucault that Jeremy Bentham, whose proposal for a panoptical prison served Foucault as a blueprint for repressive modernity, roused public opinion against the harsh penalty for people stealing food, fought to keep children out of jail, demanded lighter sentences for sex offenders, opposed the judges' arbitrary exercise of power, and worked to curtail corruption in the legal profession. Nor are we told that Rousseau, the man of reason par excellence, rejected the notion of progress as a historical universal, blamed science for the increase in deprivation, cut reason down to size for its excessive reliance on cognition, and propagated emotional, intuitive knowing as indispensable for a genuine reformer. The postmodernist exegesis tells us little about such quintessentially modern figures as Hume, Blake, Novalis, Schleiermacher, Schopenhauer, Kierkegaard, Stirner, Dostoyevsky, to mention just a few names whose counter-enlightenment is part and parcel of the historical modernity. Long before postmodernists, Blake ([c. 1790] 1957, p. 459, 451) wondered aloud, "What is General Nature? is There Such a Thing? What is General Knowledge? is There Such a Thing? Strictly Speaking All Knowledge is Particular .... To Generalize is to be an Idiot." It was Schleiermacher ([1805-10] 1977, p. 64) who insisted on "understanding an author better than he understands himself"; Goethe ([1826] 1940, p. 72) who declared, "The highest wisdom is to realize that every fact is already a theory"; and Stirner ([1845] 1971, p. 219) who called for an "insurrection [which] leads us no longer to let ourselves be arranged, but to arrange ourselves, and sets no glittering hopes on 'institutions.'" In Kierkegaard ([1846] 1941, p. 182), we find this radical challenge to truth-as-correspondence: "*An objective uncertainty held fast in an appropriation process of the most passionate inwardness is the truth*, the highest truth attainable for an *existing* individual." One of the early heroes of the Age of Reason, David Hume, compared the self to a republic which constantly changes its laws, so that "the same person may vary his character and disposition, as well as his impressions and ideas, without losing his identity" ([1739] 1978, p. 261). Let us not forget also Ludwig Tieck (1797] 1978, pp. 14, 87) who celebrated irony as a handy weapon "to overthrow the boundaries which rightfully surround us in everyday life" and who extolled in his plays the multiple realities, where a modern hero could wonder, "Look—here we sit watching a show; in this show more people sit watching a show, and in this third show, the third actors are watching still another show." And how about this pre-postmodern insight into the vanishing self:

> It is all role, the role itself and the play actor who is behind it, and in him in turn his thoughts and plans and enthusiasms and buffooneries—all belongs to the moment and swiftly flees, like the word on the comedian's lips.... Does no I stand in the mirror, when I step before it—am I only the thought of a thought, the dream of a dream—can you not help me to find my body ... ? It is indeed terribly lonely in the ego, when I clasp you tight, you masks, and I try to look at myself—everything echoing sound without the disappeared note—nowhere substance, and yet I see—that must be nothing that I see! Away, away from the I—only dance on, you masks! (Anonymous [1805] 1971, pp. 209 169)

Historical modernity, as we can see, signs in every style and leaves ample room for countercultural expressions.[2] Its two most prominent intellectual currents are the Enlightenment that inaugurated the Age of Reason and the counter-Enlightenment articulated in Romanticism (Gouldner 1973; Shalin 1986). Whereas the former has been overplayed, the latter has been consistently downplayed by the postmodernists, who derive their inspiration from Nietzsche, this genius-freak credited with moving philosophical discourse single-handedly beyond rationalism. Postmodernists tend to overlook movements like pragmatism which eschewed both hyperrationalism and irrationalism and sought to combine the Enlightenment's commitment to rational inquiry with the Romanticism's critique of rationalism and capitalist modernity. A blueprint for a better life that we find in these pragmatic currents (we can call them "enlightened romanticism") diverged sharply from Nietzsche's (1968, p. 331) dark premonition that "humanity ... is on the point of changing suddenly into nihilism—into the belief in absolute *worth*lessness, i.e., *meaning*lessness." Radical postmodernists court ethical nihilism when they embrace deconstruction by innuendo and the politics of insult. As long as postmodernists remain deconstructive in their engagement, they are likely to remain on the margins of whatever may pass for social reconstruction in our time.

"I lay it down as a fact that there never has been a real complete skeptic," Pascal once observed [1670] 1941, p. 143). "Nature sustains our feeble reason, and prevents it raving to this extent." With Pascal, we can question the radical postmodernists' willingness to follow their skeptical convictions to the end. Even though our world might be lacking in logos, we should not turn our backs on reason. Indeed, we may need it all the more now that we know that ours is a damaged universe. With Pascal, Montaigne, Kant, Kierkegaard, James, Shestov, and Sartre, I conclude that because our world is wrought with uncertainty, what we need is not "will to power" but "will to believe" James ([1897] 1956, pp. 1-31). We will never bring this teaming chaos to heel, let alone make it fully rational, but with irony, good faith, and "a little help from our friends" (Beattles), we can find the courage to live and bring some sanity into this world. This is the pragmatist text for our time, as I read it.

Conclusion

It would be unfortunate if the above discussion led someone to conclude that what is right about postmodernism is old-hat and what is new is wrong-headed. Postmodernism is a protean intellectual movement from which interactionists stand to learn a good deal. I agree with Manning (1993, p. 88) that the "task of creating an orderly integration of the seminal and central ideas of postmodernists and powerful feminist critiques of androcentric social science knowledge with symbolic interaction remains before us." So, here are some thoughts on the issues where the cross-fertilization between interactionism and postmodernism may be productive.

Mass media analysis is one research area where interactionists stand to learn from postmodernists. Instant communications and replays (an air pilot who could watch on his monitor just as his disabled plane hits the ground), the media reporting that shape the covered events (the 1991 Russian Revolution), multiple and virtual realities (a white house official impersonating himself on a TV show), staged realities (a TV station simulating a car crash), radically self-referential realities (the media reporting about the media reporting about the media)—these startling phenomena proliferating in the mass media age can add fresh wrinkles to the interactionist notion of multiple realities and pluralistic universe. How does the explosion of the electronic media affect our sense of what is real; to what extent people realize that their perceptions are being manipulated; and what can they do to fight back?

A closer scrutiny bears the claim that the interactionist distinction between the generalized other, the significant other, and the self is getting blurred in the hypermodern world. How generalized is the generalized other; is the sense of community diminished in today's society; what role do convictions play in managing self-identity; are humans more likely to take moral holidays today than in the past?

The issue of postmodern self-identity and ontological insecurity invites further research. Is there a loss of agency; has the difference between "to be" and "to seem" lost its meaning; is ironic detachment more prevalent today; do individuals feel they have an identity or care to have any; which practices help sustain the sense of identity in today's chaotic environment?

The question of power requires more attention than the interactionists have been willing to give it. Who wields power in our age; does the postmodern condition promote the concentration of power; which counter-strategies enable agents to resist domination; how can we challenge power in the name of truth without endorsing the truth-as-correspondence thesis?

Of particular interest (to me at any rate) is the problem of chaos. In the Nietzsche-inspired postmodern discourse chaos appears as a negative reference frame, something to surmount or to bow to, rather than as a valuable resource in managing uncertainty. Are there constructive forms of chaos; can uncertainty be patterned and indeterminacy structured; which logic (fuzzy logic, informal logic) applies to the world of indeterminacy; how does the breakdown in the structures of (in)determinacy affect social change?

A host of methodological problems arise for interactionists taking up the postmodernist challenge. Is there such a thing as a forced or repressive reading of the text; how can the reader overcome the power asymmetry endemic to deconstructive reading; should the narrative emerging from an ethnographic study be seen as a collaborative product; does ethnography presuppose mutual disclosure between the ethnographer and the respondent; if participant observers learn something about themselves in the course of inquiry, will such an insight count as a discovery and should they be included in the report?

These are just some of the problems we face when the postmodern world-under-erasure meets the interactionist world-in-the-making. Let us hope this meeting will prove transformative for both sides.

Notes

1. Derrida has pointed out that this is a mistranslation of his words, that what he meant was that the text has no outside ("there is no outside of the text"). I do not find this explanation entirely convincing. Deconstructive procedures enjoin us to treat every thing, feeling, or event as just another text and forbid references to anything outside the text, except for other texts. Thus, texts are the only reality given to us, and whatever else there might be in the world has no expression in deconstructive philosophy. This perspective fails to recognize the vital role that qualitatively different interpretants play in our interpretative practices.

2. These historical realities make certain statements by postmodernists look anachronistic. Thus Gergen (1991, p. 7) singles out among the features distinguishing the postmodern self "the emergence of ironic self-reflection," while Denzin (1986, p. 194) observes, "Since Foucault, correspondence theories of truth have been seriously challenged." (What about pragmatism?) Nor can I fully comprehend this statement: "[T]he individualism of the Chicago School will hopefully expire" (Fee 1992, p. 37).

References

Agger, Ben. 1990. *The Decline of Discourse: Reading, Writing, and Resistance in Postmodern Capitalism.* New York: Palmer Press.

Anonymous. [1805] 1971. *The Nightwatches of Bonaventura.* Austin: University of Texas Press.

Barthes, Roland. 1977. *Image, Music, Text.* New York: Hill and Wang.

Baudrillard, Jean. 1987. *Forget Foucault.* New York: Semiotext(e).

_____ 1983. *Sumulations.* New York: Semiotext(e)

_____ 1981. *For a Critique of the political Economy of the Sign.* St. Louis, MO: Telos Press.

_____ 1975. *The Mirror of Production.* St. Louis, MO: Telos Press.

Bauman, Zygmunt. 1990. "Philosophical Affinities of Postmodern Sociology." *Sociological Review* 38:411-44.

_____ 1988. "Is There a Postmodern Sociology." *Theory, Culture and Society* 5:217-39.

Benhabib, Seyla. 1984. "Epistemologies of Post-modernism: A Rejoinder to Jean-François Lyotard." *New German Critique* 33:103-26.

Blake, William. 1957. *The Complete Writings of William Blake. With All the Variant Readings.* New York: Random House.

Dickens, David and Fontana, Andrea, eds. 1994. *Postmodernism and Social Inquiry.* New York: Guilford Press.

Clough, Patricia Ticineto. 1992a. "A Response to Farberman's Distinguished Lecture: A Closer Encounter with Postmodernism." *Symbolic Interaction* 15:359-66.

_____. 1992b. *The End(s) of Ethnography.* Newbury Park, CA: Sage.

_____. 1989. "The Movies and Social Observation: Reading Blumer's Movies and Conduct." *Symbolic Interaction* 11:85-97.

Denzin, Norman K. 1992. "The Conversation." *Symbolic Interaction* 15:135-49.

_____. 1991. *Images of Postmodernism: Social Theory and Contemporary Cinema.* London: Sage.

_____. 1990a. "The Spaces of Postmodernism: Reading Plummer on Blumer." *Symbolic Interaction* 13:145-54.

_____. 1990b. *Interpretive Biography.* Newbury Park, CA: Sage.

_____. 1990c. "Empiricist Cultural Studies in America: A Deconstructive Reading." *Current Perspectives in Social Theory* 11.

_____. 1989. "Reading/Writing Culture: Interpreting the Postmodern Project." *Cultural Dynamics* 11:9-27.

_____. 1986. "Postmodern Social Theory." *Sociological Theory* 4:194-204.

Derrida, Jacques. 1973. *Speech and Phenomena and Other Essays on Husserl's Theory of Signs.* Evanston, IL: Northwestern University Press.

_____. 1976. *Of Grammatology.* Baltimore, MD: Johns Hopkins University Press.

Dewey, John. 1946. *Problems of Men.* New York: Philosophical Library.

_____. [1929] 1958. *Experience and Nature.* New York: Dover 1958.

_____. [1929] 1960. *Quest For Certainty: A Study in the Relation of Knowledge and Action.* New York: Capricorn Books.

_____. [1927] 1950. "Pragmatic Acquiescence." In *Pragmatism and American Culture,* edited by Gail Kennedy. Boston: D. C. Heath.

Durkheim, Emile. [1915] 1965. *The Elementary Forms of Religious Life.* New York: The Free Press.

Ellis, John. 1989. *Against Deconstruction.* Princeton, NJ: Princeton University Press.

Farberman, Harvey A. 1991. "Symbolic Interaction and Postmodernism: Close Encounter of a Dubious Kind." *Symbolic Interaction* 14:471-88.

_____ 1992. "The Grounds of Critique: A Choice Among Metaphysics, Power, and Communicative Action; Reply to Fee and Clough." *Symbolic Interaction* 15:375-79.

Featherstone, Mike. 1988. "In Pursuit of the Postmodern: An Introduction." *Theory, Culture and Society* 5:195-217.

Fee, Dwight. 1992. "Symbolic Interaction and Postmodernist Possibilities: A Comment on Harvey Farberman's Distinguished Lecture." *Symbolic Interaction* 15:367-73.

Fontana, Andrea and Preston, Frederick. 1990. "Postmodern Neon Architecture: From Signs to Icons." *Studies in Symbolic Interaction* 11:3-24.

Foucault, Michel. 1973. *The Order of Things.* New York: Vintage Books.

_____ 1980a. *Power/Knowledge.* New York: Pantheon Books.

_____ 1980b. *The History of Sexuality.* New York: Vintage Books.

_____ 1980c. *Language, Counter-Memory, Practice.* Ithaca, NY: Cornell University Press.

Gergen, Kenneth 1. 1991. *The Saturated Self.* New York: Basic Books.

Goethe, Johann Wolfgang von. 1940. *Schriften zur Naturwissensehaft, Erster Teil. Geothes Samtliche Werke.* Stuttgart: J.G. Goethe'sche Buchhandlung Nachfolger.

Gouldner, Alvin. 1973. *For Sociology: Renewal and Criticism in Sociology.* New York: Basic Books.

Habermas, Jürgen. 1987. *The Philosophical Discourse of Modernity.* Boston: MIT Press.

Heller, Agnes and Feher, Ferenc. 1989. *The Postmodern Political Condition.* New York: Columbia University Press.

Heraclitus. [c. 500 B.C.] 1960. Pp. 69-89 in Philip Wheelwright, ed. *The Presocratics.* Indianapolis, IN; Bobbs-Merrill.

Hume, David. [1739] 1978. *A Treatise of Human Nature.* Oxford: Oxford University Press.

James, William. [1909] 1967. *The Meaning of Truth.* Ann Arbor: The University of Michigan Press.

_____ . [1904] 1970. "Does Consciousness Exist." Pp. 3-22 in *Essays in Radical Empiricism and Pluralistic Universe.* Gloucester: Peter Press.

_____ . [1909] 1970. *Essays in Radical Empiricism and Pluralistic Universe.* Gloucester: Peter Press.

_____ . [1897] 1956. *The Will to Believe.* New York: Dover.

Katovich, M. A. and C. MacMurray. 1990. "Toward a Postmodern Theory of the Past." *Studies in Symbolic Interaction* 12.

Kellner, Douglas. 1989. *Jean Baudrillard: From Marxism to Postmodernism and Beyond.* Stanford, CA: Stanford University Press.

Kierkegaard, Søren. [1846] 1941. *Concluding Unscientific Postscript.* Princeton, NJ: Princeton University Press.

Krug, Gary and Graham, Laurel. 1989. "Symbolic Interactionism: Pragmatism for the Postmodern Age." *Studies in Symbolic Interaction* 10 (Part A): 61-71.

Manning, Peter K. 1993. "Drama = Life? The Drama of Social Life in Postmodern Social Psychology, by T. R. Young." *Symbolic Interaction* 16:85-89.

_____ 1989. "Strands in the Postmedern Rope: Ethnographic Themes." *Studies in Symbolic Interaction* 12.

Mead, George Herbert. 1938. *The Philosophy of the Act*. Chicago: University of Chicago Press.

_____. 1934. *Mind, Self and Society*. Chicago: University of Chicago Press.

_____. 1929. "Bishop Berkeley and His Message." *Journal of Philosophy* 26:421-30.

_____. (n.d.) George Herbert Mead Papers. University of Chicago Archives.

Nietzsche, Friedrich. 1968. *The Will to Power.* New York: Vintage Books.

_____. [1886] 1966. *Beyond Good and Evil: Prelude to a Philosophy of the Future.* New York: Vintage Books.

Pascal, Blaise. [1670] 1941. *Pensées*. New York: Random House.

Peirce, Charles. [1877] "The Fixation of Belief." Pp. 5-22 in *Philosophical Writings of Peirce*, edited by Justus Buchier. New York: Dover.

_____. 1931-1958. *Collected Papers of Charles Sanders Peirce*, 8 vols. Cambridge, MA: Harvard University Press.

Plato. [c. 430-350 B.C.] 1963. *The Collected Dialogues of Plato*. Princeton, NJ: Princeton University Press.

Rosenau, Pauline Marie. 1992. *Postmodernism and the Social Sciences: Insights, Inroads, and Intrusions*. Princeton, NJ: Princeton University Press.

Shalin, Dmitri N. 1986a. "Romanticism and the Rise of Sociological Hermeneutics." *Social Research* 53:77-123.

_____. 1986b. "Pragmatism and Social Interactionism." *American Sociological Review* 51 (1986a), 9-29.

_____. 1988. "G. H. Mead, Socialism, and the Progressive Agenda." *American Journal of Sociology* 92:913-951.

_____. 1991. "The Pragmatic Origins of Symbolic Interactionism and the Crisis of Classical Science." Pp. 225-253 in *Studies in Symbolic Interaction*, Vol. 12, edited by Norman K. Denzin. Greenwich, CT: JAI Press.

_____. 1992a. "Critical Theory and the Pragmatist Challenge." *American Journal of Sociology* 98:237-279.

_____. 1992b. Review: The Heidegger Controversy: A Critical Reader." *American Journal of Sociology* 98:409-411.

Stirner, Max. [1845] 1971. *The Ego and His Own*. New York: Harper & Row.

Tieck, Ludwig. [1797] 1978. *The Land Upside Down. London: Dickerson University Press.*

Wellmer, Albrecht. 1990. *In Defense of Modernity*. London: Blackwell.

Young, T.R. 1991. *The Drama of Social Life: Essays in Postmodern Social Psychology*. New Brunswick, NJ: Transaction Publishers.

6

Signing in the Flesh: Pragmatist Hermeneutics, Embodied Sociology, and Biocritique

"Gradually it has become clear to me what every great philosophy so far has been: namely, the personal confession of its author and a kind of involuntary and unconscious memoir…"
—Friedrich Nietzsche

"The key to a personal poetic attitude of a philosopher is not to be sought in his ideas, as if it could be deduced from them, but rather in his philosophy-as-life, in his philosophical life, his ethos."
—Michel Foucault

Introduction

For several decades social scientists have been criticizing the disembodied view of society and human agency. "We now realize," observed Mary Douglas (1978: 298), "that we have unduly privileged the verbal channel and tended to suppose that it could be effective in disembodied form." In a similar spirit, Jenkins (1994: 319) objected to the view of culture as "located from the neck up" and the "traditional dualist idea

---

An earlier version of this chapter was presented in 2001 at the annual meeting of the Society for the Advancement of American Philosophy. A revised and extended text appeared as "Signing in the Flesh: Notes on Pragmatist Hermeneutics," *Sociological Theory*, 2007, Vol. 25, pp. 193-224. I wish to thank my UNLV students who took part in the 2003 graduate seminar on pragmatist hermeneutics where the ideas of this paper were fleshed out. I am also grateful to Vincent Colapietro, Hans Joas, Bruce Mazlish, and Erkki Kilpinen for their comments on an earlier draft of this essay.

that the closer we come to the body, the further away we must be from culture." Richard Shusterman (1997: 31) challenged "philosophy's image as an essentially linguistic discipline" and called to refocus philosophical investigation on "the nondiscursive somatic dimension of life." Kindred sentiments reverberate throughout the social sciences where scholars express their dissatisfaction with "the text metaphor [that] has virtually ... gobbled up the body itself" (Csordas, 1999: 146), highlight "the crucial role of emotion in the being of the body in society" (Lyon and Barbalet, 1994: 63), and advocate "the turn to the body as a primary site of social and cultural theorizing" (Turner, 1994: 32).

This chapter builds on the incipient movement in the social sciences aiming to complement the traditional concern for discursive dimensions of cultural life with the embodied forms of social phenomena. In particular, it seeks to extend the "paradigm of embodiment" (Csordias 1990) and the pragmatist notion of "bodymind" (Lakoff and Johnson, 1999) to interpretation theory, suggesting the way we can turn body and emotion into a hermeneutical resource. The discussion begins with classical hermeneutics which equates meaning with authorial intent and logical sense and then contrasts this tradition with the pragmatism-inspired approach that brings into the interpretation process somatic, emotional, and behavioral signs. After outlining pragmatist hermeneutics and biocritical analysis based on it, I focus on postmodernism as a discourse and an embodied practice. Next, I propose a line of inquiry grounded in the hermeneutics of embodiment, discuss its potential as an alternative to depth hermeneutics, and explore interfaces between pragmatist hermeneutics and kindred theoretical perspectives. The chapter concludes with a list of questions central to hermeneutical analysis in a pragmatist key.

Reason, Body, and Emotions
in Classical and Contemporary Perspectives

From its inception in Greek antiquity, Western philosophy has expressed deep reservations about body and emotions. Plato (1963: 62-63) set the tone in this debate, admonishing the knower to stay clear from somatically grounded evidence as inimical to sound interpretive practices: "[W]hen the soul uses the instrumentality of the body for any inquiry, whether through sight or hearing or any other sense—because using the body implies using the senses—it is drawn away by the body into the realm of the variable, and loses its way and becomes confused and dizzy, as though it were fuddled, through contact with things of a similar nature" (1963: 62). No one should trust knowledge compromised by the "contamination of the body," nor should any philosophically minded knower mind parting with the body when his time is up, for body as *soma* (flesh) is ultimately indistinguishable from the body as *sema* (entombment), which is why Socrates facing death calmly takes his poison as *pharmakon* (medicine) that once and for all will set his soul free from its corporeal body-prison (Plato 1963: 64-65).

We find a similar attitude toward body and emotion in the Stoic thinkers who insisted that "reason itself, entrusted with the reins, is only powerful as long as it remains insulated from the affection.... Once the intellect has been stirred up and shaken out, it becomes the servant of the force which impels it" (Seneca 1995: 25). The same concern animates the rationalist claim that the human agent is "a substance the whole essence or nature of which is to think, and that for its existence there is no need of any place, nor does it depend on any material thing; so that this 'me,' that is to say, the soul by which I am what I am, is entirely distinct from body" (Descartes 1955: 101). The prejudice against body and affect is evident in Kant's insistence that "[t]o be subject to emotions and passions is probably always an illness of mind because both emotions and passion exclude the sovereignty of reason" and in his commitment to the principle of "moral apathy" according to which "the prudent man must at no time be in a state of emotion, not even in that of sympathy with woes of his best friend, [such] is an entirely correct and sublime moral principle of the Stoic school because emotion makes one (more or less) blind" (Kant 1978: 155, 174).

Such a fastidious attitude toward the corporeal and the affective has clear implications for hermeneutics, which finds itself stirred toward the meaning uncontaminated by mundane confusions, transparent to all rational minds, and impervious to corrosive doubt. Spinoza, who paid much attention to the role of affect in ethical life, articulated with admirable clarity the rationalist hermeneutics' concern for logically purified meaning exemplified by Euclid's geometry. The latter "can easily be comprehended by anyone in any language; we can follow his intentions perfectly, and be certain of his true meaning.... We need make no researches concerning the life, the pursuit, or the habits of the author; nor need we inquire in what language, nor when he wrote, nor vicissitudes of his book, nor its various readings, nor how, nor by whose advice it has been received" (Spinoza 1909: 113). This logocentric perspective persisted well into the twentieth century, beginning with

Frege's identification of meaning with "logical sense" (Frege 1970) and Husserl's differentiation between "noema" and "noesis" (Husserl 2001), through Saussure's famous distinction between "linguistic structure and speech" (Saussure 1986) and Levi-Strauss's application of the binary linguistic codes to myth (Levy-Strauss 1963), and all the way to Gadamer's conflation of meaning with "what is fixed in writing" (Gadamer 1982: 354), Ricoeur's refocusing of hermeneutics on the "distanciation by which a new being-in-the-world, projected by the text, is freed from the false evidence of everyday reality" (Ricoeur, 1981: 113), and Habermas's equation of meaning with "propositional content" that has "*identical meanings* for different users" and lends itself to an unambiguous "true-false" adjudication (Habermas 1998: 10-13).

The desire to ban body and affect from interpretive practice does not guarantee that rationalist thinkers freed themselves from their pernicious influence. The very passion with which rationalists affirm their commitment to logos begs the question. As William James (1956: 63-72) astutely noted, philosophers with a logocentric bias display a peculiar "sentiment of rationality," "the craving for rationality," the ardent desire to make "the concrete chaos rational," "fuse the manifold into a single totality," and "banish puzzle from the universe." Dispassionate discourse plays here the role of an analgesic alleviating "a very intense feeling of distress," bringing about "a certain pleasure," and engendering the "peace of rationality." This passionate resistance to passion may have something to do with the world the rationalists inhabited, the world that was neither rational nor sane. Just think about Socrates condemned to death by the Athenian authorities, Seneca forced to commit suicide by the Emperor Nero, Spinoza excommunicated by his religious community, Descartes fleeing civil war to save his life....

The craving for pure meaning and scientific rationality bears further scrutiny when juxtaposed to the emotional turbulence stirring the rationalists' lives. Take Immanuel Kant, an unwavering champion of reason for whom murder was supreme injustice and human dignity the highest value. This is the same man who inveighed against "the disgrace of an illegitimate child [whose] destruction can be ignored" (Kant 1980: 106), urged a woman facing sexual assault "to give up her life rather than dishonor humanity in her own person" (Kant 1996: 178-179), and condemned masturbation and homosexuality as *crimen carnis contra naturaem* rivaling in insidiousness crimes against humanity (Kant 1980: 124). Hardly dispassionate, the tone in which Kant discusses these issues is bordering on shrill.

Now consider Karl Marx's disdain for bourgeois morality, his commitment to universal brotherhood and scientific rationality, and cross-reference these enlightened ideations with their progenitor's flesh and blood speech acts. Marx the man refused to acknowledge paternity of a child he sired with his housekeeper, declining to meet his son even after his wife's death. The founder of the First International enthusiastically supported his buddy Engels's ranting about the inferiority of Slavic people whom the "coming world war will cause ... to disappear from the face of the earth." With merry abandon he hurled racial epithets at his rival, Ferdinand Lassalle, calling him "the little kike," "water-polack Jew," "Jew Braun," "Barron Izzy," and opined about his son-in-law running for a municipal office that "[b]eing in his quality as a nigger a degree nearer to the animal kingdom than the rest of us, he is undoubtedly the most appropriate representative of that district [which happened to house a city zoo]" (quoted in Weil, 1970: 245, 23, 22). The crying gap between Marx's theoretical commitments and his recorded actions adds a wrinkle to his life's project.

Such examples are not meant to denigrate the rational procedures guiding our quest for knowledge, nor do they obviate the need to rein in emotions threatening to overload an inquiry. The point of the exercise is to illuminate rationalism's blind spots, its proponents' failure to apply their principles to themselves, as well as to furnish a backdrop against which we can better understand the somatic-affective underpinnings of interpretive practice and the embodied nature of reason central to pragmatist philosophy. Pragmatists resolutely eschew the "hypostatization of cognitive behavior" (Rorty 1982: 201). According to Peirce (1976: xxi), "reasoning has no monopoly of the process of generalization," "[s]entiment also generalizes itself." Consciousness, for pragmatists, "is only a very small and shifting portion of experience" which belongs to a far larger "universe of nonreflectional experience of our doings, sufferings, enjoyments of the world and of one another" (Dewey 1916: 6, 9). "Reason, anyway, is a faculty of secondary rank.... Cognition is but the superficial film of the soul, while sentiment penetrates its substance" (Peirce 1976: xxi). "'Reason' as a noun signifies a happy cooperation of a multitude of dispositions, such as sympathy, curiosity, cooperation, exploration, experimentation, frankness, pursuit—to follow things through—circumspection, to look about at the context, etc., etc. ... Rationality, once more is not a force to evoke against impulse and habit. It is the attainment of a working harmony among diverse desires" (Dewey 1950: 198, 195-196). When pragmatists talk about reason, they make sure to link it to desire; where cognition comes to the fore, the subtext is affect; and if mindful conduct is thematized, you can be certain that the specter of the body is rising in the wings: "Mental processes imply not only mind but that somebody is minding" (Mead 1938: 69). "The mother minds her baby; she cares for it with affection. Mind is care in the sense of solicitude, anxiety, as well as of active looking after things that need to be tended" (Dewey 1958: 263).

These philosophical intuitions have been vindicated in recent studies by sociologically minded brain researchers working in the field alternatively called "neurosociology," "neurocognitive sociology," "ethnoneurology," and "pragmatist neuroscience" (Brothers 1997; Massey 2001; Franks and Thomas Smith 1999; Franks and Ling 2002). The inquiry into bodily sources of reasoning has furnished evidence that somatic and cognitive processes work in tandem, that reason "arises from the nature of our brains, bodies, and bodily experience," that the "structure of reason itself comes from the details of our embodiment" (Lakoff and Johnson 2001: 4; see also Shalin 1986a, 1992a), and that the "common origins of emotions and intellect demand a conception of intelligence that integrates those mental processes that have been traditionally described as cognitive and those qualities that have been described as emotional, including the sense of self or the ego, the awareness of reality, conscience, the capacity of reflection, and the like. The mind's most important faculties are rooted in emotional experiences from very early in life" (Greenspan quoted in Franks and Thomas Smith 1997: 119).

These momentous developments call for a fresh look at hermeneutics as a theoretical discipline and a fully embodied practice.

The Project of Pragmatist Hermeneutics

What is pragmatist hermeneutics? In keeping with the traditional agenda (Bruns 1992; Ferraris 1996; Gadamer 1982; Ricoeur 1981; Shalin 1986b), pragmatist hermeneutics focuses on meaning, on discourse products, but it does so in the pragmatist spirit, that is, it broadens the notion of meaning beyond its familiar identification with linguistic intent and logical sense to include affective narrative, body work, and behavioral performances. Pragmatist hermeneutics builds on Charles Peirce's precept that "the ultimate meaning of any sign consists either of ... feeling or of acting or being acted upon" (Peirce, 1931-1935: 5.7). There is more to meaning than conceptual signification; the latter must be situated alongside feelings, sentiments, actions—nonlinguistic interpretants which go beyond symbolicity and have the power to signify through their iconicity and indexicality. Iconic, indexical, and symbolic signs are vital links in the semiotic chain (Peirce 1991: 239-240, 249-252; 270). When this chain is broken, when its links are no longer interlocked, the meaning process shows strain, and so does a larger social formation where this semiotic process is embedded.

The pragmatist emphasis on feeling and action runs contrary to Saussurean semiotics which privileges linguistic codes and reduces meaning to the play of difference between linguistic signs (Saussure, 1959; Derrida 1974: 30-44). Saussure warned us that "in a language there are only differences" and these differences are between units internal to the linguistic structure, i.e., "between sound patterns (e.g. *père* vs. *mere*), or between ideas (e.g. "father" vs. 'mother')" (Saussure 1986: 118-119). For all his critique of Ferdinand de Saussure, Derrida remains locked in the theoretical space of structural linguistics, and his equivocal acknowledgement that "Saussure opens the field of general grammatology" (Derrida 1974: 43) has more truth to it than Derrida is ready to concede. Nor is his gesture toward Peircean semiotics—"Peirce goes very far in the direction that I have called the de-construction of transcendental signified" (Derrida 1974: 49)—convincing, for the founder of deconstruction does not square off with the distinct character of various interpretants crucial to Peirce, assimilating instead all sign types to linguistic signifiers. Pragmatist semiotics, by contrast, works with iconic and indexical signs as well as their symbolic counterparts, and it holds the interplay between these embodied signifiers and linguistic symbols to be constitutive of meaning. The tension between logical-symbolic, bodily-emotional, and behavioral-performative interpretants is key to the pragmatist inquiry into signifying practices. Pragmatist hermeneutics stipulates that every sign has a body, that its corporeality matters, that the flesh of the sign interpolates its meaning, and that the signs of the flesh are what we must look for to understand signifying acts in their embodied richness.

In many ways this pragmatist precept is common sense. What Peirce advises us to do is to consider linguistic signs in the larger context of human practice, align verbal claims with embodied actions. The pragmatist maxim stipulates that each pragmatically meaningful term must set forth empirical indices bearing on overt conduct and engendering practical consequences some total of which exhausts the concept's meaning (Peirce 1955: 23-41). When empirical indicators comprising meaning work at cross purpose, we are forced to reexamine what and how we mean. There are sign-symbols, sign-indexes, and sign-icons, which sometimes mesh and sometimes get in each other's way. The interplay of these signs constitutes meaning in its embodied fullness. Considered from the pragmatist perspective, the hermeneutic process consists in the ongoing triangulation that allows the interpreter to check a particular sign against other sign types and ascertain their (mis)alignment at a particular point in time.

It might be useful to distinguish three basic types of the signifying media available to pragmatist hermeneutics: (1) the symbolic-discursive; (2) the somatic-affective; and (3) the behavioral-performative. Each signifying media is marked by a special relationship between signs and their objects. The symbolic interpretants include direct speech, verbal accounts, written communications, fictional writing, acoustic and nonpictorial visual signs—all markers that signify by virtue of a convention, a designated code. Thus, the word "love" designates a particular state of mind and body, the swastika represents fascism, a war medal vouches for its holder's valor, yet none of these symbols have a necessary physical connection between the sign's body and its agreed-upon meaning.

The somatic indices encompass emotional indicators, facial expressions, neurochemical processes, hormonal outlays, dreams and various bodily states. The relationship between indexical signs and their objects is marked by a certain compulsion; there is a dynamic force, Peirce (1991: 239-240) tells us, that binds this kind of sign to its object, with the index sign more or less directly partaking in the life of its object. Such is the relationship between smoke and fire, the weathervane and the wind, the thermometer and the temperature, the blushing and the embarrassment—the body of the sign is physically, or as Peirce would say "energetically," linked to the object it stands for.

The behavioral-performative signs refer to acts, deeds, habits—behavior insofar as it constitutes a role performance and establishes an iconic relationship of resemblance or likeness between the deed in question and a role model. Behavioral-performative signs are related to their objects through the agent's will that redeems a self-claim pragmatically through a string of actions that vouch for person's social qualities or underscore their absence. Helping a disabled person reads as a compassionate deed, volunteering for a tour of duty signals patriotism, regular attendance at your child's baseball games testify to committed parenting, refusal to return borrowed money to the rightful owner suggests dishonesty—such behavioral-performative signs have an iconic dimension insofar as they hark back to a prototype, invoke a cultural model which they resemble to a variable extent.

No clear line separates the interpretants comprising each signifying media—this distinction is largely analytical. Social behavior is a compound sign that mixes symbolic, indexical, and iconic elements which routinely shade into each other within the context of daily interactions. Thus, words have an illocutionary force of a deed when a person enunciates "I do" in a wedding ceremony or swears "I promise" while making a pledge. Verbal insults hint at an emotional state, eyes rolled behind somebody's back communicate exasperation, and a kiss on the forehead acquires symbolic value as a token of affection. Context determines the semiotic status of signifiers undergoing change across space and time, as attention shifts back and forth between the nondiscursive properties of discourse and discursive aspects of nondiscursive practices. By focusing on the trimedia, pragmatist hermeneutics enjoins us to explore the word-body-action nexus—something we can do only if we contemplate the full range of significant events, with meaning conceptualized as an emergent artifact that is historically constituted, interactionally sustained, and situationally reinterpreted. The task is to comprehend how various sign types complement each other and watch for inconsistencies and contradictions in the agent's semiotic output. Understood pragmatically, meaning is a multi-media event open to an ongoing revision rather than a Platonic idea or Frege's sense inherent in the symbolic structure and independent from its mundane interpretations.

In the past, the U.S. Constitution was deemed to be compatible with slavery, racism, ethnic discrimination, economic monopoly, limited political suffrage—none of these readings have survived the test of time. New interpretations continuously emerge on the hermeneutical horizons of the U.S. constitutional history. Rather than assuming that any one reading is authentic, irrefutably compelling, true to the framers' intent, or (which is the same thing) is the property of the text, pragmatists take the totality of its practical interpretations and embodied renderings as encompassing the Constitution's meaning at any given point in the U.S. history (Holmes 1982; Shalin 2005). The past interpretations lay out precedent-samples that guide agents seeking to instantiate a legal universal in concrete situations or predict the court's holding in a particular case. As the hermeneutical horizons within which the concepts are interpreted expand, the hermeneutical resources of society are mobilized, the interpretive skills of its agents activated, the new readings challenge the established order. Novel interpretations are apt to focus on the contradictions in familiar signifying chains, on the inconsistent biosocial performances of the key players in the established semiotic order. This is where the hermeneutical process becomes biocritical and hermeneutics turns into biocritique.

Biocritique and Biocritical Hermeneutics

Biocritical studies are a part of pragmatist hermeneutics devoted to the investigation of how various historical agents—from Greek sophists and Roman stoics to Nazi-era public intellectuals and Soviet dissidents—answered the challenges of their time by forging an identity for themselves and incarnating cherished creeds in their particular biographical circumstances. An offshoot of pragmatist hermeneutics, biocritique differs from zoosemiotics and biosemiotics (Sebeok and Umiker-Sebeok, 1991) in its emphasis on the interplay between the discursive, affective, and somatic signifying practices, on symbolically mediated behavioral processes conspicuously absent in lower organisms (e.g., in fish extensively studied by biosemioticians), or present only in a rudimentary fashion (e.g., in proto-sapient primates studied by ethologists). Biosocial semiotics is an exercise in pragmatist hermeneutics that examines symbolic systems by systematically linking the agent's symbolic corpus to its emotional-behavioral output. This can be a body of fiction, an ideological creed, a theoretical program—any conventional semiotic product found in society whose meaning is interpreted not only from the standpoint of logical coherence and discursive intent but also in light of nondiscursive practices embedded in the author's life. Affective ambivalence and behavioral non-sequiturs are as central to biocritical inquiry as discursive contradictions and grammatical inconsistencies.

The biocritical approach does pretty much the same thing as standard biographical accounts, except that it frames the Greek *bios*—life—in the broadest possible sense and pays close attention to the discrepancies between biographical corpus and theoretical output. Biocritical analysis explores *bios theoretikos* and *bios philosophicus*—life informed by principles and principles embodied in life. The inquiry centers on the manner in which historical agents integrate their *vita activa, vita contemplativa,* and *vita voluptuosa,* with the authorial discourse systematically examined in light of the author's bodily, emotional, and behavioral outputs. Biocritics sample the agent's discursive tokens, emotional markers, bodily indicators, ingrained habits, and discrete acts in an attempt to figure out how they hang together, what a given theoretical precept means in practical terms. Surveying the semiotic continuum, one zeros in on the breaks in the agent's semiotic production, the ever-changing gap between words, emotions, and deeds. Selfhood sheds here its appearance as an incorrigible identity, while human agency reveals itself as a stochastic phenomenon marked by indeterminacy, creativity, and hubris—just as Michel de Montaigne saw it some four hundred years ago:

> [A]ny one who turns his prime attention on to himself will hardly ever find himself in the same state twice.... Every sort of contradiction can be found in me, depending on some twist or attribute: timid, insolent; chaste, lecherous; talkative, taciturn; tough, sickly; clever, dull; brooding, affable; lying, truthful; learned, ignorant; generous, miserly and then prodigal—I can see something of all that in myself, depending on how I gyrate; and anyone who studies himself attentively finds in himself and in his very judgment this whirring about and this discordancy. There is nothing I can say about myself as a whole simply and completely, without intermingling and ad-mixture. The most universal article of my own Logic is DISTINGUO. (Montaigne 1987: 377)

Pragmatist hermeneutics is built on the premise that the pragmatic-discursive misalignment is an ontological condition. No matter how hard we try to practice what we preach, we find ourselves in situations where our deeds do not match our words, where our affective indices are at cross-purpose with our verbal stance. Or else, we may deliver more than we promise, more than anybody had reason to expect, sur-prising ourselves in the process. It is the mark of ethical life that we not only try to resolve discursive contradictions but also track emotional ambivalence and behavioral non-sequiturs, and then seek to realign our verbal attitudes with our emotional posture and practical conduct. When we fail to bring our discursive-symbolic corpus in line with our behavioral-affective indicators, we are reminded about the inconsisten-cies across the signifying media and the need to work harder in bodying forth our discourse.

Embodied Agency and the Economy of Signification

Take a routine speech act in which we focus on the speaker's verbal intent and try to figure out what the interlocutor has in mind. As we come to terms with a stated meaning, we also listen carefully to the voice, to its illocutionary thrust, and watch for translocutionary signs, eager to grasp the mind as a totality of the agent's mindings. "I love you" is a string of characters in English language that triggers in the person for whom the words are intended certain attitudes and expectations. These are verbal tokens waiting to be redeemed in the flesh. It matters how the love is professed, what the body posture says, whether the agent's voice trembles or evinces signs of irony. One wants to make sure that discursive tokens of affection are reinforced by emotional offerings, that the body indicia vouchsafe for the words of love. We know what it means to *talk the talk* and *walk the walk*, but this dyad is incomplete without the third leg—to *rock the rock*. Those unwilling or unable to sweat it out, to assume a proper bodily stance and generate a believable affective display, risk having their performances doubted. By professing love, we open the hermeneutical horizons onto the future and imply certain lines of conduct which can redeem discursive tokens in the flesh and practically validate emotional displays. You better know how to swoon and sway if you wish your love declaration to mean pragmatically what it signifies discursively, and when your relevant body indicia point in the wrong direction, your love proclamations will leave something to be desired.

Steven Gordon (1990: 154) suggests that body arousal is not required for an emotion. This valid point threatens to obscure the invaluable contribution that somatic markers make to ascertaining emotionally-charged significations. When Louis Renault (Claude Raines), a police inspector from the movie "Casablanca," walks into Rick's joint and says, "I'm shocked, shocked to see that gambling is going on here!" we know he does not really mean it because the discourse work is not matched by somatic performances or reflected in the inspector's subsequent deeds. The practical interpretive process scans the entire word-body-action arc, ascertaining the alignment between symbolic, indexical, and iconic signs.

Action-qua-role performance mobilizes all three signifying media—it entails a symbolic code, a somatic-affective display, and a behavioral-agentic performance. Behavior is iconic insofar as the typical course of action it follows "resembles" (in the Peircean sense of the word) a role model performance expected in a given culture under certain circumstances. Like a moving picture, proper social behavior exhibits likeness to its prototype. The fewer the points of similarity between the presented behavioral icon and a culturally certified role model, the weaker the agent's claim to a given selfhood. Words, emotions, and actions each signify in their special ways, forcing us to watch closely how the discursive, the affective, and the behavioral signs coalesce into a whole. Both as interpreters and as performers, human agents continuously triangulate the signifying markers, check for the (mis)alignment across the signifying media, and look for breaks in the semiotic chain casting shadow on the true meaning of agent's words. These gaps are rarely absent; they keep reemerging, resurfacing, straining the fragile semiotic chains that bind us into a social whole, all the while reminding us that the pragmatic-discursive misalignment is at the heart of the human condition.

Our emotional experience is sedimented in the soma; it leaves traces in the body circuits and manifests itself in the functional brain networks, the hormonal equilibrium, the neurochemical balances, the affective structures, persistent moods and mood disorders. The sociological theory sensitive to the corporeal dimension of the social order cannot confine itself to the imprints that culture makes on its normative, discursive by-products but must look for the characteristic signatures that culture leaves on the human body through which human agency signs itself in the flesh (Bourdieu 1977, 1984). The historically situated agency mobilizes the semiotic resources of the body, integrates them into a corporeal selfhood, and thereby reproduces the social order in the process that continuously loops onto itself. The physiological machinery is set in motion to assure the agent strikes a proper attitude, the body indicia vouchsafe the affective stance called for by the situation, the verbal narrative grounds the body posture in the appropriate discourse, and overt behavior reinforces the assumed emotional stance through a line of action amenable to further discursive and affective validation. Human agency achieves its goal when the principal signifying practices—discourse work, body work, and action work—operate in concert to produce a selfhood the agent can legitimately claim its own in the situation at hand. This identity does not automatically transcend the situation; it is good until further notice, and it must be reconstituted with every new encounter.

Affect and Action as Vital Links in the Semiotic Chain

Now picture the televangelist Jimmy Swaggart, a one-time crusader against filth in America. His message had an explicit discursive content—prostitution, pornography, sex outside marriage are loathsome acts violating Christian teachings. This message was delivered in a strenuous fashion, the speaker's voice evincing the powerful affect the subject evoked in his body. You could sense the agent's wet-wiring moving into high gear—the man's blood pressure rising, the adrenaline surging through his body, the feelings amplified by the powerful feedback from the live audience and millions more watching his histrionics on national TV. The outward emotions functioned here as indices, biosocial signs simultaneously conveying emotional intensity and the message's social import. The fleshed-out image the speaker communicated to the audience served as an icon exemplifying the lofty role of a committed preacher that this agent sought to impersonate.

As it turned out, Jimmy Swaggart did not practice what he preached. While he was exhorting Americans to cleanse themselves from sexual filth, Swaggart was patronizing prostitutes. When the truth came out, urgent steps had to be taken to bridge the gap between the discursive self and its profane incarnations. At first, we were led to believe that the alleged sexual acts with prostitutes did not happen. Then, one could have inferred from the explanations proffered that this man of the cloth was visiting with prostitutes to save their immortal souls. Finally, Jimmy Swaggart broke down and reverted to the tried and true: "The devil made me do it."

Most would agree that it is none of our business what people do in their private lives with other consenting adults—except when they take a public stance against the practices they carry out in private. Reverend Ted Haggard, senior pastor of New Life Church, put himself on record as the opponent of gay marriage and questioned whether gays have a place in the world to come, only to be exposed as an unfaithful husband and someone practicing nonconventional sexuality. As soon as this happened, he was reminded about his book, *Foolish No More*, where he warned his followers that "lying about a sexual affair produces 'the stinking garbage of a rotten sin'," that "if a church leader sins ... everyone within the church's influence pays" (Goodstein 2006: A22). And when Günter Grass belatedly revealed to his stunned compatriots that as a young man he served in the Waffen SS, he had to account for the gap between his current and former selves: "This teacher of generations of young Germans, who taught them to ask freely at home, 'What did you do in the war, Daddy?' failed to obey his own injunction!" (Gay 2006: A24). As such inconsistencies come to life, repair work gets under way. Patching the misalignment between discourse and body work requires tinkering with both sides of the equation—the linguistic stance and its pragmatic renderings. This is a standard strategy deployed in such situations. We offer discursive tokens redeemable in the flesh and perform deeds amenable to discursive validation, and all along "give" and "give off" emotions called for by the situation (Goffman 1959: 32-51) as a running commentary on the ever-changing gap between our words and deeds. Emotions are bodily indices that let us know when mind is out of joint with its mindings.

To be sure, we can separate the pragmatically rendered self from the discursive claims to a selfhood, the meaning of what Jimmy Swaggart was saying from the practical significance of what he was doing outside the glare of TV cameras. While this standard practice suffices for many purposes, glossing over the pragmatic output short circuits the interpretive process and impoverishes the hermeneutical resources available to us in everyday life. Pragmatist hermeneutics bids us to treat mind's discursive offerings as tokens or verbal claims waiting to be redeemed in the flesh, to be vouchsafed by iconic behavioral performances that replicate in deed a symbolic chain the agent inserts itself in or sets in motion. Such a pursuit of meaning encompasses the semiotic life of the entire body, its voice as well as its discourse. Voice contrives to turn our attention away from itself toward the intended conceptual meaning, but it is hardly a neutral carrier indifferent to the encoded message. We take special care to track both voice and discourse, intonation and reference, significant and nonsignificant gestures. Having mastered communication based on intentional signifying acts, humans did not lose their capacity or need to interpret unencoded gestures and unscripted enselfments, which furnish an invaluable context for our linguistic behavior (Mead, 1934; Shalin 2000). Pragmatist hermeneutics grasps communication in its totality, as an embodied semiotic event whose constituent parts are separable only in abstraction. The semiotic chain signifies conceptually as well as corporeally, its tonal substance bearing on its ideational content.

We may say that voice is silently present in every discourse; the two carry on a dialogue, constantly reminding us that every sign has a body which no discursive efforts can completely efface. This dialectic of voice and discourse is central to pragmatist hermeneutics as a hermeneutics of historically corporealized agency and to biocritique as a study of live semiotic chains. The focus is on signifying (intentionally communicative) and asignifying (unintentionally meaningful) acts that form a semiotic chain comprised of verbal symbols, emotional displays, body language, neurophysiological processes, behavioral forays, dissimulative gambits, immediate consequences, and long-term unanticipated outcomes. The rhetoric of "unconscious" comes in handy here, as it thematizes the nondiscursive properties of discourse and illuminates the discursive-pragmatic misalignment. We should note that Freudian and pragmatist hermeneutics have a certain affinity, especially when it comes to ambivalence as a sign of conflicted agency, although the psychoanalytic craving for "depth" wedded to "reductionist" methodology and privileging of sexual affect over other somatic-affective indices are inimical to the pragmatist interest in phenomena insofar as they come to the surface and embody themselves in overlaying signs. "Depth" can be a shallow metaphor we resort to when we get impatient with the bewildering array of surfaces vying for our attention. Hence, I will call the present undertaking "surface hermeneutics."

The pragmatist perspective on meaning brings into sharp focus a special role that our feelings, sentiments, and emotionally charged narratives play in forging semiotic chains. It is sensitive to emotional overtones signaling behavioral proclivities enciphered in discursive products. In this respect, pragmatists follow Spinoza the ethicist with his keen awareness of body affections rather than Spinoza the metaphysician with his craving for logically immaculate meaning. As Spinoza pointed out in his *Ethics*, emotion is a substance that diminishes or increases our capacity for action: "By Emotion (affectus) I understand the modification of the body by which the power of action in the body is increased or diminished, aided or restrained, and at the same time the ideas of these modifications" (Spinoza 1910: 84-85). Notice that ideas, according to Spinoza, are emotionally charged, and emotions are discursively framed. Looked at from this angle, bodies poised for action are affectively wound; the emotions they evince serve as clues to the kind of selfhood one is apt to body forth. Emotions are bound to the corporeal and ideational processes, serving as their virtual indexes waiting to be eventualized. Emotions signal that things are getting personal, that stakes are rising, that body circuits are activated, that one may be forced to take a stance, that behavioral options are being considered, evaluated, aborted, tried out and acted upon. Affective reason does not have much respect for the boundaries set by pure reason; it is more sensitive to the demands of practical reason, but the latter has to pay heed to emotions, lest the latter overwhelm the agent's moral commitments. Emotions are nondiscursive narratives, exquisitely expressive means through which primates sign in the flesh their motions to themselves and to others. The agent attuned to its own ambivalence will not be content to straddle discourse but will ride an emotion toward a fresh narrative and an alternative paradigm. Affective narratives are only partially accessible to consciousness; the experienced onlookers may glean emotional stirrings which escape the agent's control and self-reflection and which furnish valuable insights into the life of meaning. Bodyminding eludes the agent's "I," which grasps its mindings indirectly and retrospectively through its "Me's" objectified in various products and reflected in other agents' reactions (Mead 1934).

With the groundwork in place, I now turn to specific domains where the project of pragmatist hermeneutics offers a potentially fruitful line of inquiry and furnish a few examples of biocritical analysis.

Postmodernism as Discourse and Embodied Practice

An intriguing feature of the postmodern discourse is its proponents' tendency to dissolve existence into discourse, into a never ending play of linguistic differences where material effects evaporate, affect is repressed, and simulation reigns supreme. With the notable exception of Michel Foucault, the pioneers of postmodernism picture human agents as talking heads who relate to the world and their fellow human beings primarily through the symbolic media. However, the deconstructive flight from corporeality into disembodied textuality does not mean that the interpreter escapes the siren voice of the flesh. Like their rationalist counterparts, postmodernist writings are dripping with raw emotionality and extratextual reference.

Consider Gilles Deleuze's memories about his college years, his reminiscences about classical philosophy and the hard time he had with mastering the masters. Here is a colorful excerpt in which Deleuze communicates his feelings about the likes of Plato and Hegel: "What got me by during that period was conceiving of the history of philosophy as a kind of assf[--]k, or, what amounts to the same thing, an immaculate conception. I imagined myself approaching an author from behind and giving him a child that would indeed be his but would nonetheless be monstrous" (Deleuze and Guattari, 1987: x). Here is another passage, a prescription that Deleuze and Guattari offer on how to become what they call "body without organs" or "masochistic body [that] has its sadist or whore sew it up; the eyes, the anus, urethra, breasts, and nose are sewn up. It has itself strung up to stop the organs from working; flayed, as if the organs clung to the sin; sodomized, smothered, to make sure everything is sealed up" (Deleuze and Guattari, 1987: 150). Whatever their propositional content, such statements are notable for their nondiscursive properties. This is the text rich in affective markers; it stands out by its raw iconicity that breathes emotional cruelty disguised as playfulness and sarcasm. The metaphors are starkly corporeal, the verbal tokens are laden with violent sentiments lurking beneath the discursive veneer.

Affectively charged metaphors leap from the pages of Lyotard's *Libidinal Economy* where the author renounces "terror" as a form of organized repression but cheerfully embraces random "violence" as an expression of unfettered political creativity. Having denounced "critique as imperialism and theory as racism," Lyotard hails "red cruelty [which] destroy[s] instantiated appropriations, powers" (Lyotard 1993: 114) and heaps scorn on Marx, who makes his appearance in this text as "the Old

Man," "a young woman," and "a stray bisexual assemblage" (Lyotard 1993: 96). This rhetorical figure of abuse is striking for a postmodernist who began his carrier as a radical left-wing intellectual only to shun his youthful Marxism, albeit without shedding the affective baggage of militant radicalism. Instructive is also the fact that the accolades once reserved for Marx, Lenin, and Mao, the pioneers of postmodernism are apt to shower on the Marquis de Sade.

The references to Sade are common in the postmodernist discourse. He is treated reverentially as a daring intellectual who envisioned "profoundly egalitarian institutions of pleasure" (Lyotard 1993: 114, 104). The man is somewhat of a patron saint to French postmodernists who find in his honest cruelties a healthy antidote to the hypocrisy and injustice of modern society. Although postmodernist writers avidly dissect the Marquis de Sade's literary corpus, they have little to say about his real-life exploits. Yet, this literary giant did not simply imagine his sadistic pleasures; at every opportunity, Sade sought to bring his fantasies to life. You can find this out by placing side by side the depositions that witnesses made at his trials and the pages from his novels (Sade 1953: 211-215). This bard of nonconsensual sexuality honestly believed that if you torture your victims physically, sexually, and emotionally, and do so imaginatively enough, they will come to love the torture and the torturer. (I will note in passing that Sade is a prototype of modern revolutionaries, all would-be Raskolnikovs whose emotional deformities acquired during the ancien régime were fanned by the revolutionary flames into a full-blown rage replete with homicidal violence, power orgies, and frustrated sexual yearnings). Postmodernists show little interest in the all too real ways in which Sade signed himself in the flesh, in the fact that the Sadean cruelties were more than literary tropes. They reassure us that "[t]he precise object of 'sadism' is not the other, neither his body, nor his sovereignty: it is everything that might have been said" (Foucault 1998: 96), that "the sole Sadean universe is the universe of his discourse," which should be treated "according to a principle of tact" (Barthes 1976: 36, 170). This indifference flies in the face of Sade's biography, and it is, in my view, indicative of the postmodernist tendency to suppress corporeality and gloss over the affective-somatic substance.

Michel Foucault, who did not use the label "postmodern" but who is often cited as the postmodern thinker par excellence, is a notable exception in that he gave a prominent place to the flesh in his writings. His perspective on the human body as subjugated flesh illuminates a psychosomatic trauma at the heart of postmodernist discourse. Foucault's fascination with death, his image of life as a "suicide orgy," his paeans to "pure violence" and "the joys of torture," his avid participation in S & M practices, his opposition to rape laws because "there is, in principle, no difference between sticking one's fist into someone's face or one's penis into their genitalia" (Miller 1992: 27, 87, 257)—all these affect-laden references and behaviorally iconic symbolizations make you wonder if the theorist's bodied existence can be fully detached from his theoretical corpus. What strikes me in Foucault's verbal imagery is not so much its sexual content, instructive though it is, as its emotional intensity and negative valence. One senses the same fierce negativity and emotional violence in many French postmodernists. Derrida's polemics against John Searle, collected in the volume *Limited, Inc.*, is a good example.

Whatever validity there is in Derrida's critique, it is drowned in his sarcastic attitude. Derrida mocks Searle's name, which he derisively links to an acronym of a French company, and lashes out against the "dangerous dogmatists and tedious obscurantists" who find his deconstructive texts dogmatic and obscure. Here, Derrida engages in that species of symbolic abuse that French intellectuals have perfected into an art form. His discursive stance packs a powerful illocutionary punch, and as such, it is a model case of a speech act that accomplishes something behaviorally significant with words—it administers a calculated insult. Later on, Derrida admitted that his polemics were "not devoid of aggressivity" (Derrida 1988: 113), but just as he owned up to "this violence of mine" and professed his aversion to the "brutality" and "violence, political or otherwise, in academic discussions" (Derrida 1988: 113, 112), he had unleashed a scathing personal attack on Habermas, accusing him of operating "in the most authoritarian manner" and failing to make "the slightest effort to take cognizance of [Derrida's works], to read them, or to listen to them" (Derrida 1988: 158). What prompted this violent outburst was Habermas's decision to square off with Derrida's theories without directly quoting his works, which, according to Habermas, disregard the communicative properties of discourse and make direct quotation pointless.

We have to be cautious reading too much into symbolic violence in the postmodernist discourse. Its practitioners' discursive and nondiscursive actions form a vast universe featuring diverse metaphors and contradictory enselfments which are to be treated in context and carefully crossreferenced. Thus, Deleuze's virulent attacks on his intellectual predecessors must be balanced against the friendly attitudes he showed toward his students. The insulting manner in which Derrida occasionally treats his opponents is no more indicative of his character than the generosity with which he reached out to his Eastern European colleagues in distress. Foucualt's violent proclivities are no more noteworthy than his work on behalf of prisoners and gays. It would be a mistake, however, to gloss over such awkward episodes, to ignore the rich indexicality and raw iconicity of the postmodernist writing and forfeit an inquiry into the possible link between these agents' symbolic and corporeal practices, between their discursive output and biographical corpus. By matching discursive and nondiscursive signs, biocritique seeks to illuminate the emotional and somatic-affective moorings of various discourses and the socio-historical conditions under which they flourish.

When Michel Foucault strikes across the face the author of a novel featuring an unflattering portrait of a Foucault-like character (Macey 1995: 191) or when he goes out of his way to prevent the publication of an article unfavorable to him (Macey 1995: 337), he deploys behavioral stratagems that bring to mind his own discourse on power. When Baudrillard (1990: 131) blames women for their failure to see that "seduction ... represents the mastery of the symbolic world" and invites the potential victims to dare the harasser and beat men by playing their own game ("Take me into your motel room and ... screw me!" p. 157), he overlooks the fact that irony, sarcasm, simulations, and other willed figures of non-identity have somatic-affective underpinnings and shows a profound misconception of sexual harassment as a playful act calling for a playful response.

We must pause here and ask whether such queries amount to ad hominem reasoning, whether the theorist's conduct has any bearing on the theorist's constructs. Would our understanding of the theory of relativity change if its author, Albert Einstein, turned out to be a moral relativist in his personal conduct, as some biographers have claimed? Hardly. But then, the theory we deal with is social through and through, it grapples with the stance the theorist takes publicly and invites scrutiny of the claims to a selfhood, which is why the question deserves—demands—a serious consideration. Michel Foucault addressed this very issue when he urged readers to judge his written output in light of his entire life. This passionate intellectual turned his body into a subject of ongoing investigation, embracing toward the end of his life a creed reminiscent of pragmatism. One year before he died, Foucault gave an interview in which he contended that "at every moment, step by step, one must confront what one is thinking and saying with what one is doing," for the meaning of the intellectual's life "is not to be sought in his ideas, as if it could be deduced from them, but rather in his philosophy-as-life, in his philosophical life, his ethos" (Foucault 1984: 374). I take this as an invitation to all those taking Foucault's project seriously to connect his discursive corpus with his broader pragmatic output—an undertaking central to pragmatist hermeneutics.

Michel Foucault died of AIDS. Although the knowledge about the disease was rather limited at the time, Foucault knew for some time that he was gravely, perhaps mortally, ill, as the rumors about the "gay cancer" spread throughout the gay community (Miller 1993: 23-36). To the dismay of his live-in partner, Foucault did not tell him about his illness until the very end when his condition was impossible to conceal. There are questions as to whether Foucault had continued to pursue casual sexual encounters with anonymous and not so anonymous partners after he realized what fate had in store for him and his lovers (Miller 1993: 26-36; Halperin 1995: 143-152; Macey 1996: 475-476). No doubt, the reality Foucault faced was complex, ethically ambiguous, and we should exercise an abundance of caution before jumping to any conclusions. Pragmatist hermeneutics does not condone zeroing in on pragmatic occasions consistent with a partisan interpretation and glossing over the agent's incongruent signings. On the contrary, it tracks the widest amplitude of signification found in a given agent or a group of agents. This is why we have to follow Foucault's advice and not shy away from examining the intellectual's biography critically—biocritically, that is—if we want to understand the full import of his life's project.

Contrary to what postmodernists tell us, the author is not dead, biography matters. Writers do not forget or efface themselves in the act of writing, and when they try to, as Paul de Man did when he assiduously dissimulated his anti-Semitic past, they are reminded, even if only posthumously, that the symbolic media cannot blot out behavioral signs. As we learned after Paul de Man's death, he had authored dozens of articles in the early 1940s in which he expressed his contempt for Jews and advocated stamping them out from the face of Europe (Burke 1992: 1-2). De Man's escape into discourse and willed forgetfulness is consistent with the agentic-discursive strategy deployed by many postmodernists, beginning with their intellectual precursor, Martin Heidegger, whose discursive stance veered away from his pragmatically rendered agency.

In his signature postwar piece, "Letter on Humanism," Heidegger ([1946] 1977: 231, 200) condemned "the blindness and arbitrariness of what is ... known under the heading of 'pragmatism'" (231), a species of a broader intellectual malaise Heidegger identified as "humanism."

He spurned pragmatism and humanism because of their proponents' tendency to equate thinking with the "l'engagement dans l'action" (Heidegger 1977: 194, 197), a stance that breeds the "peculiar dictatorship of the public realm." To counter the humanistic bias, Heidegger urged the human agent to choose a heroic solitude where it turns itself into "the shepherd of Being" and a guardian of "Language [a]s the house of Being" who pursues "the world's destiny" and "the truth of being" forever denied to practically engaged thought (Heidegger 1977: 211, 193, 219, 213).

Heidegger's disquisitions are thought provoking, riveting at times. Yet, there is something of a reaction formation in his strenuous opposition to politically engaged life. Heidegger's verbiage would make better sense were his exhortations not conspicuously at odds with his hyper-activist past as a fascist intellectual and Nazi functionary. Heidegger's veneration of thinking ("Thinking towers over action") and his exhortation of memory ("Being is entrusted to recollection") underscore his abject failure to think through and recollect his own public engagement during the Nazi era—paeans to Hitler, tacit endorsement of book burning, willingness to inform on his colleagues, the pointed refusal to renounce or even to acknowledge the Holocaust (Wolin, 1991; Shalin 1992b, 2004). Like de Man's theory of writing as forgetting, Heidegger's programmatic anti-humanism and anti-pragmatism appear in a different light when placed in the historical context and aligned with his practical actions.

A closer look at the postmodernists' practices suggests that their symbolic utterances are rich in indexical-affective reference, that their emotionally charged discourse morphs into behavioral performances just as their affectively-charged deeds are encrypted in their texts. Derrida's ironically detached analysis of John Searle's speech act theory amounts to a violent deed calculated to deliver a symbolic blow (Searle has refused to discuss Derrida ever since). Lyotard's virulent attacks on Karl Marx have the affective markings of a true believer poised to trade the prophet he once worshipped for the one he is about to embrace (Mao Zedong took Marx's place in Lyotard's pantheon). The carnal imagery embedded in Deleuze's reminiscences about rival thinkers alludes to a poisonous experience of growing up within the French academia (a system notorious for its intellectual snobbery and ritualized abuse). Styling human conduct as an interminable simulation raises questions about Baudrillard's tendency to gloss over the somatic-affective cost of our supposedly simulative actions (one wonders if Baudrillard is familiar with sexual harassment first hand). Foucault's contempt for modernity, which he juxtaposes to the more tolerant ways of yesteryear, takes on an added meaning when judged against his programmatic celebration of tormented flesh (consider from this angle an excruciatingly detailed description of Damiens' death by torture in *Discipline and Punish*). Heidegger and de Man proved themselves superior intellects, yet some of the discursive coins they brought into circulation—"recollection," "forgetfulness of being," "writing as self-effacement"—are hardly redeemable at face value given these agents' incarnate lives. The stakes in the game of meaning are high; we are all inexorably drawn into this game as we make discursive self-claims and redeem them in the flesh, and the best way to approach this game is in the spirit of pragmatism.

The framers of postmodernism like to talk about "absence," "simulation," "fictitious presence," and disclaim references to reality beyond discourse. Judged from the emotional indicators permeating their texts and the material traces their actions have left, something appears to be lurking in the interstices of the postmodernist discourse, something tangible and real, a presence that refuses to go away. I sense here strong feelings and strenuous bodywork with which the harbingers of postmodernism are not always in touch, the body-language games that remain decidedly undertheorized. This is why I propose to complement the postmodernist notion of "simulacrum" with the pragmatist concept of "dissimulacrum."

If simulacrum is a copy masquerading as reality, then dissimulacrum is reality pretending to be a fiction. A simulator claims something to be there when it is not, a dissimulator pretends that there is nothing when there is something. The former wishes to pass one's mask for a face, the latter intimates that his is merely a mask. One is busy feigning enthusiasm and constructive activity, while the other rushes to dissemble pesky corporealities overloading the speaker's emotional circuits. One fakes total presence, the other feigns total absence, and each conceals and suppresses its affective-somatic substance. In short, the two are twins: the simulator always dissimulates just as the dissimulator invariably simulates; theirs is a sibling rivalry, the one can hardly do the job without the other, as they continue to pretend that they pretend or that they don't. Culture does not so much lose its body in these exercises as it whittles down its emotionally laden substance and masks its all too real affective-somatic deformities.

Like any historical movement, postmodernism has been bodied forth by disparate individuals who were often at odds with each other, pursued different political agendas, and left in their wake institutions, programs, and texts of vastly different quality. We should resist the urge to lump them together and cast their still evolving project in definitive terms. The strength of postmodernism is in its proponents' ear for ideological cant and power plays behind discursive production. Its weakness lies in the tendency to privilege the symbolic signifying media, neglect the corporeal forms of signification, and gloss over their own embodied agency and its socio-historical underpinnings. It is my belief that the early postmodernists and their intellectual forerunners sought to escape from historical trauma into a disembodied discourse, that their infatuation with sadism and penchant for violence constitute a willful gloss over the corporeal memories tormenting these historical agents condemned to live through the all too real horrors and assorted gulags of the twentieth century.

Pragmatist Hermeneutics and Ethics of Embodiment

"Gradually it has become clear to me what every great philosophy so far has been: namely, the personal confession of its author and a kind of involuntary and unconscious memoir" (Nietzsche, 1966: 13). This bold statement draws attention to its author's life, to the relationship between his discursive and nondiscursive significations. As Nietzsche's biography suggests, this relationship is anything but straightforward. The man who may have never known a woman in the biblical sense, who "derived his intimate knowledge of the female sex from hearsay only" (Kohler 2002: 73), solemnly intones, "Thou goest to women? Do not forget thy whip!" (Nietzsche, 1938: 70). A notorious social climber who craved academic prestige and failed in his professional aspirations, Nietzsche would come to renounce such worldly pursuits and resentment left in their wake, finding solace in philosophical musings about illustrious Zaratustra, "blond beasts" and "triumphant monsters who perhaps emerge from a disgusting procession of murder, arson, rape and torture, exhilarated and undisturbed of soul, as if it were no more than a student's prank" (Nietzsche 1969: 40). Should we pass in silence his confessions about the "terrible mixture of lust and cruelty which was always for me 'the witch's potion" (Nietzsche, quoted in Kohler, 2002: 72)?

This is exactly what Heidegger urges Nietzsche scholars to do: "What we must do is turn away from Nietzsche the man and Nietzsche the author, inasmuch as these are fields that lie within a context of human dimension" (Heidegger, quoted in Kohler, 2002: xvii)—strange advice, given Nietzsche's insistence on the biographical nature of thought. But then, we need not endorse Nietzsche's interpretive strategies that

reduce hermeneutics to "the exercise of suspicion" aimed at reality disguised under clamorous appearances (Ricoeur, 1978: 214). Nietzsche's
genealogical analysis is premised on the notion that thinking is but a
subterfuge for the "will to power," that primordial drives propelling our
thinking can be unearthed if we follow proper hermeneutical procedures.
Psychoanalysis is another example of what Paul Ricoeur called the
"hermeneutic of suspicion"—an interpretive practice that more or less
dismisses discursive products as rationalizations whose manifest content
conceals their true meaning. Pragmatism parts company with such depth
hermeneutics that finds its primary methodological tool in this reductionist suspicion. Nor is it to be confused with the "wild psychoanalysis"
(Freud, 1959) exemplified by lay practitioners rushing in their diagnosis
where the afflicted need lengthy professional treatment to come to grips
with the true significance of their symptoms. Pragmatist hermeneutics
offers no cure. It opens up the hermeneutical circle wide enough to include alongside discursive tokens the agent's bodily effects and thereby
expands semiotic resources available to the interpreter without assigning
a higher dignity to any one signifying media. Sign-symbols, sign-indexes,
sign-habits are all real after their fashion; they cannot be reduced to each
other or arranged in a hierarchical order. Pragmatist hermeneutics does
not pretend to get a hold of reality itself or reveal an authentic character.
It gauges an emotionally laden substance, bears witness to a presence
(fleeting though it might be), and highlights the contradictory ways in
which we sign ourselves in the world, all along trusting the agents to
connect the dots and realign their significations.

Anton Chekhov, the Russian short story writer and playwright, is
an artist who made much of the fact that our words are all too often at
odds with our deeds and at cross-purposes with our emotions. His stage
characters incessantly talk about falling in love, taking grand stands,
making amends, and going places, while they fritter their lives away,
betray confidences, attempt suicide, or dance all night long to forget
about the grim realities waiting for them in the morning—all that against
the backdrop of continuous emoting that clues the audience in on the
perennial misalignment between the actors' utterances and deeds. As
his diaries and correspondence show, Chekhov was very much aware
of the pragmatic-discursive misalignment in his own life. He equated
a responsible being in the world with the ability to take stock of and
realign one's words, deeds, and feelings—even though such efforts all
too often prove futile in the end. It is startling to see how this iconic
humanist who urged the Russian intelligentsia to aid cholera-stricken

peasants and worked tirelessly for the cause confesses to a friend that he felt "utterly indifferent to this disease and the people whom one is compelled to serve" (Chekhov 1977: 104). Chekhov's writing offer an invaluable insight into the historically shaped bodymind of the Russian intelligentsia: its somatic ailments, bipolar tendencies, emotional volatility, moral maximalism, ironic detachment and sarcastic vigilantism, the disparity between word and deed, the tendency to build castles in the air and sink into hopelessness (Shalin, 1986).

As Dewey (1950: 198) pointed out, people focused on discursive production may be sending different messages through their body language and actions: "Men who devote themselves to thinking are likely to be unusually unthinking in some respects, as for example in immediate personal relationships. A man to whom exact scholarship is an absorbing pursuit may be more than ordinarily vague in ordinary matters. Humility and impartiality may be shown in a specialized field, and pettiness and arrogance in dealing with other persons." The misalignment between our deeds, emotional stirrings, and public pronouncements renders human identity perennially problematic. This programmatic insight nourishes the pragmatist inquiry into embodied significations that seeks to reconstruct the long semiotic chains, pinpointing historical junctures where the cord binding disparate significations grows threadbare or breaks entirely. The interpretive process is focused here on the iconic markers, indexical expressions, metaphorical statements, and illocutionary acts embedded in a discourse. Of signal importance are also actions undertaken in line with and in the name of a given discourse, as well as somatic-affective indices that distinguish the standard bearer and the hanger-on. The failure to spell out the pragmatic interpretants of a discursive stance invites scrutiny, as when the Bush administration professes its adherence to the international law prohibiting torture while resolutely refusing to clarify whether "waterbording" counts as an instance of this kind. Such "escape from the pragmatic" (also known as "stonewalling") will be instantly evident to the interpreter operating within the horizons of pragmatist hermeneutics.

The same goes for the Christian doctrine that exhorts you to "love your neighbor as yourself," "turn the other cheek," "submit to the church doctrine," "walk in Christ's way." What exactly do these precepts mean pragmatically? Check the discursive-pragmatic alignment, and you will discover that the Christian Crusaders shredded these precepts during their jihad against the infidels, as they raped and pillaged all the way to the Holy Land. That did not prevent Crusaders from calling themselves "good Christians" and having their actions sanctified by the church. In the sixteenth century, the Holy Inquisition approved torture as an expedient means to extract confessions from the witches, conjuring up a macabre visage of a man invoking the name of Jesus as he tightens the screws on a hapless victim. The meaning of Christianity has evolved through the ages, with the violence against Native Americans and the antislavery movement, unbridled capitalism and progressive reforms, rank xenophobia and bold ecumenism receiving a nod from church authorities at one point or another. The pragmatist question of what it means to be a Christian (What would Jesus do?) is as problematic in our times as it has ever been.

The same multivocity is embedded in Marxist discourse. Its favorite shibboleths—"the end to alienation," "universal brotherhood," "authentic existence," "freedom from exploitation," "economic egalitarianism"—promise a pristine communist world to come. Frame these discursive markers in their twentieth century context and you will see that people claiming to be Marxists have relished violence, wasted millions in the gulags, tolerated hidden and not-so-hidden inequality, and abused power in every way imaginable. While Mao carried out his cultural revolution under Marxist banners, he enjoyed living in palaces and was served by an army of servants, artists, and mistresses. As Marx's own racist statements suggest, he was very much the man of his age, unable to shed its prejudices as he struggled to expand its hermeneutical horizons. What it means to be a Marxist (What would Gramsci do?) is the question yielding as many answers today as ever.

When Republicans take a stance on counting all the absentee ballots from overseas military personnel while working behind the scenes to invalidate such ballots in predominantly Democratic counties, we can spot a semiotic forgery and see through their grandstanding in the Florida presidential election. When Democrats clamor for recounting ballots only in the counties that favor their presidential candidate and maintain a stony silence about potential miscounts elsewhere, they invite a biocritical look at the incongruities between their verbally articulated and extra-discursive postures. When the sworn-to-chastity and committed-to-moral-uplift clergy abuse their charges, the misalignment between their preaching and actions is painfully obvious. The same goes for police using their night sticks for purposes unspecified in their manuals, judges whose court behavior mocks the notion of judicious temperament, teachers and parents whose emotional littering vitiates the emotional intelligence they seek to impart to their charges—the pragmatist imperative of watching how we sign across the signifying media applies to all of us insofar as we conduct an everyday hermeneutical inquiry into our discourse-body-action language games.

It would be ghoulish to take the cruelties committed in Christ's name as an interpretant of Christianity's significate value, just as it would be hasty to equate Marxism with human rights violations. There is more to these intellectual currents than witch-hunting and the power-monger-ing, but that is what each signified pragmatically at certain historical junctures. The incarnate actions undertaken in the name of Christian-ity and Marxism are tethered to their practitioner's somatic-affective a priori no less than to their discursive-theoretical assumptions. We can debate forever what this or that concept means, how much truth a theory in question has to offer—all such debates, as Marx pointed out in one of his pragmatism-tinged passages, would remain "scholastic" as long as they are "isolated from practice" (Marx 1947: 197). The meaning of a social theory, a political platform or a state constitution is ultimately predicated on the embodied actions rather than on logi-cal inquiry, on the actions that historical agents undertake within the hermeneutical horizons opened up by a theory and subject to collective experimentation.

The strictures of pragmatist hermeneutics apply to pragmatism as well. It is a historical enterprise like any other, championed by fallible agents eager to place their names on its masthead but not always ready, willing, or able to practice what they preach. Nor can we be certain about policy options the pragmatic stance necessitates, as the following statements by signature pragmatist indicate:

> Monopolies, such as can be created in our days, are most beneficent for the public [and it is only] the miserable tyranny exercised over the great businessmen [that prevents people from seeing this]. (Peirce, quoted in Kilpinen, 2000: 89)

> [A]ctual and concrete liberty of opportunity and action is dependent upon equaliza-tion of the political and economic conditions under which individuals are alone free in fact, not in some abstract metaphysical way. (Dewey 1946: 116)

Over the course of its history, pragmatism furnished theoretical ammu-nition for Dewey's socialism, Mead's social democratic agenda, Hook's liberal Marxism, Rorty's libertarianism, and Cornel West's prophetic pragmatism. What pragmatism calls for is an inquiry, prior to which our policies and plans are but hypothetical constructs waiting to be validated through concrete behavioral sequences. If pragmatists share any politi-cal sensibility, it is "civility," or if you will—"emotional intelligence"

(Shalin 1992a, 2004, 2005). To the extent that pragmatists display it on their banners, they will be judged by how well they body forth this civic virtue in their personal conduct. We discover what pragmatism means by following the pragmatist maxim for ascertaining meaning in live semiotic chains, that is, by measuring its proponents' discursive tokens with their emotional offerings and judging their creedal statements by the behavioral bounty their actions reap. We cannot allow inquiry to be short-circuited on meaning in itself and poke deconstructively at the theory's semantic contradictions; rather, we must explore how theorists exemplify their theoretical commitments in their own conduct, what performative contradictions they run into, and how the practitioners bridge the gap between their verbal and nonverbal renderings. Wherever the agent's theory and agent's action work at cross-purposes, we gauge the intellectual enterprise by the theorist's ethos and willingness to realign one's signifying acts. Meaning sheds here its privileged status as a logical construct existing outside time and space. It grows, expands, opens up to the future; it points to the deeds yet to be undertaken; it invites actions that may lend new life to the old meanings. To grasp meaning as an actual occasion in its corporeal forms, we have to examine its life *in situ* and *in actu*. We grasp the life of meaning—the meaning of life—by surveying the full range of its discursive and nondiscursive interpretants, tracking the widest possible dispersion of its pragmatic renderings, and assessing the contradictory ways in which it is bodied forth by the historical agents who have incorporated given symbolic frames into their personal projects. Meaning is the emotionally charged and somatically grounded actions carried out within the ethico-hermeneutical horizons opened up by a historically situated discourse. This concerns actions that were, are, or will be undertaken and legitimated within a given political-theoretical perspective. Hermeneutical horizons are ultimately the horizons of practical action, which expand and contract, merge with other horizons, or disappear altogether, as historical practitioners pursue their discursive practices. These practices are thoroughly somatized, inscribed in the body circuits continuously renewed by the agents through their discourse work, face work, emotion work, body work, action work, perhaps even gut work—any somatic practice amenable to semiotic control. For the hermeneutical horizons to change, it is not enough to advance a novel ideology, to legislate politically correct discourse. Rooted in our bodies, the old discursive forms continue to seep into our emotions and drive our conduct long after the new symbols come into vogue. This stance has implications for a theory of democracy.

As an embodied phenomenon, democracy calls for an affective presence. Its agentic texture is irreducible to a constitutional text severed from its nondiscursive moorings. "Judaism," "Islamism," "Christianity," "Marxism," "capitalism," "liberalism"—these are abstractions waiting to be redeemed in the flesh. Their embodiments depend on historical agents whose conduct is affected by the social currents passing through them but whose "conductivity" is a factor to be reckoned with, as we belatedly discovered in Vietnam and are now rediscovering in Iraq and Afghanistan. Society's fuses are apt to blow when its members' somatic-affective circuits are overloaded. No Bill of Rights can prevent a Columbine High massacre; charting clear legal boundaries and strenuously enforcing the laws can get us only so far in combating violence and abuse. Nor do political desiderata encoded in the nation's foundational texts relieve us from the need to muddle through, to act as "strange attractors" willing to embody democracy in the flesh, to repair the inanities of history and inequities of being.

If politically pragmatist hermeneutics is a quest for the emotionally intelligent democracy, then sociologically it is an inquiry into the somatic-affective conditions of its possibility, and philosophically it is a critique of disembodied reason. It matters for its practitioners whether society's members embody trust, tolerance, prudence, compassion, humor, or are weaned on suspicion, hatred, vanity, cruelty, and sarcasm (see mission statement of the UNLV Center for Democratic Culture, http: //www.unlv.edu/centers/cdclv). For the democratic project pragmatists champion to fulfill its promise, they have to find ways to realign, starting with themselves, the agentic substance of democracy with its normative-discursive canon.

The Embodiment Paradigm
and the Hermeneutics of Embodiment

The project of pragmatist hermeneutics builds on the embodiment movement that has been invigorating the social sciences in recent years. It has particularly benefited from the ideas articulated by Bourdieu (1990) and Goffman (1959), Shusterman (1997) and Colapietro (1989), Alexander (2003, 2006) and his colleagues developing the paradigm of cultural pragmatics (Alexander, Giesen and Mast 2006), as well as many scholars who have taken the somatic-affective turn in social science (Csordas 1990, 1999; Featherstone, Hepworth and Turner 1991; Schilling 1993; Lyon and Barbalet 1994; Turner 1994; Lakoff and Johnson 1999).

Common to social scientists in this nascent movement is the understanding of human agency as a somatically grounded, emotionally laden, discursively framed, historically rooted, self-referentially guided, and structurally constrained capacity for action. Taking their cue from Saussure, social scientists, working with the embodiment paradigm, angle to revise his structuralist tenets in the spirit of pragmatic paradigmatism. In most general terms, it is appropriate to say that the relationship between grammar and speech is analogous to the relationship between culture and body practices—both are mutually constitutive yet neither can be reduced to the other. But the seminal distinction between language structure and language-in-use draws too sharp a line between the privileged linguistic system based on binary oppositions and embodied speech acts relegated to the linguistic science's periphery. The chess metaphor Saussure invokes while elucidating his theory is particularly instructive here. "[A] state of the board in chess corresponds exactly to a state of language," observes Saussure (1986: 88, 22). "If pieces of ivory are substituted for pieces made of wood, the change makes no difference to the system." This metaphor shows exactly where the analogy between the language/speech and culture/body practices breaks down. While pieces on the Saussurean chessboard are dumb and mute, the pieces on the cultural board are self-propelling agents capable of transforming the normative structure that set them in motion.

Rules of chess are the same for everyone, they are generally closed to revision, those who violate them will be barred from the game. Rules of society are open to (re)interpretation and frequently ignored. As an approximation (and contestable one at that), one can say that all members of a language community play the same language game. That is not the case with society, which is comprised of many games corresponding to various cultural domains, each one anchored in its own code, with new grammars coming into being incessantly. As emergent grammars clamor for attention and siphon off resources from the dominant ones, the agents' creativity is tapped. The paradigmization-grammatization process we observe in the cultural realm bears little resemblance to the world of structural linguistics. A metaphor more appropriate for this domain would be society as a system of overlapping networks whose members are at once nodal points, transmitters, and traffic controllers. That is to say, we are all live wires through which social currents pass, but our conduct—conductivity—feeds back and reshapes the social networks from which we have sprung. Studying grammars-in-the-making casts the interplay between agency and structure in a new light.

Pierre Bourdieu has given a major boost to reconceptualizing the relationship between social structure and body. He took his cue in part from Mauss's work on body techniques—"I can ... recognize a girl who has been raised in a convent [for] she will walk with her fists closed" (Mauss 1978: 35), and in part from Marx, specifically from his *Theses on Feuerbach* that calls for "taking back from idealism the 'active side' of practical knowledge that the materialist tradition has abandoned to it. This is precisely the function of the notion of habitus, which restores to the agent a generating, unifying, constructing, classifying power, while recalling that this capacity to construct social reality, itself socially constructed, is not that of a transcendental subject but of a socialized body" (Bourdieu 2000a: 136). Habitus is the concept Bourdieu uses to bring into one continuum agency and structure, to demonstrate that "[t]he body is in the social world but the social world is in the body" (152). Habitus is variously defined as "history incarnated," "corporeal knowledge," "a kind of infallible instinct," or "deep-rooted bodily dispositions" which are triggered by social situations "without passing through consciousness and calculations" in a manner akin to an athlete making a split-second decision (151, 135, 159, 177). Armed with this concept and an ingenious theory of practice, Bourdieu (1984: 157) outlines a social structure in which dominant classes perpetuate their hegemony through the privileged access to "economic capital," "symbolic capital" and "cultural capital in its incorporated form." "[The individual's] position in the relations of production governs practices, in particular through the mechanisms which control access to positions and produce or select a particular class of habitus. ... the most typically bourgeois deportment can be recognized by a certain breath of gesture, posture and gait ... contrasting with working class haste or petty bourgeois eagerness" (Bourdieu 1984: 102, 218).

Bourdieu's research program was a step forward that led inquiry beyond Levi-Strauss whose preoccupation with myth and the discursive forms of culture closely mirrors Saussure's disembodied structuralism. But his socio-corporeal determinism came under criticism because it threatened to reduce agency to its reproductive function and left little room for self-transformation and radical political engagement (Jenkins 1992; Shusterman 1997; Hoy 1999; Alexander 2006: 561-562). Indeed, Bourdieu's own surveys show that the amount of variance in overt conduct which can be traced to class/field positions is relatively trivial, with plenty of border crossing between social groupings when it comes to taste if not deportment. Responding to this criticism, Bourdieu sought to clarify his position, pointing out that "[h]abitus is not a destiny," that "a habitus [can be] divided against itself," that uncalculating agents can "improvise," act "strategically," use their "sense for the game," and that "the homology between the space of positions and the space of dispositions is not perfect and there are always some agents out on the limb" (Bourdieu 2000a: 180, 157; 1999: 511). This move made his account more realistic but it was achieved at the price of stretching his paradigm to a point where the meaning of socially corporealized agency becomes elusive, for talking about "primary habitus" (Bourdieu 2000a: 157) inevitably raises the question about "secondary habitus," "tertiary habitus," and so on. Even in its amended form, Bourdieu's paradigm has drawbacks—it downplays the discursive dimension of human agency (the intellectually undemanding game like tennis is no better approximation of strategically enacted agency than the calculation-driven games of Scrabble or poker); it overlooks the multiple group affiliation and crosscutting identifications characteristic of modern societies (Friedrich Engels was a capitalist who used the surplus value he had extracted from his workers to foment the proletarian revolution); and it unduly spurns the commitment to universalism and critical discourse as the self-serving exercise of intelligentsia (the historical struggle for the universal human rights, equality before law, and human dignity did more than perpetuate the domination of well-healed classes).

One last critical point to be brought up here, the one especially attuned to the biocritical agenda articulated in this paper, concerns the performative contradiction endemic to Bourdieu's embodied practice. I am talking about the fact that for all his personal charm and charisma, Bourdieu "enjoyed his power as star intellectual," was "brutally intolerant of rival views," and given to "vicious invective" against his opponents whose "imbecilic misinterpretation" he was quick to denounce (Shusterman 2002b)—all this while he was condemning his academic rivals for their "symbolic violence" and hunger for "academic supremacy."

There are many passages in Erving Goffman's writings that bear an uncanny resemblance to Bourdieu's work, as for instance this prominently displayed Bourdieuesque quote from Adam Smith where the latter describes a well-bred eighteenth-century gentleman whose "air, his manner, his deportment, all mark that elegant, and graceful sense of his superiority, which born to inferior stations can hardly ever arrive at" (Goffman 1959: 34). Yet, Goffman's take on embodied interactions differs from that of his French associate (the two met at the University of Pennsylvania where Goffman offered his junior colleague a job).

While Bourdieu stresses the indelible nature of the marks society leaves on the human body, Goffman is fascinated with the body's malleability, with agent's prodigious capacity to adjust its demeanor to situational demands. Goffman's research program is focused on face-to-face inter-actions marked by "a brief time span involved, a limited extension in space, and a restriction to those events that must go on to completion once they have began"; it uses as its data "behavioral materials [such as] the glances, gestures, positionings, and verbal statements that people continuously feed into the situation, whether intended or not"; and it is grounded in the premise that "the individual is likely to present himself in a light that is favorable to him [with his performance split] into two parts; a part that is relatively easy for the individual to manipulate at will, being chiefly his verbal assertions, and a part with regard to which he seems to have little control, being chiefly derived from expression he gives off. The others may then use what are considered to be ungov-ernable aspects of his expressive behavior as a check upon the validity of what is conveyed by the governable aspects" (Goffman 1967: 1; 1959: 7). The visible body resources the agent mobilizes to communi-cate the intended self-image are conceptualized as "face" while staged performances are referred to as "face-work," with the proviso that "the person's face clearly is something that is not lodged in or on the body but rather something that is diffusely located in the flow of events in the encounter" (Goffman 1967: 7). The ultimate discerner and noticer, Goffman furnished many a vivid account of interaction rituals in which humans deploy their bodies and mobilize their verbal skills to construct desired appearances. Goffman's naturalistic methodology dovetails with the pragmatist inquiry, as does the semiotic turn his theory took in the latter stages of his intellectual career when he focused on the "framing process," "sign production," and "[t]he natural indexical signs given off by objects and animals (including, and primarily, man)" (Goffman 1974; 1979: 7). Nonetheless, Goffman's approach diverges from pragmatist hermeneutics in several ways.

The focus on short-term transactions and immediate presence makes the dramaturgical approach less suitable for tracking the long semiotic chains unfolding in historical time —a task central to pragmatist herme-neutics. There are tantalizing remarks on biography and reputation in Goffman's writing, notably in *Stigma* (Goffman 1963: 66-71), but they need to be expanded and revised to facilitate the biocritical analysis outlined in this study. Problematic from the standpoint of pragmatist hermeneutics is Goffman's decision to sever the specific "content" of interactions from their "dramaturgical" characteristics, which pushes aside the dialectical relationship between form and content (Goffman 1959: 15). To cite his own examples, a waiter can display a snazzy front in the hopes of earning better tips, a plumber may surreptitiously take off his glasses to protect his manly image, and a prostitute could spend extra time validating a customer's self-image, but the waiter's job will be ultimately judged by the food quality and timely delivery, the plumber will earn respect by stopping the leak, and ego-stroking is not the only skill bearing on a sex worker's performance. The exclusive focus on "the expressive costume that individuals are expected to wear whenever they are in the immediate presence of others" (Goffman 1967: 133) also raises the question as to the role that agent's body plays in society. "The world, in truth, is a wedding," Goffman (1959: 36) assures us, but such statements underscore the dramaturgical analysis's tendency to disembody human agency and etherealize the agent, for "he and his body merely provide a peg on which something of collaborative manufacture will be hung for a time" (Goffman 1959: 253).

When Bourdieu posits too rigid a link between the body and its social role, Goffman treats this bond as somewhat perfunctory. This becomes especially troublesome when Goffman theorizes mental illness, as he assures us in his famous study *Asylum* that "the 'mentally ill' ... and mental patients distinctly suffer not from mental illness, but from contingencies," that "the craziness or 'sick behavior' claimed for the mental patient is by and large a product of the claimant's social distance from the situation that the patient is in, and is not primarily a product of mental illness" (Goffman 1961: 135, 130). As fate would have it, biographical circumstances forced Goffman to revise his views (Goffman's wife developed a serious mental illness and committed suicide in 1964). An apparently autobiographical account of his painful experience surfaces in a poignant essay "The Insanity of Place" where Goffman (1971: 389) extricates mental illness from quotation marks, although his statement still sounds equivocal as to the somatic dimension of mental disorders: "Whatever the cause of the offender's psychological state—and clearly this may sometimes be organic—the social significance of the disease is that its carrier somehow hits upon the way that things can be made hot for us."

The (mis)alignment between Goffman the scholar, the teacher, and the man is one more facet of his prodigious output crying for a biocritical analysis. The incongruous impressions Goffman left on his contemporaries—some remember him as "a warm, friendly, modest, considerate man" (Bourdieu 2000b: 4) while others recall him as "cynical, ironical, duplicitous, deceptive, unserious, nonpersuasive" (MacCannell 2000: 13)—would present a worthy challenge for a student of pragmatist hermeneutics and biocritique.

Richard Shusterman (1997, 2000a) has shown how pragmatism can incorporate somatic practices into the analysis of culture, art, and society. An admirer of the socially grounded theory of art developed by Bourdieu, Shusterman felt the need to distance himself from his French colleague's views as incompatible with the pragmatist perspective on body and popular art. Shusterman's position is close to that of Dewey who criticized the academic treatment of canonical art and stressed the importance of popular art forms (Shusterman 1992: 183). By contrast, Bourdieu sides with those who "loath to recognize that there are humanly worthy and esthetically rewarding activities other than intellectual excursion" found in high-brow art, whose proponents look down at their popular counterpart as aesthetic travesty. In a series of critical essays on rap, country music, and body arts, Shusterman validates their aesthetic appeal, demonstrating why Bourdieu's approach "wrongly essentializes the nature of artistic understanding by affirming that there is only one legitimate way of understanding art—'a science of works'" (Shusterman 2000a: 223). Starting with the premise that "body was always the primordial *paradigm* of the media," "a medium of aesthetic self-fashioning," and "a means of aesthetic pleasure," Shusterman (2000a: 138-141, 1997: 9) proposes somaesthetics as a scholarly field exploring the relationship between somatic practices (meditation, physical exercise, body styling, sexual performance, ascetic self-control) and traditional philosophical subjects (perception, ratiocination, and self-consciousness).

Of particular interest from the standpoint of pragmatist hermeneutics is the question Shusterman (1997: 9) raises: "What is the connection between the views of a philosopher and his or her life?" His comparative biography of Dewey, Wittgenstein, and Foucault is a fine example of how philosophers' private pursuits feed their public engagements and shore up their theoretical commitments. Shusterman differs from Bourdieu and Goffman in his willingness to engage in autobiography and show how his location in historical time and space, specifically his split persona as a secular Zionist American Jew, drove him to resolve the contradictions in his self-identity by "integrating the self's conflicting roles and stories into [a] narrative coherence" and committing himself to a life of "[a]esthetic self-creation" (Shusterman 1997: 195). This frank discussion goes a long way to expose "the philosophy's deep seated prejudice for universality," "[t]he taboo of the personal and contingent" (Shusterman 2000a: 181). While it suggests new avenues for the pragmatist inquiry into embodiment and body practices, Shusterman's approach raises difficult questions about a self-interpretation performed in the pragmatist key.

If for Bourdieu the body is a semiconductor programmed early on to pass a limited set of social currents and for Goffman it is a superconductor instantly switching to an appropriate semiotic display in response to situational pressures, then for Shusterman the agent's body is a transistor conducive to various social circuits whose response to societal pressures and cultural imperatives is mediated by self-direction, askesis, and exercise modulating bodily competences throughout the agents' life span. The emphasis on auto-reflection and self-styling exposes the ethical ambiguities of biocritical research. When does a legitimate self-exploration turn into a narcissistic navel gazing; how much frankness is too much/too little; what makes the personal account self-serving or insincere? For instance, Shusterman (2000a: 183) mentions "populating [Israel] with three children" without telling us with whom, under what circumstances, or which kind of relationship he has with his children. Do we need to know such details, is the "narrative unity" the author strives for achieved at the price of glossing over the incongruent and painful strands of his enselfment? In keeping with biocritical hermeneutics, we must do the reverse editing here to restore the redacted materials that promise to recover less auspicious enselfments and rescue from oblivion more encompassing self-framings. The goal is reconstruction rather than deconstruction here. I hope Shusterman will address these issues in his future work, incorporate into his study the distinction between the signifying media suggested by pragmatist hermeneutics, and trace in a more systematic fashion the tension between *vita activa*, *vita contemplativa*, and *vita voluptuosa* in the lives of famous and not so famous thinkers (e.g., is Dewey's extramarital affair and Wittgenstein's frustrated homosexuality a proper subject of somaesthetics?).

Jeffrey Alexander's magisterial treatise on the civic sphere which includes "structures of feelings that permeate social life and run just below the surface of strategic institutions and self-conscious elites" zeroes in on the issues central to pragmatist hermeneutics (Alexander 2006a: 54). "Civil hermeneutics," as Alexander (2006a: 550) conceives it, examines how the civic ideals have been sabotaged by the dominant elites' visceral reactions that have engendered exclusionary and hegemonic practices. Further inquiry along these lines could benefit from comparison between the semiotic resources of the body and the textual authority of scriptural signs. The role of civility as an embodied virtue deserves special attention in this regard, more so than it has been accorded in the book. Also, it would be interesting to expand Alexander's study of the social construction of the Holocaust (2003: 24-84) so that it squares off with the Torah commandment to exterminate the Amalekites, the Jewish people's response to this commandment, and the manner in which this biblical narrative has been reconstructed over the course of time.

Of particular relevance to the line of inquiry outlined in this essay is the research program designated as "cultural pragmatics" (Alexander, Giesen, and Mast 2006). Building on the ideas of Erving Goffman, Victor Turner, and Kenneth Burke, sociologists comprising this school study culture as it comes across in strategic performances staged by skillful agents who deploy their symbolic and emotional resources in the bid to dramatize meaning structures embedded in cultural scripts. "Cultural pragmatics accounts for how meaning, in the form of background collective representations, shapes social actors and audiences' interpretations in a deeply structural way [while allowing] for contingency by reconciling culture's constitutive power with social actors' abilities to creatively and agentically situate and strategize vis-à-vis the symbolic structures in which they are embedded" (Mast 2006: 138-139). "To take meaning seriously," according to this outlook (Alexander and Mast 2006: 2, 32, 39), requires not only deciphering society's cultural codes but also showing how agents manage to "offer plausible performances," "not only metaphorically but literally [becoming] the text," "creatively citing hegemonic codes in order to play upon and subvert them" (Alexander 2006b: 14). Pragmatist hermeneutics shares with cultural pragmatics an abiding interest in "the incongruities between words and deeds" (Mast 2006: 120), although the cultural pragmatics' agenda is closer to depth hermeneutics with its focus on *background structures of immanent meaning*" (Eyerman 2006: 195) while the pragmatist approach hews closer to surface hermeneutics that concerns itself with body language games and emergent grammars exerting cross-pressures on agents caught in their gravitational pull. Since each approach suggests complementary solutions to the problem of agency and structure, there are ample opportunities for cross-fertilization.

Recent research on body metaphors (Lakoff and Johnson 1999), pragmatist neuroscience (Brothers 1997), neurosociology (Franks and Thomas Smith 1999), somatic markers and unconscious memory (Massey 2001) has opened new vistas for understanding our interpretive practices. What these studies tell us is that "the conscious mind is a monkey riding a tiger of unconscious decisions and actions in progress, frantically making up stories about being in control" (Overbye 2007: D1). Once reason grasped the situation discursively, it has already been powerfully influenced by emotions. The mammalian brain continuously bombards the cerebral cortex with strong signals waiting to be rationalized, which explains why emotions have a far more powerful impact on logical reasoning than the other way around. The affect will undergo changes once it has been subsumed under a proper label, but its somatic presence will inform conduct in a way that resists conscious control. We need to adjust our theoretical schema to account for the role that unconscious affect and somatic markers left by historical upheavals have on our interpretive practices.

Finally, pragmatist hermeneutics needs to acknowledge its debt to twentieth-century hermeneutics. Gadamer and Ricoeur have taught us much about the historical nature of meaning appropriation and the role of language in interpretative reconstruction, but the master metaphor of "text" and "textuality" that animates structural hermeneutics is overdue for pragmatist revision. "In writing, th[e] meaning of what is spoken exists purely for itself, completely detached from all emotional elements of expression and communication," explains Gadamer (1982: 357, 350). "In this sense understanding is certainly not concerned with understanding historically, ie reconstructing the way the text has come into being. Rather, one is understanding the text itself." As this programmatic statement shows, structuralist hermeneutics privileges written tradition over the oral one. Indeed, Gadamer (1982: 251) goes as far as to contend that "tradition is linguistic in nature." Pragmatist hermeneutics, by contrast, insists that textualized cultural forms fail to capture the vibrancy and contradictions of lived experience. Written traditions tend to distort voices that fail to come to language and articulate their own emergent grammars, voices obscured and suppressed by dominant discourses.

Ricoeur's formulation is more balanced. He is particularly helpful in explaining how actions become a matter of record, how they bear on the agent's reputation and disclose the agent's historical world. Pragmatists agree that "action itself, action as meaningful, may become an object of science ... through a kind of objectification similar to the fixation which occurs in writing" (Ricoeur 1981: 203). But the fact that "a text breaks the ties of discourse to all the ostensible references" and secures the "emancipation from the situational context" (Ricoeur 1981: 207) spells trouble for pragmatists who situate historical agents on the intersection of multiple discourses/paradigms and resist assigning an agent to any one "world." As is the case with most theorists who take their cues from Frege's view of meaning qua logical sense, there is also little room in Ricoeur's framework for nondiscursive significations and affective narratives that propel pragmatist inquiry.

Pragmatist hermeneutics has more affinity with early Heidegger who stressed the vital link between our moods and interpretive practices. "It is precisely when we see the 'world' unsteady and fitfully in accordance with our moods, that the ready-to-hand shows itself in its specific mood-hood, which is never the same from day to day.... Yet even the purest *theoria* has not left all moods behind it.... Indeed from the ontological point of view we must as a general principle leave the primary discovery of the world to 'bare moods'" (1962: 177). Heidegger abandoned this existentialist stance once he took a linguistic turn, but its unmistakably pragmatic thrust calls for further investigation. This bold move invites a fresh look at the hermeneutical circle which, as Heidegger (1962: 95) warned us, "is not to be reduced to the level of vicious circle, or even of a circle which is merely tolerated, [for in this] circle is hidden a positive possibility of the most primordial kind of knowing." I take this to mean that tracking the embodiment-disembodiment-reembodiment arc requires that we insert ourselves—our bodies—into the hermeneutical circle and ensure that our affections serve as indexes of being and our deeds feed back into our discursive commitments. As we enter the hermeneutical circle, we need to ask ourselves if we are ready to spell out our commitments pragmatically, join issues with opponents, bring all evidence to bear, make room for the honest difference of opinion, affirm dignity of the parties involved, and body forth in deed what we profess in theoria. These quasi-discursive properties of discourse comprise what can be called the *ethos of pragmatist hermeneutics*. Exploring such pre- and postinterpretive practices surrounding the interpretation process will add a welcome dimension to hermeneutical inquiry.

Conclusion

As is the case with every theoretical enterprise, the project of pragmatist hermeneutics and biocritique is bound to raise more questions than it answers.

How do we match icons, indexes, and symbols? Which actions comprising the universe of embodied significations bear on a given discursive stance? Cannot some affective indexes be discarded or bracketed as exceptions (a Mel Gibson's moment), certain deeds set aside as aberrations

(Billy Graham's anti-Semitic slur)? How far can a particular enselfment stray from the self one aspires to be before the agent has to renounce its claim to a given selfhood, ceases to reveal a pragmatic identity? Would it help to separate the universal-logical-extratemporal content of a theory from its mundane-contingent-pragmatic incarnations? Shouldn't we draw a line between public actions and private deeds to avoid airing dirty linen and running roughshod through a person's private life? How can we honor the time-proven injunction against ad hominem reasoning while sustaining a responsible inquiry into the affective-behavioral underpinnings of a theoretically articulated and politically grounded enterprise? Isn't it imperative for someone bent on exploring biosemiotic raptures in other people's lives to start with one's own discursive-pragmatic misalignments and bare one's own somatic/affective a priori? Given Foucault's commitment to living his own philosophy and the extensive use he made of other people's archives, was he justified in destroying his diaries, correspondence, and manuscripts before he died and demanding that his friends do the same with the personal communication bearing Foucault's signature? Should we keep our personal archives in good shape and be prepared to open them up for inspection, if so—when? How can one counter the tendency to moralize and judge implicit in the hermeneutical procedures that are focused on the pragmatist-discursive misalignment?

I cannot pretend to know answers to all these queries. My hope is that the questions raised here will engender a viable line of inquiry into the scope and the meaning of pragmatist hermeneutics.

References

Alexander, Jeffrey C. 2003. *The Meaning of Social Life: A Cultural Sociology*. Oxford: Oxford University Press.

Alexander, Jeffrey C. 2006a. *The Civil Sphere*. Oxford: Oxford University Press.

Alexander, Jeffrey C., Bernhard Giesen and Jason L. Mast, eds. *Social Performance. Symbolic Action, Cultural Pragmatics, and Ritual*. Cambridge: Cambridge University Press.

Alexander, Jeffrey C. 2006b. "Cultural Pragmatics: Social Performance between Ritual and Strategy." Pp. 29-90 in Alexander, Jeffrey C., Bernhard Giesen and Jason L. Mast, eds. *Social Performance. Symbolic Action, Cultural Pragmatics, and Ritual*. Cambridge: Cambridge University Press.

Alexander, Jeffrey C. and Jason L. Mast. 2006. "Introduction: Symbolic Action in Theory and Practice: The Cultural Pragmatics of symbolic action." Pp. 1-28 in Alexander, Jeffrey C.,

Bernhard Giesen and Jason L. Mast, eds. *Social Performance. Symbolic Action, Cultural Pragmatics, and Ritual*. Cambridge: Cambridge University Press.

Barthes, Roland. 1976. *Sade/Fourier/Loyola*. New York: Hill and Wang.

Baudrillard, Jean. 1990. *Revenge of the Crystal: Selected Writings on the Modern Object and Its Destiny, 1968-1983*. London: Pluto Press.

_____. 2000a. *Pascalian Meditations*. Stanford, CA: Stanford University Press.

Bourdieu, Pierre. 2000b. "Erving Goffman: Discoverer of the Infinitely Small." Pp. 1-4 in Gary Alan Fine and Gregory W. H. Smith, eds. *Erving Goffman*. Vol. 1. London: Sage Publications.

_____. 1999. *The Wight of the World. Social Suffering in Contemporary Society.* Stanford, CA: Stanford University Press.

_____. 1990. *The Logic of Practice*. Stanford, CA: Stanford University Press.

_____. 1984. *Distinction. A Social Critique of Judgment of Taste*. Cambridge, MA: Harvard University Press.

Brothers, Leslie. 1997. *Friday's Footprint: How Society Shapes the Human Mind.* New York: Oxford University Press.

Bruns, Gerald L. 1992. *Hermeneutics Ancient and Modern*. New Haven, CT: Yale University Press.

Chekhov, Anton P. 1977. *Pisma*, Vol. 5. Moskva: Nauka.

Colapietro, Vincent. 1989. *Peirce's Approach to the Self: A Semiotic Perspective on Human Subjectivity*. New York: State University of New York Press.

Csordas, Thomas. 1990. "Embodiment as a Paradigm for Anthropology." *Ethos* 18: 5-47.

Dewey, John. 1950. *Human Nature and Conduct*. New York: The Modern Library.

Deleuze, Gilles and Felix Guattari, 1987. *A Thousand Plateaus: Capitalism and Schizophrenia*. Minneapolis: University of Minnesota Press.

Derrida, Jacques. 1974. *Of Grammatology*. Baltimore, MD: Johns Hopkins University Press.

_____. 1988. *Limited Inc*. Evanston, IL: Northwestern University Press.

Descartes, René. 1955. *Philosophical Works of Descartes.* New York: Dover.

Dewey, John. 1916. *Essays in Experimental Logic.* New York: Dover.

_____. 1946. *Problems of Men*. New York: Philosophical Library.

_____, 1958. *Art and Experience*. New York: Dover.

Douglas, Mary. 1978. "Do Dogs Laugh? A Crosscultural Approach to Body Symbolism." Pp. 295-303 in Ted Polhemus, *The Body Reader: Social Aspects of the Human Body*. New York: Pantheon Books.

Eyerman, Ron. 2006. "Performing Opposition or, How Social Movements Move." Pp. 193-217 in Alexander, Jeffrey C., Bernhard Giesen and Jason L. Mast, eds. *Social Performance. Symbolic Action, Cultural Pragmatics, and Ritual*. Cambridge: Cambridge University Press.

Featherstone, M., M. Hepworth, and B. S. Turner, eds. 1991. *The Body: Social Process and Cultural Theory*. Sage Publications.

Ferraris, Maurizio. 1996. *History of Hermeneutics*. Atlantic Highlands, NJ: Humanities Press.

Foucault, Michel. 1984. *The Foucault Reader*. New York: Pantheon.

_____. 1998. *Essential Works of Foucault 1954-1984*. Volume 2. New York: The New Press.

Franks, David and Thomas Smith. 1997. *Mind, Brain, and Society: Toward a Neurosociology of Emotion*. Vol. 5, *Social Perspectives on Emotion*. Stamford, CT: JAI Press.

Franks, David and Stephen Ling. 2002. *Sociology and the Real World.* Boulder, CO: Rowman & Littlefield.

Freud, Sigmund. 1959. "Wild Psychoanalysis," Pp. 221-227 in *The Standard Edition of the Complete Works of Sigmund Freud*. London: The Hogarth Press, Vol. 11.

Gadamer. 1982. *Truth and Method*. New York: Crossroad.

Gay, Peter. 2006. "The Fictions of Günter Grass." *New York Times*, August 20.

Gadamer, Hans-Georg. 1982. *Truth and Method*. New York: Crossroad.

Goffman, Erving. 1979. *Gender Advertisements*. New York: Harper & Row.

_____. 1974. *Frame Analysis*. New York: Harper & Row.

_____. 1971. *Relations in Public*. New York: Harper & Row.

_____. 1967. *Interaction Rituals: Essays in Face-to-Face Behavior*. Garden City, NY: Doubleday.

_____. 1963. *Stigma: Notes on the Management of Spoiled Identity*. Englewood Cliffs, NJ: Prentice-Hall.

_____. 1961. *Asylums*. Garden City, NY: Doubleday.

_____. 1959. *The Presentation of Self in Everyday Life*. Garden City, NY: Doubleday.

Goodstein, Laurie. 2006. "Minister's Own Rules Sealed His Fate." *New York Times*, November 19.

Gordon, Steven L. 1990. "Social Structural Effects on Emotions." Pp. 145-179 in *Research Agenda in the Sociology of Emotions*, ed. by Theodore D. Kemper. New York: State University of New York Press.

Habermas, Jürgen. 1998. *Between Facts and Norms: Contribution to a Discourse Theory of Law and Democracy*. Cambridge, MA: MIT Press.

Halperin, David M. 1995. *Saint Foucault: Towards a Gay Hagiography*. New York: Oxford University Press.

Heidegger, Martin. 1961. "Letter on Humanism," Pp. 190-242 in D. F. in D. F. Krell, ed. *Martin Heidegger: Basic Writings*. New York: Harper & Row.

Heidegger, Martin. 1962. *Being and Time*. Harper & Row Publishers.

Holmes, Oliver Wendell. 1992. *The Essential Holmes: Selections from the Letters, Speeches, Judicial Opinions, and Other Writings of Oliver Wendell Holmes*. Richard A. Posner ed. Chicago: University of Chicago Press.

Hoy, David Couzens. 1999. "Critical Resistance: Foucault and Bourdieu." Pp. 3-2 in Gail Weiss & Honi Fern Haber, eds. *Perspective on embodiment. The Intersection of Nature and Culture*. London: Routledge.

Husserl, Edmund. 2001. *Logical Investigations*. London: Routledge. Krell D. F., ed. 1971. *Martin Heidegger: Basic Writings*. New York: Harper & Row.

Jenkins, Janis. 1994. "Culture, Emotion, and Psychopathology." Pp. 307-335 in Shinobu Katayama and Hazel Rose Markus, eds., *Emotion and Culture: Empirical Studies of Mutual Influence*. American Psychological Association: Washington, DC.

Jenkins, Richard. 1992. *Pierre Bourdieu*. London: Routledge.

Kant, Immanuel. 1965. *The Metaphysical Elements of Justice*. Macmillan Publishing Co.

Kant, Immanuel. 1978. *Anthropology from a Pragmatic Point of View*. Carbondale: Southern Illinois University.

_____. 1996. *The Cambridge Edition of the Works of Immanuel Kant. Practical Philosophy. The Metaphysics of Morals*. Cambridge: Cambridge University Press.

Kilpinen, Erkki. 2000. *The Enormous Fly-Wheel of Society. Pragmatism's Habitual Conception of Action and Social Theory*. Helsinki: University of Helsinki Press.

Kohler, Joachim. 2002. *Zarathustra's Secret: The Interior Life of Friedrich Nietzsche*. New Haven, CT: Yale University Press.

Lakoff, George and Mark Johnson. 1999. *Philosophy in the Flesh: The Embodied Mind and Its Challenge to Western Thought*. New York: Basic Books.

Lévi-Strauss, Claude. 2000. *Structural Anthropology*. New York: Basic Books.

Lyon, M. L. and J. M. Barbalet. 1994. "Society's Body: Emotions and the 'Somatization' of Social Theory. Pp. 48-66 in Thomas J. Csordas, ed., *Embodiment and Experience: The Existential Grounds of Culture and Self*. Cambridge: Cambridge University Press.

Lyotard, Jean-Francois, 1993. *Libidinal Economy*. Bloomington: Indiana University Press.

MacCannell, Dean. 2000. "Erving Goffman (1922-1982)." Pp. 8-37 in Gary Alan Fine and Gregory W. H. Smith, eds. *Erving Goffman*. Vol. 1. London: Sage Publications.

Macey, David. 1995. *The Lives of Michel Foucault: A Biography*. New York: Vintage Books.

Massey, Douglas S. 2002. "A Brief History of Human Society: The Origin and Role of Emotion in Social Life." *American Sociological Review* 67: 1-29.

Mast, Jason L. 2006. "The Cultural Pragmatics of Event-ness: the Clinton/Lewinsky Affair." Pp. 115-145 in Alexander, Jeffrey C., Bernhard Giesen and Jason L. Mast, eds. *Social Performance. Symbolic Action, Cultural Pragmatics, and Ritual*. Cambridge: Cambridge University Press.

Mauss, Marcel. 1978. "The Technique of the Body." *The Body Reader. Social Aspects of the Human Body*. Ted Polhem, ed. New York: Pantheon Books.

Mead, George H. 1938. *The Philosophy of the Act*. Chicago : University of Chicago Press.

Mead, Geroge H. 1934. *Mind, Self, and Society*. Chicago: University of Chicago Press.

Miller, James. 1993. *The Passion of Michel Foucault*. Cambridge, MA: Harvard University Press.

Montaigne, Michel de. 1987. *The Complete Essays*. London: Penguin Books.

Nietzsche, Friedrich. 1966. *Beyond Good and Evil: Prelude to a Philosophy of the Future*. Vintage Books.

Overbeye, Dennis. 2007. "Free Will: Now You Have It, Now You Don't." *New York Times*, January 2.

Peirce, Charles Sanders. 1931-1935. *Collected Papers of Charles Sanders Peirce*, Vols.1-6. Cambridge, MA: Harvard University Press.

_____. 1976. *The New Elements of Mathematics*. Atlantic Highlands NJ: Humanities Press.

_____. 1991. *Peirce on Signs*. Chapel Hill: University of North Carolina Press.

Plato, "Phaedo," 1963. *The Collected Dialogues of Plato*, ed. by E. Hamilton and H. Cairns. Princeton, NJ: Princeton University Press.

Ricoeur, Paul. 1978. *The Philosophy of Paul Ricoeur: An Anthology of His Works*. Boston: Beacon Press.

_____. 1981. *Hermeneutics and the Human Sciences*. Cambridge: Cambridge University Press.

Rorty, Richard. 1982. *Consequences of Pragmatism*. Minneapolis: University of Minnesota Press.

Sade, Marquis. 1953. *Selections form His Writings and a Study by Simone de Beauvoir*. New York: Grove Press.

Saussure, Ferdinand de. 1986. *Course in General Linguistics*. New York: Chicago: Open Court.

Sebeok T. A. and J. Umiker-Sebeok. 1991. *Biosemiotics: The Semiotic Web*. Berlin: De Gruyter.

Seneca. 1995. *Moral and Political Essays.* Cambridge: Cambridge University Press.

Shalin, Dmitri N. 1986a. "Pragmatism and Social Interactionism." *American Sociological Review* 51: 9-30.

_____. 1986b. "Romanticism and the Rise of Sociological Hermeneutics." *Social Research* 53: 77-123.

_____. 1992a. "Critical Theory and the Pragmatist Challenge," *American Journal of Sociology* 96: 237-279.

_____. 1992b. Review: "The Heidegger Controversy. A Critical Reader," edited by Richard Wolin. *American Journal of Sociology* 98: 409-411.

_____. 1996. "Intellectual Culture." Pp. 41-98 in *Russian Culture at the Crossroads: Paradoxes of Postcommunist Consciousness*. Edited by Dmitri N. Shalin. Boulder: Westview Press, 1996.

_____. 2000. "George Herbert Mead." Pp. 302-344 in George Ritzer, ed. *The Blackwell Companion to Major Social Theorists*. Malden, MA: Blackwell Publishers.

_____. 2004. "Liberalism, Affect Control, and Emotionally Intelligent Democracy." *Journal of Human Rights* 3: 407-428.

_____. 2004a. "The Hermeneutics of Prejudice: Heidegger and Gadamer in Their Historical Setting." Paper presented at the Annual Meeting of the American Sociological Association, San Francisco.

_____. 2004b. "Hermeneutics and Prejudice: Heidegger and Gadamer in Their Historical Setting." Paper presented at the Annual Meeting of the American Sociological Association, San Francisco.

_____. 2005. "Legal Pragmatism, an Ideal Speech Situation, and the Fully Embodied Democratic Process." *Nevada Law Journal* 5: 433-478.

Shilling, Chris. 1993. *The Body and Social Theory*. London: Sage Publications.

Shusterman, Richard. 2002a. *Surface & Depth: Dialectics of Criticism and Culture*. London: Routledge.

_____. 2002b. "Pierre Bourdieu: Reason and Passion." *Chronicle of Higher Education*. February 8.

_____. 2000. *Performing Live. Aesthetic Alternatives fro the End of Art*. Ithaca, NY: Cornell University Press.

_____. 1997. *Practicing Philosophy: Pragmatism and the Philosophical Life*. London: Routledge.

_____. 1992. *Pragmatist Aesthetics: Living Beauty, Rethinking Art*. Cambridge: Blackwell Publishers.

Spinoza, Baruch. 1909. *A Theological-Political Treatise*. London: George Bell & Sons.

Spinoza, Baruch. 1910. *Ethics*. London: J. M. Dent & Sons Ltd.

Turner, Terence. 1994. "Bodies and Anti-bodies: Flesh and Fetish in Contemporary Social Theory." Pp. 27-47 in Thomas J. Csordas, ed., *Embodiment and Experience: The Existential Grounds of Culture and Self*. Cambridge: Cambridge University Press.

Weyl, Nathaniel. 1979. *Karl Marx: Racist*. New York: Arlington House.

William, James. 1956. *The Will to Believe*. New York: Dover Publications.

Wolin, Richard. 1991. *The Heidegger Controversy: A Critical Reader*. New York: Columbia University Press.

7

Reframing the Law:
Legal Pragmatism, Juridical Moralism,
and the Embodied Democratic Process

I. Introduction

Few philosophies can rival pragmatism in its influence on American popular culture. Pundits routinely invoke this down-to-earth creed to label certain twentieth-century intellectual currents, although they disagree on whether pragmatism bears good tidings. A pragmatic attitude comes in handy, many feel, when we confront a problem that defies easy solutions and calls for a novel, experimental approach. Others see pragmatism as a slippery slope that will lead astray undisciplined minds unwilling to fortify their judgment with firm principles. Which position one takes depends in part on one's political leanings.

Few commentators on the right would go as far as Edward Cline in condemning pragmatism as "the school of thought which dispenses with the need for moral values,"[1] but it is common for conservative pundits to lament the baleful impact of this philosophical movement on American legal thought. Witness Thomas Bowden's derisive comments about "the grandfather of Supreme Court Pragmatism, Justice Oliver Wendell Holmes," whose distaste for formal reasoning has reverberated throughout twentieth-century jurisprudence and is now starkly on display in the Rehnquist Court which succumbed to "pragmatism, the

---

This chapter was published as "Legal Pragmatism, an Ideal Speech Situation, and the Fully Embodied Democratic Process" in the *Nevada Law Journal*, 2005, Vol. 5, pp. 433-478.

philosophy that claims there are no absolutes and no principles, only subjective opinions guided by expediency."[2]

Critics on the left are also uneasy about pragmatism, seeing its penchant for compromise as a sell-out. The so-called "moderate," explains one commentator, is apt to slip "into the managerial technique that constitutes pragmatism in recent American politics: succumbing to the delusion that he has transcended ideology, he accepts status quo injustice in the name of hardheaded realism."[3] The Clinton administration came under criticism for its excessive pragmatism from those on the left of the political continuum. "Stephen Breyer was the candidate who could win praise from Orrin Hatch," Lincoln Caplan noted wryly, as he berated Bill Clinton for his failure to "display principles," "a needless sacrifice of idealism," and a precipitous slide into the "paralyzing, even cynical, pragmatism that many have criticized in the Administration [and that] has shown up unmistakably in its handling of legal issues."[4]

Political moderates, by contrast, have few qualms about the pragmatic sensibilities which shaped the legal culture of the Clinton era, as evidenced by the welcome they gave to Breyer's appointment to the Supreme Court. "His legal culture is more liberal, and his very flexible pragmatism will enable him to give things a gentle spin in a liberal direction," opined David Margolick, adding only half in jest that Breyer "is a person without deep roots of any kind. He won't develop a vision."[5] Linda Greenhouse, the *New York Times*' legal correspondent, concurred: "Stephen G. Breyer is a judge of moderate leanings, a self-described pragmatist interested more in solutions than in theories.... His avoidance of any single approach to legal interpretation places judge Breyer squarely within the tradition of legal pragmatism that, on the Supreme Court, has included Justices like Oliver Wendell Holmes and Benjamin N. Cardozo."[6]

If news analysts disagree about the pragmatist promise, so do scholars, who are divided about the meaning of pragmatism and its value for the field of law. Once they are through compiling a glossary of key concepts, legal scholars dabbling in pragmatism and pragmatist philosophers expounding the law are apt to caution against expecting much from this creed. "[T]o say that one is a pragmatist is to say little," admonishes Richard Posner, a prominent figure in the legal pragmatist camp.[7] Richard Rorty concurs, "I agree with Posner that judges will probably not find pragmatist philosophers—either old or new—useful."[8] "Indeed, if you take the antifoundationalism of pragmatism seriously," Stanley Fish pushes the argument a step further, "you will see that there is absolutely nothing you can do with it."[9]

Skepticism about legal pragmatism may carry a sharper edge. Donald Dworkin, who gave a good deal of credit to legal pragmatism in his *Laws' Empire*,[10] has little use for self-described pragmatists like Posner, whose work he finds "erudite, punchy, knock-about, witty, and relentlessly superficial."[11] Dworkin is equally blunt about Rorty's philosophy, for "what Professor Rorty calls 'new' pragmatism has nothing to contribute to legal theory, except to provide yet another way for legal scholars to be busy while actually doing nothing."[12]

A more upbeat brand of legal pragmatism is associated with the German political philosopher Jürgen Habermas who developed an elaborate discourse concept of law.[13] A group of American legal scholars influenced by Habermas has been pushing his discourse theoretic framework in new directions, applying it to a broad range of democratic processes.[14] What is interesting about this movement is that its proponents seek to transcend the court-centered approach with its adversarial culture and practice law in a pragmatist key in alternative dispute resolution forums where pragmatist insights are applied to grass root democratic processes. A lecture Carrie Menkel-Meadow recently gave at the Saltman Center for Conflict Resolution at the William S. Boyd School of Law highlights a wide range of experiments currently underway that promise to give legal pragmatism a wider resonance.[15]

This chapter is about jurists' encounter with pragmatism and pragmatist philosophers' grappling with law. It reviews the range of discursive and nondiscursive practices associated with the pragmatic perspective on law and democracy. Section II begins with Kant's legal philosophy and its peculiar relevance for pragmatism as a negative reference frame. Section III shows how philosophers responded to Kant. Section IV tracks the jurists' reaction to pragmatism. Section V analyzes recent trends in legal pragmatism. Section VI discusses the place of principles in pragmatic jurisprudence. Section VII focuses on attempts to reclaim the Kantian insights in the discourse theory of law and democracy. Finally section VIII joins issues with the process theorists of democracy and appeals to the legacy of John Dewey and George Herbert Mead as theoreticians of the fully embodied democratic process.

II. Kant's Juridical Moralism

Pragmatism and transcendental idealism are commonly seen as antithetical creeds in philosophy, one committed to a priori principles independent from experience, the other sacrificing philosophical abstractions to practical wisdom. Thus, it is all the more intriguing that Charles

Sanders Peirce, the pioneer of pragmatist thought, not only spoke highly of Kant but also saw him as something of a precursor. "Kant (whom I *more* than admire) is nothing but a somewhat confused pragmatist,"[16] intimated Peirce, who did not mean this as a backhanded compliment.

Kant was probably the first to use "pragmatic" as a philosophical term, notably in his *Critique of Pure Reason*, where he juxtaposed "*pragmatic laws* ... recommended to us by the senses" and "practical laws ... given by reason entirely a priori."[17] This opposition recurs in all three of Kant's *Critiques*, as well as in his *Metaphysical Elements of Justice, Doctrine of Virtue*, and his lesser known *Anthropology from a Pragmatic Point of View*, which draws a contrast between pragmatic (*pragmatisch*) considerations rooted in everyday experience and practical (*praktisch*) motives ennobled by theoretical reflection.

Another angle that makes Kant a good starting point for the present inquiry is the pervasive legalism of his thought. Legal metaphors are among Kant's favorites. When he is groping for rhetorical tools equal to the task he set for himself in his path-breaking *Critique of Pure Reason*, he summons legal imagery to communicate the exalted place critical reason is destined to play in human affairs: "The critique of pure reason may really be looked upon as the true tribunal for all disputes of reason ... [which] secures to us the peace of a legal status, in which disputes are not to be carried on except in the proper form of a *lawsuit*."[18] Positive or civil law has a power to coerce conduct, but it does not have the dignity that the testimony of pure reason lends to our decisions. Substantive law must perfect itself by hewing closely to the a priori moral principles dormant in every citizen who, upon transcendental reflection, discovers "that he has a universal legislation within himself"[19] and imposes his rational will on the world at large.

Kant's strategy here is to intermesh as much as possible law and morality. He is cognizant of the fact that law can be immoral and moral action illegal, but he sees the best hope for the future in suffusing legal matters with moral precepts and imparting formal-logical rigor to moral reasoning. The result is a kind of "juridical moralism" or "ethical legalism" which endows conscience with legislative powers and turns every citizen into a lawgiver.

While morality and law are mutually constitutive in a perfectly rational state—the former asserts the dignity and universal rights of every human being, the latter backs the dictates of reason with administrative power—the relationship between the two is not symmetrical. Civil courts apply the extant corpus of laws without passing judgment on their wisdom. Moral practical reason, by contrast, gives laws their ultimate justification by furnishing an a priori true foundation for the entire legal edifice. While the tribunal of practical reason cannot prescribe to laws their empirical content, reason enlightened by transcendental reflection is well equipped to formulate its constitutive principles, such as respect for civil rights, reverence for human dignity, abhorrence of violence, and control over the legitimate means of coercion. Hence, Kant draws a rather invidious comparison between "civil court" and the "court of conscience,"[20] the "authorization [that] is wholly external" and "freedom according to universal laws,"[21] and the "mere agreement or disagreement of an action with the law ... called *legality*" and conduct motivated by "the Idea of duty ... [that] is called the *morality* of the action."[22]

Politically, Kant is treading here on ground well traveled by natural law theorists who sought constitutional limits on political absolutism. He is particularly indebted to Rousseau, who blended a sovereign and a subject into a citizen called upon to obey no law except the self-legislated one. Such a citizen will reside in a blessed republic where the general will coincides with the will of everyone.

Kant, however, parts company with his predecessors on several fronts when he deals with practical ("pragmatic" in his terms) adjudication and what we would call today "judicious temperament." People well versed in theoretical matters may follow general rules, but they are not necessarily good judges when it comes to particulars, Kant astutely observes—"the faculty of judgment is a special talent which cannot be taught, but must be practiced."[23] Hence, his advice to judges is to take special care "in order to guard the faculty of judgment against mistakes (*lapsus judicii*)."[24] Even supple minds should heed this advice when they step into the pragmatic domain: "A physician, therefore, a judge, or a politician, may carry in his head many beautiful pathological, juridical, or political rules, nay, he may even become an accurate teacher of them, and he may yet in the application of these rules commit many a blunder..."[25] To guard against *lapsus judicii* one has to cultivate a judicious temper that eschews negative emotions and cultivates "the habitually cheerful heart,"[26] a "kind of *hygiene* that man should practice to keep himself morally *healthy*."[27] Kant is adamant about temperamental preconditions for sound judgment. He calls upon all citizens, professional or otherwise, to exercise a judicious attitude, which requires taming emotions and ruthlessly suppressing passions:

Passions are cancerous stores for pure practical reason, and most of them are incurable.... Therefore passions are not, like emotions, merely unfortunate moods teeming with many evils, but they are without exception bad. Even the most well-intended desire if it aims ... at what belongs to virtue, that is, to charity, is nevertheless ... as soon as it changes to passion, not merely pragmatically pernicious, but also morally reprehensible.[28]

If passion is the enemy of reason, then freedom is first and foremost freedom from passion—indeed, from negative affect in general, for "what we do cheerlessly and merely as compulsory service has no intrinsic value for us."[29] Even when it comes to positive emotions, reason has to assert its mastery. Moral practical reason has nothing to learn from affect. However benign this affect might be, it will not pass the test of practical reason unless it is thoroughly infused with a sense of duty. Helping a friend out of sympathy would be morally reprehensible on this account, as would be tending for a child with mere affection as a guide. In a juridically moral state based on the categorical imperative we all can be "cheerful in the consciousness of our restored freedom,"[30] as every citizen's action attests to "the purity of his moral purpose and the sincerity of his attitude."[31]

There is a political dimension to Kant's thought that has appealed even to those who rejected his philosophical method, a dimension that foregrounds free inquiry and promotes speech conditions conducive to democracy. At least in theory, Kant is committed to a deliberative process in which "everybody has a vote,"[32] which allows "no other judge but universal human reason,"[33] and which "grant[s] to reason the fullest freedom, both of enquiry and of criticism."[34] Closely related to this theme is the strategically important distinction between an act of "justification" which grounds a policy in moral concerns for universal rights and an act of "adjudication" which squares off conduct with existing laws without questioning their raison d'être. This activist approach explains the continuous relevance of Kant to the ongoing debates about deliberative democracy. The pragmatic question that Kant bequeathed to his successors is whether society can be organized around the discursive principles grounded in moral concerns, and if so, how we go about instituting such a society.

Kant is fully aware that history falls short of what pure practical reason mandates, that "what one himself recognizes on good grounds to be just will not receive confirmation in a court of justice" and "what he must judge unjust in itself will be treated with indulgence by the court."[35] Still, Kant is sanguine about the pragmatic import of his theory. He stakes his hopes on social pedagogy, on a broadly conceived educational practice that cultivates respect for human autonomy, rouses moral imagination, promotes peace in international relations through a "league of nations,"[36] and pursues similar lofty causes. The concept of human liberty under universal law might be utopian, Kant admits at some point, but at the very least it can serve as a worthy ideal.

The problem with Kant's theory is that it does not square very well with his more specific recommendations. Contemporary readers are bound to wince when they follow Kant into the pragmatic realm and check his path-breaking intellections against his legal and political opinions. I am not talking about the misogynistic witticisms jumping from the pages of Kant's *Anthropology From the Pragmatic Standpoint* where he pokes fun at "scholarly women ... [who] use their books somewhat like a watch ... [which they wear] so it can be noticed that they have one, although it is usually broken or does not show the correct time."[37] Nor is it his questionable endorsement of "the people's duty to endure even the most intolerable abuse of supreme authority"[38] or his support of the estate-based society with "a superior class (entitled to command) and an inferior class (which, although free and bound only by public law, is predestined to obey the former)."[39] Inconsistent though such judgments are with Kant's appeal to universal human dignity, they might have something to do with his anxiety about the Prussian authorities' reaction to his free-spirited discourse, the reaction that was negative at times. What makes one cringe, however, is the cruelty ingrained in specific legal opinions he ventured at the time. For the very man who theorized human dignity enthusiastically endorsed the death penalty, insisted that a woman should die rather than submit to rape,[40] and ranted about "the disgrace of an illegitimate child ... [who] has crept surreptitiously into the commonwealth (much like prohibited wares [contraband]), so that its existence as well as its destruction can be ignored."[41] Equally troubling are his ravings against *crimen carnis contra naturam*, which cover among other things homosexuality and masturbation, two crimes against nature Kant went to a great length to expose, condemning the former as a disgrace to the human race and the latter as an abomination worse than suicide.[42]

To the modern conscience such counsel sounds like the very *lapsus judicii* Kant warned against in his theoretical discourse. What his legal opinions show is that, for all his bold theoretical statements, Kant could not escape the hermeneutical horizons of his time, that he shared the prejudices of his age which drove him to pragmatic judgments inconsistent with his theoretical views. The broader issue that this pragmatic-discursive misalignment raises is whether Kant erred in assigning priority to abstract formula over pragmatic considerations. The late nineteenth and early twentieth centuries saw a robust philosophical critique of Kant. One philosophy that challenged Kant's apriorism and influenced legal thought in early twentieth-century America was "pragmatism."

III. Pragmatists Respond to Kant

Before we examine the issues over which pragmatist philosophers parted company with Kant, let's review the premises they all share. One such premise is "universalism" which asserts that knowledge is public, that the knower who raises a truth claim brings it on behalf of the entire community. Herein lies the sociological import of the judgment a priori: it is made by an individual but stakes a claim valid for everyone. We see the shades of this conviction in Peirce, who thought that the knowledge pragmatists strive for—whether they labor in the vineyards of philosophy, politics, or law—must be valid for the entire human race. The pragmatic attitude embedded in logic and guiding public affairs, according to Peirce, "inexorably requires that our interests shall not be limited," that they "embrace the whole community. The community, again, must not be limited, but must extend to all races of beings with whom we can come into immediate or mediate intellectual relation. It must reach, however vaguely, beyond the ideological epoch, beyond all bonds."[43]

Another pragmatist insight traceable to Kant concerns the key role pragmatists assign to free inquiry as fodder for scientific and social progress. John Dewey tirelessly spread the gospel of inquiry as a tool for gaining knowledge and furthering commonwealth. Science, in this respect, is not so much a store of reliable truths as a model of democracy in action, a blueprint for a community where free discourse flourishes and all assertions are subject to critical inquiry: "[F]reedom of speech, toleration of diverse views, freedom of communication, the distribution of what is found out to every individual as the ultimate intellectual consumer, are involved in the democratic as in the scientific method."[44]

A quintessentially modern belief in the right of every citizen to participate in the national conversation and directly inform the political process is yet another point on which Kant and pragmatists converged: "The idea of democracy as opposed to any conception of aristocracy is that every individual must be consulted in such a way, actively not passively, that he himself becomes a part of the process of authority."[45]

One more paradigmatic conviction that pragmatists share with Kant is that education rather than coercion is the way to improve social conditions and bring about a better social order. The prospect for a better future "rests upon persuasion, upon ability to convince and be convinced,"[46] upon "the improvement of the methods and conditions of debate, discussion, and persuasion. That is *the* problem of the public."[47]

Besides these similarities, several philosophical, methodological, and political tenets separate pragmatists from Kant. The latter's apriorism came under attack for its tendency to anoint as transcendentally valid precepts that passed for settled knowledge at one point in time, be this women's inferiority, crimes against nature, or immovable ether permeating physical space. To this speculative approach pragmatists juxtaposed an experience-oriented philosophy that acknowledged the constitutive role reason plays in production of the meaningful world but that fastened attention on the socio-historical nature of the categories and practices humans rely on to find their way in the continuously evolving universe. The pragmatist alternatives to the Kantian transcendental idealism can be summed up under the following headings: (1) philosophical antifoundationalism; (2) epistemological consequentialism; (3) emergent determinism; (4) embodied rationalism; (5) social perspectivism; and (6) political progressivism.[48]

A. Philosophical Antifoundationalism

Philosophical antifoundationalism rejects the notion that our knowledge must be grounded in the immutable principles discovered a priori via transcendental reflection, logical deliberation, or any other abstract theoretical procedure. Kant's metaphysics draws attention away from the empirical world, wasting an inordinate amount of time on first principles and a priori categories. Pragmatists, by contrast, shun "terms abstracted from all their natural settings."[49] Pragmatist philosophy "has no dogmas, and no doctrines save its method," according to William James; it is *"looking away from first things, principles, 'categories,' supposed necessities; and of looking towards last things, fruits, consequences, facts."*[50] General principles and abstract ideas have their place in knowledge, but only insofar as they prove themselves in experience, in public affairs.

B. Epistemological Consequentialism

Epistemological consequentialism counsels caution regarding truth claims whose status cannot be empirically validated. While Kant opposed "inferring the truth of some knowledge from the truth of its consequences,"[51] pragmatists turn such an inquiry into a maxim. They will not admit a synthetic (nonanalytical) statement as true unless it can be demonstrated in concrete situations, through practical consequences vouching for the proposition's validity. "The truth of an idea is not a stagnant property inherent in it. Truth happens to an idea. It *becomes* true, is *made* true by events.... Its validity is the process of its valid-*ation*."[52] Peirce extends epistemological consequentialism to all scientific concepts, whose meaning he proposes to ascertain via this famous pragmatist maxim: "Consider what effects, that might conceivably have practical bearings, we conceive the object of our conception to have. Then, our conception of these effects is the whole of our conception of the object."[53] James, who did much to popularize Peirce (sometimes to the latter's great consternation), rephrases this maxim as follows: "the meaning of any proposition can always be brought down to some particular consequence in our future practical experience, whether passive or active."[54] That is, we should not admit in scientific discourse concepts which cannot be spelled out in operational terms, nor should we waste time on propositions which stake demonstrably unverifiable truth claims.

C. Emergent Determinism

Emergent determinism rejects the idealist view of the universe as fully determined in its internal structure and waiting to be apprehended in a final theoretical schema. "[F]or rationalism reality is ready-made and complete from all eternity while for pragmatism it is still in the making."[55] Our world is in flux, its natural state is that of indeterminacy, and it remains indeterminate until the knower terminates this "buzzing confusion" by imposing on it a terminological scheme that foregrounds some elements just as it backgrounds others. Or as James put it in one of his poetic moments: "Other sculptors, other statues from the same stone! Other minds, other worlds from the same monotonous and inexpressive chaos! My world is but one in a million alike embedded, alike real to those who may abstract them."[56] We can put this precept in a more contemporary idiom by saying that reason is a participant observer, an agency that leaves its mark on the world, even though the agent is often oblivious of its constitutive role. "[A]ny view that holds that man is part of nature, not outside it," explains Dewey, "will certainly hold ... that indeterminacy in human experience, once experience is taken in the objective sense of interacting behavior and not as a private conceit added on to [sic] something totally alien to it, is evidence of some corresponding indeterminateness in the process of nature within which man exists (acts) and out of which he arose."[57] Whatever determinacy we find in this "pluralistic universe"[58] is of our own making. We put a perspective on the world to render it meaningful, make a choice between conflicting experiences to make sense of them, and choose a terminological frame to bring out one or another pattern submerged in chaotic crosscurrents.

D. Embodied Rationalism

Embodied rationalism reconnects reason to the rest of the human body. Reason is at its best when it harnesses its affect, reins in its cold-blooded abstractions through intelligence native to sentiment. For a rationalist like Kant, reason is a disembodied agency that deliberately suppresses its passions to gain a clear picture of objective reality. Pragmatists, on the other hand, protest the "hypostatiz[ation] of cognitive behavior,"[59] warn against "imminent extinction at the hand of unhinged reason,"[60] and claim along with Peirce that "[r]eason, anyway, is a faculty of secondary rank. Cognition is but the superficial film of the soul, while sentiment penetrates its substance."[61] "'Reason' as a noun," Dewey concurs, "signifies the happy cooperation of a multitude of dispositions, such as sympathy, curiosity, exploration, experimentation, frankness, pursuit—to follow things through—circumspection, to look about context, etc., etc."[62] New pragmatists like Richard Rorty built on this premise their critique of conventional rationality: "Another meaning of 'rational' is, in fact, available. In this sense, the word means something like 'sane' or 'reasonable' rather than 'methodical.' It names a set of moral virtues: tolerance, respect for the opinions of those around one, willingness to listen, reliance on persuasion rather than force."[63] This pragmatist emphasis on the noncognitive sources of intelligence thematizes the discrepancy between our discursive and affective performances. It also rehabilitates passion as an embodied state compatible with virtue and conducive to social change.

E. Sociological Perspectivism

Sociological perspectivism reminds us that, contrary to Kant, the knower does not cogitate in isolation, alongside equally autonomous subjects, that "the very origin of the conception of reality shows that this conception essentially involves the notion of community,"[64] and the real problem is "how to fix belief, not in the individual merely, but in the community."[65] The individual belongs to society, and society stamps each mind with its blueprints, so that "the mind that appears *in* individuals is not as such [an] individual mind."[66] A modern individual belongs to several groups at once, each one furnishing a different perspective on reality. It is on the intersection of such publicly defined perspectives that we discover what reality is, and this reality is bound to be multiple, pluralistic, tinged with uncertainty, and open to conflicting interpretations. Our take on the world is mediated by a historically constituted collectivity that supplies us with terminological frames in terms of which we terminate indeterminacy to produce a meaningful world. As community members, we rely on language, and "[l]anguage does not simply symbolize a situation or object which is already there ... it makes possible the existence or the appearance of that situation or object, for it is a part of the mechanism whereby that situation or object is created."[67] This approach to reality as socially bound and continuously emergent engenders a pragmatist conception of society as social interaction. Institutional realities, according to pragmatist sociology, should not be treated as entities hovering above our heads. Social structures must be traced all the way down to face-to-face interactions and redeemed in experiential terms and affect-laden observations. "Society not only continues to exist *by* transmission, *by* communication, but it may be fairly said to exist *in* transmission, *in* communication."[68]

F. Political Progressivism

Political progressivism is one more feature present in historical pragmatism, whose proponents are generally open to change and social amelioration. At the same time, pragmatists do not espouse a definite political creed or urge specific policies. Peirce was probably the least progressivist in his political instincts. He disdained trade unionism, fretted about "the lowest class insist[ing] on enslaving the upper class," and expressed "hopes that the governing class will use some common sense to maintain their rule."[69] His fellow pragmatists were more in tune with the changing times and mores, convinced that the social structure of American capitalism had to be updated, that "ideas are worthless except as they pass into actions which rearrange and reconstruct in some way, be it little or large, the world in which we live."[70] Toward the end of his life, James came close to endorsing "the more or less socialistic future towards which mankind seems drifting."[71] Dewey was also deeply impressed with socialism before he rallied behind a robust social democratic agenda premised on the notion that "liberalism must become radical in the sense that, instead of using social power to ameliorate the evil consequences of the existing system, it shall use social power to change the system."[72] Today's pragmatists stress with Richard Posner that pragmatist philosophy has "no inherent political valence,"[73] an observation borne out by a broad spectrum of political beliefs found among pragmatists, ranging from Rorty's aesthetically tinged libertarianism[74] to Cornell West's "prophetic pragmatism."[75] This political ambivalence notwithstanding, pragmatist thinkers of the old and new school have been critical of existing institutions and open to ameliorative social change, even though the direction of this change and its specific forms are subject to a continuous debate.

A note of caution about the suggested six-point list is in order—it should not be taken as exhaustive. The best way to see it is as an "ideal type" or a theoretical construct which judges an empirical phenomenon by the extent to which it approximates the construct, even though no claim is made that the case in point is a pure instance of a given kind.[76] Pragmatists do not see eye to eye on every issue. Some may well disavow a particular premise on the six-point list.[77] With the possible exception of Habermas, few would endorse today Peirce's Kantian belief that "[t]he opinion which is fated to be ultimately agreed by all who investigate, is what we mean by truth, and the object represented in this opinion is the real."[78] Nor is every pragmatist comfortable with James's freewheeling pragmatism that "is willing to take anything, to follow either logic or the senses and to count the humblest and most personal ... [even] mystical experiences if they have practical consequences."[79] In today's pragmatist camp, some are uneasy about Rorty's libertarian aestheticism, others feel Fish has gone too far deploring theory, and quite a few disavow Posner's market-knows-best perspective on law. What pragmatists share is a set of attitudes present to various degrees in individual thinkers, yet revealing enough of a common ferment to suggest a "family resemblance."[80] I borrow this last metaphor from Ludwig Wittgenstein, whom pragmatists readily claim as their own.[81] If we push this metaphor a bit further, we can say that things aren't always tranquil in the pragmatist family. Indeed, they get rather nasty at times, as family members fight for a competitive advantage and promote their own brand of pragmatism. With this in mind, we now turn to legal pragmatism.

IV. Jurists Respond to Pragmatism

The term "legal pragmatism" is of relatively recent vintage. It did not come into wide circulation until the 1980s, though the phenomenon itself is at least a hundred years old, dating back to Oliver Wendell Holmes and Benjamin Cardozo, two distinguished American legal minds who gave pragmatic jurisprudence a strong impetus still felt today. Holmes was a founding member of the Metaphysical Club (along with Peirce, James, Green, and Chauncey Wright), where the pragmatist salvo first sounded in the early 1870s. Yet, Holmes had few good things to say about fellow pragmatists. He found James's *Pragmatism* superfluous and confided to a friend that "the judging of law by its effects and results did not have to wait for W[illiam] J[ames] or Pound for its existence."[82] Although Cardozo was more indebted to legal realism than to pragmatism, he, unlike Holmes, cited Dewey and James as philosophical authorities and fondly repeated the pragmatist maxim.[83] When it comes to their pronouncements on law and specific legal holdings, however, both Holmes and Cardozo displayed the signature pragmatic skepticism about immutable principles, a respect for changing community mores, an appetite for fact-finding inquiry, and a willingness to support reform. Holmes's celebrated opening in his *Common Law* can be read as a creedal statement of legal pragmatism:

> The life of the law has not been logic: it has been experience. The felt necessities of the time, the prevalent moral and political theories, institutions of public policy, avowed or unconscious, even the prejudices which judges share with their fellow-men, have had a good deal more to do than the syllogism in determining the rules by which men should be governed.[84]

From his early years as a private attorney and throughout his distinguished service on the Supreme Juridical Court of Massachusetts and the United States Supreme Court, Holmes practiced the jurisprudence of pragmatic compromise, refusing to privilege civil rights, judicial discretion, political expediency, or any other principle while drawing freely on them when the situation warranted. In keeping with epistemological consequentialism, Holmes redefined concepts like "right," "liberty," "contract," and "property" in a way that stripped them of their metaphysical halo and brought to the fore their hard-boiled practical implications. "But for legal purposes a right is only the hypostasis of a prophecy," proclaimed Holmes, and it owes its efficacy to "the fact that the public force will be brought to bear upon those who do things said to contravene it."[85] When the right in question is enforced intermittently, its objective status comes into question, and when a specific liberty is no longer backed by administrative force, it matters not if society continues to pay lip service to it—such a liberty is but a legal fiction. Looked at from this angle, the meaning of a legal principle no longer pivots out on itself. Rather, it grows with the circumstances and absorbs the changing historical climate, its objectivity treated as a variable reflecting specific context and not as a property inherent in the principle.

"Contract" is another legal precept which does not owe its efficacy to some major premise enshrined in constitutional tracts and guiding inquiry to an inevitable conclusion. Contract ultimately refers to the practical consequences likely to befall those who enter a legal agreement. An unscrupulous businessman—a "bad man" as Holmes called him famously, "does not care two straws for the axioms or deductions, but ... he does want to know what the Massachusetts or English courts are likely to do in fact. I am much of his mind. The prophecies of what the courts will do in fact, and nothing more pretentious, are what I mean by the law."[86] To determine what restraints the government can impose on the freedom of contract, it is not enough to perform a logical syllogism, to construe a statute in light of its plain language, to let a constitutional principle speak for itself—one also has to take into account changing community standards and the statute's impact on the parties involved.

The voluminous batch of legal opinions bearing his name attest to Holmes's pragmatic convictions that "[g]eneral propositions do not decide concrete cases," that courts had rightfully been "cutting down the liberty to contract by way of combination," and that a statute limiting working hours under hazardous conditions was not an infringement on the employers' constitutional rights to contract freely but a "proper measure on the score of health."[87] In a dissenting opinion Holmes entered in *Adkins v. Children's Hospital*, he appeals to the "industrial peace" as the ground for rejecting the constitutional reasons the majority invoked to strike down a law "forbid[ding] employment at rates below those fixed as the minimum requirement of health and right living."[88] The same activist reasoning informs his numerous judgments, many held in dissent, that endeared Holmes to progressive politicians of his time and infuriated laissez-faire supporters. A rare occasion on the U.S. Supreme Court, dissent would become increasingly common after Holmes, who used it to articulate the nascent community values inviting a fresh look at the Constitution. Rationales behind his specific decisions varied, but the willingness to go beyond the precedent, to give a novel reading to time-honored principles in light of changing community standards, remains the hallmark of Holmes's method throughout his tenure on the U.S. Supreme Court.

Following his illustrious predecessors on the Supreme Court, Cardozo linked his judicial perspective to the common law tradition with its benign view of judicial discretion and sensitivity to evolving policy concerns. More than Holmes, Cardozo was willing to theorize the principles underlying his jurisprudence, to trace their intellectual roots and credit his philosophical comrades in arm: "[T]he juristic philosophy of the common law is at bottom the philosophy of pragmatism. Its truth is relative, not absolute. The rule that functions well produces a title deed to recognition."[89] His is a theory of the legal process that focuses on law-in-use or law-in-the-making—law as it manifests itself in a judgment rendered upon a particular situation with a specific set of circumstances to contend with. Cardozo captured the emergent determinism germane to the legal system in this trenchant formula: "Law never *is*, but is always about to be. It is realized only when embodied in a judgment, and in being realized, expires. There are no such things as rules or principles: there are only isolated dooms."[90] Law, in other words, becomes pragmatically meaningful when applied to the full range of cases whose adjudication determines the proper scope and meaning of the law. Before a legal judgment is passed, the situation remains open to multiple determinations just as the law invites disparate, conflicting interpretations. The judge terminates indeterminacy by selecting a terminological frame from the current stock of laws, principles, and precedents, achieving in the process what Dewey calls in his theory of inquiry the "transformation of an indeterminate unsettled situation into a determinate unified existential situation."[91] To "terminate" means two opposite things here: "to define, to delimit the sense" as well as "to extinguish, to bring to an end." By choosing particular terminological means of discursive production, we do justice to the situation at the cost of doing violence to its alternative determinations, some of which, preserved for posterity in dissenting opinions, might ground future determinations. Laws and legal canons we use to terminate the indeterminacy may be thoroughly codified, but for all their formal rigor legal principles routinely get in each other's way, leaving professionals ample room to argue which one takes precedent in the case at bar. Indeed, the function the legal lore plays in juridical practice is not altogether dissimilar to the folklore where proverbs strategically contradict each other, and where this very multivocity serves a practical purpose by allowing the user to invoke a maxim most suitable for the situation and amenable to the interpreter's agenda. By rendering the situation officially meaningful, legal judgment bears the double burden of doing justice to the unique fact pattern and sustaining law as a semi-coherent system—the two objectives that often work at cross-purpose.

With this turn of argument, the locus of the judicial process shifts to legal judgment which instantiates a universal law in a particular case just as it universalizes the case particulars into court certified facts. The law in question may seem to leave little or no room for disagreement, but the determinacy the legal judgment confers on the situation is something socio-historically emergent rather than a priori—ahistorically—true. This certainty is a product of the ongoing interpretation process that stretches back for generations. Once the community sense of right and wrong has changed, the interpretive process ceases to be routine, novel fact patterns are discerned, and old principles are given new ostensible definitions. Legislators play their part in codifying the most enduring social changes, but the logistics of statutory law enactment is too slow and unwieldy to keep pace with the continually evolving reality. And so, it often falls on the courts to lead the way in articulating the changing community values and establishing in situ the emergent meaning of a particular law and of the Constitution as a whole. Justice John Marshall is one example Cardozo cited to illustrate how a judge at once expresses emerging national needs and helps channel them along: "He gave to the constitution of the United States the impress of his own mind; and the form of our constitutional law is what it is, because he moulded it while it was still plastic and malleable in the fire of his own intense convictions."[92] Judges are more than neutral transmitters for immutable principles; they apply the rules in situ, remaining faithful to the constitutional ethos while adjusting the settled principles to the community mores continuously evolving with the passage of time. Thus, it is imperative for judges to ask, "Does liberty mean the same thing for successive generations? May restraints that were arbitrary yesterday be useful and rational and therefore lawful today? May restraints that are arbitrary today become useful and rational and therefore lawful tomorrow? I have no doubt," Cardozo concludes, "that the answer to these questions must be yes."[93]

This pragmatic jurisprudence was marked by an increasing reliance on social science research used by judges to justify their ruling. Economic, sociological, and epidemiological data was in particular demand, as legal scholars angled for a construction promising to breathe new life into the old laws:

> Courts know today that statutes are to be viewed, not in isolation or *in vacuo*, as pronouncements of abstract principles for the guidance of an ideal community, but in the setting and the framework of present-day conditions, as revealed by the labors of economists and students of the social sciences in our own country and abroad.[94]

Legal inquiry extends beyond the study of relevant statutes and precedents—it encompasses the legislative history, the present day social conditions, and the latest empirical data bearing on the pending judgment.

An increased attention to speech conditions advancing the democratic process is another prominent feature of pragmatist jurisprudence. When government or corporate interests work to suppress critical opinions, judges should err on the side of allowing even extreme views (like those of the socialist leader Eugene Debs) to reach the public ear. This is what Justice Holmes urged when he wrote in his famous dissent in *Abrams v. United Sates* that "the ultimate good desired is better reached by free trade in ideas—that the best test of truth is the power of the thought to get itself accepted in the competition of the market.... That at any rate is the theory of our Constitution."[95]

One more aspect of the pragmatist current in legal thought needs to be singled out. I am talking about the oft admired rhetorical power of the written corpus Holmes and Cardozo left to posterity. Posner believes that Holmes is read today not so much because he spawned innovative legal opinions but because of the superb style in which his judgments are clothed, even when his specific legal opinions are flawed.[96] I see this dimension of early legal pragmatism as reflecting its proponents' commitment to embodied reasonableness. However intellectually grounded, a constitutional principle or a statutory enactment cannot be effective unless it affects our minds as well as emotions. This is where rhetoric is called upon to play a part, for its office is to shake our convictions, move us toward a new way of seeing, and stir one into actions that change the shape of things. Good rhetoric is something you cannot readily ignore. It plants in your soma the nagging seeds of doubt and tender hooks of hope which pull you by your guts, compelling you to confront your prejudices and realign your action with you beliefs. Cardozo urged jurists to pay close attention to the noncognitive springs of other people's—and their own—conduct: "Deep below consciousness are other forces, the likes and the dislikes, the predilections and the prejudices, the complex of instincts and emotions and habits and convictions, which make the man, whether he be litigant or judge."[97] Mastering rhetorical tools is one way legal professionals can achieve their ultimate goal of furthering justice, order, and peace in society.

As for their political agenda, we should not take the legal pragmatists' openness to change as a sign of their personal political preferences. Holmes's dicta often sound progressive, as when he opines "that legislation should easily and quickly, yet not too quickly, modify itself in accordance with the will of the de facto supreme power in the community and ... spread ... an educated sympathy [to] reduce the sacrifice of minorities to a minimum."[98] But if you read closely the rationales he proffers for desired policy objectives, you discover how firmly his sentiments were rooted in nineteenth-century Social Darwinism.[99] Holmes was a true believer in the struggle for survival that demands the sacrifice of the weakest. The law should interfere in this evolutionary struggle only to the extent necessary to give all groups a fair chance to compete. Society is within its rights to enlist law to expedite the extinction of a group no longer able to fight for itself or contribute to societal welfare. This is why Holmes voted to uphold a Virginia law permitting involuntary sterilization in *Buck v. Bell*, with this rationalization to buttress his case: "We have seen more than once that the public welfare may call upon the best citizens for their lives. It would be strange if it could not call upon those who already sap the strength of the State for these lesser sacrifices."[100]

As a member of the religious minority who saw discrimination first-hand, Cardozo showed no traces of nativism found in the upper-crust American progressivism of this era. He was not given to doubt about the wisdom of reform afflicting his distinguished predecessor on the Supreme Court. To the end he remained convinced that "[t]he final cause of law is the welfare of society."[101] He supported wholeheartedly the New Deal laws, often finding himself in the minority on the Court, yet pressing his case with dignity and flair, occasionally convincing the majority to reverse itself and endorse his views. There is a warmth to his prose, an apparent absence of malice disguised as humility that sometimes mars Holmes's judgment. You sense this in his demeanor as well as his rhetoric; you want to believe that Cardozo embodied in personal conduct the pragmatist virtues he professed in theory. This alignment between pragmatist discourse and practical action would not become an issue until legal pragmatists were ready to move beyond the traditional legal venues into town halls and mediation forums where they could rejoin other citizens in shaping America's democratic process.

V. The Resurgence of Legal Pragmatism

Legal pragmatism is much in the news these days, in both the popular and scholarly press. It raises unsettling questions, fights an established dogma, yet offers few clear-cut solutions to the problems afflicting today's jurisprudence. And these problems are legion, according Richard

Posner. The U.S. legal system is "much too solemn and self-important," "too marmoreal, hieratic, and censorious," "too theocratic," while its practitioners are apt to show "too much confidence," "too little curiosity," "too much emphasis on authority, certitude, rhetoric, and tradition," and "too little on consequences and on social-scientific techniques."[102] In sharp contrast to this moribund picture is a paradigm Posner offers to his colleagues as a philosophical alternative which invites a sober look at "the limitations of human reason," accepts "the unattainability of 'truth'," takes "problems concretely, experimentally, without illusions," acknowledges the inexorable "'localness' of human knowledge," and urges that "social thought and action be evaluated as instruments to valued human goals rather than as ends in themselves."[103] The name of this paradigm is pragmatism. Alas, if you are a lawyer or a judge, there is not much you can do with it. It is more of an attitude than a creed, more a mood than a practical guide to action; its most trenchant advice to professionals curious about a "method of pragmatic jurisprudence" is to practice "kicking ... sacred cows"[104] and keep "muddling through."[105]

Kicking sacred cows is indeed a favorite pastime of many legal pragmatists, so much so that you begin to wonder if such cruelty to animals is really conducive to reasoned discourse. Fortunately, there is more to pragmatist jurisprudence than name calling and the avowal of faith. We get a better sense of what legal pragmatists are up to when we move beyond their programmatic statements and examine their specific legal judgments. A good place to start is the robust pragmatist defense Stanley Fish offers to laws supporting affirmative action.[106]

In a piece titled *When Principles Stand in the Way*, Fish takes to task both the proponents and opponents of affirmative action for their misguided efforts to ground their policy objectives in a priori principles. One example of the futile search for such a neutral standard is Wechsler's article about the decision in *Brown v. Board of Education*, where the author, troubled by the Supreme Court's failure to procure a major theoretical premise for its pragmatic decision to allow school integration, offers a "general principle whose application would yield that result independently."[107] The principle general enough to allow the right deduction, Wechsler proposed, is "the right of freedom of association." However, the application of the principle yielded paradoxical results: If segregation denies excluded minorities the right to free association, then forced integration coerces into an association those who wish to avoid it. Either way, the facts on the ground would not square off with the Constitutional principle, which sounds unimpeachable in formal theory but proves to be divisive in real-life situations. The solution Fish offers is pragmatic: Don't let a good principle stand in the way of a sound policy. "A principle scorns actual historical circumstances and moves quickly to a level of generalization and abstraction so high that the facts of history can no longer be seen."[108] The policy in question is a sound one—to remedy the insidious consequences of institutional racism that marred social relations in America for generations. You get nowhere when you have "substituted philosophical urgencies for social urgencies" in such cases. Worse than that, you give ammunition to and stir up bitter opposition from the opponents of social integration who are only too happy to cover their bigoted motives by taking refuge in hallowed principles. Fish quotes Justice Stevens's plain words that set the matter straight in the controversies surrounding affirmative action: "There is no moral or Constitutional equivalence between a policy that is designed to perpetuate a caste system and one that seeks to eradicate racial subordination."[109] By reverting to neutral principles like "fairness," "equality," "merit," or "color-blindness," Fish contends, you are really "playing on your opponent's field and thus buying into his position."[110] The brief for pragmatist jurisprudence concludes with this plea:

> Let's be done with code words and concentrate on the problems we face and on possible ways of solving them. Those who support affirmative action should give up searching for theoretical consistency—a goal at once impossible and unworthy—and instead seek strategies with the hope of relieving the pain of people who live in the world and not in the never-never land of theory.[111]

Less hostile to legal principles and theoretical considerations is the position articulated by Orlando Patterson. His article titled "Affirmative Action: The Sequel," defends affirmative action on the pragmatic ground of policy objectives and cost effectiveness. Several decades after the courts threw their support behind affirmative action, we can see the progress made: fewer ethnic riots, racial integration at major universities, more heterogeneous professional elites, gains in the African-American middle class, and the emergence of a global popular culture where minorities play a key role. This progress has had its cost born in part by the whites, but this cost was modest. As befitting a pragmatically driven legal argument, Patterson cites research data to back up his claim: "[N]o more than 7 percent of Americans of European heritage claim to have been adversely affected by affirmative action programs."[112] While Patterson acknowledges that "affirmative action violates fundamental principles that have guided this country" and that it is "difficult to reconcile affirmative action with the nation's manifest ideals of individualism and merit-based competition," he does not shrink from the challenge, pointing out that "America's history is replete with just such pragmatic fudging of these ideals."[113] Congress has not hesitated in passing legislative acts that support special interests—multinational corporations, millionaire farmers, oil well drillers, mortgage owners, and war veterans have benefited from these statutory enactments with dubious Constitutional provenance. But there are red flags for the African-American leaders who search for an overarching principle like "diversity" in which to ground programs favoring minorities, for "many whites who were otherwise prepared to turn a pragmatic blind eye to their principled concerns about affirmative action" will not stand for ever-expanding entitlements benefiting minorities who stake no claim to have been wronged in the past.[114] The affirmative action legislation is unique, its purpose is "to redress the past wrongs," not to indulge in "the celebration of separate identities." Henceforth, one should stay clear of "affirmative action as an entitlement, requiring little or no efforts on the part of minorities."[115] Patterson concludes with an appeal to our pragmatic wisdom, which does not require throwing away principles and bravely embraces the inevitable clash between the cherished ideals enshrined in our Constitution:

> Americans have always recognized that high ideals, however desirable, inevitably clash with reality, and that good public policy requires compromise. But only through the struggle of affirmative action are they coming to realize that such compromises, wisely pursued, can actually serve a higher principle: the supreme virtue of being fair to those who have been most unfairly treated.[116]

Posner's latest book, *Law, Pragmatism, and Democracy*, offers more examples of the pragmatic approach to litigation on highly divisive issues facing our nation. On *Bush v. Gore*, Posner offers "a pragmatic defense of the Supreme Court's controversial decision."[117] He agrees with the critics that the Court's rationale for its majority decision was flawed. This decision shows how perilous the judgment often is when reached in haste under the conditions of national emergency. "[T]he Justices' choice of the ground of decision, and other strategic choices that various Justices made in the course of the litigation, turned *Bush v. Gore* into a pragmatic donnybrook."[118] Spurious though the foundation on which the holding rests, it led to the right outcome. "The result was defensible—and that matters a great deal to a pragmatist! It was not the outrage to democracy and the rule of law that the critics of the decision have claimed it was, unless the Justices' motives were as malign as some of their critics have charged."[119] The due attention to the consequences is what makes the ultimate decision, if not the Court's reasoning, correct, for "the danger that there would be a Presidential succession crisis if the Court failed to intervene was one of the pragmatic considerations that should have weighed (and perhaps did weigh) with the Supreme Court..."[120]

The opposite is true of the outcome in *Clinton v. Jones* where the Court failed to weigh the likely consequences of its decision to force the sitting president to testify in a private law suit. It is fine to invoke principles like "no one is above the law," but when the Supreme Court denied President Clinton the narrowly crafted temporary immunity he sought from testifying in Paula Jones's sexual harassment suit, it plunged the nation into the paralyzing spectacle which lead to Clinton's impeachment.[121]

Posner also brings up kindred pragmatic arguments in cases involving the First Amendment issues. He rejects the notion that "First Amendment freedoms are 'absolute',," urging attention to "the relationship between pragmatic adjudication and the use by judges of cost-benefit analysis in 'noneconomic' cases."[122] On national security legislation like the Patriot Act, Posner defends government actions, citing "the urgent need for taking a pragmatic approach to cases that arise out of national emergencies—cases involving war, terrorism, economic depression."[123] He asks judges to weigh carefully the consequences that the constraints imposed on individual rights will have on the quality of life and advocates measured, revisable compromises that reflect the nation's security needs while preserving our liberties.

Pragmatic jurisprudence has secured a foothold in the nation's highest judicial body. "The Supreme Court that upheld the new campaign finance law on Wednesday," announces a typical newspaper article, "was a pragmatic court, concerned less with the fine points of constitutional doctrine than with the real world context and consequences of the intensely awaited decision."[124] Popular press credits several Justices with pragmatist virtues. David Souter receives accolades from liberal commentators for his "brand of moderate pragmatism and his willingness to engage Justice Scalia in direct intellectual combat,"[125] and so does Justice Sandra O'Connor—"the court's leading pragmatist [who] cast only five dissenting votes in the entire term, far fewer than anyone else, and was in the majority in 13 of the 18 most closely decided cases."[126] But it is Justice Breyer who is rightly considered the premier theoretician of legal pragmatism on the nation's highest court. His recent exchange with Justice Scalia—the Court's chief opponent of pragmatic jurisprudence—brings into sharp focus the constitutional issues involved.

Scalia is a formidable opponent. His powerful—or sinister, as critics allege—attacks on legal realism and its pragmatist heirs show the real stakes we all have in this debate. In a speech Scalia gave at the University of Chicago Divinity School, the justice dramatized the constitutional issue involved:

> As it is, however, the Constitution that I interpret and apply is not living but dead—or, as I prefer to put it, enduring. It means today not what current society (much less the Court) thinks it ought to mean, but what it meant when it was adopted. For me, therefore, the constitutionality of the death penalty is not a difficult, soul-wrenching question. It was clearly permitted when the Eighth Amendment was adopted...[127]

As this statement attests, Scalia is a proponent of "originalism"—an influential constitutional doctrine that appeals to the framers' original understanding embodied in the text of the Constitution and steadfastly resisting efforts to tailor its meaning to the changing community mores.[128] Scalia forswears attempts "to impose our 'maturing' society's 'evolving standards of decency'" on our Constitution. "That moral obligation may weigh heavily upon the voter, and upon the legislator who enacts the laws," he states,

> [b]ut a judge, I think, bears no moral guilt for the laws society has failed to enact. Thus, my difficulty with *Roe v. Wade* is a legal rather than a moral one: I do not believe (and, for two hundred years, no one believed) that the Constitution contains a right to abortion. And if a state were to permit abortion on demand, I would—and could in good conscience—vote against an attempt to invalidate that law for the same reason that I vote against the invalidation of laws that forbid abortion on demand: because the Constitution gives the federal government (and hence me) no power over the matter.[129]

In the widely read Tanner Lecture on Human Values he delivered at Princeton University, Scalia articulated his "philosophy of statutory construction in general (known loosely as textualism) and of constitutional construction in particular (known loosely as originalism)."[130] He did not spare sarcasm about the brand of jurisprudence championed by Holmes and Cardozo and now taught to first year law students who are plowed with stories about a wise judge "running through earlier cases that leaves him free to impose that rule—distinguishing one prior case on his left, straight-arming another one on his right, high-stepping away from another precedent about to tackle him from the rear until (bravo!) he reaches his goal: good law."[131]

Scalia takes pains to distinguish his "textualism" from "strict constructionism," the latter obstinately holding onto a literal sense of the law, the former allowing that statutes "should be construed reasonably, to contain all that it fairly means"[132] in line with the established "rules of interpretation called the canons of construction."[133] The point he strains to make is that we should beware of adapting the Constitution to the political moods of the country, for:

> It surely cannot be said that a constitution naturally suggests changeability; to the contrary, its whole purpose is to prevent change—to embed certain rights in such a manner that future generations cannot take them away.... If the courts are free to write the Constitution anew, they will, by God, write it the way the majority wants.... This, of course, is the end of the Bill of Rights, whose meaning will be committed to the very body it was meant to protect against: the majority.[134]

Stephen Breyer responded to Scalia's spirited defense of originalism and textualism in the James Madison Lecture he gave at the New York University Law School, where he spelled out the interpretation cannons guiding jurisprudence steeped in the pragmatist ethos.[135] This particular brand of jurisprudence espouses "an approach to constitutional interpretation that places considerable weight upon consequences—consequences valued in terms of basic constitutional purposes," a perspective that "disavows a contrary constitutional approach, a more 'legalistic' approach that places too much weight upon language, history, tradition, and precedent alone while understating the importance of consequences."[136] Central to Breyer's argument is the contention that the U.S. Constitution embodies several complementary principles which sometime work at cross-purpose. He lists five such objectives: "(1) democratic self-government, (2) dispersion of power (avoiding concentration of too much power in too few hands), (3) individual dignity (through protection of individual liberties), (4) equality before the law (through equal protection of the law), and (5) the rule of law itself."[137] According to Breyer, the problem with legal formalists is that they fail to appreciate the importance of giving all these objectives fair play. They focus on the dispersion of power and the rule of law yet overlook other values encysted in the Constitution, particularly the need to foster democratic self-government. Nevertheless, formalists cannot escape the very fallacies of which they accuse their opponents, since their "'literalism' tends to produce the legal doctrines (related to the First Amendment, to federalism, to statutory interpretation, to equal protection) that ... lead to consequences at least as harmful, from a constitutional perspective, as any increased risk of subjectivity."[138] Appealing to the plain meaning supposedly inherent in the constitutional and statutory documents, the originalists conveniently gloss over the inconsistencies and ambiguities abounding in such texts. Breyer notes,

> The more literal judges may hope to find in language, history, tradition, and precedent objective interpretive standards; they may seek to avoid an interpretive subjectivity that could confuse a judge's personal idea of what is good for that which the Constitution demands; and they may believe that these more "original" sources will more readily yield rules that can guide other institutions, including lower courts. These objectives are desirable, but I do not think the literal approach will achieve them, and, in any event, the constitutional price is too high.[139]

With his interpretive weapons drawn, Breyer proceeds to analyze several key legislative acts that have come before the Supreme Court—campaign finance reform, the disposal of toxic substances, federal minimum standards, equal protection and voting rights, and laws infringing on privacy rights—showing in each case how the decisions he recommended, some reflecting the minority opinion, navigate between the equally sound yet conflicting objectives propounded by the framers. Breyer's overriding concern in all these decisions was to promote "the Constitution's general democratic participatory objectives [which] can help courts deal more effectively with a range of specific constitutional issues."[140]

There is the story of a British official entrusted to hold court in India who asks his more experienced colleague for advice. "Use your common sense," the esteemed judge tells him, "and you will almost always be right, but never give reasons for your rulings, for they will almost always be wrong." That is, pretty much, what radical pragmatists at law advise us to do. It is easier to see what they oppose—originalism, textualism, formalism—than to grasp any alternatives they put forward. Legal pragmatists reject originalism on the ground that we could not possibly fathom the primordial constitutional understanding, not with fifty-five framers struggling to reach a compromise over the Constitution and some 1,500 delegates bitterly contesting its meaning at the state ratifying conventions. Nor can we rely on the plain language of the final document to yield its timeless meanings to honest textualists willing to set aside their prejudices and let the Constitution speak for itself. Pragmatists are skeptical about any doctrine that casts the judge as a faithful agent carrying out the legislative will by applying formal rules while ignoring the ambiguities inherent in legislative acts and conflicting special interests embodied in their provisions. Pragmatist jurists see the judicial process as part of a national conversation in which they take part as legal professionals entrusted to guard the tradition and as citizens sensitive to evolving community standards. They are eclectic in the choice of tools,[141] ready to reach for whatever helps advance the democratic process in a manner consistent with the framers' ideals. An ethos more than a theory, pragmatism invites judges to cultivate an inquiring mind, consult empirical research, and accept all conclusions as provisional in the face of the semi-chaotic world we inhabit. Sometimes that means drawing on "the ragtag bag of metaphors, analogies, rules of thumb, inspirational phrases, incantations, and jerry-built 'reasons' that keep the conversation going and bring it to temporary, and always revisable, conclusions."[142]

One senses this pragmatic attitude in Justice Breyer's contention that laws change "in the context of a national conversation involving, among others, scientists, engineers, businessmen and women, the media, along with legislators, judges, and many ordinary citizens"[143]; in his willingness to enlist rhetorical devises like "metaphor [which helps] avoid the more rigid interpretations to which greater reliance upon canons alone would lead"; and in his determination to "harmonize a court's daily work of interpreting statutes with the Constitution's democratic, and liberty-protecting, objectives."[144] As Breyer's analysis suggests, there is more to the pragmatist method than blowing with the political winds. Legal pragmatists need not dispense with principles or ditch theory altogether, as Stanley Fish would have it. Principles have their rightful place in the pragmatist analysis, provided we understand that they do not coalesce into an immaculate logical system and are often at loggerheads. Theory comes in handy too, especially if it is open to nonclassical insights into the objective indeterminacy of the situation. Dewey urged judges to adopt "a logic *relative to consequences rather than to antecedents*, a logic of prediction of probabilities rather than one of deduction of certainties," but he also maintained that "in judicial decisions the only alternative to arbitrary dicta, accepted by the parties to a controversy only because of the authority or prestige of the judge, is a rational statement which formulates grounds and exposes connecting or logical links."[145] The search for pragmatically understood principles and a logic of inquiry consistent with emergent determinism remains on the legal pragmatists' research agenda.

VI. The Place of Principles in Pragmatic Jurisprudence

Rightly or wrongly, weighing consequences is perceived as the chief method of pragmatist adjudication that lets a cost-benefit analysis tip the scales toward a particular holding. But do we not endorse the facts-speak-for-themselves positivism when we claim "[t]here are bad pragmatic decisions as well as good ones"[146] without spelling out the accounting principles to guide the evaluation? Zeroing in on legal outcomes and their long-term impact on society poses serious challenges.

For one thing, the consequences a legal ruling is likely to engender are often hard to fathom, and when they loom large, it is difficult to calculate their true cost. Just try to balance the risk of plunging the country into a presidential succession crisis against the damage to the rule of law the Court's decision in *Bush v. Gore* could have precipitated. Biases affecting decision calculus are another difficult-to-gauge factor in high-wire balancing acts, like the one the Supreme Court had to perform in *Roe v. Wade*.[147] According to Posner, the justices failed to reach a pragmatically viable decision in this crucial case. When they overturned the Texas statute prohibiting abortion (except where a woman's life is endangered), the Justices underestimated the moral outrage their decision was likely to provoke in certain religious circles. Nor did the Court weigh the positive impact on sexual habits that letting the Texas statute stand could have had, such as "to make girls and women somewhat more careful about sexual activity than if they still had access to abortion on demand as a backup to contraception...."[148] Above all, Posner contends, the justices failed to consider the "stifling effect on democratic experimentation of establishing a constitutional right to abortion."[149] It was wrong, in other words, to stop a state from pursuing its own policy and finding out whether it works in practice.

Posner does not dwell on the negative consequences that upholding the Texas antiabortion statute could have produced—outrage among the pro-choice activists, grim prospects of back alley abortions, the difficulty of monitoring compliance with the Texas statute. Yet, the cost of such consequences was hardly negligible, and weighing it against the cost of the decision the Court handed down in *Roe v. Wade* would have been a contentious exercise without a principle to anchor the holding. Whether it is an unconscious bias or an explicitly stated rationale, some sort of perspective is bound to guide the evaluation process. Even Stanley Fish cannot avoid recourse to general principles when he talks about "long-standing injustices" as a reason for pressing on with affirmative action,[150] to say nothing of Orlando Patterson's appeal to "the supreme virtue of being fair."[151] And if we add up all the pragmatic consequences Posner cites in his opposition to *Roe v. Wade*, it would not seem outlandish to infer that their combined effect dovetails with conservative principles.

Matching legal decisions with their consequences is indeed a hazard-ous enterprise. Based on the "If X, then Y" logic, such an exercise tends to run afoul of the *ceteris paribus* clause, the assumption that other things are being equal. If the world consisted of two variables only—X and Y, the presence of X would indeed likely affect the behavior of Y. Other factors are rarely equal in the real world, however, where an indefinite number of variables are at work and where the events cannot be readily broken down into logical antecedents and outcomes. In the real world, we are forced to deal with causal networks that produce wide-ranging, often unanticipated consequences which leave ample room for partisan squabbling about which outcome can be credited to what decision. It took time for economists to realize that unregulated markets produce monopolies inimical to free trade and for social scientists to figure out that releasing the mentally ill from hospitals turns prisons into mental wards. Reckoning with this perennial uncertainty, pragmatists learned to mistrust broad theoretical claims, stick close to particulars, and keep tracking the unanticipated consequences our informed decisions rou-tinely produce. Still, pragmatists are not ready to give up on principles altogether.

Posner is well aware that pragmatic jurisprudence cannot confine itself to weighing consequences, which is why he rejects crude consequential-ism and embraces a qualified consequentialism he credits to a genuinely pragmatic approach, which is not above borrowing wisdom from any creed. In this spirit, Posner adopts a not-that-I-am-against rhetorical strategy designed to prove legal pragmatism's moderate bona fide. "It would not be unpragmatic to prefer the rule to the standard," he writes. "Nor would it be unpragmatic to refuse to recognize any but the most excruciatingly narrow exception to the rule."[152] "Nor is it unpragmatic to worry ... about constitutional doctrines that are so loose that they give judges carte blanche to decide cases any way they want..."[153] Moreover, "legal pragmatism is not always and everywhere the best approach to law ... in some circumstances formalism is the best pragmatic strategy."[154] There is no analytical arrow, it seems, which would not fit into the prag-matist quiver. With the conceptual net spread so widely, legal pragmatists make their claims sound plausible, but such an ecumenist strategy has its cost: it blurs the pragmatic jurist's identity, turns legal pragmatism into a hodge-podge of ad hoc practices, and unwittingly refocuses attention on the moral underpinnings of law. Posner shows little interest in juridical moralism, resolutely rejecting Kant's "moralistic conception of law far removed from pragmatic considerations."[155] But scholars sympathetic to the pragmatism's progressive agenda are willing to give the Kantian perspective on human autonomy another chance.

The natural law tradition from which Kant derived his inspiration had furnished a theoretical groundwork for modern republicanism. The inalienable rights verbiage helped safeguard human autonomy against absolutism, and as such, it aided the movement toward civil society which gave citizens the liberties necessary to advance their private goals with minimum state interference. Natural law shored up capitalist markets, providing the bourgeoisie with the enforceable legal constructs to support their entrepreneurial ventures. Unfettered commerce, industrial buildup protected from state interference, labor free to sell itself in the marketplace, freedom to enter contractual relations anywhere in the nation—such laissez-faire principles inscribed into law did their magic with little public outcry well into the nineteenth century, when the harsh realities of unbridled capitalism began to ignite a serious opposition. As capitalism went through its natural cycles of multiplying goods and profits, it also left in its wake a trail of human misery which the custodians of law were no more eager to acknowledge than the captains of industry. The U.S. Supreme Court steadfastly invoked the freedom of contract to rebuff legislative efforts to soften the impact of round-the-clock manufacturing on children and women while citing the same natural law to keep women from entering the legal profession as inimical to "the nature of things" and the "functions of womanhood" which mercifully consigned women to "the domestic sphere."[156] Meanwhile, free competition bred fierce battles for the markets, and free markets begot cartels and trusts, whose monopolistic proclivities encouraged price fixing and pushed upward the cost of living, most ominously for labor, whose deteriorating working conditions stirred unrest at the century's end. The cause of human dignity that liberalism took for its guiding star was hard to reconcile with children working overtime on the factory floor and in shops throughout the country. Such was the fate of the "18th century doctrine of natural rights," Dewey charged, "which began as a liberal doctrine and is now the dogma of reactionaries."[157] Child labor legislation, the federal workmen's compensation program, the Adamson Act reducing working hours on interstate railroads, Sherman Antitrust regulations, food and drug laws—every statute passed during the Progressive era was at some point challenged in court as inimical to constitutional principles or stalled by legislators eager to please special interests. It was up to Holmes, Cardozo, and other juridical mavericks to nudge the Constitutions in a new direction to meet public concerns.

At first decried as *lapsus judicii*, their unconventional opinions would in time become mainstream.

Not that the rights natural law bestowed upon humans ceased to be valued. What happened was that the routine interpretation and enforcement of these rights produced consequences the American public came to judge injurious to its other rights. And that, I believe, is the point legal pragmatists like Holmes and Cardozo (and more recently Breyer) were trying to make in their defense of the consequence-oriented yet constitutionally grounded legal reasoning. The need for such jurisprudence becomes clear at major historical junctions. That is when new principles are invoked to offset old ones and fresh metaphors deployed to fire up moral imagination and spur legal creativity. It is at such a turning point in our legal history that pragmatic jurisprudence first came into its own.

This momentous historical transformation exemplifies the pragmatist notion of emergent determinism which, we may recall, suggests that our principles do not merely describe the world out there but also help usher it in, lend it determinacy. "Indeterminacy" does not mean the paucity of terms as much as their overabundance, with antithetical terminologies vying for attention and forcing themselves on the public mind. While the social world appears to its producers as a thing itself, it owes its being to terminological practices—and law is a paradigmatic example of a formal terminological practice—through which historical agents continuously frame themselves and their situations as objective and meaningful. Applied and enforced, a principle brings in tow an objective reality which appears to stand on its own, blinding its producers to the constitutive role their sense-bestowing interpretation and law-abiding action play in generating the world as a sheer fact. What humans discover at major historical junctions is that this facticity is a historical accomplishment, that as sense-making creatures we all take part in the production of objective social reality. We do so by applying the taken-for-granted values, principles, laws—the terminological means of production that generate the world as a readily recognizable, affectively saturated, behaviorally fleshed out historical construct. Such terminological props do not form a coherent system, although contradictions enciphered in the text remain hidden for the time being. Meanwhile, these contradictions do their subterranean work, as principles bump up against each other, with some forced into plain view, others pushed down, and new ones working their way into public discourse.

A good example of constitutional principles working at cross purpose is the slogans the French Revolution proudly placed on its masthead—*lib-*

erté, egalité, fraternité. Far from being mutually reinforcing, these principles subtly undermined each other. Civil liberties that allowed citizens to pursue their private interests without state interference did little to mitigate inequality. The material inequalities, in turn, handicapped the ability of the poor to redeem their constitutional rights and, in the absence of a meaningful safety net, dimmed prospects for social peace. Taking a clue from Isaiah Berlin we can say that by maximizing one value we are likely to undermine some other value, by doing justice to one right we may have to abridge another. The relationship between the antithetically paired principles is that of uncertainty—the two cannot be maximized simultaneously with an arbitrary precision. Clean environment, we all agree, is a good thing, but so is chip oil and energy self-sufficiency, and it is not until the issue of oil drilling in Alaska comes up that we are forced to judge which value must in the end trump the other. By the same token, we all value liberty and equality, yet pushing one principle to its limit will inevitably set it on a collision course with the other. And when principles we act upon bring forth conflicting realities, we cannot readily appeal to "facts" to resolve the tension between valued objectives, for these facts are propped up by the very principles we espouse. To deal with social strain, we must engage in a moral discourse about the first principles, their relative weight, and the kind of society they engender.

Herein lies the significance of the Kantian distinction between adjudication and justification, between positive law that treats reality as a fact determined in itself and moral law that lends to things themselves their humane significance. Both types of law rely on force to achieve their goals. In one case this is the administrative force that secures compliance through violence; in the other—the force of reason which appeals to nothing but our moral imagination or compassion with fellow human beings. Eclipsed by the utilitarian and pragmatic philosophies, this Kantian perspective has made a comeback. It shines through in contemporary thinkers like Ronald Dworkin who calls for "the moral reading of the Constitution"[158]; it is evident in John Rawls's commitment to "Kant's [and] Rousseau's idea that liberty is acting in accordance with a law that we give to ourselves"[159]; and it is most palpable in Jürgen Habermas who "demands a *remoralization* of politics"[160] and grounds his theory in the "principle, that—expressed in the Kantian manner—only reason should have force."[161] These authors seek to restore the debate about principles to its rightful place in jurisprudence, as well as widen public discourse on the meaning of justice. Each one uses a different strategy for reintegrating moral deliberation into the legal process.

VII. Juridical Moralism Reconsidered

In his influential monograph, *Law's Empire*, Dworkin outlines three competing perspectives on law—legal positivism, legal pragmatism, and what he calls "law as integrity."[162] Legal positivism has several strains, all converging on the premise that in any historical community there is one correct statement as to what the law is or what it requires, and it is up to jurists to discover and apply this correct reading to the case at bar. Legal positivists do not agonize about the law's ambiguities or the need to reconcile statutes with nascent mores. They simply follow the "plain-fact view of law" and enforce statutes in line with established conventions, relevant precedent, and the brute facts of the case.[163] Legal pragmatism, by comparison, is "a skeptical conception of law" premised on the notion that judges "should make whatever decisions seem to them best for the community's future, not counting any form of consistency with the past as valuable for its own sake."[164] The principle of right does not play a prominent role in this legal approach. Its proponents treat civil liberties as legal fictions filled with specific meaning by the judges who "sometimes act *as if* people had legal rights" but who are generally free to invoke or ignore any principle as the situation warrants, consistent with the overall objective of furthering social change.[165] This perspective, according to Dworkin, ignores the systemic properties of law, the paramount objective of reconstructing the legal corpus as a coherent system aimed to (a) produce predictable outcomes; (b) clarify the overall constitutional architecture; and (c) regenerate the nation's liberal culture. Such is the burden of the third legal perspective Dworkin calls "law as integrity which accepts law and legal rights wholeheartedly,"[166] "demands consistency with decisions already made by other judges and legislature,"[167] and claims that "law's constraints benefit society not just by providing predictability or procedural fairness, or in some other instrumental way, but by securing a kind of equality among citizens that makes their community more genuine and improves its moral justification for exercising the political power it does."[168]

In his subsequent works, Dworkin grounds law as integrity in liberal values and principles he finds central to the U.S. Constitution. Chief among these is the "general principle that the government should not act out of prejudice against any group of citizens."[169] Doing so would violate human dignity and moral autonomy—values consistent with "the ideal of ethical individualism"[170] that Dworkin finds at the core of the U.S. Constitution interpreted in moral terms. With this move, Dworkin hopes to avoid the pitfalls of originalism, notably its proponents' reluctance to extend the reach of a constitutional principle beyond the matters it was meant to address by those who framed the principle. The fact that the Fourteenth Amendment aimed to remedy racial injustice and said nothing about gender discrimination should not handicap future generations from mobilizing the moral force built into this principle for a fight against the prejudicial, unequal treatment of women. The very abstract nature of moral principles codified in the Constitution serves as an interpretive resource, for "once we have defined the principle we attribute to the framers in the more abstract way, we must treat their views about women as misunderstandings of the force of their own principle, which time has given us the vision to correct, just as we treat their views about racially segregated education."[171] The adjudication process, then, focuses on the structure of constitutional principles, with the expectation that judges will justify every decision by explicitly anchoring it in a suitable moral principle and applying the same moral standard consistently to the full range of relevant cases.[172]

John Rawls takes a different route toward restoring the moral dimension of law. He enlists Kant's categorical imperative, the principle that bids us to contemplate the maxim guiding our conduct as if it were a universal law and measure our own conduct by what we are willing to tolerate in others. Applying this principle to law in his monumental treatise *Theory of Justice*, Rawls develops "a justice as fairness" thesis that invites adjudicators to place themselves in "the original position" or a purely deliberative state where one can "set up a fair procedure so that any principles agreed to will be just."[173] The justification discourse succeeds when "the parties are situated behind the veil of ignorance," that is, when they "do not know how the various alternatives will affect their own particular case [and] are obliged to evaluate principles solely on the basis of general considerations."[174] Under such idealized conditions of unconstrained discourse propelled by arguments alone, participants are expected to establish a hierarchy of universal rights reasonable enough to secure consent from the parties involved and to insure distributive justice. Legal practice will be guided here not just by positive laws but by the adjudicators' sense of justice, the fair standards articulated in the ongoing national discourse about moral goods and the way these goods ought to be distributed among community members.

The strategy Rawls favors in implementing the justification process is different from the one advocated by Dworkin. The latter recognizes that discourse on justice is part of a broader democratic process, but he addresses his model primarily to legal professionals whom he expects to shoulder the main burden of upholding fairness in the community: "[I]ndividual citizens can in fact exercise the moral responsibilities of citizenship better when final decisions involving constitutional values are removed from ordinary politics and assigned to courts, whose decisions are meant to turn on principle, not on the weight of numbers or the balance of political influence."[175] Rawls, on the other hand, wants to draw into justification discourse a far broader constituency. Lawyers are not accorded a privileged role in his schema, nor are philosophers, who may initiate the discussion but who otherwise play no special part in this process which includes legislators, executives, judges, party leaders, and citizens engaged in a discourse about public good and rational principles: "In justice as fairness there are no philosophical experts. Heaven forbid! But citizens must, after all, have some ideas of right and justice in their thought and some basis for their reasoning. And students of philosophy take part in formulating these ideas but always as citizens among others."[176]

Habermas is even more adamant about the importance of engaging the entire body politic in justification discourse. Combining Kant's commitment to a disinterested moral deliberation where everybody has a vote with Peirce's vision of a research community ceaselessly advancing toward truth, Habermas calls for a public discourse in an ideal speech situation found "under the *pragmatic* conditions of rational discourses in which the only thing that counts is the compelling force of the better argument based on the relevant information."[177] "In this speech situation, persons for and against a problematic validity claim thematize the claim, and, relieved of the pressures of action and experience, adopt a hypothetical attitude in order to test with reasons, and reasons alone, whether the proponent's claim stands up."[178] Habermas does not offer a comprehensive account of the conditions under which the justification discourse achieves its goals, but drawing on his various works we can say that ideal speech conditions exist in a situation where: (1) every interested party has a say; (2) no force is admitted except the force of reason; (3) all statements are sorted out into factual, normative, and expressive validity claims; (4) propositions are methodically redeemed through rational arguments; (5) the discussion continues until a collective consensus is reached; and (6) conclusions are revised in light of experience and further deliberation.[179]

The ideal speech situation can be approximated only in a thoroughly modern society which has replaced "the weight of tradition with the weight of arguments..."[180] A society that clears this threshold no longer accepts positive law in its unexamined facticity, as a natural state enforced by administrative power, but demands judgment about the law's legitimacy based on rational considerations. That is when the perennial "tension between facticity and validity built into law itself, between the positivity of law and the legitimacy claimed by it"[181] comes to the fore. For centuries this tension has been building in the Occidental world, which saw European states undergo the juridification process. Following Max Weber and Otto Kirchheimer, Habermas identifies this process with "the tendency toward an increase in formal (or positive, written) law that can be observed in modern society."[182] The juridification has unfolded in stages, beginning with the creation of a centralized state under Absolutism, followed by a constitutional monarchy, in turn supplanted by a democratic constitutional state, which evolved into a contemporary democratic welfare state.

The juridification process has produced mixed results. On one hand, it codified civil rights (protecting individuals from arbitrary state interference), political rights (securing citizens' ability to participate in the political process), and social rights (spreading the safety net underneath the most vulnerable social strata). On the other hand, by extending law into life domains previously immune to legal rational authority, the juridification process has weakened the bond between the lifeworld and the normative system, between personal values and impersonal regulations, between individual identities and bureaucratic rationalized classifications. To offset the insidious consequences of juridification and bureaucratization, one has to find ways to reengage alienated citizenry in justification discourse about the laws' rationality. According to Habermas, "the legitimacy of law ultimately depends on a communicative arrangement: as participants in rational discourses, consociates under law must be able to examine whether a contested norm meets with, or could meet with, the agreement of all those possibly affected."[183] To be sure, communicative practices are unlikely to render positive law and administrative force completely obsolete—in modern society with its staggering complexity, "the increasing need for integration must hopelessly overtax the integrating capacity of communicative action."[184] But the justification discourse conducted under the conditions approximating ideal speech empowers the subjects of law, particularly those dependent on the largesse distributed by the welfare administration, and thus promises to lend legitimacy to the thoroughly bureaucratized, impervious-to-scrutiny legal system. In a democratic state, "the *legitimacy* of statutes is measured against the discursive redeemability of their normative validity claims—in the final analysis, according to whether they have come about through a rational legislative process, or at least could have been justified from pragmatic, ethical, and moral points of view."[185]

Contemporary juridical moralism deplores the situation where "the court serves as nothing more than an ad hoc arbiter of issues it finds too difficult to decide in a principled way."[186] At the same time, legal moralism moves beyond Kant's moral apriorism, shows how moral principles can undergo historical reinterpretation without losing their universal appeal, suggests standards by which one can assess the practical consequences of various legal decisions, integrates the legal process into a community-wide justification discourse where citizens as well as institutional agents take part, and it captures certain features of justification discourse in our legal and political community. As far back as the 1858 Lincoln-Douglas debates, the discussion about the most urgent legal issues confronting the nation featured a clash of moral principles. Judge Stephen Douglas articulated one such principle when he appealed to "popular sovereignty"[187] as a constitutional warrant allowing citizens of each state to decide whether they wish to retain the institution of slavery.[188] Abraham Lincoln offered an alternative moral vision, one based on the hermeneutical strategy highlighting "the abstract moral question"[189] that the Declaration of Independence raised and that required new answers from successive generations:

> I think the authors of that notable instrument intended to include all men, but they did not intend to declare all men equal in all respects. They did not mean to say that all men were equal in color, size, intellect, moral development, or social capacity. They defined with tolerable distinctness in what respects they did consider all men created equal—equal in certain inalienable rights, among which are life, liberty, and the pursuit of happiness. This they said, and this they meant. They did not mean to assert the obvious untruth, that all were then actually enjoying that equality, nor yet that they were about to confer it immediately upon them. In fact, they had no power to confer such a boon. They meant simply to declare the right, so that the enforcement of it might follow as fast as circumstances should permit. They meant to set up a standard maxim for free society which should be familiar to all and revered by all—constantly looked to, constantly labored for, and even, though never perfectly attained, constantly approximated; and thereby constantly spreading and deepening its influence and augmenting the happiness and value of life to all people, of all colors, everywhere.[190]

This is as good an approximation of the law-as-integrity model as you can find in U.S. political history. But as the above example suggests, juridical moralism runs into problems of its own. After all, it was not the force of reason that allowed Lincoln to impose his moral vision on this reluctant nation. It was the Civil War which required the suspension of habeas corpus, interdiction of enemy food supplies, burning of Atlanta to the ground, and the sacrifice of more than half a million lives. The fight for moral principles can be costly.

The moral reading of the Constitution raises the question how to balance moral precepts vying for supremacy at any given historical junction. Dworkin is aware that ethical principles enciphered in our Constitution routinely clash, that they send mixed signals to interpreters facing specific legal problems. Where one adjudicator favors human autonomy, another may stress equal opportunity, and still others opt for security, safety, or social justice as a moral guide. The ethics of conviction and the morality of ultimate ends breed bitter disagreements, especially when we deal with hot-button issues like reproductive rights, gay marriage, and sexually explicit materials. Sometimes these moral disagreements evolve into full-blown uncivil wars. The bitter polemics between Dworkin and MacKinnon, one taking liberty as a paramount value and another placing social justice above individual autonomy, is the case in point.[191] It would be hard to avoid self-righteousness and acrimony in ethics-centered judicial discourse without a meta-discourse justifying a hierarchy of moral principles and settling conflicts between competing value claims. Or else, we need to make ample room for the honest difference of opinion in situations where consensus about moral priorities proves elusive.

Another objection to current efforts to remoralize legal practice concerns the division of powers in our political system which explicitly empowers legislators to deliberate on the moral questions. According to the tripartite system of government, the judges' responsibility is to make sure that the legislative will, provided it comports with basic constitutional requirements, is correctly interpreted and properly executed. That is what Justice Scalia advocates in his textualist approach to adjudication. Once the legislature passes the law, judges must squelch their personal preferences and exercise judicial restraint, applying unswervingly the moral guidelines spelled out by the Congress. But as Scalia's critics are quick to point out,[192] he did not live up to his commitment when he joined the majority decision in *Bush v Gore* that contradicted the Court's and Scalia's longstanding deference to states' rights in matters within their jurisdiction, which state election procedures clearly exemplified. For all their dedication to the rule of law, originalists cannot evade their biases in situations marked by indeterminacy. Indeed, textualists never cease to be community members, and their legal judgments are bound to reflect, albeit in a well disguised form, their sense of what is fair and just for their own time and place.

One can also object to the moral reasoning in law on the ground that its proponents privilege consensus over dissent. Habermas cites Günther Frankenberg to the effect that justice as fairness underestimates the fact that "law is not a rule system but chaos" marred by "the radical indeterminacy" which precludes a rational consensus about "equal treatment and justice."[193] But this criticism applies to Habermas even more so than to Dworkin, who has to contend with the problem of consensus building among a handful of appellate judges (or just one "judge-Hercules"), whereas Habermas anticipates a community-wide agreement as the ultimate test for the rationality of a particular legal opinion or policy decision. Habermas does not sound very pragmatic when he contends that "majority decisions are held to be only a substitute for the uncompelled consensus that would finally result if discussion did not always have to be broken off owing to the need for a decision."[194] And he is theoretically vulnerable when he holds rational consensus rather than reasonable dissent to be the touchstone of democratic politics. Certain locutions which crop up in his texts—"the costs of dissensions are quite high," "the risk of dissension is growing," "[one has to] counter the risk of dissension and therewith the risk of instability built into the communicative mode of social reproduction in general"[195]—makes one wonder if dissent has any conceptual footing in his theory as a vital element in the judicial and democratic process.

Finally, the contemporary juridical moralists like Habermas and Rawls remain faithful to the Kantian program that bypasses emotions and frames every dispute as a "*lawsuit.*"[196] Fashioned on the anvil of rationalism, the ideal speech situation appears to be thoroughly emptied of its affective content. Emotion shows up in the theory of communicative action in a truncated form as the "sincerity of the expressions"[197] and in the justice-as-fairness paradigm as the "principle-dependent and conception-dependent desires."[198] But theories that "attribute to reasons the force to 'move' participants, in a nonpsychological sense"[199] run the risk of reducing moral agents engaged in the justification process to talking heads—disembodied creatures listening only to the voice of reason and ordering themselves into action by the sheer power of their will. References to "motivation through 'good reasons'"[200] beg the question as to where theory-driven desires come from and how they mesh with more mundane motives and partisan interests. Perhaps realizing this, Habermas amends his wording in the postscript to his treatise on law, which contains several tantalizing references to the habits of freedom and a population schooled in liberty:

> [C]onstitutional democracy depends on the motivations of a population *accustomed* to liberty, motivations that cannot be generated by administrative measures....[201] [F]or only a population *accustomed* to freedom can keep the institutions of freedom alive....[202] [C]onstitutionally protected institutions of freedom are worth only what a population *accustomed* to political freedom and settled in the "we" perspective of active self-determination makes of them.[203]

Italicized in the original, the word "accustomed" tacitly grounds communicative action in the nondiscursive properties deliberating agents are expected to bring to justification discourse. Communicative practices embedded in democratic deliberation are to be carried out by the agents whose embodied habits have already met the demands of the democratic process. This circular, untheorized premise exposes the Achilles heel of the deontological tradition in moral philosophy and the theory of democratic justice that takes its cue from ethical formalism.

VIII. The Fully Embodied Democratic Process

The deontological tradition in ethics stipulates that duty trumps inclination whenever the two are in conflict.[204] Kant, the radical exponent of this view, would have us believe that only by suppressing passions and cultivating "*moral apathy*" or complete "freedom from agitation"[205] can we have confidence in the verdict rendered by "the court of justice of morality."[206] The moral philosophy privileging reason over emotions has its counterpart in ethical emotivism whose proponents mistrust reason's propensity to rationalize and seek to check its intellectual proclivities by "moral sense," "moral sentiments," "the sentiment of the heart," and kindred forms of affective reasonableness "upon which each particular virtue is found."[207] David Hume, with whom Kant carries a tacit polemics, captured the antirationalist pathos of this approach: "'Tis not contrary to reason to prefer the destruction of the whole world to the scratching of my finger."[208] Pushing ethical emotivism to its logical extreme, Hume stands the deontological maxim on its head: "Reason is, and ought only to be the slave of the passions, and can never pretend to any other office than to serve and obey them."[209] The point is that our sentiments, desires, and passions must be of the kind that makes for social peace and justice—reason alone will not suffice.

Thus, deontological ethics and ethical emotivism are set on a collision course. Whereas Kant etherealizes human agency into pure reason to achieve a worthy moral aim, Hume and Adam Smith call on natural sentiments to resist imperious reason's self-aggrandizing claim to pursue nothing but the public good. Hume's polemical stance downplays the emotional littering that befouls discourse, but then he readily admits passion's destructive potential when he deals with anger or envy. Neither can Kant escape the recalcitrant reality of strong affect, which worms itself back into his ethical rigorism disguised as moral agent's passion for justice. And yet the two perspectives owe each other more than their proponents are willing to admit. Incompatible at first blush, both ethical systems are dialectically bound to each other. This dialectic comes to the fore in the pragmatist view of reason as an embodied, historically emergent, biosocial structure that channels emotions along intelligent pathways and simultaneously taps affect's sensitivity to the indeterminacy of the situation.

That passions can disrupt human intercourse is obvious, and Kant makes a sensible point when he appeals to judicious temperament. However, it is his unwillingness to accommodate strong emotions that raises the red flags. As Dewey warned us, "[T]he conclusion is not that the emotional, passionate phase of action can be or should be eliminated in behalf of a bloodless reason. More 'passions,' not fewer, is the answer.... Rationality, once more, is not a force to evoke against impulse and habit. It is the attainment of a working harmony among diverse desires."[210]

There is more to reason than intellect and analytical skills which help us simplify reality, impose a rational schema on the world, and gloss over its chaotic properties. The human mind thrives on "emotional intelligence"[211]—an enlightened affect that readily transgresses borderlines imposed by reason, reclaims the world's unfathomable complexity, and treats uncertainty not as an indicator of our limited knowledge but as a birthmark of the world-in-the-making, the world in which embodied human agents act as participant observers. Extreme rationalism, in this reckoning, is a mark of self-deception. A desire to suppress the somatic-affective dimension of human existence is the sign of a troubled mind. Behind "the craving for rationality" hides what James calls "the sentiment of rationality," a passionate desire to make "the concrete chaos rational" and "banish puzzle from the universe" which serves as a kind of analgesic promising to alleviate "a very intense feeling of distress" and bring about the "peace of rationality."[212] The life of the man who took the categorical imperative for his North Star offers an instructive illustration to this pragmatist insight.

The moral heights Kant sought to scale were lofty indeed. He demanded that we treat human beings as ends in themselves, cultivate a judicial temper in interpersonal communications, and squelch malignant passions defiling our moral agency. According to his contemporaries, Kant did not always follow his own counsel. Curled under the thick layer of rationalism was a man "passionate and impulsive—both in the way in which he lived his life and the way in which he philosophized."[213] The theoretician of categorical imperative called upon his fellow citizens to foreswear treating others as means, yet he leaned heavily on his reluctant ex-students to confront his critics and write "apologia" for his controversial theories.[214] An eager conversationalist, Kant liked talking better than listening, acted in an increasingly overbearing fashion as his fame spread, and on occasion behaved "almost rudely and uncivilly" toward those who disagreed with him.[215] We will never know for sure whether Kant managed to free himself from the pernicious habits which "give our imagination free play in sensual pleasures," breed "vices ... contrary to nature," and precipitate "most serious offenses against the duties we owe to ourselves,"[216] but it wouldn't be unreasonable to conjecture that he hadn't an easy time ridding himself from carnal images through the superior power of his rational will. Once again, we are reminded of Dewey's pragmatist warning: "Men who devote themselves to thinking are likely to be unusually unthinking in some respects, as for example in immediate personal relationships. A man to whom exact scholarship is an absorbing pursuit may be more than ordinarily vague in ordinary matters. Humility and impartiality may be shown in a specialized field, and pettiness and arrogance in dealing with other persons."[217]

Prudence requires that we exercise an abundance of caution sorting through the testimonies left by Kant's contemporaries. A balanced biocritical account has to include conflicting testimonies and avoid rash generalizations. Bear in mind, also, that what is at issue here is not the truth of Kant's theory prescribing a moral attitude but the extent to which the author of categorical imperative integrated his theoretic stance with his pragmatic existence. We need to undertake this inquiry to find out how much fiber there is in Kant's morality. Looking from this angle at the discourse theory of law and the ideal of a morally grounded democracy, one can see what it sorely misses—embodied reasonableness. There is more to democracy than redeeming discursive claims by rational arguments. Democracy is also a demeanor, a system of government sustained by citizens who sign themselves in the flesh as well as in well-formed propositions. The same applies to law as an embodied practice that thrives on the corporeal habits not always abounding in its most successful practitioners. The moral approach to adjudication must extend beyond theoretical integrity to encompass an emotional stance that embodies the ethical principles the adjudicator bids us to accept.

Dworkin is right to protest MacKinnon's attacks on his moral commitments and intellectual integrity,[218] yet he needs to be careful to treat his opponents with the dignity he expects for himself. Suspect are the motives of those who commit themselves to a truth and then take "dissent from that truth [a]s treason," but those who bristle at dissenting views as an evidence of opponent's stupidity and urge that disagreeable arguments be "discredited by the disgust, outrage, and ridicule"[219] risk falling into the same trap. Considering how Dworkin sometimes puts down his opponents, one is compelled to ask if he has not crossed the line separating principled exchange from name calling. According to the student of law as integrity, Posner is "relentlessly superficial."[220] Rorty's followers pretend to be "busy while actually doing nothing."[221] MacKinnon deploys "bad arguments," engages in "plain non sequitur," and reveals a "single-minded concentration on lurid sex."[222] Bork is a "crude moral skeptic" given to "empty" rhetoric, advancing "meager" and "shabby" ideas of "unsurpassed ugliness" and entertaining bogus arguments the way "alchemists once used phlogiston."[223] Again, I am not concerned with the substance of Dworkin's judgment, which has merit, only with the emotional attitude his polemical stance embodies. It would be unfortunate if "vicious conservatism," assuming there is such thing, springs a counterpart on the liberal side.

Just think about First Amendment lawyers eloquently defending free speech while repeatedly cutting off their opponents arguing the limits of free expression. Performative contradictions of this kind abound among legal professionals who may extol judicious temperament in theory while abusing power vested in the judge, who fight for civil liberties around the world while ignoring the rights of their own employees, who pass professional ethics exams with flying colors only to engage in grossly unethical legal practices. Chief Justice Warren Burger had some of these embodied virtues in mind when he urged that "civility is to the courtroom and adversary process what antisepsis is to a hospital and operating room. The best medical brains cannot outwit soiled linen or dirty scalpels—and the best legal skills cannot either justify or offset bad manners."[224] The larger pragmatist point here is that we ought to move beyond the purely discursive mode in which democratic deliberation is locked in discourse-centered accounts and open the affective-behavioral channels through which we communicate our attitudes in all their complexity and contradiction. The research focus thereby shifts from discourse ethics to the "ethics of embodied interaction," from verbal communication to "the word-body-action nexus," from textual interpretation to "pragmatist hermeneutics," and from the discursive regime of democratic governance to "emotionally intelligent democracy."[225] This is the direction in which democratic theory has been moving in recent years.

The discourse theoretic turn has influenced several legal practitioners in this country who agree with Habermas and Rawls that "citizens owe one another justifications for the laws they collectively enact"[226] but seek to expand the deliberative process to make room for affect and emotions alongside principles and reasoned arguments.[227] According to pragmatism-conscious thinkers, "democratic theory needs to learn from dispute resolution theory, that positions and parties may be multiple, that processes of deliberation may range from principled argument to interest-based bargaining and coalition behavior, to appeals based on emotions, faith and belief, as well as fact."[228] American scholars working in this tradition call on participants in democratic discourse "to renew their dedication to honesty, self-criticism, civility, good faith, and respect for their opponents..."[229] In keeping with this agenda, they search for "a distinctively democratic kind of character—the character of individuals who are morally committed, self-reflective about their commitments, discerning of the difference between respectable and merely tolerable differences of opinion, and open to the possibility of changing their minds or modifying their positions at some time in the future if they confront unanswerable objections to their present point of view."[230]

Unlike their continental counterparts, however, scholars influenced by American pragmatism recognize that legal professionals have to act as "mood scientists,"[231] that "sometimes [it is] necessary not only to 'promote mutual respect...' but also to achieve authenticity, to reveal (as in 'testimony') the pain and anger ... that someone actually feels, when expression or knowledge of those feelings furthers the understanding that is the goal of deliberation."[232]

Legal pragmatists follow John Dewy and George Herbert Mead, the two preeminent pragmatist theorists of the fully embodied democratic process, who advocated the "passing of functions which are supposed to inhere in government into activities that belong to the community" and called for "the readjustments of personal interests that have come into conflict and which take place outside of court ... [and] is not dependent upon an act of legislature."[233] Hence, the preference to work outside traditional legal venues where citizens can assemble to resolve their disputes over proposed dump sites and highway roads, parking garages and half-way houses, health issues and waste disposal, inter-group and neighborhood conflicts, city-wide ordinances and national legislations.[234] Alongside citizens gathered in these venues toil legal professionals who, according to Menkel-Meadow, have a role to play in local justification discourses, for "lawyers may be particularly well suited to the design, management and facilitation of consensus building process, especially those which implicate law, such as environmental, regulatory, governance, land-use, and other 'legal' problems."[235] Lawyers are expected to do more than provide legal expertise in the deliberation process. They have to model democracy in the flesh, find a way to embody the virtues of reciprocity, mutual understanding, and respectful disagreement where consensus eludes the parties in dispute. The process in such a deliberative practice is every bit as vital as its outcome, and often more so, for the consensus is bound to break down when we move to implement the mediated agreement, but the goodwill the well-executed deliberations engender may last beyond the fragile understanding reached on any given occasion.

The mediation and settlement movement that takes its cue from pragmatism has many critics, including some legal pragmatists,[236] who point out that "[d]eliberation is not an activity for the demos,"[237] that "the best thinking of the best thinkers, deliberating under the best conditions, reflects nothing more than the interests of the powers-that-be,"[238] and that public deliberations "confront the problems of demagoguery, of sound-bite democracy, of the persistent inability of facts and evidence to transcend background normative belief, and of the extent to which the inequalities of society in general are reflected and replicated in its deliberative environments."[239] There is merit to this critique, and pragmatists should to take it seriously. They will also have to contend with the old query that John Dewey addressed to legal professionals: "How are we to explain the fact that to such a large extent the lawyers who have had a professional and supposedly a competent professional education seem to be the advocates of the most reactionary political and social issues of the community at any given time?"[240] But then, half a century has passed since Dewey raised the issue, and it is now fairly obvious that lawyers are not beholden to any given political cause. Still, the challenges legal pragmatists face when they opt to facilitate the fully embodied democratic process are great.

"In our own time," Justice William Brennan warned at the end of his illustrious career, "experience may signal that the greatest threat to due process principles is formal reason severed from the insights of passion."[241] To reconnect reason with the rest of the body, to realize the ideal of embodied reasonableness, legal professionals need to check their discursive stance against the messages they are signing in the flesh, and when the gap grows wide, work to realign mixed signals. Whether they toil at the bar, on the bench, or inside mediation forums, jurists must hone their people skills and act as "strange attractors" willing to remedy the laws' intractable contradictions with emotions that are intelligent and intellect that is emotionally sane. Research on the place of emotions in the legal process continues to emerge, and there is much that legal scholars and social scientists can learn from each other in this area.

Architects of deliberative democracy are likely to be frustrated as long as they continue to measure their success by the actually achieved consensus. Nine Supreme Court Justices, some of the best and the brightest in legal profession, routinely fail to reach an agreement, delivering an increasing number of split-decisions in recent years. Do we really think the rest of us can do better? The law often appeals to reasonable persons' judgment, yet one thing that stands out about reasonable people is that they agree to disagree. It is heartening to see that deliberative democracy theorists shift their emphasis away from rational consensus and move beyond "*mere* toleration" toward "mutual respect (which is a more demanding form of agreeing to disagree)."[242]

Integrating emotions and reasons into a coherent conceptual schema also presents a problem. Menkel-Meadow divides modes of deliberation into principle-based, bargain-oriented, and emotion-driven.[243] However, this classification creates an impression that principled discourses and interest-driven negotiations are devoid of emotions while emotional conflicts or faith-based disputes are bereft of principles. A robust yet flexible theoretical schema that can accommodate logical, affective, and behavioral dimensions of deliberative process may take time to articulate.

The biggest challenge facing legal pragmatists determined to insert themselves into the embodied democratic process is modeling its values in their conduct. They have every right to do so. They need to remember Judge Learned Hand's advice, however, "[l]iberty lies in the hearts of men and women; when it dies there, no constitution, no law, no court can save it; no constitution, no law, no court can even do much to help it."[244] Democracy is not held together by just laws, nor does it spring from wise constitutions. The genius of the framers has less to do with the clever foundational documents they cobbled together than with their embodied virtues, painfully limited though these proved on occasion (why else would countries that copy our constitution have hard time bodying forth its democratic ethos?). The framers' chief strength was in their readiness to compromise, to accommodate each other, and to go on searching for elusive answers in the face of the bitter disagreements over principles. Therein lies the lesson for pragmatists, discourse theorists, social justice champions—all democracy boosters of our time.

No one holds a monopoly on democratic virtue. We should not assume that pragmatists are more ethically gifted or deliberatively savvy than the proponents of other philosophical brands.[245] Pragmatist hermeneutics will have to tell us how to study the relationship between our discursive, affective, and behavioral performances while dodging the dangers of *ad hominem* reasoning. As the case of Immanuel Kant suggests, the misalignment between a theoretical corpus, affective attitude, and behavioral performance is part of the human condition. But the challenge is worth taking, and I hope that all those who understand democracy as the fully embodied democratic process will not shrink from it.

IX. Conclusion

Over two millennia ago Aristotle observed that "all things are not determined by law," that "about some things it is impossible to lay down a law," and that we must undertake "a correction of law where it is defective owing to its universality."[246] Pragmatists have been expounding on this premise for just over a century, providing legal scholars with ammunition in their polemics against legal formalism. Although there is no consensus about legal pragmatism's tenets, jurists identifying with this movement tend to be skeptical about immutable principles, mindful of their historical meaning, sympathetic to judicial discretion, attentive to legal outcomes' likely consequences, and open to social science findings illuminating the relationship between law and society.

As I tried to make clear in this essay, legal pragmatists cannot dispense with principles altogether. The theoretical nihilism Stanley Fish urges us to embrace as a shortcut to justice is no more viable than the principled textualism Justice Scalia proposes as a solution to the reigning judicial chaos. Legal consequences do not come to us with price tags attached, ready to be sorted out into pragmatically sound or pragmatically spurious ones. Someone has to judge the consequences, figure out their cost, and such an evaluation requires a contestable standard. By the same token, pragmatist jurisprudence rejects the notion that laws are to be interpreted by some immutable principles lodged in a timeless legal canon. The rule of law does not dispense with women and men who lend it its time-bound agentic substance. Laws do not interpret themselves, nor do they enforce their own strictures. Laws are applied by fallible human beings who need room for honest differences of opinion. As Justice Breyer pointed out, we should strive to do justice to the competing constitutional principles as well as to the historical consequences of specific legal holdings.

I have also tried to articulate another strain in legal pragmatism, the one that casts our political system as an embodied phenomenon. Democracy is more than a discourse. It is also a civic culture "which encourages trust, tolerance, prudence, compassion, humor, and withers away when overexposed to suspicion, hatred, vanity, cruelty, and sarcasm."[247] This pragmatist perspective on democracy bids us to look for its somatic-affective, behavioral-performative, as well as ethical-discursive equivalents. One can only get that far redeeming reasons with reasons, words with more words. "[T]he life according to virtue lived without impediment,"[248] which the author of the *Nicomachean Ethics* took for the highest ideal, requires that we redeem our discursive claims with emotionally intelligent attitudes, affective offerings with bold behavioral commitments, and behavioral performances with principled arguments, as we travel the full hermeneutical circle where embodied meaning acquires its concrete historical shape. To achieve its pragmatic end, an ideal speech situation must include logos, pathos, and ethos, leaving ample room not only for intellectual prowess but also for emotional creativity and moral imagination.

Once again, we find a precursor for this line of reasoning in Aristotle. This proto-pragmatist taught us that "each government has a peculiar character which originally formed and which continue to preserve it. The character of democracy creates democracy, and the character of oligarchy creates oligarchy; and always the better the character the better the government."[249] We might want to reexamine the legal process in line with this premise, and that means recasting democratic justice as both a discursive and nondiscursive practice in the course of which legal professionals shape—or misshape—the social order they are sworn to protect. Jurists are engaged in a continuous production of social reality as objective and meaningful. They play a special role in this process as guardians of cherished terminologies waiting to be applied to contested situations whose indeterminacy jurists terminate not only discursively but also somatically, affectively, and behaviorally. The promise of legal pragmatism will not be fulfilled until its proponents grasp democratic justice as an embodied process.

Notes

1. Edward Cline, "Acclaimed Films Not at Bottom of the Barrel, But Beneath It," *Las Vegas Rev.- J.*, Apr. 9, 1995, at 3C.
2. Thomas A. Bowden, "An Overview of Nation's Highest Court," *Las Vegas Rev.- J.*, Dec. 28, 1997, at 1E.
3. Jackson Lears, "Golden Mean," *New York Times*, Dec. 15, 1996, §7, at 28 (reviewing Alan Wolfe, *Marginalized in the Middle* [1996]).
4. Lincoln Kaplan, "Lawyers Without a Cause," *New York Times*, Aug. 14, 1994, at A19.
5. David Margolick, "Scholarly Consensus Builder," *New York Times*, May 14, 1994, at A19.
6. Linda Greenhouse, "Portrait of a Pragmatist," *New York Times*, Jul. 14, 1994 at A1.
7. Richard A. Posner, *The Problems of Jurisprudence* 28 (1993).
8. Richard Rorty, "The Banality of Pragmatism and the Poetry of Justice," in *Pragmatism in Law and Society 89, 92* (Michael Brint and William Weaver eds., 1991).
9. Stanley Fish, "Almost Pragmatism: The Jurisprudence of Richard Posner, Richard Rorty, and Ronald Dworkin," in *Pragmatism in Law and Society,* supra note 8, at *47, 63.*
10. See generally, Dworkin, supra note 10.
11. Ronald D. Dworkin, "Pragmatism, Right Answers, and True Banality," in *Pragmatism in Law and Society,* supra note 8, *359, 385* n.17.
12. Id. at 359.
13. Jürgen Habermas, *Between Facts and Norms: Contribution to a Discourse Theory of Law and Democracy* 84 (William Rehg trans., 1998).
14. Joshua Cohen, "Reflections on Habermas on Democracy," 12 *Ratio Juris* 385 (1999); Stuart Hampshire, *Justice is Conflict* (Princeton University Press 2000); Carrie Menkel-Meadow, "The Trouble with the Adversarial System in a Postmodern, Multicultural World," 38 *Wm. & Mary L. Rev.* 5 (1996); Jon Elster, *Solomonic Judgments: Studies in Limitations of Rationality* (Cambridge University Press 1989).
15. Carrie Menkel-Meadow, "The Lawyer's Role(s) in Deliberative Democracy," 5 *Nev. L. Rev.* 0 (2005).
16. Charles S. Peirce, *Philosophical Writings of Peirce* 299 (Justus Buchler ed., Dover Publications 1955 [1940]).
17. Immanuel Kant, *Critique of Pure Reason* 513 (F. Max Müller trans., Anchor Books 1966 [1781]).
18. Id. at 486.
19. Immanuel Kant, *The Metaphysical Elements of Justice: Part I of The Metaphysics of Morals* 16 (John Ladd trans., Macmillan Pub. Co. 1965 [1797]).
20. Id. at 41.
21. Id. at 36.
22. Id. at 19.
23. See Kant, supra note 17, at 119. "Deficiency in the faculty of judgment is really what we call stupidity, and there is no remedy for that." Id.
24. *Id.* at 120.
25. Id. at 119.
26. Immanuel Kant, *The Doctrine of Virtue: Part II of the Metaphysics of Morals* 159 (Mary J. Gregor trans., Harper & Row 1964 [1797]).
27. *Id.*
28. Immanuel Kant, *Anthropology from a Pragmatic Point of View* 174 (Victor Lyle Dowdle trans., Southern Illinois University Press 1978 [1798]).

29. See Kant, supra note 26, at 158.
30. Id. at 159.
31. Id. at 52.
32. Kant, supra note 17, at 486.
33. See *id.*
34. Id. at 482.
35. *Id.*, Kant, supra note 19, at 42.
36. Id. at 116.
37. See Kant, supra note 26, at 221.
38. Kant, supra note 19, at 86.
39. See *id.* at 95-6.
40. According to Kant, if "a woman cannot preserve her life any longer except by sur-rendering her person to the will of another, she is bound to give up her life rather than dishonour humanity in her own person, which is what she would be doing in giving herself up as a thing to the will of another." Immanuel Kant, *Lectures on Ethics 156* (Louis Infield trans., 1979 ed., Hackett Publishing Co. 1980) (1930).
41. See Kant, supra note 19, at 106.
42. See Kant, supra note 40, at 124. Kant views masturbation as perverse desire stirred up by illicit imagination: "Lust is called *unnatural* if one is aroused to it not by a real object but by his imagining it, so that he himself creates one, contrapurposively [sic]; ... for in this way imagination brings forth a desire contrary to nature's end..." Immanuel Kant, *The Cambridge Edition of the Works of Immanuel Kant, Practical Philosophy, The Metaphysics of Morals* 178-79 (Mary Gregor trans., Cambridge University Press 1996 [1797]).
43. Charles S. Peirce, *Collected Papers of Charles Sanders Peirce* (1931-58) 398 (Charles Hartshorne & Paul Weiss eds., Harvard University Press 1960) (1931).
44. John Dewey, *Freedom and Culture* 102 (Capricorn Books 1963 [1939]).
45. John Dewey, *Problems of Men* 35 (Philosophical Library, Inc. 1968 [1946]).
46. John Dewey, "Organization in American Education," 17 *Tchrs Coll. Rec.* 127, 134 (1916).
47. Dewey, supra note 44, at 102.
48. A more detailed discussion of the pragmatist premises can be found in Dmitri N. Shalin, "Pragmatism and Social Interactionism," 51 *Am. Soc. Rev. 9* (1986). See also Hans Jonas, *Pragmatism and Social Theory* (1993); Eugene Rochberg-Halton, *Meaning and Modernity: Social Theory in the Pragmatic Attitude* (1986); Richard Shusterman, *Practicing Philosophy: Pragmatism and Philosophical Life* (1997).
49. William James, *The Meaning of Truth* 283 (University of Michigan Press, 1970 [1909]).
50. William James, *Pragmatism & Four Essays From the Meaning of Truth* 47 (Ralph Barton Perry, ed., Meridian Books 1955 [1907]).
51. See Kant, supra note 17, at 507.
52. See James, supra note 50, at 133.
53. See Peirce, supra note 16, at 31.
54. See James, supra note 49, at 210.
55. See *id.* at 167.
56. William James, *The Principles of Psychology* 289 (Dover Publications 1950 [1890]).
57. See Dewey, supra note 45, at 351.
58. William James, *Essays in Radical Empiricism and Pluralistic Universe* (P. Smith 1967 [1912]).
59. Richard Rorty, *Consequences of Pragmatism* 201 (1982).

60. Eugene Rochberg-Halton, *Meaning and Modernity: Social Theory in the Pragmatic Attitude* 144 (1986).
61. Charles S. Peirce, *The New Elements of Mathematics,* at xxi (Carolyn Eisele ed., 1976).
62. John Dewey, *Human Nature and Conduct: An Introduction to Social Psychology* 196 (Modern Library ed., Random House 1950 [1922]).
63. Richard Rorty, "Science as Solidarity," in *The Rhetoric of the Human Sciences: Language and Argument in Scholarship and Public Affairs* 40 (John S. Nelson et al. eds., 1987).
64. See Peirce, supra note 16, at 247.
65. Id. at 13.
66. John Dewey, *Experience and Nature* 219 (Dover Publications 1958 [2d ed. 1929]).
67. George Herbert Mead, *Mind, Self and Society from the Standpoint of a Social Behaviorist* 78 (1934).
68. John Dewey, *Democracy and Education: An Introduction to the Philosophy of Education* 5 (1916).
69. Charles S. Peirce, *Letter to Victoria Welby* (Dec. 14, 1908), in *Semiotics and Significs: The Correspondence Between Charles S. Peirce and Lady Welby* 79 (Charles S. Harwick ed., 1977).
70. John Dewey, *Quests for Certainty: A Study of the Relation of Knowledge and Action* 138 (Capricorn Books ed., G.P. Putnam Son's 1960 [1929]).
71. William James, *The Moral Equivalent of War, in The Progressive Years: The Spirit and Achievement of American Reform* 488 (Otis Pease ed., 1962).
72. See Dewey, supra note 45, at 136.
73. See Posner, "What Has Pragmatism to Offer Law?" in *Pragmatism in Law and Society,* supra note 8, at 29, 35.
74. Richard Rorty, *Contingency, Irony, and Solidarity* (1989).
75. Cornel West, *The Cornel West Reader* 147 (1999).
76. See Max Weber, *The Methodology of the Social Sciences* 104-05 (Edward A. Shils & Henry A. Finch trans., Free Press 1949).
77. "Neither the old nor the new pragmatism is a school," writes Posner. "The differences between a Peirce and a James ... and a Dewey, are profound. The differences among current advocates of pragmatism are even more profound, making it possible to find greater affinities across than within the 'schools.'" Posner, supra note 73, at 34.
78. See Peirce, supra note 16, at 38.
79. See James, supra note 50, at 61.
80. *Ludwig Wittgenstein, Philosophical Investigations* 32e (G.E.M. Anscombe trans., 2d ed. 1958 [1953]).
81. See Rorty, supra note 8, at 96 n.17; Posner, supra note 7, at 464.
82. Richard A. Posner, "Introduction to Oliver Wendell Holmes, Jr.," *The Essential Holmes: Selections from the Letters, Speeches, Judicial Opinions, and Other Writings of Oliver Wendell Holmes, Jr.,* at xxiv (Richard A. Posner ed., 1992).
83. See Benjamin N. Cardozo, "Growth of the Law" 46 (1924), reprinted in *Selected Writings of Benjamin Nathan Cardozo* 205 & n. 21 (Margaret E. Hall ed., 1947); *Benjamin N. Cardozo, Paradoxes of Legal Science passim* (1947), reprinted in *Selected Writings of Benjamin Nathan Cardozo,* supra, *passim.*
84. Holmes, supra note 82, at 237.
85. Oliver Wendell Holmes, Jr., *Natural Law,* 32 *Harv. L. Rev. 40, 42 (1918),* reprinted in *Holmes,* supra note 82, at 182.

86. Oliver Wendell Holmes, Jr., *The Path of the Law*, 10 *Harv. L. Rev.* 457, 460-61 (1897), reprinted in *Holmes*, supra note 82, at 163.
87. Lochner v. New York, 198 U.S. 45, 75-76 (1905) (Holmes, J., dissenting), reprinted in *Holmes*, supra note 82, at 306.
88. Adkins v. Children's Hosp. of the District of Columbia, 261 U.S. 525, 570-71 (1923) (Holmes, J., dissenting), reprinted in Holmes, supra note 82, at 308-09.
89. Benjamin N. Cardozo, The Nature of The Judicial Process 102-03 (1921), reprinted in *Selected Writings of Benjamin Nathan Cardozo*, supra note 83, at 149.
90. Id. at 126.
91. John Dewey, *Logic: The Theory of Inquiry* 296 (1938).
92. See Cardozo, supra note 89, at 169-70, reprinted in *Selected Writings of Benjamin Nathan Cardozo*, supra note 83, at 179.
93. Id. at 76-77.
94. Id. at 139.
95. Abrams v. United States, 250 U.S. 616 (1919) (Holmes, J., dissenting), reprinted in Holmes, supra note 82, at 320.
96. Richard A. Posner, Introduction to Holmes, supra note 82, at xvi-xvii. Elsewhere, Posner asserts that the nations' most esteemed and rhetorically gifted Justices—Holmes, Cardozo, Jackson, Hand, and Brandeis—were pragmatist in their legal practice if not in their philosophy. See Richard A. Posner, *Law, Pragmatism, and Democracy* 84 (2003) [hereinafter Posner, *Law*].
97. Cardozo, supra note 89, at 167, reprinted in *Selected Writings of Benjamin Nathan Cardozo*, supra note 83, at 178.
98. Holmes, supra note 82, at 122.
99. "Why should the greatest numbers be preferred?," asks Holmes. "Why not the greatest good of the most intelligent and most highly developed? The greatest good of a minority of our generation may be the greatest good of the greatest number in the long run." Oliver Wendell Holmes, Jr., "The Gas-Stokers' Strike," 7 *Am. L. Rev.* 582, 584 (1873), reprinted in Holmes, supra note 82, at 122.
100. Buck v. Bell, 274 U.S. 200, 207 (1927), quoted in Louis Menand, *The Metaphysical Club: A Story of Ideas in America* 66 (2001).
101. See *Cardozo,* supra note 89, at 66, reprinted in *Selected Writings of Benjamin Nathan Cardozo*, supra note 83, at 133.
102. Posner, supra note 7, at 465.
103. Id.
104. Id. at 466.
105. Posner, supra note 72, at 43.
106. Stanley Fish, *When Principles Stand in the Way, New York Times,* Dec. 26, 1996, at A27.
107. Id.
108. Id.
109. Id.
110. Id.
111. Orlando Patterson, "Affirmative Action: The Sequel," *New York Times*, June 22, 2003, at 11.
112. Id. at 4-11.
113. Id.
114. Id.
115. Id.
116. Id.
117. Posner, *Law,* supra note 96, at 22.
118. Id. at 22-23.

119. Id. at 22.
120. Id.
121. Id.
122. Id. at 23.
123. Id. at 386.
124. Linda Greenhouse, "A Court Infused with Pragmatism," *New York Times*, Dec. 12, 2003, at A38.
125. See David J. Garrow, "Justice Souter Emerges," *New York Times*, Sept. 25, 1994, § 6 (Magazine), at 64 (quoting Linda Greenhouse).
126. Linda Greenhouse, "The Year Rehnquist May Have Lost the Court," *New York Times*, July 5, 2004, at A12.
127. Antonin Scalia, "God's Justice and Ours," *First Things,* May 2002, at 17-18, http://www.firstthings.com/ftissues/ft0205/articles/scalia.html (last visited Feb. 15, 2005).
128. See David Hoy, "Is Legal Originalism Compatible with Philosophical Pragmatism?" in *Pragmatism in Law and Society,* supra note 8, at *343* (describing the doctrine of originalism).
129. Scalia, supra note 127, at 18.
130. Antonin Scalia, "Common-Law Courts in a Civil-Law System: The Role of United States Federal Courts in Interpreting the Constitution and Laws," Tanner Lecture at Princeton University (Mar. 8-9, 1995), *in* 18 *The Tanner Lecture on Human Values* 79 (1997).
131. Id. at 85.
132. Id. at 98
133. Id. at 100.
134. Id. at 114, 120.
135. Stephen Breyer, "Our Democratic Constitution," Fall 2001 James Madison Lecture at New York University Law School (Oct. 22, 2001), at http://www.supremecourtus. gov/publicinfo/speeches/sp_10-22-01.html (last visited Nov. 23, 2004).
136. Id.
137. Id.
138. Id.
139. Id.
140. Id.
141. Special mention in this regard deserves Sunsteins's attempt to articulate "incompletely theorized agreements," which can be seen as an alternative to the kind of extreme positions we find in Stanley Fish (who favors "completely untheorized" decisions) and Justice Scalia (who insists on "completely theorized" judgments). See Cass R. Sunstein, "Agreement Without Theory," in *Deliberative Politics: Essays on Democracy and Disagreement* 128 (Stephen Macedo ed., 1999).
142. See Fish, supra note 8, at 67.
143. See Breyer, supra note 135.
144. Id.
145. John Dewey, *The Middle Works, 1899-1924,* at 72-73, 75 (Jo Ann Boydston ed., 1983).
146. See Posner, *Law,* supra note 96, at 125.
147. 410 U.S. 113 (1973).
148. See Posner, *Law,* supra note 96, at 125.
149. Id. Another pragmatist alternative available in this case, Posner suggests, was to invalidate the Texas law but uphold a less stringent Georgia statute which allowed abortions in cases involving rape and incest. Id. at 126.
150. See Fish, supra note 106, at A27.

151. See Patterson, supra note 111, at 11.
152. See Posner, *Law,* supra note 96, at 339.
153. Id. at 374.
154. Id. at 94.
155. Id. at 251.
156. Bradwell v. Illinois, 83 U.S. 130, 141-42 (1872) (Bradley, J., concurring); see also Daniel R. Oritz, *Deadlock in Constitutional Theory, in Pragmatism in Law and Society,* supra note 8, at 314.
157. Dewey, supra note 145, at 234.
158. See Ronald Dworkin, *Freedom's Law: The Moral Reading of the American Constitution* 72-76 (1996) (describing the idea of a natural reading of the Constitution).
159. *John Rawls, Theory of Justice* 225 (1999).
160. Jürgen Habermas, *Autonomy and Solidarity: Interviews with Jürgen Habermas* 71 (Peter Dews ed., 1986).
161. Jürgen Habermas, *Toward a Rational Society; Student Protest, Science, and Politics* 7 (Jeremy J. Shapiro trans.,1970).
162. Dworkin, supra note 10, at 94.
163. Id. at 33; see also *id.* at 37-43.
164. Id. at 95.
165. Id. at 152.
166. Id. at 95.
167. Id.
168. Id. at 95-96.
169. See supra note 157, at 118.
170. Id. at 250.
171. Dworkin, supra note 158, at 270.
172. See id. at 271.
173. Rawls, supra note 159, at 118.
174. Id.
175. See Dworkin, supra note 158, at 344.
176. John Rawls, *Political Liberalism* 427 (1995).
177. Habermas, supra note 13, at 103.
178. Id. at 228.
179. See Jürgen Habermas, *Autonomy and Solidarity: Interviews with Jürgen Habermas* 90 (Peter Dews ed., 1986); see also Jürgen Habermas, *The Theory of Communicative Action* 72-74 (Thomas McCarthy trans., 1987) [hereinafter Habermas, *Theory*]; Dmitri N. Shalin, "Critical Theory and the Pragmatist Challenge," 98 *Am. J. Soc.* 237 (1992) (discussing Habermas's theory of communicative action and the ideal speech situation); "Habermas, Pragmatism, and Critical Theory," in *15 Symbolic Interaction* 1 (Dmitri N. Shalin ed., 1992).
180. Jürgen Habermas, *Communication and Evolution of Society* 113 (Thomas McCarthy trans., 1979).
181. See Habermas, supra note 13, at 95.
182. See Habermas, *Theory*, supra note 179, at 357.
183. Habermas, supra note 13, at 104.
184. Id. at 26.
185. Id. at 30.
186. Charles Field, "Courting Confusion," *New York Times,* Oct. 21, 2004, at A29. Field takes to task the present-day Supreme Court for "defending principles in theory but abandoning them in fact [which] points to a court that has lost its will to protect and explain the nuanced doctrinal constructions that have threatened their way past opposing extremes." Id.

187. "Fifth Joint Debate, at Galesburgh, Illinois," (Oct. 7, 1858), in Abraham Lincoln, *The Complete Works of Abraham Lincoln 427-28* (John G. Nicolay & John Hay eds., The Century Co. 1894). Countering Lincoln, Douglas plausibly claimed that "this government was made by our fathers on the white basis. It was made by white men for the benefit of white men and their posterity forever, and was intended to be administered by white men in all time to come." Id. at 434.

188. Id. at 435.

189. Id. at 438.

190. Speech in Springfield, Illinois (June 26, 1857), in Lincoln, supra note 187, at 226, 232.

191. See generally Dworkin supra note 158, at 195-243.

192. Alan Dershowitz points out that Scalia's vote in *Bush v Gore* contradicts his own pronouncement that "[o]nly by announcing rules do we hedge ourselves in" and that whenever "my political or policy preferences regarding the outcomes are quite opposite, I will be unable to indulge those preferences; I have committed myself to the governing principle." Antonin Scalia, "The Rule of Law as a Law of Rules," 56 *U. Chi. L. Rev.* 1175, 1179-80 (1989), quoted in Alan Dershowitz, *Supreme Injustice: How the High Court Hijacked Election 2000,* at 123-24 (2001).

193. Gunther Frankenberg, "Down by Law: Irony, Seriousness, and Reason," 83 *Nw. U. L. Rev.* 360, 392-93 (1988), quoted in Habermas, supra note 13, at 216.

194. *Jürgen Habermas, Toward a Rational Society: Student Protest, Science, and Politics* 7 (Jeremy J. Shapiro trans., 1970).

195. See Habermas, supra note 13, at 21, 26, 36.

196. Kant, supra note 17, at A29.

197. Jürgen Habermas, *The Theory of Communicative Action* 41 (Thomas McCarthy trans., 1984).

198. Rawls, supra note 176, at 85.

199. Habermas, supra note 13, at 227.

200. Habermas, supra note 180, at 200.

201. Id. at 461.

202. Id. at 513.

203. Id. at 499.

204. See Robert D. Olson, "Deontological Ethics" in *Encyclopedia of Philosophy* 343 (1967).

205. See Kant, supra note 26, at 70.

206. See Kant, supra note 40, at 213.

207. Adam Smith, *The Theory of Moral Sentiments* 508, 511, 518 (Arlington House 1969) (1853).

208. David Hume, *A Treatise of Human Nature* 416 (Prometheus Books 1992).

209. Id. at 415.

210. Dewey, supra note 62, at 195-96.

211. See Daniel Goleman, *Emotional Intelligence* (1995); Howard Gardner, *Multiple Intelligences: The Theory in Practice* (1993); Rob Bocchino, *Emotional Literacy: To Be a Different Kind of Smart* (1999).

212. See William James, *The Will To Believe: And Other Essays in Popular Philosophy* 63-75 (1956).

213. Manfred Kuehn, *Kant: A Biography* 319 (2001).

214. See id. at 320-22.

215. See id. at 319.

216. See Kant, supra note 40, at 142.

217. Dewey, supra note 70, at 198.

218. See Dworkin, supra note 158, 227-243.

219. Id. at 238, 252.
220. See Dworkin, supra note 11, at 377 n. 17.
221. Id. at 359.
222. Dworkin, supra note 158, at 233, 243.
223. Id. at 273-75.
224. Warren E. Burger, "The Necessity for Civility," 52 F.R.D. 211, 215 (1971).
225. See Dmitri N. Shalin, "Liberalism, Affect Control, and Emotionally Intelligent Democracy," *J. Hum. Rts.* 420-25 (2004); see also Shalin, supra note 177, at 254-75; see also Dmitri Shalin, "Discourse, Emotion, and Body Language of Democracy," paper presented at the SSSI Stone Symposium (1999); Dmitri Shalin, "Signing in the Flesh: Notes on Pragmatist Hermeneutics," a revised version of the paper presented at the annual meeting of the Society for the Advancement of American Philosophy (2001). The impact that the emotional heritage of the past has on building democracy in Russia is discussed in Dmitri N. Shalin, *Intellectual Culture, in Russian Culture at the Crossroads: Paradoxes of Postcommunist consciousness* 41-98 (1996).
226. Amy Gutmann and Dennis Thompson, *Democratic Disagreement, in Deliberative Politics,* supra note 141, 243, 244.
227. For a general overview, see two representative collections, *Deliberative Politics,* supra note 141, and *Deliberative Democracy* (Jon Elster ed., 1988). An early example of an attempt to move beyond Habermas can be found in Amy Gutmann and Dennis Thompson, *Democracy and Disagreement* (1996). See also Menkel-Meadow, supra note 15 (reviewing the pragmatism-influenced dispute resolution theory).
228. See Menkel-Meadow, supra note 15, at 0.
229. Robert P. George, *Democracy, and Moral Disagreement: Reciprocity, Slavery, and Abortion, in Deliberative Politics,* supra note 223, at 184, 194.
230. Amy Guttman and Dennis Thompson, *Moral Conflict and Political Consensus, in Why Deliberative Democracy* 64, 76 (1990).
231. See Clark Freshman et al., "The Lawyer-Negotiator as Mood Scientist: What We Know and Don't Know About How Mood Relates to Successful Negotiation," 2002 *J. Disp. Resol. 1* (2002); see also Scott R. Peppet, "Contract Formation in Imperfect Markets: Should We Use Mediators in Deals?" 19 *Ohio St. J. on Disp. Resol.* 283 (2004).
232. James Mansbridge, *Everyday Talk in the Deliberative System, in Deliberative Politics,* supra note 223, at 211, 223.
233. George Herbert Mead, "Natural Rights and the Theory of the Political Institution," *in Selected Writings: George Herbert Mead* 150, 166-67 (Andrew J. Reck ed., Phoenix ed., Univ. Chicago Press 1981) (1964). See also Dmitri N. Shalin, "G. H. Mead, Socialism, and the Progressive Agenda," 92 *Am. J. Soc.* 913-951 (1988).
234. See Menkel-Meadow, supra note 15, at 363-66.
235. Id. at 367.
236. See Posner, *Law,* supra note 96, at 130-57.
237. Michael Walzer, "Deliberation, and What Else?" *in Deliberative Politics,* supra note 141, at 58, 68.
238. Id. at 67.
239. Frederick Schauer, *Talking as a Decision Procedure, in Deliberative Politics,* supra note 141, at 17, 23.
240. Dewey, supra note 45, at 54.
241. The speech on the judicial role that Justice Brennan gave in 1987 at the Association of the Bar of the City of New York, *New York Times,* July 25, 1997, at C19.

242. Gutmann and Thompson, supra note 226, at 251.

243. See Menkel-Meadow, supra note 15, at 365-366.

244. Learned Hand, *The Spirit of Liberty: Papers and Addresses of Learned Hand 190* (3d ptg. 1974).

245. An interesting example is the debate about Justice Cardozo's legal practice that according to some feminist critics shows a gap between his publicly espoused principles and certain legal decisions he rendered. See Catherine Weiss and Louis Melling, *The Legal Education of Twenty Women*, 40 *Stan. L. Rev.* 1299 (1988) (debating Justice Cardozo's legal practice in light of his holding that allegedly shows a gap between his publicly espoused principles and certain legal decisions he rendered); but see Richard A. Posner, *Cardozo: A Study in Reputation* (1990) (giving an alternative look at this controversy).

246. Aristotle, *Nicomachean Ethics, in The Basic Works of Aristotle* 935, 1020 (Richard McKeon ed., 28th prtg. 1941).

247. Mission Statement of The UNLV Center for Democratic Culture, *at* http://www. unlv.edu/centers/cdclv/mission/index.html (last visited Jan. 21, 2005).

248. Aristotle, *Politica, in The Basic Works of Aristotle,* supra note 246, at 1127, 1220.

249. Id. at 1305.

8

Cultivating Democratic Demeanor: Liberalism, Affect Control, and Emotionally Intelligent Democracy

"Those to whom evil is done
Do evil in return"
—W. H. Auden

If ancient Greece is the birthplace of democracy and Athens its earliest incarnation, which deity in the illustrious pantheon of Greek gods and goddesses qualifies as its benefactor? No major figure inhabiting Olympus comes to mind, but once you consider the second-tier deities, you find a plausible candidate in Peitho, the goddess embodying "the spirit of agreement, bargain, contract, consensus, exchange, and negotiation in a free *polis*," which, according to Alexander Mourelatos, makes her "the patron of civilized life and of democratic institutions."[1] What makes Peitho such an intriguing candidate for the part is that she is also the attendant and companion of Aphrodite, whose capacity to attract and persuade, it would seem, has something to do with the art of living in a democratic polis.[2]

The discursive strategy linking democracy, civility, and affect is central to the thesis I wish to develop in this chapter, namely, that democracy is an embodied process that binds affectively as well as rhetorically and that flourishes in places where civic discourse is not an expedient means to be discarded when it fails to achieve a proximate goal but an end in

This chapter was presented in 2003 at the Rockefeller Archive Center's Conference on "Globalization, Civil Society, and Philanthropy." It was later published as "Liberalism, Affect Control, and Emotionally Intelligent Democracy" in *Journal of Human Right*, 2004. Vol. 3, pp. 407-428.

itself, a source of vitality and social creativity sustaining an emotionally intelligent democratic community. I begin my discussion with a blueprint for democratic polity formulated in ancient Greece and its critical reception at the time. Then I consider the difficulties that fledgling democracies encounter on the way to civil society as they struggle to put behind their historical legacy. Next I make the case that civic discourse is inseparable from the civic body which has been misshapen by past abuses and which takes a long time to heal. And finally, drawing on Norbert Elias's work on the civilizing process, I speculate about the emotion, demeanor, and the body language of democracy, and explore from this angle the prospects for democratic transformation in countries that are struggling to shake off their totalitarian past.

Athenian Democracy and Its Critics

The earliest sustained defense of the democratic ethos in the Occidental world dates back to 424-403 B.C. It comes to us via Thucydides,[3] who offers a spirited defense of the Athenian democracy in his *Peloponnesian War* where he pictures an Athenian statesman Pericles railing against the despotic Sparta. "Here each individual is interested not only in his own affairs but in the affairs of the state as well," explains Pericles the ways of Athens, "even those who are mostly occupied with their own business are extremely well-informed on general politics—this is a peculiarity of ours: we do not say that a man who takes no interest in politics is a man who minds his own business: we say he has no business here at all." "When it is a question of settling private disputes, everyone is equal before the law," Pericles continues.[4] "We give our obedience to those whom we put in positions of authority, and we obey the laws themselves, especially those which are for the protection of the oppressed, and those unwritten laws which it is an acknowledged shame to break." Poverty is not an obstacle for participating in the democratic process, the orator goes on to say. "No one, so long as he has it in him to be of service, is kept in political obscurity because of poverty.... [W]hat counts is not membership of a particular class, but the actual ability which the man possesses.... We regard wealth as something to be properly used, rather than as something to boast about. As for poverty, no one need be ashamed to admit it: the real shame is in not taking practical measures to escape from it."

Astutely, Pericles ties democracy to unfettered commerce—a key benefit, if not a precondition, of democratic living. "Then the greatness of our city brings about that all the good things from all over the world flow in to us, so that to us it seems natural to enjoy foreign goods as our own local products." Equally prescient in light of the issues confronting democracy today appears Pericles' defense of tolerance and diversity:

> Our city is open to the world, and we have no periodical deportations in order to prevent people observing or finding our secrets.... We do not get into a state with our next-door neighbor if he enjoys himself in his own way, nor do we give him the kind of black looks which, though they do no real harm, still do hurt people's feelings. We are free and tolerant in our private lives.... [O]ur city is an education to Greece, and I declare that in my opinion each single one of our citizens, in all the manifold aspects of life, is able to show himself the right lord and owner of his own person, and do this with exceptional grace and versatility.... When we do kindnesses to others, we do not do them out of any calculations of profit or loss; we do them without an afterthought, relying on our free liberality.... This makes our friendships all the more reliable.[5]

One more feature distinguishing the democratic lifestyle needs to be singled out here—its affinity with art and recreation. This is how Pericles renders this point, according to Thucydides: "When our work is over, we are in a position to enjoy all kinds of recreation for our spirits. There are various kinds of contests and sacrifices regularly throughout the year; in our own homes we find a beauty and a good taste which delights us every day and which drives away our cares.... Our love of what is beautiful does not lead to extravagance; our love for the affairs of the mind does not make us soft."[6]

As one can gather from the above, the political, economic, social, and cultural domains are intertwined in the Athenian polis where all citizens partake in politics and are equal before law, where merit drives political appointment and commerce ranges free and wide, where diverse lifestyles are respected, individual autonomy is supreme, and domestic life is infused with good sense and beauty.

If this paean to democracy sounds like wartime propaganda, it is probably because it was just that. The contemporary reality in Athens was far less benign, with slaves, women, and servants excluded from civil exercises, laws applied selectively, judges influenced by the powerful, and public offices far more accessible to the propertied classes than to the lower orders of society. Fittingly, one critic calls it "the first Cold War document."[7] We can find a more skeptical account of democracy in Pericles' contemporary, Socrates, whose views were preserved for posterity by his student Plato (or so we are asked to believe).

Efforts to run society democratically are doomed, explains Socrates to his interlocutor enamored of democracy. They run afoul of the hard facts of human nature. The "madness of the multitude" is incurable, "the inevitableness of the degeneracy of the multitude"[8] can be gleaned from the regularity with which democratic governments degenerate into a tyranny. This debacle happens because "democratic city athirst for liberty gets bad cupbearers for its leaders and is intoxicated by drinking too deep of that unmixed wine."[9] People drunk on liberty follow their own counsel, ignoring the voice of reason. In time, they come to resemble

> horses and asses [which] are wont to hold on their way with the utmost freedom and dignity, bumping into everyone who meets them and who does not step aside. And so all things everywhere are just bursting with the spirit of liberty [which] render[s] the souls of citizens so sensitive that they chafe at the slightest suggestion of servitude and will not endure it.... [T]hey finally pay no heed even to the laws written or unwritten, so that forsooth they may have no master anywhere over them.... And so the probable outcome of too much freedom is only too much slavery in the individual and the state.[10]

This pernicious dialectics of freedom and slavery is set in motion whenever the *demos* finds itself in power. Democracy pushes up side down the natural order of things: "And the climax of popular liberty, my friend, I said, is attained in such a city when the purchased slaves, male and female, are no less free than the owners who paid for them. And I almost forgot to mention the spirit of freedom and equal rights in the relation of men to women and women to men."[11] (A prospect so ludicrous requires no further comment, Plato thought). Thus, it is only a matter of time before "the demos trying to escape the smoke of submission to the free would have plunged into the fire of enslavement to slaves, and in exchange for that excessive and unreasonable liberty has clothed itself in the garb of the most cruel and bitter servitude."[12]

If the blueprint offered by Pericles/Thucydides lays emphasis on diversity, civility, and individual autonomy, the guidelines laid down by Socrates/Plato underscore uniformity, compliance, and the authority of the elite. Both blueprints for good government make room for social pedagogy, but where the former presupposes a liberal education infused with aesthetic sensibilities, the second requires an illiberal schooling that nurtures intellect and suppresses emotions. The "scientific art of statesmanship"[13] practiced in "a well-governed city" calls for schooling that permits "only pleasures which reason approves."[14] Traditional art, like poetry, is to be shunned, for it "associates with the part in us that is remote from intelligence."[15] Music is to be indulged in gingerly, with the enthusiasm-filled Phrygian mode strongly favored over others.

Even gymnastics commonly taught in school at the time is suspect on this account because it "is devoted to that which grows and perishes, for it presides over the growth and decay of the body."[16] The problem with all such disciplines is that they leave too much room for emotions and sensual desires threatening to overwhelm the intellect. The latter must assert its mastery over the senses, turn the soul toward the eternal and everlasting good:

> And so in regard to the emotions of sex and anger, and all the appetites and pains and pleasures of the soul which we say accompany all our actions, the effect of poetic imitation is the same. For it waters and fosters these feelings when what we ought to do is to dry them up, and to establish them as our rulers when they ought to be ruled.... [W]e can admit no poetry into our city save only hymns to the gods and the praises of good men. For if you grant admission to the honeyed Muse in lyric and epic, pleasure or pain will be lords of your city instead of law ... and the general reason as the best.[17]

One more ancient authority to be cited here weighed in on the debate about the merits of democracy. I am talking about Aristotle who broke new grounds relevant to our argument. You cannot call Aristotle a friend of democracy; his own preference is for what he calls "polity"—the "limited monarchy, or kingship according to law,"[18] which designates a constitutional government strong enough to rein in the destructive social forces. Democracy, in this reckoning, is a deficient form of constitutional government in which "the many and the poor are the rulers" and in which "the authority of every office is undermined [by] demagogues [who] make the decrees of the people override the laws." These conditions are conducive to civil unrest, anarchy, and usurpation.[19]

While it is classified among the three known "perversions" of government (the other two being "tyranny" and "oligarchy), "democracy is the most tolerable of the three."[20] At some point Aristotle appears to be making a case for the "constitutional government to be really a democracy,"[21] i.e., a democracy constrained by laws and governed by elected representatives. This is not to suggest that we are dealing with a precursor of modern constitutional democracy—Aristotle thought that "no labourer can be a citizen" and that "the working classes had no share in the government—a privilege which they only acquired under the extreme democracy."[22] But his willingness to acknowledge democracy's strength is important, and so is his emphasis on the middle class as a backbone of the sound government:

Thus it is manifest that the best political community is formed by citizens of the middle class, and that those states are likely to be well-administered, in which the middle class is large, and stronger if possible than both the other classes, or at any rate than either of the extremes form being dominant. Great then is the good fortune of a state in which the citizens have a moderate and sufficient property; for where some possess much, and the others nothing, there may arise an extreme democracy, or a pure oligarchy; or a tyranny may grow out of either extreme...[23]

Aristotle makes one more point bearing on our subject, which postulates a bond between government and character: "For each government has a peculiar character which originally formed and which continue to preserve it. The character of democracy creates democracy, and the character of oligarchy creates oligarchy; and always the better the character the better the government."[24] Character is what sustains political institutions, character is what makes political discourse civil or uncivil, character is a personal space where both citizen and the state show their true colors. Building the right character, henceforth, is a paramount goal for every constitutional state. Aristotle does not say much about the characters bred by the inferior forms of government, although his treatment of tyrants, oligarchs, and demagogues makes it clear,[25] but he talks a great deal about character traits befitting a mature polity—a gift for friendship and prudence, a capacity for compromise and rhetorical persuasion, an ability to manage one's emotions and show civic courage, as well as "doing kindnesses; doing them unasked; and not proclaiming the fact when they are done."[26] His social pedagogy spells out the sensibilities on which good government thrives, character traits that would come to be associated with civility and civitas.

While Thucydides seems content to let diverse tastes flourish in Athens and Plato sets out to regulate tastes by decrees, Aristotle looks for a middle path between the two extremes. A well-thought education is crucial for turning the populace into virtuous citizens, aesthetic education no less so than the intellectual one. Since human nature has rational and irrational parts, it is not enough to shape pupils' minds—their bodies and senses must be engaged through habit-forming, emotion-ennobling, taste-refining exercises which enable citizens to function in the public and private spheres. "Again, from the exercise of any faculty or art a previous training and habituation are required; clearly therefore for the practice of virtue.... And as the body is prior in order of generation, so the irrational is prior to the rational.... Wherefore, the care of the body ought to precede that of the soul...."[27] Alongside traditional gymnastics, exercises must extend to arts, including poetry and music, which have "the power of forming character, and should therefore be introduced into the education of the young."[28] Whereas Plato was willing to admit into his utopian city only the martial Phrygian mode, Aristotle endorsed the mild Dorian and the mournful Mixolydian musical tone systems.[29] There are limits to what Aristotle was willing to tolerate in matters of taste. Thus he opined against the harp that requires learning too complicated skills, cast aspersion on the flute as "too exciting,"[30] and demanded to "banish pictures or speeches from the stage which are indecent."[31] Still, the notion that training minds as well as forming corporeal habits and refining emotions is essential to happy life—"the life according to virtue lived without impediment"[32]—was a significant departure from his philosophical predecessors.

I have descended into this well-mined historical shaft not so much to unearth the new veins of discursive ore as to show how relevant this ancient debate is for the age of democratic revolutions. All three perspectives on democracy have retained some currency in our time. The Thucydides/Pericles thesis offers us a benign view of democratic society whose strength derives from its citizens' direct involvement with politics, their willingness to accept alternative lifestyles, pursue their private interests without state interference, and cultivate civic virtue and esthetic sensibilities. This civility-centered approach grounding government in civic virtue comes in for a sober appraisal in Socrates/Plato who finds the masses inherently unfit for self-government. According to this view, a sound government must put limits on individual freedom, shrink the private sphere, and vest authority in the hands of the philosophically minded elite empowered to suppress destructive emotions and tastes in the name of reason and the public good. Then there is a third way endorsed by Aristotle who splits the differences between the Scylla of unbridled democracy and Charybdis of the administered state by valorizing a constitutional polity based on law, eschewing the extremes of wealth and poverty, and providing for a personal space where well-educated citizens can enjoy leisure consistent with the demands of decency and civic virtue. The fate of liberal democracy in modern times gives substance to these abstract creeds.

Democratic Reform and Illiberal Democracy

Few would argue today that democracy inexorably breeds tyranny (more commonly known today as totalitarianism), but most would agree that democracy unfettered by constitutional guarantees and unleavened by civic virtue can be a cruel affair. Here is a smattering of headlines appearing in the *New York Times* in the last few years: "In Failed States, Can Democracy Come Too Soon?" "When Democracy and Liberty Collide," "America Finds Democracy a Difficult Export," "Democracies That Take Liberties," "What is Democracy Anyway?" "Does Democracy Avert Famine?" "What Makes Nations Turn Corrupt?"[33] The recurrent refrain in this discourse is that placing power in the hands of the people does not a viable democracy make.

"Elections are only one element in a democracy; others include a free press, an independent judiciary, and respect for minorities," writes *New York Times* columnist Nicholas Kristoff, "Without these checks, countries can end up with elections that (as in Pakistan) are used by drug lords as a convenient way to install their pals in important offices. Once in place, they can use their power to steal money and murder critics."[34]

"From Haiti in the Western Hemisphere to the remnants of Yugoslavia in Europe, from Somalia, Sudan and Liberia in Africa to Cambodia in Southeast Asia, a disturbing new phenomenon emerging: the failed nation-state, utterly incapable of sustaining itself as a member of the international community," concurs Steven Ratner, a fellow at the Council on Foreign Relations.[35]

"Law and order must be first priority," agrees Morton Halperin, who headed the policy planning stuff in Clinton administration. "The main thing is developing a capacity to help a country through a transitional period in a way that allows a democratic process to take hold."[36]

Politicians and civic leaders in ex-communist countries have sounded a similar alarm about the treacherous path toward civic society and the dearth of viable democratic institutions. Ex-dissidents whose commitment to liberty and justice seem beyond reproach have found the realities of democratic governance bewildering and frustrating. This is how Alexander Solzhenitsyn summed up his impressions upon returning from exile to his native Russia:

> The price of human life has dropped to zero in a country where criminal bandits have unleashed their deadly cynicism. From the start of great reforms, criminals have been thriving in Russia.... The general atmosphere is that of utter disunity, of the complete indifference toward each other, with each person licking his own wounds and nurturing his own pains; the feeling of hopelessness and psychological exhaustion drives everybody to a morbid thought that life has come to naught, that control over one's existence is totally lost.[37]

From Victor Pelevin, an intellectual of a different generation and completely different aesthetic sensibilities, comes a kindred judgment.

"Living in Russia drains you if you are an intelligent person. We have no civil society, and people have no protection from corrupt rule. Ordinary people are much worse off than they were under Communism; you simply cannot survive on your pension or money from the state."[38]

Vaclav Havel, a man who saw first hand the democratic transformation in the Czech Republic, is also full of foreboding and doubts about the outcome of the Velvet Revolution. Now that the "transition from epic poetry to the tedious and tawdry details of everyday political life" is under way, it becomes painfully clear that "freedom of speech and a free vote do not easily translate into wealth, foreign investment or happiness, that totalitarian habits of mind die hard and that Western Europe, with its own divisions and economic problems, is in no hurry to bring them into full membership in the European Union."[39]

Jere Pehe, a former Havel aid, concurs as he looks wistfully on the aftermath of Havel's first presidential term: "People don't yet understand that democracy is more than just democratic institutions, but the democratic spirit of compromise and tolerance."[40]

Disappointment with the pace and direction of reforms in fledgling democracies has given rise to a current of opinion among experts in this country who urge politicians to give the benefit of the doubt to authoritarian states which in some cases offer more protection to their citizens than their quasi-liberal counterparts. The gist of their argument is that neither well-drafted constitutions nor reasonably free-elections automatically produce a society free from human rights abuses and political corruption. Saddam Hussein's Bill of Rights guaranteed Iraqis basic freedoms on paper while denying them in practice, elections in Kazakhstan are technically free, and the Russian army's brutal actions in Chechnya enjoy popular support.[41] By contrast, authoritarian governments in China and Singapore have secured for their citizens a modicum of freedoms and economic rights lacking in some openly democratic nations. "Were China to have suddenly become a parliamentary democracy in 1989 at the time of the Tiananmen Square uprising," contends Robert Kaplan, "the average Chinese citizen would likely to be worse off today, and dramatically so."[42]

Fareed Zakaria is probably the best-known advocate for this view. In his much-quoted 1997 essay in *Foreign Affairs* and subsequent articles, he points out that "Democratically elected regimes, often ones that have been reelected or reaffirmed through referendums, are routinely ignoring constitutional limits on their power and depriving their citizens of basic rights and freedoms. From Peru to the Palestinian authority, from Slovakia to Sri Lanka, from Pakistan to the Philippines, we see the rise of a disturbing phenomenon in international life—illiberal democracies.... Democracy is flourishing; constitutional liberalism is not."[43] Half of the democratizing countries these days fall into the category of illiberal democracies, according Zakaria, and even though their rulers spurned democratic tenets, their populace often fair better than people who enjoy the right to vote and say what they wish. "Despite the limited political choice they offer, countries like Singapore, Malaysia and Thailand provide a better environment for the life, liberty and happiness of their citizens than do illiberal democracies like Slovakia and Ghana. And the pressures of global capitalism can push the process of liberalization forward. Markets and morals can work together."[44]

There is more than a whiff of elitism in the notion that flesh and blood democracies are marked by crude tastes, messy politics, and unpredictable outcomes, that people in emerging democracies may be better off with authoritarian leaders. One also senses here a tacit polemics with Isaiah Berlin who famously contended that "negative liberty" protecting the individual from state encroachment is more precious than "positive liberty" empowering the elites to impose on society a scheme that allegedly benefits everybody.[45] The list of philosophers, intellectuals, and politicians willing to sacrifice "freedom from" to "freedom for" is long indeed, going back to Plato's *Republic* and sporting such landmarks as Thomas More's *Utopia,* Campanella's *The City of the Sun*, Saint-Simon's musings about the United States of Europe, Comte's anthem to the New Christianity, and Marx's vision of the communist paradise. There is a reason why Marx and his followers render Hegel's *Burgerliche Gesellschaft* not as "civil society" but as "bourgeois society," which belongs to the past and must disappear with an onset of a glorious post-capitalist future.[46] Looked at from this angle, individual liberty is but a means to be deployed for the purposes of achieving a true goal—social harmony, and when the former gets in the way of the latter, the collective well-being takes precedence.

I am not suggesting that those endorsing the illiberal democracy thesis see China or Singapore as "eutopian" places. Zakaria knows how abusive authoritarian governments can be, casting such regimes chiefly as a detour on the way to more democratic mores. But the accent on the collective well-being achieved at the expense of individual liberties and the benign neglect with which these theorists view civil rights' abuses in authoritarian states reveal this paradigm's blind spot. This narrative pictures civilized classes spreading liberal values throughout society, sometimes in defiance of the popular will, but it ignores the pressure from bellow that has kept liberalism honest, socialized opportunity, and turned privileges into universal rights. Looking back on the history of civil rights, we can see that every major statute designed to promote freedom in the West constituted a system of privileges that the upper orders of society held onto till the bitter end. Earls and barons coerced King John into signing the Magna Carta that granted them wonted liberties; the Glorious Revolution of 1688 forced the nobility to share their privileges with the propertied classes; the American Revolution spread liberties among the wider social strata; the Civil War extended civil rights to the blacks; the suffrage movement gave women voting privileges; and the 1964 *Civil Rights Act* put into place legal mechanisms to insure that all U.S. citizens could actually exercise their right to vote, use public facilities, attend desegregated schools, resolve racial disputes, petition the Civil Rights Commission, access federal assistance programs, and work in an environment free from religious, racial, sexual, and ethnic discrimination.

Zakaria credits U.S. Congress for the latter achievement yet characteristically fails to mention the Civil Rights movement, as if Rosa Park and Martin Luther King had less to do with the civil rights revolution than Lyndon Johnson and Hubert Humphrey. Nor does he bring up the fact the 1964 Civil Rights Act exempted the U.S. Congress, Judiciary, and Executive Branch from compliance with the Title VII provisions banning discrimination in the workplace (it was not until 1991 that the federal government yielded to public pressure and extended the statute's provisions to its employees).

There is much to be said about the role that global markets can play in improving people's lot. But then, one can also argue that illiberal practices in authoritarian states corrupt their politics, hamper progress toward civil society, and ultimately stymie economic development.[47] Critics of this model, which offers itself as "a new theoretical foundation for American foreign policy,"[48] rightly point out its tenuous empirical base and the undue optimism about the free markets' ability to foster civic virtue. To expand the latter argument, I wish to lay out the thesis that repressive regimes reproduce the affective-somatic conditions injurious to civil society, that citizens unwilling or unable to learn Peitho's art of compromise, persuasion, and emotional intelligence are likely to relive their authoritarian past.

Shedding the Totalitarian Legacy

Consider Vladimir Putin, Russia's president who took over from Boris Yeltsin and now presides over the country's reform in the post-perestroika era. Confident, level-headed, hard-working, Putin exemplifies the qualities associated with the new breed of leaders pushing beyond totalitarianism without completely discarding their authoritarian heritage.

He came to power promising to bring stability to a country ravaged by doubt and mismanagement in the go-go days of the Yeltsin's hyperliberal democracy. So far as popular opinion is concerned, he delivered on his pledge. In 2001, rejoiced the labor daily *Trud*, "Russia objectively lived the best year in its modern history."[49] In less than two years, Putin affirmed Kremlin's authority in the restive regions, reined in provincial governors, clamped down on the privatization excesses, brought some sanity to the tax legislation, pushed for legal reforms allowing jury trials, submitted a package of laws promoting market relations in agriculture, encouraged foreign investment, and aligned Russia with the West in the struggle against terrorism.[50] Private markets, stock exchange, futures trading, foreign trade—the signs that the market economy is getting entrenched in today's Russia are multiplying daily. The same cannot be said about civil society whose institutions have been retrenching ever since Putin came to power.

Having disposed of economic tycoons Boris Berezovsky and Alexander Gusinsky, Putin moved against the independent media outlets which dared to quarrel with the president. NTV and Channel 6, the country's only privately owned TV stations, are now owned by private companies in which the Russian government holds majority stock.[51] Radio Echo of Moscow noted for its free-wheeling interviews and innovative cultural programming had its board of directors pushed aside.

War in Chechnya continues unabated, as government troops wage their battle against the rebels, matching them in ruthlessness and disregard for the civilians' plight. Journalists reporting the unvarnished truth about daily life in Chechnya, human rights activists interviewing civilians, foreign observers seeking access to the region, find themselves harassed by the local and federal authorities.[52]

Putin's administration moved aggressively to prosecute scholars for alleged violations of the newly buttressed secrecy laws, obtaining convictions in several dubious cases clumsily put together with the express purpose of dissuading others from fraternizing with foreigners.[53] In a parallel move, the Russian Academy of Sciences issued a directive requiring scholars to stay away from foreign nationals and report on their trips abroad. They also have to submit their papers for prepublication review, even if they are not based on classified data.[54] Russian intellectuals and civil rights activists now take for granted that their telephone lines are tapped and their correspondence surveyed.[55]

Pro-Putin activists from government-inspired youth groups (sometimes called "Putin-Jügend") conduct demonstrations calling on patriotic forces to unite against cosmopolitan intellectuals and decadent writers. The young nationalists rail against popular tastes, sexually explicit publications, and the influx of foreign movies, their biggest gripe being the dearth of patriotic themes in Russian art. Relentless attacks on Igor Kon, the country's leading sociologist and sex educator, is one example. Another is a lawsuit against Vladimir Sorokin whose novel *Blue Lard* the self-appointed defenders of Russian mores condemned for indecency and pornography.[56]

There has also been a dramatic rise in ethnic strife, pro-fascist gatherings, and skinhead demonstrations which often turn violent. Their favorite targets are Jews and people from the Caucuses. Most such events proceed under the watchful eyes of the police and go unreported, except when the victims are foreign diplomats, as in the recent case involving Ghana's envoy to Moscow who was severely beaten at the World War II memorial.[57] Since 2000, there have been over 149 racially motivated attacks against foreign students, diplomats, and business people in the Russian capital.[58]

Then there is a wave of assassinations, often carried out in broad daylight, flooding the nation's political arteries. "Politics in Moscow More Dagger than Cloak," reads a headline of an article reporting gruesome assassination statistics against Russian businessmen, state officials, and parliamentarians.[59] Most politicians murdered are associated with shady economic transactions; some are shot because they knew too much, others because they refused to accommodate a favor-seeking tycoon. But several victims, like Galina Starovoitova and Sergei Yushenkov, are politicians with no stakes in business and impeccable liberal credentials who happen to criticize the Russian government.

Add to this Putin's successful campaign to restore the Soviet era national anthem, to place the hammer and sickle back onto the state regalia, and to allow the red star as an official symbol of the Russian armed forces, and you will agree that reasons are ample to sound alarm about the state of civil society in the Russian Federation.[60]

Notice that this precipitous decline in civic society runs parallel to the upswing in the Russian economy. Private markets are chugging along, foreign contracts are being signed, the country continues to pull its weight in the international arena (thanks in part to the high oil prices on the world market), but the promised civilizing effect that the globalization and market economy are supposed to have brought in their wake has failed to materialize. Members of the liberal faction in the Russian parliament headed by Grigory Yavlinsky declared at a meeting in St. Petersburg that "Russia was becoming a society with the trappings of freedom, but controlled in reality from the top."[61] Boris Nemtzov and his colleagues from the Union of Right Forces representing middle of the road reformers have expressed a similar concern that "Russia could become a liberal economic state controlled by an authoritarian regime."[62] Whether Russia's economy will continue to grow after the sky-high oil prices come down to earth is uncertain, as is the health of Russian market economy in the wake of recent attacks on Yukos Oil and its owners. What is not in doubt is that its civic culture will be stifled as long as the authoritarian tendencies in Russian society continue unabated. The behavior of top Russian leaders furnishes ample proof for this conclusion.

Soon after Putin came to power he warned the Chechen rebels, "If we catch them in the toilet, we will rub them out in the outhouse."[63] This is a well-known taunt in Russian criminal slang, promising murder, torture, personal vendetta. The nation loved the tough language. Following the episode, the president's popularity topped the 80 percent mark. Meanwhile, civilians in Chechnya began to disappear at an even more alarming rate.

During his recent trip to Brussels, Putin came up with this remark in response to a reporter's query about the human rights situation in Chechnya: "If you are determined to become a complete Islamic radical and are ready to undergo circumcision, then I invite you to Moscow. We are multi-confessional. We have experts in this sphere as well. I will recommend to conduct the operation so that nothing on you will grow again."[64] This insult came out of nowhere, with nary a provocation, revealing the Russian president's not-so-quiet rage waiting to burst out at an opportune, or inopportune, moment. It is hard to say whether the remarks were calculated (they were excised from the official text that appeared on the Kremlin's web site), but they tell volumes about the Russian president's—and the nation's—mood. This temper tantrum reminds one of Aristotle's advice to ladle your anger with care. Passions are to be displayed properly, counseled Aristotle, "to feel them at the right times, with reference to the right objects, towards the right people, with the right motive, and in the right way is ... virtue."[65] Indeed, character and government are intertwined.

The verbal violence cited above offers an insight into the emotions ravaging today's Russia. We are not talking here about "black looks which, though they do no real harm, still do hurt people's feelings" that Pericles warned against in his famous oration, but about verbal attacks that stop just short of physical violence. Putin's threat to rub out in the toilet Russia's enemies and castrate recalcitrant journalists is a study in incivility, featuring a calculated display of ill-will toward anyone who dares to differ. One wonders if the Russian president's schooling in the KGB arts has something to do with such emotional displays. Putin's demeanor brings to mind what Jack Katz calls "hardman," a personality marked by an impenetrable countenance, a readiness to strike without warning, and a determination to "seize ... on chaos as a provocation to manifest transcendent powers of control."[66] For all its heart-rending complexity, Putin's decision to poison the attackers, which left over a hundred innocent people dead in the October twenty-three hostage taking in Moscow, illustrates this point. The government's steadfast refusal to conduct an independent investigation of the hostage relief operation is also hardly reassuring.

A country's president, Putin serves as an emotional beacon shaping civil discourse in the nation, his intolerance reverberating throughout the republic. We can see this is in Vladimir Zhirinovsky's performance in the Russian parliament where he grabbed a colleague by her hair and slammed her face to the table. A calculated threat can be inferred from the menacing treatment Sergey Grigoryants received from the security police when they took him off the plane bound for Washington DC, interrogated him for five hours about a seminar he was going to attend, warned him to watch his step, and then let him go. A well-known figure in the Russian civil rights community who spent ten years in the Soviet Gulag, Grigoryants was spared the physical abuse that might have befallen someone without his name recognition. Other victims sustain more than emotional wounds.

Symbolic violence at the top is fanned throughout the country, multiplying exponentially as we descend the layers of hierarchy. It comes to the fore in vicious attacks against foreigners, senseless beatings of innocent passerby, arbitrary arrests of people with non-Russian facial features, ritual humiliation of young recruits in the army, booby-trapped anti-Semitic placards along the highways, Chechen civilians seized from their homes and murdered by Russian soldiers—the indicia of the civil decay are everywhere.

Not that Vladimir Putin single-handedly plunged the country into this emotional cesspool. He is a symptom more than a cause of the civic crisis sweeping though his country. His personality disorder, if such can be identified, must be traced back to the Soviet regime and its experimentations with the "New Soviet Man" whose uncivil descendants roam the Russian landscapes today.

"Those to whom evil is done / Do evil in return," wrote W. H. Auden in his poem "September 1, 1939." We should bear this dictum in mind when we try to fathom the Russian people's struggle with their harrowing past.

Emotional Footbinding in a Totalitarian State

Aristotle talks about "character"—sum total of emotions, habits, and beliefs—that informs, and in turn is informed by, a political system. I want to expand on this precept, beginning with the observation that the term should be applied cautiously to the personality type forged in the pedagogical furnaces of Soviet society. Men and women who came of age under the communist regime developed a chameleon-like quality that enabled them to conceal their true feelings, suppress politically incorrect thoughts, and engage in behavioral gambits dramatizing authorized identities. The very inconstancy and duplicity transpired here as the citizen's most characteristic feature.[67]

Soviet citizens evolved remarkable flexibility and nimbleness, qualities that enabled them to switch on a moment's notice from lavish praise for a politician in good standing to an equally extravagant contempt for the same personage after the individual suddenly fell from grace. The peace treaty the Russian prime minister, Molotov had signed with Hitler's Germany was the toast of the town in 1939; those murmuring doubts about it faced reprisals, but the moment Germany invaded Russia, any reference to the ill-fated pact had to be suppressed. Soviets knew how to squelched most natural sentiments, like the love for their parents, when the father, mother or both were pronounced enemies of the people and carted away to the Gulag. Simulation and dissimulation were the order of the day, the twin marks of a psyche in distress. The two combined to produce a kind of determined spinelessness steeped in repressed anger and nourished by fear that would mark survivors of the communist ordeal. Even those bent on doing everything the regime prescribed could not be sure of their fate.

The years 1937-1938 ("Ezhovshchina") nurtured in people a life-long horror as well as a peculiar indifference to one's conduct because a person's fate did not depend on his words, thoughts, or deeds. One would grow accustomed to daily horror and at the same time was not afraid to recount anecdotes or name names in personal conversations: if you tell a joke—you find yourself in prison, if you don't—you find yourself in the same place.... You write a letter to Ezhov defending a friend, and nothing happens to you; or as a faithful informer you put behind bars one friend after another and still find yourself arrested.... That is why it is so hard to understand this period, unique in the annals of history: the bond between cause and effect was completely broken.[68]

The Pavlovian dogs exposed to conflicting stimuli show signs of a nervous breakdown. Humans conditioned by Stalin's pedagogues revealed similar symptoms. The Soviet pedagogy was working overtime to "publish," in Trotsky's memorable phrase, "a new, improved edition of Man,"[69] to secure what the Soviet psychologist, Lev Zalkind, called the "mass construction of New Man," or as Stalin's preeminent pedagogue, Anton Makarenko, would have it, to shape "that type of behavior, those characters and qualities of personality, which are necessary for the Soviet state."[70]

This pedagogical system included sophisticated techniques designed to mobilize affect and harness it to the communist cause, including the notorious "criticism and self-criticism" which called for periodic denunciations and self-denunciation, spying on your home folks as exemplified in Pavel Morozov's heroic betrayal of his relatives reluctant to join a collective farm. Then there were show trials punctuated by requisite self-incriminating statements, public display of remorse, the pressure put on the country's leading artists to produce works flattering the national leaders' egos. In the perverse glasnost of the Stalin's era, one had to praise the very people who had stolen your dignity.

People gifted with a voice faced the worst possible torture: their tongue was ripped out and with the bloody stump they had to praise their master. The desire to live was irrepressible, and it coerced people into this form of self-annihilation, just to extend one's physiological existence. The survivors turned out to be as dead as those who actually died.[71]

Soviet biologists renouncing the idealist genetics, physicists decrying the bourgeois theory of relativity, engineers railing against capitalist cybernetics—the debased discourse sucked oxygen from the air, backed by the requisite body language and affective display. Many victims of the high-pressure tactics would eventually identify with the oppressor, join the enemy's camp. "[Osip] Mandelstam always tried to make up his mind freely and check his actions against reality," remembers Nadezhda Mandelstam, the widow of the great Russian poet who perished in Stalin's concentration camp, "but even he was not an entirely free person: the noise of time, the noise of life conspired to suppress his inner voice: 'How could I be right if everybody thinks otherwise?'"[72] Boris Pasternak wrote verses glorifying Stalin,[73] and so did Anna Akhmatova to ease the plight of her son languishing in the Gulag. Mikhail Bulgakov wrote a play about Stalin's heroism,[74] Mikhail Zoshchenko tried to win reprieve by writing children's stories about Lenin, Yuri Olesha took part in the literary venture that glorified the infamous Belomor-Baltic Canal project built by political prisoners. The struggle between the old and the new self was fierce. "I seize my own self, reach out to strangle that part of myself which suddenly balks and stirs its way back to the old days. I wish to stifle that second 'self,' and the third self, and every 'self' which comes to haunt me from the past."[75]

"Is there anybody among us," recalls Zinaida Gippius, "the most farsighted and incorruptible person imaginable, who is not haunted by the memories of the compromises we were forced to make in the St. Petersburg's captivity, who did not plead ... for something or other or ate stale bread from the enemies palms? I know the taste of such bread, of this damn ration, as well as the feel of Soviet money in my hands..."[76] Very few could withstand this pressure. "Theoretically, I know that one should not compromise, but how could I urge somebody to throw caution to the wind and not to compromise, to forget about your children. To all my friends I counsel—compromise," wrote Nadezhda Mandelstam. "There is one more thing I can add: do not bring children into this monstrous world."[77]

Soviet pedagogy had a profound impact on the Soviet character, on the demeanor of autocracy, with its signature capacity to mobilize affect in the service of the state. This kind of "emotional labor" points to "the emotional surplus meaning systematically extracted by the state from its members, condemned to work overtime in Potemkin-portable villages and dramatize the official reality as the only meaningful one."[78] To one extent or another, this phenomenon is present in all totalitarian systems, which use mass hysteria to buttress state policies and hunt down dissidents, preventing critics from airing their doubts publicly. What people lacked in conviction they could compensate by emotional violence. It was hard to know who was sincere in doing the required emotion work and who was not. "Putting the show on," to use Erving Goffman's term,[79] would become a second nature, and so was lying, feigning, scheming. "Without lying I would not have survived in those horrible days. I lied throughout my life—at work, to my students, to my acquaintances whom I couldn't trust completely, and those were the majority.... [Such] was the common mendacity of our age, the commonplace politeness of sorts. I am not ashamed of those lies."[80] Others feel more ambivalent about this defense mechanism as they look back on the horrific days when they had to keep quiet in the face of preposterous charges leveled against their friends and relatives. "Even now, as I look back at my thinking, I am ashamed of myself," confesses a survivor. "I shied away from the truth [and] publicly repented, trying not to go beyond certain limits of decency."[81]

Olga Fridenberg, a Russian literary scholar, summed up the noxious emotional climate suffocating the country after the first few decades of the Bolshevik rule:

> Everywhere, in all organizations and homes, a nasty squabble [*skloka*] is raging on, the poisoned fruit of our social order, a new concept hitherto unknown to civilization and untranslatable into any other language. It is hard to explain what it really is: a mean-spirited, petty rivalry, venomous factionalism that sickens all against each, an unscrupulous envy that breeds endless intrigues. It is sycophancy, libel, informers, the desire to unseat the rival, deliberate feeding of ugly passions, nerves perpetually set on edge, and moral degeneration that makes a person or a group run amok. Squabble is a natural state for people who are rubbing against each other in a dungeon, helpless to resist the dehumanization they have been subjected to. Squabble—is the alpha and omega of our politics. Squabble—is our methodology.[82]

This climate of fear and self-abasement changed after Stalin's death. Khrushchev's thaw brought a reprieve from the psychosis-inducing strictures of early Soviet pedagogy. It was now possible to close off the outside world and confide to a friend one's true feelings, as long as one refrained from overly critical gestures in public. But in some ways the situation got worse, for the gap between one's feelings and thoughts and the conformist public behavior grew wider, increasing the cognitive dissonance and requiring greater effort at justifying one's conduct to oneself and others. Cynicism, corrosive irony, and self-destructive behavior would spread throughout society. "In the atmosphere of mendacity, all-consuming irony becomes a universal self-defense mechanism."[83] Disaffected Soviet citizens, especially from the younger generation, would resort to voluntary self-alienation, which is what Russian irony achives as it bridges the gap between the public and the private domains. Sarcasm and black humor blossomed among the Soviet intellectuals who took to parodying official symbols when they could not openly fight them. Emotional deviance would become ubiquitous. One of its more insidious forms was withdrawing from the official world, going underground, and in some cases drinking oneself into oblivion. A paradigm for such ritual self-destruction can be found in the dissident classic *Moskva-Petushki*, a novel by Venedikt Erofeev, whose hero drives himself into the ground, and destroys his family in the process, by fanciful drinking, in much the same way as the author himself did some years later.

I wish to underscore that a merely discursive performance would not suffice to insure one's bona fide as a Soviet citizen . One had to sign in the flesh no less eloquently than in plain language, with the devastating impact on the person's body and mind. The normative system burrowed into the corporeal lifeworld where it shaped the neurochemical and hormonal circuits in a manner that would scar a person for life. Neurological and psychological studies have demonstrated the toll that high stress has on people enduring "emotional footbinding" for lengthy periods of time.[84] Among the more insidious consequences are persistent irritability, anxiety attacks, difficulties with retrieving old and forming new memories, depressive episodes alternating with the aggressive outbursts, the increase in escapist and self-destructive behavior, the immune system breakdown, heightened susceptibility to infection, and lowered life expectancy.[85] Many leading social and emotional indicators in Gorbachev's and post-Soviet Russia point in this direction. We can see this in the precipitous drop in life expectancy, pervasive alcoholism, skyrocketing suicide rates among children, increase in violent crime, and family breakdown.[86] Here is how Grigory Pomerants, one of Russia's sanest minds, diagnoses the country's mood in the post-Soviet era:

> Where simulation and pretension once ruled the day, the inertia of decay has settled in, the lust for seeing things unravel, something I try to counter as best I can. So much in our life compels you to give up and embrace the chaos, no rational measures can stop this death spiral. What does the future has in store for Russia if this chaos continuous unabated? Neither preaching nor censorship can turn things around. What is to be done? How can we counter the will to death?[87]

Masha Gessen writing for *Newsweek* on the contemporary Russian rock scene (the article is titled "Rocking to Sad Songs") observes the morbid quality of current lyrics. She quotes a radio programmer, Mikhail Kozyrev: "Russian rock is a very sad thing. If you take the Russian greatest hits of all time, made about 20 years ago, and today's songs that are likely to be remembered, you will see that they are all united by a single mood: profound regret—perhaps for lost opportunities, perhaps for the land we call home."[88]

Mikhail Zhvanetsky, Russia's beloved satirist, has a more humorous take on the nation's predicament, although his outlook is also drenched with despair:

> Our complaint has been diagnosed as being still uncivilized. The percentage of toilet-bowl, spittoon and trashcan misses is much too high. The language we use is much too coarse. We translate from Four-letterese. We readily understand and appreciate strength, and so we submit to dictatorship and criminals. In prison and in life. This is what I think.
>
> 1. We should stop hating each others.
> 2. Stop getting peeved.
> 3. Stop rushing about.
> 4. Stop feeling scared.
> 5. Stop listening to and start simply listen.
> 6. Stop begging.
> 7. Stop demeaning ourselves.
> 8. We should smile. Even if the smile is forced. Affected. As long as it is a smile.[89]

Abused children tend to grow up into abusive adults who extend the cycle of emotional violence by abusing subsequent generations—a vicious circle that defies well-meaning efforts to plant democratic institutions on the infertile affective-corporeal soil. If rebuilding civil society took far longer than expected and more frustrating than reformers hoped for, it is in part because people in places like Russia, Rumania, Nigeria, or Palestine have the habits of the heart going back for generations, in some cases for centuries. This concerns not only common folks but reformers as well, whose malignant emotional cysts have never been completely drained, whose conduct is sometimes every bit as uncivil as that of their arch-enemies, and who put too much stock in fighting the "system" while ignoring festering wounds inside.

Discourse, Emotion, and Body Language of Democracy

"Emotional footbinding" is an apt metaphor for the process through which social forces inscribe themselves in the body. The impact is gradual, incessant, debilitating, and often irreversible. People surviving the emotional Gulags are affectively pockmarked and spiritually crippled to the point when they cannot function outside the familiar environs. They are also apt to misrecognize their feelings, experience wild mood swings, and are slow to develop emotionally intelligent ways of coping essential to deliberative democracy. The quality that they need the most—civility—is conspicuously missing from their emotional tool kit. "Civility is the outlook which attempts to do justice to all the interests—which involves also holding them in check," writes Edward Shils, "and thus maintaining the traditional pattern of plurality within a common society which is of intrinsic value."[90]

Uses of civility are many. Civility can be used as a weapon—the weapon of the powerful, just as it can be a healing medium in which civil discourse flourishes. In this final section, I would like to join issue with Norbert Elias and build on his theory of the civilizing process that intertwines social structure and affective life, a central theme of this essay. My objective is to show how Norbert Elias's insights bear on the prospects for building civic society in ex-totalitarian countries and suggest some revisions of his thesis.[91]

Norbert Elias's theory traces the historical progression from "courtesy" to "civility," two key junctures in the history of Western civilization.[92] Courtesy is the first stage on the road toward psychological modernity, an affective-behavioral structure presupposing a sophisticated ability to monitor affect, your own and that of other people, as well as to control one's body. Early advice to manner-conscious courtiers would include the following ditties:

> It is very impolite to keep poking your finger into your nostrils, and still more insupportable to put what you have pulled from your nose into your mouth.... It is very contrary to decency to blow your nose with two fingers and then to throw the filth onto the ground and wipe your fingers on your clothes.... Moreover, it does not befit a modest, honorable man to prepare to relieve nature in the presence of other people, nor to do up his clothes afterwards in their presence.... Listen to the old maxim about the sound of wind.... The sound of farting, especially of those who stand on elevated ground, is horrible. One should make sacrifices with the buttocks firmly pressed together.[93]

With time, such crude points would be replaced with more sophisticated counsel, centered on court appearances, suggesting that the more basic points were now well rehearsed. Keeping the proper posture during a court pageant, holding a fork properly, moving gracefully on a dance floor—such disciplines would grow in importance throughout the late medieval Europe, becoming mandatory by the sixteenth century. The *English Book of Courtesye* rendered detailed instructions on how courtiers can put on a show to please their superiors and pacify their equals. Special emphasis was placed on avoiding scenes and defusing tension. "Say nothing that can arouse conflict, or anger others."[94] Refined demeanor did more than assure others that the courtier was not harboring hostile intent (the ritual of shaking hands originally meant "no knife"). It also marked class boundaries separating the higher orders of society from the lower ones. Wielding a fork or sporting a suave move on a dance floor would become more important as a status symbol in a court society than wielding a sword or dressing down a hapless subordinate.

Along with courtesy comes a new sensitivity to embarrassing conduct, in oneself and others, as the civilized body would respond spontaneously to situations where one's demeanor did not accord with the etiquette: "...[T]he embarrassment threshold is raised. The structure of emotions, the sensitivity, and the behavior of people change, despite fluctuations, in a quite definite direction."[95] The heightened sensitivity to embarrassing situations signaled a new stage in affect refinement—the willingness to exercise restraint. With time, skills crucial for courtiers would spread throughout society, preparing the grounds for the emergence of civil discourse in society at large.

> The king requires this conduct as a 'mark of respect' from his courtiers. In court circles this sign of their dependence, the growing compulsion to be restrained and self-controlled, becomes also a 'mark of distinction' that is immediately imitated below and disseminated with the rise of broader classes. And here, as in the preceding civilization-curves, the admonition 'That is not done,' with which restraint, fear, shame, and repugnance are inculcated, is connected only very late, as a results of a certain 'democratization' ... to an argument that applies to all men equally, regardless of their rank and status.[96]

I would like to point out that courtesy and verbal wit functioned as substitutes for violence, or perhaps a sublimated form of violence, a point that remains implicit and can be lost in Elias's account. One of the absolutism's key accomplishments was forcing destructive urges and conduct into new, acceptable channels. The same cannot be said about totalitarian polities, for they are steeped in an arbitrary, whimsical authority that flouts convention and common sense. Thus Stalin could order Nikita Khrushchev to dance a Ukrainian folk dance or make Politburo members dance with each at a party as a way to humiliate them. Repressed and driven inside, emotions did not loose their power to shape conduct and nourish imagination. However civilized, strong emotions—anger, rage, fear, envy, contempt—continue to work behind the façade, engendering complicated moods, fantasies, and discourses. A fine rendition of this precept can be found in the French movie *Ridicule* where the art of verbal insult serves as a substitute for, and in some cases a prelude to, a highly scripted physical violence epitomized in dueling.

Civility closely follows courtesy in its emphasis on body control and emotion management, with the steadily growing pressure to show consideration and polite inattention. In his famous treatise on manners,

Erasmus offers this advice to his upper class charges: "Be lenient toward the offenses of others. This is the chief virtue of *civilitas*, of courtesy. A companion ought not to be less dear to you because he has worse manners. There are people who make up for the awkwardness of their behavior by other gifts.... If one of your comrades unknowingly gives offense ... tell him so alone and say it kindly. That is civility."[97] The main difference between courtesy and civility is that the latter is no longer reserved for individuals of equal status, it is no longer a mark of blue blood. Civility is courtesy democratized, extended first to the third estate, then to the professional classes, and ultimately to all educated members of society. To be civil was to affirm the dignity of the other whatever the person's class affiliation. Civility is what we owe to any person simply as a citizen in a nation state, and ultimately to every person as a member of the human race, a class to which every civilized person belongs alongside more immediately felt and less inclusive affiliations.

The term still carries a certain class connotation. "Nonpersonhood" so obvious under the regime of courtesy (an aristocratic lady may feel no qualms about disrobing in front of a male servant) reappears here in a more subtle way. A civilized person tends to hide one's indifference, if not contempt, behind politeness. There is also a good deal of smoldering resentment and hatred waiting to burst out at an opportune moment—the point that Elias seems to overlook. Civility tends to be applied selectively. Someone acting civilly in public can be cruel behind the scenes toward a person lacking in power. Civility has not yet worked all the way into the body—it did not become a habit. It often works against character, which is why there is usually an element of hypocrisy in civility, a fact widely noticed in the Romantic era. The Romantic and bohemian intellectuals decried civility as superficial, rejected contrived rituals of courtesy, and opted for naturalness in the expression of emotions, which sometimes bordered on rudeness. Civility continues to be a sticky issue for the Old and the New Left,[98] whose members show the Bohemian predilection for physically, emotionally, and discursively violent means in furthering their professed humanistic agenda.

How do these observations link with the problems of building civil society?

A Harvard scholar, Samuel Huntington, has pointed out that countries that did not pass through a full-fledged aristocratic phase have a hard time grappling with democratic institutions.[99] I think he has a point. The civilizing process makes room for sentiments and body language that the Greek goddess Peitho would recognize as conducive to exchange, civilized discourse, reasoned negotiation. Civil society is not in substance what it is in name until its members have mastered the art of dialogue and compromise, until they have agreed to disagree. The skills that make civil society possible are grounded in the habits of emotional intelligence which sometimes part company with intellect and logical calculations.[100] Reformers seeking to overcome the totalitarian legacy need to focus on the affect dysfunctions and somatic ailments formed during earlier stages of a country's history. They need to consider what Antonio Dadamasio, a prominent neuroscientist, calls "somatic markers"[101] whose network frames body politic in the corporeally affective manner, not just discursively and normatively. Exporting U.S. institutions to countries where citizens are "wet-wired" for emotional violence and self-destruction, be this Iraq or Russia, is likely to backfire. We must pause to consider the full range of relevant structures in place—the normative system (constitutional, institutional, rational), the lifeworld (attitudinal, value-oriented, identity-fostering), and the bodymind (affective, somatic, neurochemical). Forcing democratic institutions on an unwilling nation risks discrediting democratic ethos before it takes hold. This is where I want to push Elias's thesis beyond his program and connect it with the pragmatist notion of civil society and emotionally intelligent democracy, that is, a society in which "[h]uman intelligence is emotional just as emotions are intelligent."[102]

Important as courtesy and civility are for the progress toward civil society, these historical formations fall short of creating an affectively-sound society. Courtesy is about court life, just as civility is about the life of the civitas—the state. Civility is what you owe to every citizen of the state, no more, no less. Violence—symbolic, affective, physical—is hiding in the interstices of civilized society. The forces of courtesy and civility were harnessed to promote centralized control, to deliver the monopoly over the means of violence in the hands of a monarch and the state. It is for the good of the state—first absolute and then constitutional—that members of society had to sacrifice their immediate gratification, rein in their violent drives. The destructive affect has not been vanquished, however. Submerged and repressed, it is lurking in the background, waiting to burst out and reveal the supposedly civilized people's darker colors. Indeed, civilized sentiments are often at odds with what the emotions concealed under civil appearances (think about German Nazis). A civilized person knows how to simulate and dissimulate—both operations implying hidden agendas, a suspicion toward others, hoarding one's resources, in short, a strategic reasoning guided by the agent's self-interest. Civil society is bound to be prone to violence and less than emotionally sane as long as the civic bodies composing it remain affectively crippled by past abuses under a civilized veneer. The emotional substance of democracy impinges on its political profile. The process of democracy—in all its embodied forms—is no less relevant than its outcome, and often it is its most salient product, as James Madison and John Dewey used to point out. When the process is unseemly, it matters little who wins—the results are likely to be flawed, the scars will be slow to heal. When the process is fair, it does not matter that much who loses—the democratic process itself will have a healing effect.[103]

Given these considerations, it seems reasonable to add the third stage to the Elias's civilizing process—"emotional intelligence."[104] If "courtesy" is about the court life (the habitus of a privileged estate), and "civility" is about the civitas (the hexis of the national state inhabitants), then "emotional intelligence" is about the humanity as a whole and the habits of the heart we body forth when we deal with every human being, no matter where the person hails from. The third stage in the evolution of the democratic body politic is distinguished by its universal application. No one is denied here a civil treatment, not even individuals lacking in civility. People handicapped physically, impaired emotionally, disadvantaged legally, or lacking in citizenship rights are part of the civic discourse. At the stage of emotional intelligence, civility inscribes itself not only in the community's legal statutes (the normative system) and our self-identities (the lifeworld), but also in our affective-somatic habits (the bodymind). Civic discourse moves beyond the exchange of formal signs of respect toward an affective-body work sustaining civil society and reproducing the affective infrastructure of democracy. Emotional intelligence relies on voice and not just discourse to achieve its civilizing agenda. It turns everybody you face into a concrete person, compels you to treat a human being not as a status holder but a flesh-and-blood individual who inhabits various social niches, ranging from membership in the species-wide category of humanity to the social configurations formed by immediate face-to-face interactions.

Sentimental education is valued here as much as intellectual and professional schooling. Emotional literacy, the backbone of civil society, is to be taught at home and in school, emotional littering tactfully exposed as emotional illiteracy. Allowed to fester, uncivilized affect breeds emotional, and eventually physical, violence. Emotional intelligence must become a habit that permeates personhood at every level, that signs itself across the signifying media—symbolic, somatic, and behavioral. Expressing ugly emotions in public would be as embarrassing as relieving body functions without regard for those present (once a routine practice). Emotions displayed will be felt and acted upon in various social situations, with the violent and intolerant sentiments recognized and dealt with at their early stages. This blueprint is not meant to proscribe emotions like anger, which plays an important part in mobilizing agency for righteous struggle, or frown upon melancholy, which may feed empathy and creativity. The point is to find the right measure or "mean," to use Aristotle's favorite term, that allows you to recognize your feelings, express them honestly, and do so intelligently and creativelyin a way that does full justice to the issues involved and at the same time affirms the dignity of the other.[105]

Implicit in this pragmatist outlook on civil society is the notion of "moral imagination," which may be construed as a phase in the evolution of a democratic polity toward an emotionally intelligent community. A society that lets itself be informed by moral imagination is marked by the equitable distribution of economic and symbolic resources which practically enable every member of society to participate in civil discourse. The political economy of civility comes to the fore here. If civility is the weapon of the powerful and the economically advantaged, then anger is the ultimate weapon of the powerless and economically handicapped. It is easy to be polite when you know your needs will be met at the end of the day, when you have enough power to ram your decision through the power circuits. It is much harder when you face unfair odds, are not allowed to do your best, struggle to speak when nobody is listening. Tempers flare more often as we descend the socio-economic ladder and so do instances of violence, emotional and otherwise. Socio-emotional indicators—physical health, emotional vitality, life expectancy—are known to correlate with the group's socio-economic status. We should heed Aristotle's warning that a democratic society stacking its economic deck in a way that benefits egregiously some while keeping others in poverty will reap the bounty of frustration it sawed. A democracy that strives to be emotionally intelligent cannot afford to leave anybody far behind. It must furnish every citizen with the capital—symbolic, economic, emotional—necessary to become a participant in a liberal democracy, as Pericles envisioned it in his paean to democracy.

Conclusion: Toward an Emotionally Intelligent Democracy

My students ask me occasionally when democracy will sink roots in Russia. The answer I like to give—when Russians stop interrupting each other and start taking turns in conversations—is not very satisfying. This surely is not a sufficient condition, but if the goal is an emotionally intelligent democracy, it is a necessary one. Achieving an emotionally intelligent democracy is a task that faces democracies all over the world. Building a legal, political, and economic framework for liberal democracy is not enough, unless we accept Columbine-style massacres as normal part of civil society. A viable political system requires changes in the citizens' affective life, in the habits of the heart. Such habits form the somatic-affective conditions of possibility for civil society—a society in which "emotions are intelligent and intellect is emotionally sane."[106]

Various organizations are dedicated to this civic ideal.[107] They ground their work in a sound premise that free speech, multi-party politics, constitutional checks and balances are central to building a viable democracy, but they tend to overlook the fact that democracy, in the worlds of Dewey, is also an "experience," an emotion, that it thrives in the emotional culture which promotes trust, tolerance, prudence, compassion, humor, and it wilts when overexposed to suspicion, hatred, vanity, cruelty, and sarcasm. Emotional sanity is as central to democracy as discursive political rationality. Mistaken are those who pin their hopes on correct political "signals" and dismiss emotional littering as mere "noise." The emotional medium is very much the message when it comes to politics. While emotions that confer dignity on the other are democracy's lifeblood, violent emotions that hold others in contempt subvert its sacred thrust. No quantum of hatred we impart to the world disappears without a trace, nor does the quantum of kindness. Affective energy is conserved like any other, aggregating along the way in a manner that can produce staggering effects. It may leave good will in its wake, as Martin Luther King's nonviolent movement has done, or it can shake the human world in a violent explosion, as the events of September 11 amply demonstrated. This is why civic reformers at home and abroad, all those who take an emotionally intelligent democracy for their North Star, need to guard civic discourse not only from political but also from emotional distortions.

I want to end this essay with a quote from Anton Chekhov, famous Russian writer, and one of the most respected figures in Russia's intellectual history. It is excerpted from a letter in which he sets up an agenda for self-transformation that a person aspiring to emotional intel-ligence—*intelligentnost* as Russians call it—ought to undertake. To use a more current expression, we might say that Chekhov was determined to turn himself into a work of art.[108] Although his efforts yielded mixed results,[109] his formulation remains apt, relying as it is on a powerfully corporeal metaphor for the task at hand and conveying a fair idea about the magnitude of the task facing reformers in fledgling, and often enough, in established democracies:

> What if you write a story about a young man, son of a serf, ex-shopkeeper, a high school and college student, brought up to honor rank, to slobber over priests' hand, to genuflect before other people's thoughts, who gave thanks for every piece of bread he received, was whipped repeatedly, walked through wet streets in leaking shoes, engaged in fights, tormented pets, loved to dine with rich relatives, casually lied to God and people just because he felt his nothingness—write how this young man squeezed the slave out of himself, drop by drop, and how one glorious day he wakes up and realizes that it is not a slave's blood that is coursing through his veins but real human blood.[110]

Notes

1. Alexander Lourelatos, *The Route of Parmenides: A Study of Word, Image, and Argument in the Fragments* (New Haven, CT: Yale University Press, 1970), p. 139.
2. See http://www.loggia.com/myth/peitho.html.
3. Thucydides, *The Peloponnesian War* (New York: Penguin Books, 1954).
4. Ibid. p. 2. The following quotations from Thucydides appear on pages 145-147.
5. Ibid.
6. Ibid.
7. *The Democracy Reader* (Diane Ravitch and Abigail Thernstrom, eds., New York: Harper Perennial, 1992), p. 2.
8. Republic," *The Collected Dialogues of Plato*, ed. by E. Hamilton and H. Cairns (Princeton, NJ: Princeton University Press, 1963), pp. 732, 726.
9. Ibid., pp. 790-791.
10. Ibid., pp. 793-794.
11. Ibid., p. 791.
12. Ibid., p. 797.
13. Ibid., p. 752; "Statesman," *The Collected Dialogues of Plato*, p. 1071.
14. Ibid., p. 814.
15. Ibid., p. 828. A fine account of Plato's problem with poetry can be found in Richard Shusterman, Performing Live. *Aesthetic Alternatives for the Ends of Art* (Ithaca, NY: Cornell University Press, 2000).
16. Ibid., p. 754.
17. Ibid., p. 832.
18. Aristotle, "Politics," *The Basic Works of Aristotle* (Random House, 1941), p. 1201.
19. Ibid., pp. 1186, 1213, 1240.
20. Ibid., p. 1207.
21. Ibid. p. 1209.

22. Ibid., pp. 1183, 1181. Along with Plato, Aristotle also believed "that some men are by nature free, and others slaves, and that for these latter slavery is both expedient and right." Ibid., p. 1133.
23. Ibid., p. 1221
24. Ibid., p. 1305.
25. More is said on the subject in Aristotle's *Rhetoric* where, for instance, he heaps scorn at the oligarch's penchant for material possessions: "In a word, the type of character produced by wealth is that of a prosperous fool," ibid., p. 1407. Worse still, are "the newly rich [who] have all the bad qualities mentioned in an exaggerated and worse form." Ibid. Elsewhere, Aristotle talks about tyrants who "are always fond of bad men, because they love to be flattered" (*Politics*, p. 1258) and demagogues who stir popular unrest to drive "out many notables in order that they might be able to confiscate their property," ibid., p. 1240.
26. *Rhetoric*, ibid., p. 1388.
27. Ibid., pp. 1305, 1300-1301.
28. Ibid., p. 1312.
29. Ibid., pp. 1312, 1316.
30. Ibid., p. 1313.
31. Ibid., p. 1304.
32. Ibid., p. 1220.
33. "Michael Massing, "In Failed States, Can Democracy Come Too Soon?" *New York Times*, February 23, 2002; Eric Alterman, "When Democracy and Liberty Collide," *New York Times*, October 3, 1998; Tina Rosenberg, "America Finds Democracy a Difficult Export," *New York Times*, October 25, 1999; Fareed Zakaria, "Democracies That Take Liberties," *New York Times*, November 2, 1997; Nicholas Kristoff, "What is Democracy Anyway?" *New York Times*, May 3, 2002; Michael Massing, "Does Democracy Avert Famine?" *New York Times*, March 1,2003; Serge Schmemann, "What Makes Nations Turn Corrupt?" *New York Times*, August 28, 1999.
34. "What is Democracy Anyway?," op. cit.
35. Quoted in Michael Massing, "Does Democracy Avert Famine?," op. cit.
36. Ibid.
37. Alexander Solzhenitsyn, "How Can We Breath Around Here?" *Argumenty i Fakty* (May 27—June 2, 1998).
38. Interview with Victor Pelevin, Jason Cowley, *New York Times Magazine* (January 23, 2000), p. 22.
39. Steven Erlanger, "A Decade After His Triumph, Vaclav Havel Is Crushed Velvet." *New York Times*, November 4, 1999.
40. Ibid.
41. Anthony DePalma, "Constitutions are the New Writers' Market." *New York Times*, November 30, 1997.
42. Robert Kaplan, "Sometimes, Autocracy Breeds Freedom." *New York Times*, June 28, 1998. See also his book *The Coming Anarchy: Shattering the Dreams of the Post Cold War* (New York: Random House, 2000).
43. Fareed Zakaria, "Democracies That Take Liberties." *New York Times*, November 2, 1997. See also his article "The Rise of Illiberal Democracy." *Foreign Affairs* (November-December, 1997).
44. Ibid.
45. Isaiah Berlin, "Two concepts of liberty," in *Four Essays on Liberty* (Oxford University Press, 1969).
46. See Peter Beilharz, "The Life and times of Social Democracy." *Between Totalitarianism and Postmodernity* (ed. by Peter Beilharz, Gillian Robinson, and John

Rundell. Cambridge, MA: MIT Press, 1992), p. 57. See also, Dmitri Shalin, "Marxist Paradigm and Academic Freedom," *Social Research* (No. 2, 1980).

47. See Eric Alterman, "When Democracy and Liberty Collide."
48 Ibid.
49. Quoted in Alison Smale, "Russia's Leaders Are Different. It's the People Who Are the Same." *New York Times* (January 6, 2002).
50. Ibid. Celestine Bohlen, "Russian Regions Wary as Putin Tightens Control." *New York Times* (March 9, 2000).
51. Michael Wines, "TV's Impious Puppets: On Kremlin's Hit List?" *New York Times* (June, 18, 2000).
52. "Michel Wines, "Chechnya Weighs a Russian Offer of Self-Rule," *New York Times* (March 23, 2003).
53. Michael Wines, "Some Russians Are Alarmed At Tighter Grip Under Putin." *New York Times* (June 14, 2001).
54. Ibid.
55. Ibid.
56. Sophia Kishkovsky, "Russian Writer, Facing Charges, Warns Free Expression Is at Risk." *New York Times* (July 16, 2002).
57. Steven Lee Myers, "Ghana's Envoy to Moscow Hurt in Latest Racial Attack." *New York Times* (November 9, 2002).
58. Ibid.
59. Michael Wines, "Politics in Moscow More Dagger Than Cloak." *New York Times* (August 24, 2002).
60. Vladimir Isachenkov, "Some See Red in Soviet Star's Return." *Las Vegas Review Journal* (November 27, 2002).
61. Michael Wines, "Some Russians Are Alarmed At Tighter Grip Under Putin." *New York Times* (Jun 14, 2001).
62. Ibid.
63. Michael Wines, "Why Putin Boils Over: Chechnya Is His Personal War." *New York Times* (November 13, 2002).
64. Ibid.
65. "Nicomachean Ethics, *The Basic Works of Aristotle*, op. cit., p. 958.
66. Jack Katz, *The Seductions of Crime: Moral and Sensual Attractions of Doing Evil* (New York: Basic Books, 1989). Quoted in Stephen Lyng and David Franks. *Sociology and the Real World* (New York: Rowan & Littlefield, 2002), p. 132.
67. For a detailed discussion of emotion work in Soviet society see Dmitri N. Shalin, "Intellectual Culture," *Russian Culture at the Crossroads: Paradoxes of Postcommunist Consciousness* (ed. by D. N. Shalin, Boulder, CO: Westview Press, 1996); and "Soviet Civilization and Its Emotional Discontents," *International Journal of Sociology and Social Policy* (Vol. 16, 1996).
68. Lidia Chukovskaya, Zapiski ob Anne Akhmatovoi 1952-1962. Vol. 2 (Moscow: Soglasie, 1997), p. 493.
69. Lev Trotsky. "Neskolko slov o vospitanii cheloveka," in *Sochinenia*, Vol. 1 (Moscow, 1927), p.110.
70. Aron Zalkind. "Psikhonevrologicheskie nauki i sotsialisticheskoe stroitelstvo." *Pedologia*, no. 3 (1930), p. 309-322; Anton Makarenko. "Tsel vospitaniia." *Izvestia* (August 28, 1937). These quotations appear in a penetrating study of early Soviet psychology by Alexander Etkind, "Psychological Culture." (ed. by Dmitri N. Shalin, *Russian Culture at the Crossroads. Paradoxes of Postcommunist Consciousness.* Boulder, CO: Westview Press, 1996), pp. 98-120.
71. Nadezhda Mandelstam, *Vospominaniia* (New York: Izdatelstvo Imeni Chekhova, 1970), p. 219.

72. Mandelstam, *Vtoraia kniga*, op. cit., p. 231.
73. Idem. p. 134.
74. Quoted in Marietta Chudakova, "Bulgakov i Lubianka," *Literaturnaia Gazeta* (December 8, 1993).
75. Quoted in Arkady Belinkov, *Sdacha i gibel sovetskogo intelligenta. Yuri Olesha* (Madrid: Esiciones Castilla, S. A., 1976), p. 264.
76. Gippius, Ibid., p. 41.
77. Nadezhda Ia. Mandelstam, *Vtoraia kniga* (Moskva: Moskovskii Rabochii, 1990), pp. 461, 482.
78. Dmitri Shalin, "Soviet Civilization and Its Emotional Discontent," op. cit.
79. Erving Goffman, *The Presentation of Self in Everyday Life* (New York: Doubleday & Co, 1959).
80. Nadezhda Mandelstam, *Vospominaniia*, op. cit., p. 25.
81. Efim Etkind. *Zapiski Nezagovorshchika* (London: Oversees Publications, 1977), pp. 196, 243.
82. Olga Fridenberg, in *The Correspondence of Boris Pasternak and Olga Freidenberg* (ed. by Elliott Mossman, New York: Harcourt, Brace, Jovanovitch, 1981), p. 291.
83. Andrey Kolesnikov, "Chelovek kak tsitata," *Panorama* (November 24, 1939).
84. Peggy Thoits, "Emotional Deviance." *Research Agendas in the Sociology of Emotions* (ed. by Theodore D. Kemper), New York: SUNY Press, 1990.
85. Bruce S. McEwen et al, *The End of Stress as We Know It* (Joseph Henry Press, 2002); Janice Kiecolt-Glaser, *Handbook of Stress and Immunity* (Academic Press, 1994); Erica Good, "The Heady Cost of Chronic Stress," *New York Times* (December 17, 2002).
86. Dmitri Shalin, "Ethics of Survival." *Christian Science Monitor* (December 4, 1990); "A Malaise that Plagues the Soviets." *Chicago Tribune* (October 19, 1990); "Perestroika's Ugly Brother, Anti-Semitism." *Los Angeles Times* (July 25, 1990); "Why Economic Reforms Have Failed." *Chicago Tribune* (May 30, 1990); "The Limits on Gorbachev's Power." *Christian Science Monitor* (April 3, 1990); "A Giant Headache for Mother Russia." *Los Angeles Times* (February 25, 1990); "Glasnost and Sex." *New York Times* (January 24, 1990). "No Meat, No Soap—and Now, a Crime Wave." *Wall Street Journal* (January 5, 1990); "Settling Old Accounts." *Christian Science Monitor* (December 29, 1990);"Soviet Economy Advancing to the Rear." *Los Angeles Times* (July 21, 1989).
87. Grigory Pomerants, quoted in Grigory Ryskin, "Ia Vernulsia v Moi Gorod..." *Panorama* (May 1-7, 2002.
88. Masha Gessen, "Rocking to Sad Song." *Newsweek* (March 19, 2001), p. 33.
89. Mikhail Zhvanetsky, "On Ourselves." *Moscow News* (February 16-22, 2000), p. 9.
90. Edward Shils, The Virtue of Civility. Selected Essays on Liberalism, Tradition, and Civil Society (Indianapolis: Liberty Fund, 1997), p. 15.
91. The concept presented in this section builds on the ideas presented by Dmitri Shalin in "Discourse, Emotions, and the Body Language of Democracy," Stone Symposium of the Society for the Study of Symbolic Interaction (Las Vegas, NV, 1999); and "Norbert Elias and George H. Mead: The Problem of Embodiment in Two Sociological Classics," Society for the Study of Symbolic Interaction (Anaheim, CA, 2001).
92. Norbert Elias, *The History of Manners. The Civilizing Process. Vol. 1* (New York: Pantheon books, 19178).
93. Ibid., pp. 147, 130-131.
94. Ibid., p. 80.
95. Ibid., p. 116.

96. Ibid., p. 159.

97. Ibid., p. 81.

98. See Edward Shills, *The Future of Civility*, op. cit., p. 8.

99. I was not able to track the source for this observation.

100. Habermas misses this point in his theory of communicative action when he appeals to logical reasoning and more or less completely ignores the role of the somatic-affective factors in social reconstruction. See Dmitri N. Shalin, "Critical Theory and the Pragmatist Challenge." *American Journal of Sociology* (96:237-279, 1992); Lyng and Franks, *Sociology and the Real World*, p. cit., pp. 158-159.

101. Antonio Damasio, *The Feeling of What Happens: Body an Emotion in Making of Consciousness* (New York: Harcourt Brace, 1999).

102. Dmitri Shalin, "Critical Theory and the Pragmatist Challenge." *American Journal of Sociology* (No. 2, 1992, p. 256).

103. See Dmitri Shalin, Opening Remarks at the Justice & Democracy Forum on "Judicial Election and Evaluation," sponsored by the UNLV Center fro Democratic Culture and William S. Boyd School of Law, *The Nevada Law Journal* (Vol. 4, No. 1, p. 62, 2003).

104. I used the term for some years before it was brought into wide circulation by David Goleman in his wonderful book *Emotional Intelligence* (New York: Bantam Books, 1995). See also Dmitri Shalin, *"Critical Theory and the Pragmatist Challenge." American Journal of Sociology* (No. 2, 1992); "Emotional Barriers to Democracy Are Daunting," *Los Angeles Times* (October 27, 1993); "Emotions and Democracy," *Sociology of Emotion, Newsletter of the American Sociological Association* (No. 4, 1995); "Emotions and Democracy." *Sociology of Emotions*. Newsletter. (No. 4, 1995); "Emotion, Agency, and the Social Production of Affect: A Research Note." *Sociology of Emotion. Newsletter of the American Sociological Association* (No. 4, 2001).

105. "Affect, Emotion, Agency: E-Motion Template Chart Methodology," Paper presented at the 2002 Annual Meeting of the American Sociological Association," Chicago, August 16. 106. Dmitri Shalin, "Intellectual Culture," in *Russian Society at the Crossroads*, op. cit. p. 91.

107. For an example, see the mission statement of UNLV Center for Democratic Culture at http://www.unlv.edu/centers/cdclv. See also Dmitri Shalin, "Emotional Barriers to Democracy Are Daunting," *Los Angeles Times* (October 27, 1993).

108. Chekhov's agenda lends political substance to what Richard Shusterman outlines in his proposal for "somatoesthetics," a discipline seeking to foster body awareness and increase one's emotional recall. See Richard Shusterman, *Performing Life*, pp. 137-153.

109. See Donald Rayfield, *Anton Chekhov: A Life* (New York: Henry Holt & Co., 1997); Dmitri Shalin, "Anton Chekhov, Russian Intelligentsia, and the Ethics of Small Deeds: A Biocritical Essay," paper presented at the Annual Meeting of the American Association for the Advancement of Slavic Studies (Washington, DC, 2001).

110. Anton Chekhov, "Letter to A. S. Suvorin, January 7, 1889." *Sobranie Sochinenii v Dvenadtsati Tomakh*, Vol. 11 (Moscow: Khudozhestvennaia Literatura, 1956), pp. 328-9.

9

Becoming a Public Intellectual:
Advocacy, National Sociology,
and Paradigm Pluralism

Introduction

The controversy over the proliferation of paradigms in sociology and the threat it poses to the theoretical unity of the discipline is an old one. According to Robert Merton (1975: 39-40), the "debate between theoretical pluralism and theoretical monism" reemerges at strategic junctions in the discipline's history when sociologists committed to "an overarching theoretical system" clash with those favoring "a multiplicity of occasionally consolidated paradigms." Russian sociologists appear to have reached such a juncture.

The current controversy follows the dissolution of the Soviet Union, a traumatic experience that provoked soul-searching among Russian intellectuals and engendered heated debates about advocacy, policy engagement, and scholars' ties to the state. While all sides in the current controversy agree on the urgent need to aid their country in the time of trouble, they part company on what exactly a national sociology agenda entails. Sociologists committed to the notion that Russia has unique historical destiny mistrust paradigm pluralism and insists on developing distinctively Russian theories and social remedies. Skeptical about Western paradigms, they press for a "national sociology" that realigns social science with the state (Dobrenkov 2007; Malinkin

Parts of this chapter were presented at the 2009 Annual Meeting of the American Sociological Association in San Francisco.

2005, 2006, Osipov 2004, 2006, 2007; Osipov and Kuznetsov 2005; Zhukov 2002).

Sociologists with liberal credentials endorse the idea of a policy-relevant sociology but are weary of too close an association with the state and decry any loyalty test aimed to establish social scientists' patriotic credentials. They also oppose theoretical monism and the notion of Russia's unique historical destiny. Social scientists committed to a liberal program believe that scholars espousing diverse theoretical views can effectively safeguard national interests (Yadov 2003, 2006, 2007; Zaslavskaya 1997, 1999; Kravchenko 2004).

Other participants in this debate stake a middle ground, endorsing the legitimacy of the multi-paradigmatic approach and policy-oriented studies while encouraging the search for a sociological theory informed by the Russian cultural tradition (Filippov 1997; Zdravomyslov 2006, 2007).

Although the debate under review reflects Russia's struggle to put behind its Soviet past, the issues at stake—advocacy, policy relevance, and the national agenda for social science—have their counterpart in the West. In his 2004 presidential address before the American Sociological Association, Michael Burawoy urged his colleagues to shun their discipline's hegemonic pretensions and articulate a distinctly national agenda: "We, therefore, have a special responsibility to provincialize our own sociology, to bring it down from the pedestal of universality and recognize its distinctive character and national power. We have to develop a dialogue, once again, with other national sociologies, recognizing their local traditions or their aspirations to indigenize sociology" (Burawoy 2005: 22).

This paper reviews the current controversy in Russian sociology—its origins, historical context, and political alignments in each camp. It also addresses the animosity that Russian intellectuals on the right and on the left have shown toward pragmatism as a philosophical teaching and a sociological perspective. "The polyparadigmatic approach is grounded in the ideological and philosophical principles of liberalism and pragmatism," asserts Aleksandr Malinkin, an opponent of paradigm pluralism, and "pragmatist philosophy is fruitless and unproductive as a theoretical and methodological foundation of sociology" (Malinkin 2006, 2005).[1] Coming from a completely different perspective, a public intellectual critical of the Putin regime warns his countrymen that "[p]ragmatism is only a polite name for the utter lack of principles" (Bukovsky 2006). The enmity toward pragmatism crosses political fault lines in today's Russia, animating conservative thinkers as well as their opponents, especially those on the traditional Left, and it offers an important gloss on the difficulties Russia faces in transitioning to democracy. The controversy under review illuminates a delicate balance between scholarship and advocacy in emerging democracies, the plight of public intellectuals in countries where social scientists are held accountable for policy advice they offer to the authorities.

My discussion starts with the historical context of the current controversy and the role of public intellectuals in the late Soviet era, after which I examine the nascent patriotic strand in Russian social thought and its opposition to paradigm pluralism. Next, I focus on the political affinities of the sociologists committed to the nationalist and liberal agendas, examine their institutional resources and relationship with the government, and connect their stance to the views that sociologists from each camp espoused under Soviet rule. After that, I discuss Russian intellectuals' attitude toward pragmatism and place the debate about advocacy and national sociology in a comparative perspective, focusing in particular on the situation in American sociology and the work of C. Wright Mills. I conclude by making the case that American sociologists need to pay closer attention to the nascent trends in Russian sociology.

Internationalism, Theoretical Monism, and Advocacy in Soviet Social Science

Soviet sociology has had a long and troubled history. It began with a fitful start after the Bolsheviks took power, went extinct in Stalin's years, reemerged as an empirical field during the Khrushchev "Thaw," took painful hits in the Brezhnev era, then gradually positioned itself as a scientific discipline affiliated with, yet autonomous from, its philosophical counterpart—historical materialism (Batygin 1999; Beliaev and Butorin, 1982; Doktorov 2007; Firsov 2001, 2003; Greenfeld 1988; Osipov 1979; Osipov and Kuznetsov 2005; Shalin 1978, 1990; Shlapentokh 1987; Weinberg, 2004; Yadov and Grathoff 1994; Zdravomyslov 2006, 2007). Internationalism has always been a hallmark of Marxist thought which styled itself as a universal doctrine that encompasses humanity at large and foretells the emergence of a global communist community. Nationalism was castigated as a vestige of the past, an obstacle in the path of the proletariat coming to terms with its world-historical mission. Bolsheviks saw themselves as Westernizers leading the fight for world revolution. Lenin in particular was determined to deliver Russia from its backwardness, to thrust his country in the forefront of the international communist movement.

Consistent with this stance was the perception of Western theories as muddled and ideologically biased. Soviet scholars cast the diversity of theoretical schemes and methodological approaches as a sign of inferiority, gleefully contrasting paradigm pluralism in the West to the united front Marxist social scientists forged in their pursuit of monistic sociological doctrine. This is how Gennady Osipov, a prominent Soviet sociologist and an acknowledged leader in today's patriotic camp, expressed his opposition to the paradigm pluralism: "The diversity of approaches and schools in bourgeois sociology ... reflects the contradictory and unstable character of contemporary capitalism, the absence of a truly scientific worldview, and it is a consequence of the anti-historical and anticommunist stance of contemporary bourgeois sociology, as well as a proof of its ideological crisis" (Osipov 1979: 64).

It is not that Soviet sociologists had nothing to learn from their Western counterparts. They all had their conceptual favorites and borrowed freely methodological tools from abroad, but Soviet scholars had to be careful in doling out praise to foreigners, lest their ideological vigilance come under suspicion. The critique of "bourgeois sociology" called for a balancing act where positive comments were punctuated by stern dressing-downs of ideological adversaries. An article reviewing Western authors or theories usually included a mandatory statement that ran something like this: "In our time of deepening ideological struggle, it is especially important to distinguish between certain positive scientific elements found in the works of bourgeois thinkers and the reactionary essence of their overall views. [A telling example] is the neo-Kantian movement that nourishes all sorts of revisionist concepts" (Malinkin 1983: 131). Bred into the Soviet sociologist's bones was the notion that Marxist scholarship was politically engaged and policy-bound, that "the party spirit of Marxist-Leninist sociology is at the same time the best guarantee of its scientific character. The Marxist-Leninist class analysis embodies the unity of partisanship and scholarship. ... Nonpartisanship and neutrality in sociology is nothing but a myth, a thin veil disguising an allegiance to a particular class" (Osipov 1979: 137, 142).

The fact that nationalism was officially out of favor in Soviet society did not mean that the humanities and social sciences were free from nativist sentiments. The latter always lurked behind the scene, bubbling up at certain historical junctures, as they did during Hitler's invasion of Soviet Union when Stalin sought support from the church leaders and appealed to Russian patriotism. The campaign against "rootless cosmopolitans" that swept the nation after World War II featured broadsides against the principles of universalism in science. The policy-setting editorial published in 1948 in the premier philosophy journal declared that "Marxism-Leninism explodes the cosmopolitan inventions regarding the classless, transnational, 'universal' science, and proves beyond a shadow of doubt that science, as the rest of culture in modern society, is national in form and class-bound in content" (Protiv burzhuaznoi 1948: 16). Endemic to the Bolshevik movement, the tension between Marxist internationalism and dormant Russian nationalism was never resolved (Shalin, 1990; Shlapentokh, 1987; Weinberg, 2004). And it is in response to the Soviet-style "nationalization of the international Left" that C. Wright Mills (1967: 222) warned his colleagues on the Left to beware "Communism [that] had become the instrument of one national elite ... as reactionary as that of any other great power."

The ambivalence toward the national and international dimensions in sociological thought was palpable in the way Soviet sociologists treated parochial developments in Western social thought. Soviet scholars welcomed national diversity in bourgeois sociology, treating it as something progressive insofar as local intellectuals sought to distance themselves from American patronage. The expectation was that national sociological currents would be eventually absorbed into the triumphant Marxist teaching. A sophisticated treatment of the subject can be found in Igor Golosenko's 1981 article titled "The Universal and the National in Non-Marxist Sociology." "Doubts about the universal validity of American sociological theories and methods are evident to sociologists all over the world, as they have discovered that many of these concepts are not applicable outside the USA. The logical conclusion was that national sociology must be grounded in the national scientific tradition, reflecting the country's heritage. In Western Europe the recent apologists of American methods have finally come to realize that the American theories of stratification, of the education crisis, and so on, do not apply to their own societies" (Golosenko 1981: 76). Hence it is entirely appropriate to "talk about 'German sociology,' 'English social anthropology,' 'American social psychology,'" continued the author, provided nationally-minded sociologists remember that "imposing national specificity as a standard is a dangerous thing, for this specifics is historical in nature, and ignoring its historical dimension obscures the true nature of the national" (Golosenko 1981: 78). Soviet scholars welcomed the fact that sociologists around the world had grown weary of American dominance, not only in world politics but also in scholarly discourse, and they sought to encourage this trend without ceding ground to ultranationalists or discarding the internationalist agenda.

At home or abroad, Soviet scholars upheld an activist vision of sociology as a discipline engaged in practice-oriented research and setting up progressive policies. Communist Party membership was not officially a prerequisite for becoming a sociologist, but almost all leading Soviet sociologists were party members duty bound to deploy their professional expertise in the service of building communist society. Reform minded sociologists exercised their critical judgment, both in professional and general circulation publications, but they had to avoid challenging the communist authorities head-on. When in 1983 Tatyana Zaslavskaya circulated a policy paper calling for "the fundamental perestroika of our economic governance," her "Novosibirsk Manifesto," as her pamphlet became known in the West, provoked heavy criticism. She and her boss received official party reprimands. However, the term "perestroika" that appeared eight times in Zaslvaskaya's document had caught the eye of Mikhail Gorbachev, a new generation party leader rapidly advancing through the party hierarchy, and when Gorbachev came to power in 1985, he adopted the term and the program articulated by Novosibirsk sociologists as a tool for reforming an unwieldy Soviet economy and society.

With the clarion call for perestroika and glasnost, sociology in Russia began to undergo momentous changes. In June of 1988, the Communist Party Politburo passed a resolution "On Strengthening the Role of Marxist-Leninist Sociology in Solving Key Problems of Soviet Society." Soon after the Ministry of Higher Education moved to establish sociology departments in flagship universities in Leningrad and Moscow. With the new trends came a more relaxed attitude toward Marxist orthodoxy and paradigm pluralism. In 1988 Soviet scholars adopted the "Professional Code of Sociologists" that struck a balance between the old and new. The preamble reiterated the familiar thesis about the "clear class position" expected from Soviet sociologists, but it also encouraged social scientists "to defend their ideas and concepts regardless of the established views" and show "moral courage and willingness to take on established opinions" (Professionalnyi kodeks 1988: 95). Vladimir Yadov, a leading Soviet sociologist, amplified this position in his programmatic article where he acknowledged that "our sociology is directly linked to dialectical materialism, to Marxist philosophy, and as such, it deserves to be called Marxist-Leninist," but in the same breath he warned his colleagues that it would be wrong to "brag about its exclusivity," for Marxist sociology had to overcome its "isolation from sociological scholarship in the rest of the world" (Yadov 1990: 6, 15-16).

Andrey Zdravomyslov (2006, 2007) concurred with Yadov on the value of paradigm pluralism but urged his colleagues to revive the national sociological tradition. Post-Soviet sociology in Russia exhibits "the polyparadigmatic orientation" marked by the competition between "French, German, American, and English sociological enclaves within Russian social thought," observed Zdravomyslov; this competition should be seen as "the intense creative process aimed at the appropriation and transformation of the world sociological perspectives so that they become relevant for the analysis of Russian social reality" (Zdravomyslov 2007).

With the winds of perestroika sweeping through Russian society, Soviet sociologists assumed greater role in articulating the national agenda. Their traditional commitment to professionalism and applied social research was now supplemented by the increasingly critical stance toward the state and the willingness to engage as public intellectuals in the civic process on both national and local levels. Tatyana Zaslvaskaya took over as head of the National Opinion Research Center (Russian acronym—VTSIOM) where she oversaw opinion polling on vital issues of the day, supplied the polling data to the government, and offered expert policy advice. Yuri Levada, one of the most respected academic sociologists in Russia who succeeded Zaslavskaya as head of VTSIOM, accepted the invitation to join Boris Yeltsin's presidential council. Galina Starovoitova, a prominent student of ethnic relations, became a member of the Russian parliament. Nikolai Girenko, an expert ethnographer, was elected to the Leningrad City Council, while Igor Kon, the nation's preeminent authority on the issues of diversity, offered expert advice to a coalition of sexual minorities seeking to repel the nation's antigay laws. The spirit of public service that permeated post-Soviet sociology had survived perestroika, engendering a lively debate about advocacy, national sociology, and scientists' responsibility to the state. At the start of the twenty-first century, these issues emerged as a major divide within the Russian sociological community.

The Patriotic Strand in Russian Sociology

As the Soviet Union collapsed, so did state funding for sciences and the humanities. Left to their own devices, Russian social scientists searched for ways to legitimize their enterprise and find new sources of income. A few were commissioned to do polling for the emerging political parties and private enterprises, some managed to subsist on scholarly grants administered by international foundations, many more had to take additional jobs just to get by, and still others left academia or the country altogether. Paradigm pluralism flourished after perestroika as Russian sociologists translated Western treatises and published long suppressed works of Russian thinkers. No theoretical or methodological strand emerged as a clear favorite. With the confusion and mounting economic hardship of the 1990s, voices began to be heard inside the academic community about the need to establish a national agenda for Russian sociology. Policy advice that perestroika intellectuals offered the government came under criticism, and so did paradigm pluralism, as self-styled patriots accused their liberal colleagues of promoting ideas alien to Russian culture and detrimental to the nation's welfare. Once perestroika leaders were pushed aside, nationalist sociologists made a move to align themselves with the increasingly nationalist, anti-Western political establishment in the Russian Federation. The sorry conditions of Russian economy and general social malaise gave the nationalists ammunition for their critique.

Among the first to sound the alarm about the epistemological chaos in post-Soviet sociology was A. F. Filippov. He contended that history does not know successful efforts to "transplant foreign concepts in their original form, and Russia cannot be an exception" (Filippov 1997: 11). There are many theories in today's Russian sociology, Filippov claimed, but no "theoretical sociology." A practical solution to the current disarray is the "creation of our own theoretical sociology as a series of ambitious concepts" (Filippov 1997: 16).

Aleksandr Malinkin is probably the most articulate opponent of paradigm pluralism who also aligns himself with Russian national so-ciology. What grates him the most is that "many middle-aged and most young sociologists in Russia are becoming converts to faddish Western teachings"—a trend that only exacerbates "the noncompetitive charac-ter of home-grown theories." He is appalled by reigning eclecticism, by the "unbridled hybridization of ideas" and "theoretical kasha in the heads of many Russian sociologists." "The polyparadigmatic approach makes virtue out of necessity," Malinkin contends, as it surreptitiously "translates the values of liberalism into the conceptual apparatus and methodology of sociological science" (Malinkin 2005: 113, 115). Ma-linkin is skeptical about the value neutrality espoused by the proponents of paradigm pluralism. The "deideologization forced upon us merely signifies that the reigning ideology is being supplanted by another one. ...

The Russian Federation has shed its ideological garments to a dangerous point where it exposed itself to anarchy and became vulnerable to the ideological manipulation from abroad" (Malinkin 2006: 116). The fact that Russia is moving away from its past does not justify the break with theoretical monism, nor should it blind sociologists to the achievement of the bygone era. "In their opposition to the 'dark,' allegedly totalitarian Soviet past, those embracing the logic of rapture promise the 'bright' democratic future. ... We are led to believe that Russia cannot escape the Euro-American style modernization. Such 'catching-on' modernization means colonization for Russia [and it] leads to the annihilation of Russian national culture along with the bulk of its population" (Malinkin 2006: 119).

A high-flying member of the academic establishment affiliated with the nationalist paradigm in sociology is Vladimir Dobrenikov, dean of the School of Sociology at Moscow State University. Dobrenkov is concerned about the tendency to undervalue the native sociological tradition in the existing sociology programs. He denounced what he perceives to be "the extremely worrisome processes in the Russian educational and scientific establishment [reflecting] the aggressive actions of foreign-based educational and scientific centers, as well as Russian organizations financed from abroad. Such organizations undermine the indigenous educational and research establishments and serve as a conduit for Western positivist perspectives and methods alien to the Russian tradition" (Dobrenkov 2007). The dean of the sociology faculty contrasted the native sociological thought dedicated to social justice and equality with the orientation that stresses pluralism in its political, economic, and cultural manifestations incompatible with the Russian tradition. According to Dobrenkov, liberal sociologists serve as purveyors of the "political technologies [that] are deployed with the purpose to mobilize extremist moods and pseudo-revolutionary movements among students" and feed "the 'color revolution' [the reference is to the Ukrainian democracy movement] spreading among Russian students" (Dobrenkov 2007). Among the key proponents of the pro-Western orientation Dobrenkov singled out "Yadov, Zaslvaskaya, and Zdravomylsov who contrive to purge Russian sociology of its Russianness" (Dobrenkov 2007).

Gennady Osipov, head of the Institute of Socio-Political Studies, is perhaps the best known figure in the patriotic sociology movement. His strong suit is Eurasianism, an intellectual current called upon to combat "the pernicious conceptual framework offered as a strategic blueprint for Russia's development where Russia is drawn into the linear,

Western-centric schema of socio-historical process" (Osipov 2006). An alternative model proposed by Osipov advocates "the multipolar world and acknowledges the civilizational polarities in contemporary society. Russia asserts itself here as the core of self-sufficient Eurasian civilization whose existence and development provide the necessary conditions for stability in the world order" (Osipov 2006).

The quest for "genuinely Russian" theories has intensified in the last decade, as nationalist sociologists looked for a conceptual framework to ground their claims about Russia's unique historical profile and destiny. Among the names most often mentioned in this connection is Pitirim Sorokin, a distinguished sociologist of Russian birth in whose reflections on civilizational dynamics patriotic sociologists discern the blueprint for a sociology steeped in Eurasian values. Emblematic in this respect is Osipov's (2000) riff on a 1922 statement where Sorokin celebrated "the heroic achievements that demonstrate the strength, creative abilities, resourcefulness of Russians and other people residing in Russia, their willingness to sacrifice themselves and forgo their wellbeing in order to salvage freedom, dignity and other great national values." A national symposium commemorating Sorokin's 120th birthday took place on March 25, 2009.[2] Sponsored by the Russian Academy of Science and organized by Osipov's colleagues, this event is indicative of what nationalist sociologists have in mind when they call for "the creation of genuinely Russian theories, concepts, and doctrines" (Malinkin 2006: 121). "We can call them 'Russian' (regardless of the percentage of the borrowed material in them) not so much because they are formulated by Russians, but because they are rooted in the national cultural and social realities, because they have emerged in response to the challenges facing Russian society and in line with the interests of Russian people, society, and the state. National rootedness of sociological theory presupposes a certain cultural-historical continuity, a positive connection with the heritage of Russia's imperial and Soviet past" (Malinkin 2006: 121).

Biographical Trajectories and Policy Commitments

As we ponder the divergent agendas informing contemporary Russian sociology, we need to take a closer look at their historical trajectories and examine how major players have arrived at their current positions. Much relevant information is supplied by the International Biography Initiative (2005), an online project that collects documents and biographical materials about leading Russian sociologists.[3] Particularly instructive for the task at hand is the life histories of two sociologists, Vladimir

Yadov and Gennady Osipov, who have come to embody the divergent intellectual currents in contemporary Russian sociology.

Yadov's path toward sociology began at the School of Philosophy, Leningrad State University, where he enrolled in the undergraduate program a few years after World War II. As a student Yadov was active in the Young Communist League, reaching a leadership position in the organization. He joined the CPSU in his second year of studies and appeared to be on his way to a promising career, possibly within the party hierarchy, when his advancement abruptly halted after he was charged with concealing his father's membership in an anti-party bloc (Yadov 2005). Purged from the Communist Party and the university, Yadov took up an apprentice job at an industrial plant. He resumed his education and restored his party membership after Stalin' death. Already as an undergraduate Yadov grew disillusioned with philosophical abstractions and turned his attention toward more empirical subjects, eventually drifting toward social sciences and writing a dissertation on the interfaces between ideology and politics.

In 1960 Yadov was appointed head of the Sociological Laboratory at the Leningrad State University where he lead a major study published under the title *Man and His Work* (Yadov, Zdravomyslov and Rozhin 1967) that explored Soviet workers' attitudes toward their work. This publication, which subtly undercut the Marxist prediction about the diminishing alienation in a nationalized economy, established his reputation at home and abroad as one of the country's leading sociologists. Around this time Yadov moved to the Academy of Sciences Institute of Concrete Social Research where he assumed directorship of its Leningrad branch, remaining in this position until the Institute merged with several other research divisions into a new organization reporting to the local party authorities. In the late Soviet era Yadov came under attack for his lack of ideological vigilance, lost control over his research division, and had to step down from his position as president of the Leningrad Sociological Association. It was not until perestroika that his contribution to the discipline was recognized once again. With Gorbachev's reforms gathering speed, Yadov was appointed director of the Institute of Sociology and elected president of the Soviet Sociological Association.

Looking back at his career, Yadov is quick to acknowledge his communist past. "At the time, I was a veritable shock trooper and happily accepted the invitation to join the party. [When] our Leader and Teacher died, I sincerely wept on that occasion" (Yadov 2005). When the tide turned and sociologists felt free to speak their mind, Yadov did not rush to disown his old views or hide his early political sympathies: "I definitely was a Marxist and in no way feel embarrassed about it today. I write a lot about the polyparadigmatic character of contemporary sociology in which Marx occupies a prominent place alongside Weber. Marx is a great thinker. His works are discussed in all Western sociology textbooks. Just his notion of alienated labor (proletariat) rivals the Weberian concept of social action" (Yadov 2005). Today, Yadov defends the view that sociology thrives in an environment conducive to political and theoretical diversity. He sees sociology as engaged in civil society and committed to social justice. While physicists tracking planets do not cause stellar objects to change their trajectories, sociological research inevitably impacts social objects under observation insofar as this research addresses social problems and informs policy. Sociologists ought to be mindful of this impact and consciously "try to alter the movement of social planets" (Yadov 2005). Yadov's commitment to the national cause is of a piece with his policy preferences: "If Russia is to find its rightful place in the world community while remaining itself, it must take into account its cultural tradition and derive a proper lesson from the seventy years of Soviet rule. We have no viable ideological alternative besides building a just society. Fighting the corruption, empowering the independent judiciary, establishing fair progressive taxes, and much more—that is what our people demand" (Yadov 2005).

Gennady Osipov's professional career began at the Moscow Institute of International Relations. After graduating in 1952, he enrolled in the Russian Academy of Sciences Institute of Philosophy where he wrote a dissertation on the problems of labor, science, and technology. In 1960 he was appointed head of a sociology division at the institute, the first of its kind in Moscow, as well as president of the Soviet Sociological Association, a position he held for the next twelve years. Osipov's presentation accentuating the role of sociology as a research tool in the party's hands paved the way to the creation of the Institute of Concrete Social Research, with Osipov designated as a deputy director in the newly founded organization. When sociology fell on hard times, Osipov was pushed aside by Mikhail Rutkevich, the new Institute director hired to reinstall the Marxist orthodoxy, but retained his job at the Institute, weathering the ideological storm without much damage to his scholarly or political credentials. With Gorbachev's call to glasnost, Osipov cast himself as a champion of perestroika, trumpeting the role sociology is destined to play in democratic reforms. In time, he secured a coveted position as a full member of the Russian Academy of Sciences and received an appointment as head of Institute of Social and Political Studies.

Osipov's achievements as a scholar do not match his organizational talents. The published corpus he accumulated during the Soviet era is vast, but much of it is filled with impersonal verbiage replete with statements whose obsequiousness exceeded the demands of the time. There may be a simple explanation for the dubious quality of the man's scholarship: many publications bearing Osipov's signature are believed to be ghost written.[4] When recently asked what he thought about scholars appropriating other people's works, Osipov replied: "My attitude toward that is strictly negative. If you appropriate someone else's work, that means you have no opinion of your own, you have no place in science" (Demina 2007). This stance is consistent with the Professional Code of Russian sociologists: "Plagiarism and appropriation in any form or shape of ideas that belong to other people are unacceptable and incompatible with the professional code of sociologists" (Professionalnyi kodeks 1988: 95). But then Osipov never tried to explain why, after *Sociology Today* was translated into Russian, Robert Merton's introduction to this milestone volume had mysteriously vanished and in its place appeared Osipov's foreword containing several pages taken from Merton's original text.

The strategy Osipov uses to reconcile his Soviet past with his perestroika persona differs from Yadov's. As soon as it became clear that Gorbachev's reforms were for real and that it was safe to speak about reform, Osipov began to lambast the "partocratic leaders of the past" and inveigh against "the betrayal of national interests by Communist Party" (Osipov 2005). He unearthed a telling quote from Lenin about the "arrogant party functionary who is ready at a moment's notice to write a 'thesis', formulate a 'slogan', or advance some abstract proposition," after which he boldly denounced "the army of sycophants who used their power to scorn dissidents for the views they themselves expounded when it was safe to do so" (Osipov 1987: 16). Apparently, he did not mean this as self-criticism. Offering a revisionist account of his Soviet past, Osipov pictured himself as a person who had always harbored contempt for the partocracy, suffered grievously for his unorthodox views, and finally unveiled his true self after perestroika. On March 26, 2008, at the meeting celebrating the fiftieth anniversary of the Soviet Sociological Association, Osipov gave the keynote address in which he traced critical junctures in the evolution of sociology in Russia, with two events in particular singled out as harbingers of the downturn in Soviet sociology: "the Levada affair" and "the Osipov affair." In this account Osipov likens himself to the legendary sociologist Yuri Levada who was forced out of the Institute of Sociology and the discipline during the ideological purges.[5]

Gennady Osipov's commitment to democratic reform did not survive perestroika. When Gorbachev' successor Boris Yeltsin lost public support and the opposition began to pose a real threat to his administration, Osipov reinvented himself once again, this time as a patriotic sociologist inspired by the nationalist agenda. Now he rails against "the warped spirituality and egoistic individualism of the West," extols "Russia's cultural uniqueness" (Osipov 2004), demands to reinstate the tsarist formula "Orthodoxy, autocracy, and the folk spirit" (1997), and spearheads a successful campaign to induct Metropolitan Kirill, head of the Russian Orthodox Church, into the Russian Academy of Social and Humanitarian Sciences (2002).

Several things stand out in these two divergent scholarly trajectories. While both sociologists stress the continuity between their old and new selves, endorse activist social science, and look for ways to aid the nation in distress, they follow different strategies of owning up to their communist past. Yadov acknowledges his old beliefs while straining to infuse Marxism with democratic values and insuring the discipline's theoretical diversity and organizational pluralism. Osipov obscures his credentials as a stalwart communist, exaggerates his exploits as an opponent of the communist regime, and glosses over his perennial willingness to align himself with the latest power swing in a bid to advance his career. Yadov aligns himself with the likes of Zaslavskaya, Shubkin, Levada, Kon— scholars whose scientific credentials are recognized at home and abroad and whose commitment to democratic ideals is beyond reproach. Osipov throws his lot with Dobrenkov, Zhukov, Glaziev and their ideological kin who often hail from Communist party affiliated institutions and whose xenophobic proclivities make it unlikely that they would be willing to settle for peaceful coexistence with their opponents. Each camp builds its program around divergent theoretical and political commitments.

Yadov and his colleagues reject the thesis advanced by patriotically minded theoretical monists according to which paradigm pluralism spells out subjectivism. The polyparadigmatic approach acknowledges local cultures without glossing over the transformation they continuously undergo. "If the world itself is constantly changing, why should sociological theory that aspires to explain the world stay the same?" asks Yadov. "Russian sociology needs no 'nationally-specific' social theory. ... If you wonder who needs today national Russian sociology, the answer is obvious—the ideologists of Russian exclusivity" (Yadov

2003; 2007). Seen from this vantage point, Russia's future is supposed to be shaped by the forces of "globalization, internet networking, the emergence of the worldwide information space, cooperation with the NATO alliance, integration into the world economy, and so on" (Yadov 2003). Policy recommendations advanced by Zasvlavskaya, Yadov, Levada and other liberal sociologists favored the radical democratization in politics, privatization of state controlled monopolies, and state protection for cultural diversity.

Gennady Osipov and his colleagues espouse a different agenda that weds methodological monism to the notion of national exclusivity and favors preserving the dominant role of the state in the political, economic, and cultural spheres. Starting with the proposition that "scientific ideas gestate in the depth of history and culture, reflect the tradition and the mentality, as well as the economic, social, and political foundations of a given state and people" (Osipov 2003a), nationalists push this thesis to an extreme, calling for a Russian social science that rejects the values of universalism. The nationalist theories and policy suggestions are grounded in the vision of Russia as a country whose cultural heritage precludes the alliance with its democratic neighbors: "The thesis about the integration of Russia into the Western civilization, which nowadays undergoes a systemic crisis, is not only historically spurious but also practically pernicious, for it destroys the singularity of Russian culture, tradition, and customs" (Osipov 2004). In the area of policy, nationalists want to reconsider the results of the privatization campaign, reintroduce the top-heavy management style, and purge civic society of the NGOs receiving foreign funding. The most pressing task confronting patriotic sociologists is to consolidate the nation around core Russian values and centralize control over sociological institutions in the country.

Institutional Resources of Liberal and Nationalist Sociologists

While the issues in the present debate about national sociology and policy engagement have an important theoretical dimension, they are hardly academic. As the participants in the ongoing debate vie for institutional resources, they draw the Russian political establishment into the debate and invite the nonacademic authorities to assume the role of an arbiter in scholarly disputes. We should note that Russian sociology today is home to diverse theoretical and methodological currents irreducible to the nationalist-liberal split (Gudkov 2006, 2009; Osipov 1997; Radaev 2009; Ryvkina 1997). However, the theoretical and organizational diversity of post-Soviet social sciences is endangered by the sociologists touting their patriotic credentials and seeking to enlist the state in settling professional disputes.

One influential sociology center that emerged in the post-Soviet era is the Institute of Sociology (IS), a research and graduate studies division within the Russian Academy of Sciences. Aligned with IS is the Russian Society of Sociologists, the successor of the Soviet Sociological Association, which serves as a national umbrella organization for regional sociological societies in the country. Initially appointed by the government, Vladimir Yadov was subsequently confirmed as IS director by a secret ballot of fellow sociologists. At Yadov's initiative, the Institute of Sociology established an open project policy allowing institute members to submit theoretical and policy-oriented proposals and compete for leadership positions, as well as seek funding through international organizations. On the issue of theoretical pluralism, the IS staff adopted Yadov's stance that acknowledged the legitimacy of articulating general sociological theory but disavowed the nationalist quest for a Russian paradigm in sociology. "Should Russia produce its own macrotheorist of note, the way we produce a recognized world champion in sports—all the better. That would be a truly national achievement. But if all we do is put on a pedestal yet another inventor of our unique (Russian) theory that is ignored by anyone but 'local' admirers, this will not be a contribution to sociology as much as to ideology" (Yadov 2007).

In the mid-90s Yadov was succeeded in his directorship by Leokadyia Drobizheva, who kept Yadov's policies and priorities in place. This situation changed after Vladimir Putin took over as Russia's president in 2000 and the new political currents began to sweep through the academia which made it harder for Russian scholars to communicate with their Western counterparts, seek foreign funding, and set up a research agenda. In 2005 the presidium of Russian Academy of Science appointed as IS director Mikhail Gorshkov. This was a leader with a different professional trajectory, whose resume included a stint as deputy director of the Institute of Marxism-Leninism and the top level position at the CPSU Central Committee department of science and education. Academic life at the Institute of Sociology did not undergo immediate change, but beginning in 2006, the new leadership began to align itself with the initiatives championed by Gennady Osipov and nationalist sociologists who moved to set up a rival national association for Russian sociologists.

A stronghold of nationalist sociology in today's Russia is the Institute of Socio-Political Studies (Russian acronym—ISPI). Gennady Osipov, ISPI director, traces his institution's program to the Gorbachev era when "the two distinct concepts of perestroika and Russian reform had been formulated," one articulated by Zaslavskaya, Yadov, and their ideological kin, the other by Osipov and his colleagues.[6] Nationalist sociologists billed their policy recommendations as focused on the "wellbeing of a real human being" in contrast to the policy agenda of the perestroika intellectuals who advocate "the forced destruction [of the old order] detrimental to society, the state, and its citizens" (Osipov 2006). "We believe that the population decline, growth of prostitution, drug abuse, homicide, and suicide are objective consequences of [liberal] reform" (Osipov 2002). Gorbachev's and Yeltsin's liberal policies had left millions of Russian citizens stranded amidst economic and political disarray, the nationalist platform asserts, and to the extent that Zaslvaskaya, Yadov and their colleagues endorsed those policies, they bear responsibilities for the outcome.

A milestone in the ISPI's history was a gathering convened in 2007 under the heading "On the Methods of Solving the 'Russian Question.'" The meeting produced a programmatic document detailing an alternative agenda for post-Soviet sociology. Those who signed on this program endorsed a rationale for a patriotic sociology aligned with the government policies (Dobrenkov 2007; Osipov 2006; Osipov and Kuznetsov 2005; Zhukov 2002). As a step toward the consolidation of patriotic sociologists, Osipov and Dobrenkov called for a "national congress of sociologists of Russia" (Dobrenkov 2007). Preparations for this meeting were shrouded in secrecy, liberal scholars were kept out, and preparatory work was coordinated with the federal agency overseeing educational institutions in the country. The congress of patriotic sociologists was convened on June 27, 2007, with an invitation-only audience comprised by sociologists close to the ISPI. The congress set up a new national organization—the Union of Sociologists of Russia (the Russian acronym—SSR), passed the organization's bylaws (Ustav 2007), and elected V. Zhukov and M. Gorshkov (present director of the Institute of Sociology) as, respectively, SSR president and vice-president.

Addressing the congress delegates, Vasily Zhukov (2007), rector of the Russian State Social University, criticized his liberal colleagues for uncritical acceptance of Western ideas, while Gennady Osipov advocated the "incorporation of Russian sociology into the system of state governance" (Demina 2007). According to Zhukov, "Russian sociology has reached a point when (1) the need for consolidation of the sociological community is fully understood, and (2) when the conditions for such consolidation are in place. The Union of Sociologists of Russia aims to unite all those who respect the history of sociology in our country, who critically appropriate its heritage, and who are ready to assume the responsibility for sociological knowledge and bear themselves with dignity as professional and moral human beings" (Zhukov 2007). The nation's top legislative and government officials hailed the creation of the new professional organization. Chairman of the Federal Council endorsed the SSR agenda, as did the deputy chair of the State Duma, all representing the ruling party "United Russia" (Demina 2007).

Several momentous events followed the establishment of the SSR. In 2007, the private St. Petersburg European University noted for its strong social science program and partial funding received from the West was closed on charges of "poor fire preparedness." In the same year a group of student activists was expelled from the Moscow State University after they protested the low quality of sociological education and the growing presence of ultranationalist and religious ideas in the School of Sociology curriculum. In the summer of 2008, five senior sociologists were laid off at the St. Petersburg-based Sociological Institute, Russian Academy of Sciences; the official reason—"a planned culling of scientific cadres." Those dismissed were sociologists with liberal credentials whose illustrious research and publication records were far superior to those who passed the review with flying colors (Alekseev 2008).[7]

These developments dovetail with the program championed by nationalist sociologists (Den Zakrytykh Dverei 2008; Otchisleny iz MGU 2008), the program that goads SSR activists to move from debates to actions in centralizing education in the country and nationalizing sociological curriculum. According to the SSR platform, time has come to drop "passive resistance [and heed] President Putin's demand spelled out in his letter to the Federal Parliament [where he called] to go on the offensive and expose the mendacious, anti-humanist and Russophobic slogans and programs" (Osipov 2007; Demina 2007). To realize its potential, the national sociology movement must utilize "all the state resources fit to advance the strategic task of moving Russia ahead according to its national interests and the traditions of its people" (Osipov 2006).

The patriotic sociology agenda got a boost after V. Dobrenkov was appointed to lead the ministerial council charged with the responsibility of selecting sociology department chairs in the Russian Federation, which gave him and his allies an opportunity to reinforce "the vertical of power" (Putin) in the nation's academic institutions. Among the top priorities of the newly established sociological association was the fight against paradigm pluralism and nonindigenous sociological theories, including those inspired by pragmatism.

Liberalism, Patriotism, and Resistance to Pragmatism

Pragmatism and its derivatives are among the most popular terms of abuse in the culture wars sweeping through Russia these days. Put into the Russian internet search engine expressions like "cynical pragmatism," "crass pragmatism," "cold pragmatism," and you will get hundreds of hits conveying an abiding contempt for everything that reeks of pragmatism in contemporary Russia. This aversion to things pragmatic is evident not only on the political right. Soviet-style communists who cast themselves as the left-wing opponents of the present political regime also show a distaste for pragmatism. Even liberals are not immune to this sentiment.

"The foundations of humanism are eroded in today's world," asserts Beliaev (2006), "in fashion these days are conformism, pragmatism, hedonism, and a complete lack of principles." "No national ideas, naked pragmatism," agrees Kolesnikov (2008). "Pragmatism is a rejection of conscience and morality" (Veller 2008). "Pragmatism is the ideology of scoundrels. 'Pragmatism' is a creed of burgers, arrogant and self-satisfied. A burger-pragmatist is a conduit of evil" (Vetrochet, 2004). "Where naked pragmatism and utilitarianism reign, the soul expires, and what is the Russian folk without a soul? Without its soul, the Russian people could not have survived under the harsh historical conditions, nor would they be able to create the treasures that have enriched the world culture" (Saveliev, 2003).

More often than not, the term "pragmatism" appears in these philippics in its non-technical sense as an all-purpose label disparaging apolitical, uncultured, money-driven, overly competitive attitudes widespread in post-Soviet Russia. It would be a mistake to assign the term's popularity as a negative reference frame to this idiosyncratic usage. Pragmatism is well known in Russian intellectual circles for its broader political and philosophical connotations, and the opposition to it closely mirrors the anti-pragmatist animus in twentieth-century European discourse. The term assumes an expressly political meaning among nationalist writers who equate pragmatism with pluralism—political, theoretical, and especially moral, in which case it signifies the utter "lack of scruples" (Osipov 1997). To grasp the ideological burden and sociological significance that the term carries in Russia's nationalistic academic circles we must turn again to Aleksandr Malinkin, the theoretician of patriotic sociology and champion of theoretical monism in social science (Malinkin 1999, 2005, 2006).

As many in Russia's nationalist circles these days, Malinkin takes his cue from I. A. Il'in, an early twentieth-century Russian philosopher who linked the nation's genius to its ethnic roots.[8] Coupled with Il'in's hyper-nationalist sentiment is the concept of "ressentiment" that Russian nationalists borrowed from Nietzsche and Max Scheler. What attracts Malinkin to Scheler (whom he used to denounce in his Soviet-era writings) is the concept of ressentiment with its jaundiced view of humanism as "a universal movement whose love for humanity masks not the *craving for positive values but a protestant sentiment, a negative impulse*—that is, hatred, envy, vengefulness, and so on—directed against the dominant minority that harbors positive values" (Malinkin 1999). In that reckoning, pragmatism is an expression of ressentiment, its commitment to liberal values and theoretical pluralism to be taken as a symptom of the soul that has lost its cultural moorings. "Behind liberalism as an ideological movement and an empty humanistic creed stands philosophical pragmatism [and] polyparadigmatism" (Malinkin 2005). The spirit of pragmatism and the invidious stirrings of ressentiment, the author claims, have polluted the cosmopolitan intelligentsia in post-Soviet Russia: "In the early 1990s, the majority of academic sociologists adopted a shortsighted, ethically warped stance. Their pragmatism is designed to curry favor with economic and political elites, to secure generous grants from the foreign donors.... The first casualty of this pragmatist indifference turns out to be truth. Philosophical pragmatism begets extreme subjectivism, relativism, and eclecticism" (Malinkin 2005).

The animosity toward pragmatism widespread in today's Russia is by no means unique to this country. It has a direct counterpart in the West, notably in the works of Max Scheler (1926), who was among the first to advance the thesis that pragmatism exemplifies positivism and the democratic spirit inimical to European culture. Scheler's writings inspired a generation of critics on the left and the right who defined themselves in opposition to American positivism and liberal leanings. An admirer of Scheler, Martin Heidegger (1977: 231, 200) built on his ideas, condemning "humanism" and "the blindness and arbitrariness of what is ... known under the heading of 'pragmatism.'" What Heidegger's nationalistic anti-humanism meant pragmatically became evident after the Nazis swept into power. Heidegger embraced fascism with a vengeance. Grounding his commitment in nativist rhetoric, he celebrated "the forces that are rooted in the soil and blood of a Volk," "the honor and the destiny of the nation," "our will to national self-responsibility," "the new German reality embodied in the National Socialist State" (Heidegger, 1991: 31, 33, 38, 48). "The Führer alone is the present and future German reality and its law," Heidegger declaimed, while he denounced the "much-praised academic freedom [which] is being banished from the German university; for this freedom was false, because it was only negative" (Heidegger, 1991: 47, 34). Under the spell of ultranationalism, Heidegger took to writing secret letters to Nazi authorities denouncing his colleagues from "that liberal-democratic circle of intellectuals around Max Weber ... closely tied to the Jew Frankel" (Heidegger, quoted in Safranski, 1998: 273).

The prejudice toward pragmatism and liberalism was every bit as strong among Left-wing intellectuals, notably those associated with the Frankfurt School. Horkheimer slammed pragmatism as "the abasement of reason," a philosophy which advocates the "reduction of reason to a mere instrument" and serves as a "counterpart of modern industrialism, for which the factory is the prototype of human existence, and which models all branches of culture after production on the conveyor belt, or after the rationalized front office" (Horkheimer, 1947: 45-54). The disillusionment with democratic liberalism led Marxism-inspired intellectuals to look for a conceptual link between repression and liberal rationalism. Indeed, "we can say that liberalism 'produces' the total authoritarian state out of itself, as its own consummation at a more advanced stage of development," asserted Marcuse (1968: 19). "The pattern of all administration and 'personnel policy,'" according to Adorno (1978: 131), "tends of its own accord ... towards Fascism." Left to its own devices," Horkheimer (1978: 219) contended, "democracy leads to its opposite — tyranny."

It took a new generation of European scholars like Apel (1981) and Habermas (1985, 1987) to shatter the old preconceptions about pragmatist philosophy and embrace its commitment to liberal values as an antidote to the authoritarian tradition of European social thought. Jürgen Habermas played a critical role in this transformation. With force and eloquence he argued that "the old Frankfurt School never took bourgeois democracy very seriously," that it "is only in Western nations that the precarious and continually threatened achievements of bourgeois emancipation and the worker's movement are guaranteed to any extent worth mentioning.... And we know just how important bourgeois freedoms are. For when things go wrong it is those on the Left who become the first victims.... I have for a long time identified myself with that radical democratic mentality which is present in the best American traditions and articulated in American pragmatism" (Habermas, 1986: 98, 42; 1985: 198; see also Shalin 1991).

While pragmatist ideas are feeding important currents in European social thought, most notably Habermas's theory of communicative action (Bernstein 1991; Joas 1993; Halton 1986; Shalin 1992), they are still largely misunderstood in Russia where intellectuals appear to be well behind the curve in their animosity toward pragmatism. This prejudice exposes Russian intellectuals to the dangers that befell the European nationalists and illiberal thinkers who failed to harness the pragmatist spirit of experimentation. Patriotic discourse that found a niche in Russian sociology is replete with statements of principle and declarations of good faith whose ominous implications invite pragmatist scrutiny. What Malinkin, Osipov, and like-minded scholars fail to appreciate is that pragmatism is first and foremost a method of establishing what and how we mean. Charles Peirce, the founder of pragmatism, looked for ways to make our ideas clear by aligning abstractions with the earthy particulars for which they stand, methodically linking conceptual entities to social actions that nudge them into being. The pragmatist agenda calls for identifying the somatic, affective, and behavioral indicators that signal the concept's meaningful occurrence (Peirce 1991; Joas 1993; Shalin 2007).

Take Joseph Stalin's constitution, for instance. On paper it promised Soviet citizens many of the rights found in the United States constitution—freedom of speech and conscience, the right to assemble and form parties, the inviolability of private homes. Yet just as this document pledged basic liberties to Russian citizens, the Soviet Union had plunged into a terror campaign of 1937 that claimed over a million lives and that belied the communists' political declarations. Or consider the current appeals to Russian values and patriotism flooding the Russian intellectual circuits. Nationalists lament "the deficit of nationally-minded intelligentsia in Russia" (Malinkin 2006: 120) but remain exceedingly vague on who merits the label "patriotic." Bring Peirce's maxim to bear on the issue, and you will discover that patriotism may refer to what Samuel Johnson called "the last refuge of a scoundrel" just as it can signify the last stance of a dissident. Patriotic sentiments goad skinheads to attack foreigners and move citizens to shield a neighbor from a pogrom. Patriotism compels a soldier to sacrifice himself on a battlefield and furnishes an excuse to a Soviet general ordering his soldiers to clear a minefield with their bodies. We cannot be sure which patriotism is in play until we examine the pesky particulars hiding behind the lofty universals.

The nationalists' take on pragmatist sociology reveals an ominous, growing influence of Russian Orthodox Church on scholarly debate. An example is a recently published monograph on George Herbert Mead where the author takes this notable pragmatist to task for his failure to reconcile his scientific evolutionism with Christian creationism (Kravchenko 2006; a review of this book can be found in Shalin 2008). The nationalist attack on pragmatism and sociology it inspired exposes the nationalist critics as ill-informed. "[T]he tainted Thomas theorem paraphrases the ancient motto according to which 'things are just as they seem to you'. It serves to justify pragmatically the idea that social reality is infinitely malleable and constructed," writes Malinkin (2006: 118) about the Chicago school of sociology built on pragmatist principles. Contrary to this claim, pragmatist philosophers and sociologists do not equate social reality with subjective whim. What they say is that reality is objective and meaningful insofar as it becomes an object of collective activity steeped in time-bound semiotic frames, that convictions we act upon and bring to bear on reality may come true as self-fulfilling prophesies—particularly when competing beliefs are ignored or suppressed. Nor are nationalists credible when, with the help of context-severed quotes from Sorokin, they extol "the Russian national *ethics* and communicative culture marked by kind-heartedness, longing for justice, catholicism, nonutilitarianism, hard work, and hospitality" (Malinkin 1999). Do they really mean to say that Russian culture is immune to sloth, cruelty, and corruption? By the same token, when nationalists slam "universal values" and "the historically obsolete idea that by nature humans are equal," they overlook that the sacredness of human life is very much a universal value.

Pragmatist inquiry also reveal the shortsightedness of liberal and left-leaning Russian reformers who juxtapose pragmatic considerations to the principled and moral stance. Andrey Sakharov believed that "pragmatic criteria are often useless, what is left are moral criteria (Sakharov, quoted in Alekseev 2005:79). Rosalina Ryvkina decries "pragmatism and indifferentism of the masses" in today's Russia (Ryvkina 2006). This gloomy picture ignores hopeful signs in post-Soviet society—a willingness to start a private enterprise, to join forces in a voluntary association, to respect privacy and tolerate odd tastes. Liberals need to be careful when they join the nationalist chorus that equates pragmatism with "the utter lack of principles" (Bukovsky 2006), for such sweeping condemnation slant historical pragmatism and effectively forestall the judicious examination of the national agenda and viable policy alternatives.[9] The problem for pragmatists is not the lack of principles but their abundance. Competing rationales vie for our attention, with the values we espouse often working at cross purpose, necessitating a compromise. Push liberal economic agenda too far, and you will end up with inequality; press too hard for equality, and you will undermine individual freedom. Hence, the pragmatist willingness to triangulate and look for middle ground.

Swearing by principles means little unless we are willing to track policy outcomes, to juxtapose discursive-symbolic, somatic-affective, and behavioral-performative signs which clue us onto the practical significance of our cherished precepts and pet projects. The penchant for disembodied abstractions has deep roots in European culture, and so is the ethic of ultimate ends that goes with it (Etkind, 1996; Kon 1996; Paramonov 1996; Shalin 2004b; Weber 1946). Such tendencies need to be countered by the ethics of responsibility—the ethics of means — whose pragmatic spirit makes room for patriotism and advocacy without pandering to xenophobia and encouraging theoretical hegemony.

Advocacy and National Sociologies in Comparative Perspective

Any attempt to analogize the situation in Russian and American sociology is bound to mislead unless we understand crucial differences in the political, cultural, and organizational contexts underlying the disciplinary developments in both nations. Once these historical differences are taken into account, however, we can examine with profit how the issues of advocacy, nationalism, and theoretical pluralism have played out in each country. Such an examination seems all the more appropriate that American sociologists have taken keen interests in the work of their Marxist colleagues. The plight of Russian sociology has figured prominently in the American debate about advocacy and national sociologies.

From the start, sociologists billed their discipline as a guide to reform and appealed to practice as the touchstone for their conclusions. August Comte, Karl Marx, Max Weber, Emile Durkheim, George Herbert Mead — sociologically minded thinkers confronted head-on the forces of modernity whose unanticipated consequences they sought to theorize, to expose, and to tame. Activist internationalism did not efface the local traditions from which the discipline of sociology sprang in a particular country, but nationalism remained muted in early sociological thought, subordinated, as it were, to a search for scientific solutions to the problems confronting industrial civilization (Freund 1978; Martindale 1981; Zeitlin 1981; Albrow and King 1990; Ritzer 2000). It was only after sociology firmly established itself as an academic discipline that its practitioners felt comfortable to claim ideological autonomy. The mantra of "value neutrality" came into vogue as practitioners focused on sociology as an academic field of study with a strong scientific agenda. About the same time sociologists began to clamor for a general sociological theory.

This transition did not dampen sociologists' commitment to applied research. Policy-oriented studies retained a strong scholarly agenda, while their critical dimension remained muted, as we can gather from William Ogburn's *Recent Social Trends in the United States* and Samuel Stouffer's *American Soldiers*. The emphasis on academism and ideological autonomy carried into the post-world war period, but sometime in the late-1950s a younger generation of American scholars rebelled against "the liberal conservatism of the earlier postwar sociology" (Burawoy 2005: 262). C. Wright Mills (1959), Irving Louis Horowitz (1964), and Alvin Gouldner (1973) were among the prominent sociologists who criticized the discipline's status quo bias and pushed for alternative programs variously identified as "radical sociology," "new sociology," and "reflexive sociology." The issues of professionalism and social criticism moved to the center stage of sociological debate in the 1960s. The shift toward reflexive social thought coincided with the rise of Soviet sociology whose plight attracted much attention in the West.

Alvin Gouldner was among the American sociologists who took a keen interest in the institutionalization of sociology in the Soviet Union and used it to clarify the national agenda for American sociology. He was particularly intrigued by the split within academic Soviet sociology between those who cast their discipline "as a technological aid in administration and management, and those, on the other hand, for whom Academic Sociology is rooted in their own liberal impulses and who want to see it developed because they believe it will contribute to a more humanistic culture." Gouldner went on to acknowledge that "[t]his is a tension by no means peculiar to Academic Sociology in the Soviet Union, for it is found throughout Europe, East and West, and in the United States as well" (Gouldner 1970: 474).

Irving Louis Horowitz was also struck by the parallels between the Soviet Union and United States. "When Khrushchev speaks of Soviet scientific achievements, it grates; it offends the American scientific mind. Rightfully one does not connect nationalism with science. But in the name of 'American' sociology there are those who would perpetuate the same nationalistic myth" (Horowitz 1964: 35). American sociologists could be as unreflexive and subservient to the state as their Soviet counterparts, Horowitz pointed out, citing Project Camelot to make his case. According to Horowitz, "Sociology has an obligation, first and foremost, to reflect upon the problems dealt with at the level they occur, and to provide the information and the theory for solutions to human problems. Problems of capitalism and socialism, underdevelopment and overdevelopment, or anomie, alienation, and anxiety, have to be met head on" (Horowitz 1964: 21).

The tendency to link the Soviet and American establishments is also evident in C. Wright Mills. "In several basic trends and official actions, the United States and the Soviet Union are becoming increasingly alike," observed Mills ([1959] 1967: 227-228). "The classic conditions of democratic institutions do not flourish in the power structure of the United States and the Soviet Union." This position bore more than a fleeting resemblance to sentiments widespread among Frankfurt School intellectuals, with some of whom Mills had close personal relationships (Horowitz 1966: 23). The ambivalent attitude toward pragmatism adopted by Mills echoed the sentiment of European critical theorists (Mills, 1966).

Calls for critical reflection and warnings about the coming crisis in Western sociology evoked a mixed reaction among sociology professionals. The older generation of sociologists reminded the Young Turks that their critical agenda threatened to undermine the discipline's hard-won ideological autonomy. "The generation which obtained its Ph.D. in the 1960s consisted of young people for whom the problem of sociology versus ideology did not have the same crucial importance as for their predecessors," pointed out Joseph Ben-David. "Lacking the experience of liberation from ideology, they could find in sociology few past achievements or great intellectual opportunities to command their loyalty to, and the unshaken belief in, sociology of the latter. Therefore, questioning the very possibility of a scientific sociology, and considering the possibility that the demarcation line between sociology and ideology drawn in the 1950s may not have been final, does not have for them the same meaning of totalitarian threat as for the older generation" (Ben-David 1973, quoted in Merton 1975: 27). Robert Merton, who cites Ben-David approvingly, weighed in on the debate. He looked skeptically at his junior colleagues in whose stance he discerned the grand theoretical and political ambitions inconsistent with scientific modesty. In a 1961 article, Merton defended American sociology "[which is] periodically subjected to violent attacks from within, as in a formidable book by Sorokin, *Fads and Foibles in Modern Sociology*, and in the recent little book by C. Wright Mills [*Sociological Imagination*] which, without the same comprehensive and detailed citation of seeming cases in point, follows much the same line of arguments as those advanced by Sorokin" (Merton 1973: 55). Merton took issue with Gouldner's thesis about the crisis looming over sociology on the ground that "the chronic crisis of sociology, with its diversity, competition and clash of doctrine, seems preferable to the therapy sometimes proposed for handling the acute crisis, namely the prescription of a single theoretical perspective that promises to provide full and exclusive access to the sociological truth. ... [I]t is not so much the plurality of paradigms as the collective acceptance by practicing sociologists of a single paradigm proposed as a panacea that would constitute a deep crisis with ensuing stasis" (Merton 1975: 28). Characteristically, Merton drew different lessons from Soviet science whose excessive ideological involvement, he insisted, threatened the ethos of science with its "institutional imperatives [of] universalism, communism, disinterestedness, organized skepticism" (Merton 1973: 270).

Fast forward to the twenty-first century, and you will find the issues of advocacy, professionalism, and national sociologies at the heart of American sociology's agenda. Those favoring activist sociology argue nowadays that the discipline must renew its critical agenda, address the needs of diverse publics, and commit itself to a robust dialogue with scholars representing different national traditions (Barlow 2007; Burawoy 2005; Clawson 2007; Nichols 2007).

Whatever their ideological differences, we can be certain that sociologists in this country will reject the noxious strand of nationalism in Russian sociology, as they will the old Soviet mantra that the "Marxist-Leninist class analysis embodies the unity of partisanship and scholarship," that "[n]onpartisanship and neutrality in sociology is nothing but a myth, a thin veil disguising an allegiance to a particular class" (Osipov 1979: 137, 142). Wittingly or unwittingly, today's Russian ultra-patriots reproduce the infamous 1948 editorial that spurred the campaign against cosmopolitanism in Soviet Russia: "The notion that democracy and science are twins, that they share an origin, that science needs democracy as much as democracy needs science, that science cannot tolerate the dictate and hegemony of one paradigm, theory, or idea—all such views fall short upon closer examination" (Malinkin 2005: 115).

For all their differences, sociologists schooled in the democratic ethos are likely to agree with Merton (1973: 269) that "science is afforded opportunity for development in a democratic order which is integrated with the ethos of democracy." We can see that clearly in Burawoy's presidential address where he points out that public sociology is "the complement and not the negation of professional sociology," as well as in his observation that the renaissance of sociology in Russia is "intimately connected to the eruption of civil society," that "[u]nder the stalwart leadership of Tatyana Zaslavskaya, Perestroika brought sociologists out in force" (Burawoy 2005: 21, 5). The consensus among American observers breaks down, however, when it comes to the wisdom of assuming a definitive political posture and aligning the discipline with a particular national agenda. The plight of perestroika intellectuals gives ammunition to those weary of the hyperpolitical stance.

Looking back at the bond Russian scientists forged with the state and society during the perestroika era and the years that followed, we find outstanding examples of sociology in action and public intellectuals' activism. Neighborhood associations, voters' clubs, national forums, scholarly think tanks, government task forces—there was hardly a civic venue sociologists ignored, a public they did not try to connect with, a state-sponsored policy institution they would refuse to join. Some sociologists took executive positions in government (Egor Gaidar even served as acting prime minister in the Yeltsin administration). But when the perestroika movement began to falter, it generated a backlash which exacted a heavy price from the public intellectuals aligned with reform and, arguably, set back sociology as a profession.

Anatoly Chubais, a scholar enlisted to oversee the nation's privatization campaign, became public enemy number one for many Russians when the voucher privatization program he oversaw bogged down in excesses, disproportionately benefiting those in power and leaving millions with worthless certificates. Galina Starovoitova was murdered in 1998, her legislation proposing to limit the former party and KGB officials' access to politics being cited among possible reasons for her assassination. Nikolai Girenko was killed in 2004 after numerous death threats occasioned by his work as a monitor of skinhead activities. Igor Kon, who had his face smashed with a cake during a public lecture, had to keep a low profile because of the smear campaign against him orchestrated by the religious right. Perestroika intellectuals would be quick to point out that their policy agenda was not necessarily the culprit, that the half-hearted manner in which politicians implemented those policies was largely to blame for reform failures. The cause-effect chains are indeed hard to trace in the social world, but one conclusion we can draw from this case study is that committed scholarship can backfire. In a fledgling democracy, if not in its mature counterpart, politically active scholars face public hostility and their discipline may be set back when the policies it sponsors produce unintended consequences. Not surprisingly, sociologists in the Russian Federation are taking a second look at the proper way to mix advocacy and scholarship.

Already in the days of perestroika some questioned whether it was wise for a sociologist "to plunge headlong into politics" (Saganenko [1990] 2008: 15). Professing sociology is one thing, putting its prestige behind a policy is another, carrying out the reforms is something else altogether. According to Galina Saganenko, Vladimir Yadov's associate, "the sociology's function is not to engage in political games but to educate society, to spread the sociological way of thinking" (Saganenko [1990] 2008: 15). Yuri Levada moved in a similar direction, his experience as member of the presidential council playing a part in his growing skepticism about the scholars' involvement with politics. "The illusion of practical utility hovered over the early sociological formulations of A. Comte and other thinkers; later on the relationship between sociology and social practice was judged to be considerably more complex. The situation repeated itself when sociology reemerged in the 1960s and the efforts to legitimize the sociological science [in the USSR] were buttressed by the promise of 'scientific management of society'. No 'scientific management' turned out to be possible under the conditions of decaying socialism—nor did such claims fare any better in developed countries" (Levada 2000: 559). In his last interview, Yuri Levada, who died in 2006, took a cautious stance toward mixing scholarship and politics. "I want to distance myself" from immediate political pressures, he intimated; the role I choose is that of "an observer—a skeptic" (Levada 1995).

Even Tatyana Zaslavaskaya appears to be chastened by her experience with reform. In a recent public lecture she surprised her followers with this pronouncement:

> Why should social science furnish advice? A physicist finds out that a star situated some 321 light years away has a double, and this becomes a major scientific event. We [sociologists] are expected to say how to run the government. Yet we are scientists, and our task is to study the real world, reality as it is. ... If Putin invites me tomorrow and asks: 'Tatyana Ivanovna, what is to be done with Russia?' [I will answer]—'Vladimir Vladimirovich, you are in a better position to figure that out, you have all the information. (Zaslavskaya 2005)

For a veteran perestroika intellectual who provided academic fodder for perestroika, this is a startling statement that seems at odds with Yadov's counsel to his colleagues "to alter the movement of social planets."

The Pragmatist Ethos and Politically Engaged Scholarship

We should proceed with caution drawing parallels between the social sciences in a country lacking in the democratic tradition and activist sociology practiced in a nation with a robust civil society. Arthur Schlesinger and Henry Kissinger worked for the U.S. government, and their executive stints did not seem to compromise their standing as public intellectuals, nor did their performance in government cast a shadow on their scholarly fields. But what about Jay Bybee, a legal scholar who signed the Bush administration's infamous "torture memo"? It surely damaged his intellectual reputation and provoked a bitter debate among his colleagues.[10] For all its peculiarities, the case study under review raises the pertinent question of how far we should press advocacy in social science.

Alvin Gouldner had sound reasons to question value neutrality, but those sympathetic with his stance need to make sure there is always room for the honest difference of opinion about the right values and policy decisions. Irving Louis Horowitz saw worrisome signs of capitalism spinning out of control, yet one has to be cautious about those social scientists who pronounced it obsolete. When Michael Burawoy invites his colleagues to think nationally, we should inquire which hat social scientists put on while articulating a national agenda and telling fellow citizens what is to be done.

I would like to suggest that the pragmatist ethos offers a useful perspective on mixing advocacy and scholarship in social science.

As we can gather from Mills's Ph.D. thesis on American pragmatism, he had misgivings about this intellectual current. The problem with pragmatism, as Mills (1967) saw it, was that its proponents preferred to tinker with social ills in the spirit of social work where radical social change is called for. Mills tempered his criticism in the postscript to his thesis and subsequent writings. He had not come out swinging for pragmatism the way Habermas did, but he acknowledged pragmatism's critical, even radical, potential. "As method, pragmatism is overstuffed with imprecise social value; as a social-political orientation, it undoubtedly has a tendency toward opportunism. It is really *not* opportunist, because in the very statement of method there lies the assumption of the Jeffersonian social world. It is quite firmly anchored. But in lesser hands than Dewey's, many things may happen" (Mills [1952] 1967: 167; 1966: 464-467). What Mills came to realize was that pragmatism's radical stance lies in its experimentalist method rather than in its substantive creed, that it works best as self-correcting inquiry and ongoing social criticism. The fact that pragmatism positions itself as a methodology for exploration and experimentation does not mean that its proponents eschew values, shy away from taking a stance, or bow to the status quo. "In order to endure under present conditions," professed John Dewey (1946: 132), "liberalism must become radical in the sense that, instead of using social power to ameliorate the evil consequences of the existing system, it shall use social power to change the system." For all its critical sensibilities, pragmatism is leery of self-righteous intellectualism. No theoretical cogency or scientific demonstration can anoint a political platform or vouchsafe a policy alternative. We owe our values to our membership in civil society, and whenever we bring those values to bear, we should acknowledge their provenance, join issues with those inhabiting different value niches, track the consequences of our policy commitments, and keep aligning our policies with changing social practice. In this reckoning, we would be too hasty dumping value neutrality in a wholesale fashion. Value neutrality does not mean that knowledge is devoid of values—any statement of fact necessarily involves value judgment, according to Weber. When he called on scientists to assume a neutral stance, he simply cautioned them against positing a particular set of values or a political platform as scientifically grounded, for doing so confuses the role of scholar with that of citizen.

Pragmatists see in scholars and public intellectuals more than experts called upon to solve social problems. According to the pragmatist theory of social reform (Mead 1915: 35; Shalin 1988), "The university is not an office of experts to which the problems of the community are sent to be solved; it is a part of the community within which the community problems appear as its own." Scholars wrapping themselves in the mantle of professional expertise while advocating a policy invite public backlash. They can also make their voice less effective in policy debates. From the pragmatist vantage point, scholars venturing into the public arena are first and foremost citizens. Scientific findings they introduce into policy debate must inform the discussion but can hardly settle it. The fact that the meritocratic system in higher education favors applicants with ample social capital does not forestall the debate about the unanticipated consequences of affirmative action any more than the scientific data on when a fetus can survive outside the uterus resolves the issue of late-term abortion.

Pragmatists recognize that all knowledge has political implications, that "ideas are worthless except as they pass into actions which rearrange and reconstruct in some way, be it little or large, the world in which we live" (Dewey [1929] 1960: 138). At the same time, they are not inclined to exaggerate the extent to which social practice can furnish unambiguous feedback to professional sociologists. Grounding theory preferences in societal practice raises as many questions as deducing policy commitments from theoretical considerations. Given many intervening variables affecting the outcomes of a given policy, the implications of social practice for social theory will always be problematic. The solution to this conundrum is not to privilege scientific knowledge but leave public debate wide open to conflicting value perspectives—religious, cultural, political, scientific.

The pragmatist willingness, indeed eagerness, to work in local venues is admirable. Pragmatist intellectuals have always gravitated to a community-wide dialogue in an effort to promote "a more balanced, a more equal, even, and equitable system of human liberties" (Dewey, 1946: 113). As the progressive era experience showed, local initiatives and state level reforms often pave the way to national policy enactments. Getting the various publics involved is crucial for achieving lasting social change. "If only it becomes possible to focus public sentiment upon an issue in the delicate organism of the modern community, it is as effective as if the mandate came from legislative halls, and frequently more so" (Mead 1899: 368). Those who subscribe to the pragmatist ethos will know, however, that the effectiveness in public venues taxes our affective skills and emotional intelligence as much as our intellectual savvy. Injecting scientific data into public debate will get us only that far if we fail to communicate effectively, connect with the parties involved, and show that we can sign in the flesh what we profess in theory. The Obama administration's avowedly pragmatic approach has given us clear indication of how important the capacity for rhetorical articulation is to multiple values. Taking the value perspective of the other can guard us from the excesses of value partisanship and help us unite scholarship with advocacy in the pragmatist spirit of value tolerance (Shalin 1979; 1986).

Conclusion

This study has examined the tangled relationship between advocacy and scholarship in Russian sociology. It drew attention to the virulent brand of patriotic social science that threatens to reduce the discipline to the subservient role it played in the Soviet Union. The discussion aimed to show that the tension between political engagement and scientific autonomy is endemic to the sociological enterprise, that political advocacy and professional autonomy have equal claims on our allegiance, and that the pragmatist ethos may clue us to practical ways of integrating various dimensions of sociological enterprise—professional-academic, critical-reflexive, policy-centered, and publicly-responsive.

I want to close this inquiry with an appeal to my colleagues to pay attention to what is happening in Russian sociology. As the above discussion demonstrated, ultra-nationalists are on the ascent in this part of the world. So far, the authorities have allowed both rival sociological associations to function, but the current trends do not bode well for their peaceful coexistence. In 2008, the Russian government asserted its control over the Association of Russian Journalists by purging its independently-minded representatives and bringing to power a more pliant leadership. In 2009, the federal court in Moscow invalidated the election results in the Russian Cinema Workers' Union, sanctioning the new election that transferred power to the nationalist leaders supported by the Kremlin. Similar developments hobbled attempts to set up independent labor unions in the Russian Federation. It may be just a matter of time before the Russian government moves to curtail the work of the Russian Sociological Association and enshrines the patriotic Union of Russian Sociologists as the sole representative of professional sociologists in the country.

In early March of 2009, Dr. Igor Kon went to Berlin to testify before the European Parliament's Commission on Human Rights about the mounting attacks on gays and lesbians and the general deterioration of the human rights situation in Russia. Given the tragic death of his publicly engaged colleagues and the prior attacks on Kon, this was a daring act by a committed public intellectual. After his testimony, Kon returned to Moscow where he faced the displeasure of the authorities and the anger of numerous fringe groups which had sprung to life in recent years. Igor Kon could surely use a word of solidarity from his Western colleagues, and so would other embattled social scientists and public intellectuals in Russia who remain committed to liberalism, paradigm pluralism, and unfettered scientific inquiry.

Notes

1.   Some of the materials cited in this paper exist only in the electronic form, in which case the source is identified by the URL. Where both printed and digital versions are available but the article appears in a limited circulation outlet, the information about the print publication source is supplemented by the URL directing the reader to the electronic version of the source.

2. Liberal sociologists are by no mean ready to cede Sorokin's legacy to their nationalist colleagues. They are keenly aware of Sorokin's prodigious, contradictory output, seeking to appropriate what they find congenial in his writings. One indicator of the growing interest in and controversy over Sorokin's legacy is the interview with Robert Merton published in a Russian sociology journal where Merton remembers his mentor (Pokrovsky 1992). To best of my knowledge, this interview has not been published in English.

3. Besides documenting the history of Russian sociology, this open source, web-based project illuminates the narrative strategies that major Russian scholars have deployed to reconcile their communist selves with their post-Soviet incarnations (Doktorov 2007, 2007b; Doktorov and Kozlova 2007; Mazlyumyanova and Doktorov, 2007; Shalin 2006).

4. "In order to emerge as author of numerous books and articles, Osipov did not have to rely on the 'copy and paste' method which, according to expert analysis, V. Dobrenkov and A. Kravchenko used in their work. Rather, he preferred the 'power play'. Witnesses report that, during his tenure as a deputy director of IKSI, Osipov repeatedly leaned on doctoral students or even an experienced scholar with the order-request: 'Do you wish to defend your thesis? Write this for me. Do you want something else? Here is what you need to do for me'" (Demina 2007).

5. It is not just that Osipov occupied high positions in the Soviet academic hierarchy and used his party connections to promote his career. Yuri Levada was also an elected party official at the Institute of Concrete Social Research, but each man used his perch to achieve different ends. As Levada (1990) recalls in his Harvard interview, "I did not feel badly because I had occupied a party leadership position in those days, because this restrained people like Osipov and helped us do our work." When Levada came under attack in the early 1970s for ideological infractions, Gennady Osipov proposed that "Y. A. Levada ought to be relieved from his duties as the Institute party secretary and member of the politburo" (Batying 1999; Shalin 2008). In a book published a few years later, Osipov brought up Levada's writings to emphasize his disagreement with the disgraced colleague, even though Osipov knew that Levada was in no position to reply to his critics at the time (Osipov 1979: 176).

6. "The first approach stressed the need to destroy everything build under the Communist Party, risking to undermine the stability and social order.... The second concept stemmed from the premise that the most important indicator of reform was the real human being, that the reforms must take into account the human dimension and aid rather than devastate the individual, whose needs were the main reasons for reform. ... In line with these two concepts, the Scientific Council of the Institute of Sociology received and reviewed two programs of scholarly development, with V. Yadov and G. Osipov serving as heads of the rival scholarly collectives. Following the narrow group interests, the new—Yadov's—Scientific Council created the climate which rendered impossible the coexistence of two programs within the confines of one institute. The ensuing conflict [lead to] the creation of two academic sociological institutes, each one pursuing a different vision of Russian reality and different schools of sociology. ... Unfortunately, the assessments and constructive recommendations offered by [the Osipov group] were not taken seriously by the country's democratic leadership. Worse than that, scholars stressing the growing negative tendencies were dismissed as 'catastrophists'" (Osipov 2006).

7. After the public outcry, the St. Petersburg administration agreed to reopen the foreign-grant-funded European University that had been closed on account of its failure to meet the fire code, but its long-term prospects appear uncertain. Students expelled from the Moscow State University were not reinstalled. Some were admitted to other educational centers in the country, others are exploring the prospects for

continued education abroad. Scholars who lost their jobs at the Institute of Sociology appealed the decision, but with one exception, their appeal was denied.

8.   "A person who can create something that is beautiful in the eyes of *all the people* must first and foremost engross himself in the creative act of *his own* people. 'A world genius' is always and invariably a *national* genus. Efforts to create something 'great' out of internationalism and its effusions will produce either dubious, ephemeral 'celebrities' or planetary evildoers. True greatness is nativist. True genius is national" (Il'in 1990). We should note that this precept has a long pedigree, especially in German culture, which exerted a tangible influence on Russian intellectuals in the last two centuries (Shalin 1996).

9.   Sergei Averintsev (1996) offers an intriguing explanation for this cultural characteristic, tracing it to Platonism permeating Russian culture and the underestimation of the Aristotelian tradition (Averintsev 1996). "Peripatetic pragmatism" of Aristotle, as Averintsev (1973: 73) aptly calls it, shares several key characteristics with the modern pragmatist tradition, including the willingness to measure ideal forms with their mundane manifestations, to conduct an empirical inquiry, to make room for emotions in political discourse, to acknowledge unforeseen circumstances which may scuttle our best-laid plans (Shalin 2005).

10. Bybee still retains his tenure at the Boyd School of Law where he teaches a class once a year, but the heated debate his work on behalf of the U.S. government provoked among his colleagues at the University of Nevada shows that mixing scholarly expertise with state imperatives can be costly. (See Coolican 2009).

References

Adorno, T. [1951] 1978. *Prisms*. London: Neville Spearman.

Albrow M. and E. King, eds. 1990. *Globalization, Knowledge and Society*. London: Sage Publications.

Alekseev, A. 2008. Sobytiia v IS RAN v zerkale dokumentov i ekspertnykh suzhdenii, IBI, http: //www.unlv.edu/centers/cdclv/archives/Supplements/si_ran.html.

Alekseeev, A. 2005. *Dramaticheskaia sotsiologia i avtorefleksiia*. Tom 4. Sankt-Peterburg: Norma.

Apel, K-O. 1981. Charles S. Peirce, *From Pragmatism to Pragmaticism*. Amherst: University of Massachusetts Press.

Averintsev, S. 1996. "Khristianskii aristotelism kak vnutrenniaia forma zapadnoi traditsii i problema sovremennoi Rossii." Pp. 319-367 in *Ritorika I istoki evropeiskoi traditsii*. Moskva, http: //forum.hnet.ru/index.php?showtopic=68997.

Averintsev, S. 1973. *Plutarch and Ancient Biography*. Moscow: Nauka.

Barlow, A. (ed.), *Collaborations for Social Justice: Professionals, Publics, and Policy Change*. Rowan and Littlefield.

Batygin, G. Ed. 1999. Rossiiskaia sotsiologiia shestidesiqtykh godov v vospominaniiakh i dokumentakh. St. Petersburg: Russkii khristianskii gumanitarnyi institut, http: //www.unlv.edu/centers/cdclv/archives/articles/batygin_intro.html.

Batygin, G. 2000. "Nevidimaia granitsa: grantovaia podderzhka i rekonstruirovanie nauchnogo soobshchestva v Rossii (zametki eksperta)." *Naukovedenie*. No. 4, http: //www.book-ua.org/FILES/sociology/5_12_2007/soc143.htm.

Beliaev, E. and Butorin, P. 1982. "The Institutionalization of Soviet Sociology: Its Social and Political Context." *Social Forces* 61.

Beliaev S. 2006. "Natiurmort s kamnem." *Znamia*, No. 12, http: //magazines.russ. ru/znamia/2006/12/be11.html.

Ben-David, J. 1973. "The State of Sociological Theory and the Sociological Community." *Comparative Studies in Society and History* 15: 448-472.

Bernstein, R. 1991. *The New Constellation. The Ethical-Political Horizons of Modernity/Postmodernity.* Cambridge MA: The MIT Press.

Bukovsky, V. 2006. "Ikh mechta — imet million." Index, No. 23, http: //www.index. org.ru/journal/23/buk23.html.

Burawoy. M. 2005. 2004 American Sociological Association Presidential Address: For Public Sociology. *American Sociological Review* 70: 4-28.

Clawson D. et al. (eds.). 2007. *Public Sociology: Fifteen Eminent Sociologists Debate Politics and the Profession in the Twenty-First Century.* Berkeley: University of California Press.

Coolican, P. 2009. "The Definition of Torture." *Las Vegas Sun.* March 22, p. 8.

Demina, N. 2007. Sovetskii Sotsiologicheski Revansh, http: //www.polit.ru/analytics/2007/07/11/soc.html.

Den Zakrytykh Dverei. 2008. V Sankt-Peterburge prokhodiat dni zakrytykh dverei Evropeiskogo universiteta, http: //www.polit.ru/science/2008/03/04/closed_doors. popup.html.

Dewey, J.1960. *Quest for Certainty: A Study in the Relation of Knowledge and Action.* New York: Capricorn Books.

Dewey, J. 1946. *The Problems of Men.* New York: Philosophical Library.

Dobrenkov, V. 2007. "O putiakh resheniia 'russkogo voprosa'," http: //www.glazev. ru/nir/2277.

Doktorov, B. 2007. "Tezisy k Mexhdunarodnoi nauchno-prakticheskoi konferentsii "Gumanitarnye strategii rossiiskoi transfromatsii." Tiuimen, 26-27 October, 2007, http: //www.unlv.edu/centers/cdclv/archives/articles/doktorov_reform.html.

Doktorov, B. 2007b. "O prave na istoriiu i ob otvetstvennostgi pered istoriei," http: //www.unlv.edu/centers/cdclv/archives/articles/doktorov_rights.html.

Doktorov, B. and Mzlumyanova N. 2006. "O tom, chto est i chego net v opublikovannykh interviu," http: //www.unlv.edu/centers/cdclv/archives/Comments/Mazlumyanova-Doktorov.html.

Doktorov B. and Kozlova, L. 2007. Zakhochet li graf Caliostro posetit moikh geroev? Rassiuzhdeniia o tom, kak i dlia chego pishutsiq biografii," http: //www.unlv.edu/ centers/cdclv/archives/Comments/doktorov_kozlova.html.

Etkind, A. 1996. "Psychological Culture." Pp. 99-986 in Shalin, D. N. ed. *Russian Culture at the Crossroads: Paradoxes of Postcommunist Consciousness.* Edited by D. Shalin. Boulder, CO: Westview Press.

Filippov, A. 1997. "Poniatie teoretichskoj sotsiologii." *Sotsiologichskii Zhurnal* No. 1, http: //www.socjournal.ru/article/323.

Firsov, B. 2001. *Istoriia sovetskoi sotsiologii 1950-1980: Kurs lektsii.* St. Peterburg: Izdatelstvo Evropeiskogo Unviersiteta v S.-Petereburge.

Firsov, B. 2003. "Istoriia i sotsiologiia: steny i mosty." *Zhurnal sotisologii I sotsialnoi antropologii.* 3: 55-68, http: //www.ecsocman.edu.ru/images/pubs/2007/09/23/000 0312447/Firsov.pdf .

Freund, J. 1978. "German Sociology in the Time of Max Weber." Pp. 149-186 in T. Bottomore and R. Nisbet, eds. *A History of Sociological Analysis.* New York: Basic Books.

Gouldner, A. 1973. *The Coming Crisis of Western Sociology.* New York: Basic Books.

Greenfeld. L. 1988. "Soviet Sociology and the Sociology of the Soviet Union." *Annual Review of Sociology* 14: 99-123.

Golosenko, I. 1981. "Universalnoe i natsionalnoe v nemarksistskoi sotsiologii." *Sotiologicheksie issledovaniia* 4: 73-79.

Gudkov, L. 2006. O polozhenii sotsialnykh nauk v Rossii. *Novoie literaturnoe obozrenie.* No. 77, http: //magazines.russ.ru/nlo/2006/77/gu23.html.

Gudkov, L. 2009. "Nasha nyneshniaia sotsiologiia—eto kompiuter na telege," Interview with Lev Gudkov, Polit.ru, http: //www.polit.ru/analytics/2008/11/13/gudkov.html.

Habermas, J. [1981] 1984. *The Theory of Communicative Action. Volume I. Reason the Realization of Society.* Boston: Beacon Press.

Habermas, J. 1985. "Questions and Counter Questions." Pp. 192-216 in Richard J. Bernstein, editor, *Habermas and Modernity.* Cambridge, MA: The MIT Press.

Habermas, J. [1981] 1987. *The Theory of Communicative Action. Volume II. Life World and System: A Critique of Functionalist Reason.* Boston: Beacon Press.

Habermas, J. 1986. *Autonomy and Solidarity. Interviews.* Ed. by Peter Dews. Verso: The Imprint of New Left Books.

Halton, E. 1986. *Meaning and Modernity. Social Theory in the Pragmatic Attitude.* Chicago: The University of Chicago Press.

Heidegger, M. [1946-47] 1961. "Letter on Humanism," Pp. 190-242 in D. F. Krell, ed. *Martin Heidegger. Basic Writings.* New York: Harper & Row.

Heidegger, M. [1945] 1991. "Letter to the Rector of Freiburg University." Pp. 61-66 in Richard Wolin, ed., *The Heidegger Controversy. A Critical Reader.* New York: Columbia University Press.

Horkheimer, M. 1947. *Eclipse of Reason.* New York: Oxford University Press.

Horowitz, I. L. Ed. 1964. *The New Sociology: Essays in Social Science and Social Theory, in Honor of C. Wright Mills.* Oxford University Press.

Horowitz, I. L. 1966. "The Intellectual Genesis of C. Wright Mills." Pp. 11-31 in C. Wright Mills, *Sociology and Pragmatism. The Higher Learning in America.* New York: Oxford University Press.

Il'in, A. 1990. Osnovy Khristianskoi kultry. Munkhen: Izdatelstvo bratstva prep. Iova Pochaevskogo, http: //rus-sky.com/history/library/iljin2.htm.

Joas, H. 1985. *G. H. Mead. A Contemporary Reexamination of His Thought.* Cambridge, MA: Polity Press.

Joas, H. 1993. *Pragmatism and Social Theory.* Chicago: The University of Chicago Press.

Kolesnikov, A. 2008. *The New Times*, No. 23, http: //newtimes.ru/magazine/2008/is-sue051/art_0025.xml.

Kon, I. 996. "Moral Culture. Pp. 185-208 in Shalin, D. N. ed. *Russian Culture at the Crossroads: Paradoxes of Postcommunist Consciousness.* Edited by Dmitri N. Shalin. Boulder, CO: Westview Press.

Krizis Sotsfaka. 2008. Krizis Sotsfaka MGU ili Rossiiskoi Sotsiologii, http: //www.polit.ru/author/2008/01/24/socfak.html.

Kravchenko, S. 2004. Sotisologiia: Paradigmy cherez prizmu sotsiolgoicheskogo voobrazheniia: Uchebnik dlia vuzov. Izdanie 2. Moskva: Ekzamen.

Kravchenko, E. 2006. *Dzhorzh Gerbert Mid. Filosof, psikholog, sotsiolog.* Moskva: Moskovskii gosudarstvennyi lingvisticheskii universitet.

Levada, Y. 1990. "Ia schital, chto bylo by ne estestvenno vesti sebia kak-to inache," http: //www.unlv.edu/centers/cdclv/archives/Interviews/levada_90.html.

Levada, Y. 2000. *Ot mnenii k ponimaniiu. Stati po sotsiologii.* Moskva: Novoe izdatelstvo.

Levada, Y. 2005. Yuri Levada v peredache 'Shkola zlosloviia,' 7 ноября, 2005, http: //www.unlv.edu/centers/cdclv/archives/Interviews/levada_tolstaya.html.

Malinkin, A. 1999. "Poniatie patriotizma: Esse po sotsiologii znaniia." *Sotsiologichskii Zhurnal* 2, http: //www.socjournal.ru/article/275.

Malinkin, A. 2005. "Poliparadigmaticheskii podhov v sotsiologii: mnimi vykhod iz mnimoi dilemmy." *Logos* 2, http: //www.ruthenia.ru/logos/number/47/10.pdf.

Malinkin, A. 2005a. "1999, Sotsialnye obshchnosti i ideia patriotizma." *Sotsiologichskii Zhurnal* 3-4, http: //www.socjournal.ru/article/261.

Malinkin, A. 2006. "Poliparadigmatiinyi podkhod i situatsiia v rossiiskoi sotsiologii," *Sotsiologicheskie issledovania*. No.1. pp. 114-123, http: //www.ecsocman.edu.ru/images/pubs/2007/12/06/0000317577/014_Malinkin_114-123.pdf.

Marcuse, H. [1934] 1968. "The Struggle against Liberalism in the Totalitarian View of the State." Pp. 3-42 in *Negations. Essays in Critical Theory*. Boston: Beacon Press.

Martindale, D. 1981. *The Nature and Type of Sociological Theory*. Boston: Houghton Mifflin Co.

Mead, G. H. 1915. "Madison: The Passage of the University of Wisconsin through the State Political Agitation of 1914; the Survey by William H. Allen and His Staff and the Legislative Fight of 1915, with the Indications These Offer of the Place the State University Holds in the Community." *Survey* 35: 349-61.

Merton. R. "Structural Analysis in Sociology." Pp. 21-52 in P. M. Blau, *Approaches to the Study of Social Structure*. New York: The Free Press.

Merton, R. *The Sociology of Science. Theoretical and Empirical Investigations*. Chicago: The University of Chicago Press.

Mills, C. Wright. 1949. *Sociological Imagination*. New York: Oxford University Press.

Mills, C. Wright. 1966. *Sociology and Pragmatism. The Higher Learning in America*. New York: Oxford University Press.

Mills, C. Wright. 1967. *Power, Politics & People*. New York: Oxford University Press.

Nazarenko, G., Nigai, Y. and Zhirina, T. 2006. "Systema stimulov dlia uchashchikhsia," http: //festival.1september.ru/2005_2006/index.php?numb_artic=310763.

Nichols, L. (ed.). 2007. *Public Sociology: The Contemporary Debate*. Transaction Publishers.

Osipov, G. 1977. *Sotsiologia i sovremennost*. Moskva: Nauka.

Osipov, G. 1979. *Teoriia i praktika sotsiologicheskikh issledovanii*. Moskva: Nauka.

Osipov, G. 1987. "Chelovecheskii factor uskoreniia uskoreniia (k voprosu o razrabotki sotsiologicheskoi kontseptsii." *Sotsiologichewskie issledovaniia* 5: 11-18.

Osipov, G. 1997. "Chto proiskhodi s sotsiologiei." Akademicheskaia tribuna, http: //www.ecsocman.edu.ru/images/pubs/2005/08/22/0000218860/001.OSIPOV.pdf.

Osipov, G. 2000. "Rossiia: Vstupaia v XXI vek," http: //www.ispr.ru/BIBLIO/JUR-NAL/Evra/eurasia103.html.

Osipov, G. 2002. Zakliuchitelpnoe slovo. Dukhovno-nravstvennye tsennosti sovremennogo rossiiskogo obshchestva, http: //www.ispr.ru/Confer/confer4_1.html#v7 .

Osipov, G. 2003. "Interviiu." Kommersant-Vlast, No. 4, 3-9 fevralia, pp. 62-67, http: //www.ispr.ru/Confer/confer15.html.

Osipov G. 2003a. Vstupitelnoe slovo, http: //www.ispr.ru/Confer/Files/osipov0511. pdf.

Osipov, G. 2004. Ot strategii razrusheniia k strategii sotsialnogo proryva, Uchenyi Soviet ISPI RAN, http: //www.ispr.ru/Confer/Osipov_strateg.html.

Osipov, G. 2005. Vstupitelnoe slovo. Evraziiskoe budushchee Rossii, http: //www.ispr.ru/Confer/EuroAsia/confer1_1.html.

Osipov. G. 2006. Institut sotsialno-politicheskikh issledovanii RAN na sluzhbe otechestvu i nauke. *Hauka-Kultura-Obshchestvo*, No. 1, http: //www.ispr.ru/ZNAMDAT/15LET/Images/Osipov_15LET.pdf

Osipov, G. 2007. "O putiakh i metodakh resheniia 'russkogo voprosa'," http: //www.glazev.ru/nir/2277.

Osipov, G. 2008. Vozrozhdenie sotsiologii v Rossii, http: //www.isras.ru/index.php?page%20id=699.

Osipov, G. and Kuznetsov, V. N. 2005. Sotsialnaia pol cotsiologii v XXI веке, http: //www.ispr.ru/Confer/Images/Osipov_Kuznezov.pdf.

Otchisleny iz MGU. 2008, "Iz MGU Otchislili chetyreh studentok aktivistok," http: //www.newsru.com/russia/13mar2008/students.html.

Paramonov, B. M. 1996. "Historical Culture." Pp. 11-40 in *Russian Culture at the Crossroads: Paradoxes of Postcommunist Consciousness*. Edited by D. Shalin. Boulder, CO: Westview Press.

Peirce, C. S. 1991. *Peirce on Signs*. Chapel Hill: University of North Carolina Press.

Pokrovsky, N. 1992. "R. Merton. Fragmenty iz vospominanii." *Sotsiologicheskie isseldovaniia 10: 128-133*.

Professionalnyi kodeks. 1988. "Professionalnyi kodeks sotsiologa." *Sotsiologicheskie islledovaniia* 4: 95-96.

Protiv burzhuaznoi, 1948. "Protiv burzhuaznoi ideologii kosmopolitizma." 1948. *Vorposy filosofii* 2: 14-18.

Radaev, V. 2009. Vozmozhna li pozitivnaia programma dlia rossiiskoi sotsiologii. *Polit. ru*, http: //www.polit.ru/science/2008/10/24/radaev_speech.html.

Ritzer, G. 1975. *Sociology: A Multiple Paradigm Science*. Boston: Allyn & Bacon.

Ryvkina, R. 1997. Paradoksy rossiiskoi sotsiologii. *Sotsiologoicheksi zhurnal*. No. 4, 197-208.

Ryvkina, Inna. 2006. "Intelligentsiia v postsovetskoi Rossii: Ischerpanie sotsialnoi roli," http: //www.ecsocman.edu.ru/images/pubs/2007/08/06/0000310334/019_Rivkina.pdf.

Safranski, R. 1998. *Martin Heidegger: Between Good and Evil*. Cambridge, MA: Harvard University Press.

Saganenko, G. and Golofast V. 2008. "Beseda o russkoi intelligentsii." *Teleskop: Zhurnal po sotsiologii i marketingovym islledovaniiam*. 5: 6-17.

Saveliev, Y. 2003. "Assotsiatsiia rabotnkov russkikh uchrezhdenii rabotnikov kultury RM," http: //www.nm.md/daily/article/2003/12/12/0404.html.

Shalin, D. 1978. "The Development of Soviet Sociology, 1956-1976." *Annual Review of Sociology* 4: 171-91.

Shalin, D. 1979. "Between the Ethos of Science and the Ethos of Ideology." *Sociological Focus* 12: 175-93.

Shalin, D. 1986. "Pragmatism and Social Interactionism." *American Sociological Review* 51: 9-30.

Shalin, D. 1988. "G. H. Mead, Socialism, and the Progressive Agenda." *American Journal of Sociology* 92: 913-951.

Shalin, D. 1990. "Sociology for the Glasnost Era: Institutional and Substantive Change in Recent Soviet Sociology." *Social Forces* 68: 1-21.

Shalin, D. 1992. "Critical Theory and the Pragmatist Challenge." *American Journal of Sociology* 96 (1992): 237-279.

Shalin, D. 1996. "Intellectual Culture," Pp. 41-98 in *Russian Culture at the Crossroads: Paradoxes of Postcommunist Consciousness*. Edited by Dmitri N. Shalin. Boulder, CO: Westview Press.

Shalin, D. 2004. "Hermeneutics and Prejudice: Heidegger and Gadamer in Their Historical Setting." Paper presented at the 2004 Annual Meeting of the American Sociological Association, San Francisco.

Shalin, D. 2004b. "Liberalism, Affect Control, and Emotionally Intelligent Democracy." *Journal of Human Rights* 3: 407-428.

Shalin, D. 2005. "Legal Pragmatism, an Ideal Speech Situation, and the Fully Embodied Democratic Process." *Nevada Law Journal* 5: 433-478.

Shalin, D. 2006. "Dmitri Shalin's Comments on the History of Russian Sociology.

Shalin, D. 2007. "Signing in the Flesh: Notes on Pragmatist Hermeneutics." *Sociological Theory* 25: 193-224.

Shalin, D. 2008. "Chelovek obshchestvenny: Garvardskoe interviiu s Yuriem Levadoi." *Sotsiologicheskii zhurnal* No. 1: 126-154.

Shalin, D. 2008b. "George Herbert Mead and Creationsim. E. I. Kravchenko, *Dzhordzh Gerbet Mid: Filosof, Psikholog, Sotsiolog*. Moskovskii Gosudarstvennyi Lingvistsicheskii Uuniversitet: Moskva 2006. 286 pp. *Symbolic Interaction* 31: 225-227.

Scheler, M. [1926] 1977. *Erkentnis und Arbeit: Eine Studie uber Wert und Grenzen des pragmatischen Motivs in der Erkentnis der Welt*. Frankfurt.

Shlapentokh, V. 1987. *The politics of Sociology in the Soviet Union*. Boulder: Westview Press.

Ustav, Ustav Soiuza Sotsiologov Rossii, http: //www.rgsu.net/souz/ystav/.

Veller, M. 2008. "Kariera v Nikuda," http: //lib.ru/WELLER/career.txt.

Vetrochet, A. 2004. "Trudnaia doroga k dobru I spravedlivosti," http: //amber-one. udmurtiya.ru/2005_013-k.htm.

Weber, M. 1946. "Politics as a Vocation." Pp. 77-128 in *From Max Weber: Essays in Sociology*. New York: Oxford University Press.

Weinberg, E. 2004. *Sociology in the Soviet Union and Beyond: Social Inquiry and Social Change* (Ashgate Publishing).

Wolin, R. 1991. *The Heidegger Controversy. A Critical Reader*. New York: Columbia University Press.

Wolin, R. 2000. "Nazism and the Complicities of Hans-Georg Gadamer. Untruth and Method" *The New Republic*, May 15, pp. 36-45.

Yadov, V. 1967. *Chelovek i ego rabota*. Moskva: Mysl (with A. G. Zdravomyslov and V. P. Rozhin).

Yadov V. 1990. Razmyshleniia o predmete sotsiologii. *Sotsiologicheskie islledovaniia* 2: 3-36.

Yadov, V. 1992. "Interviu s V. A. Yadovym. Gumanitarnoe napravlenie v sociologii." *Sotsiologicheskie islledovaniia* 4: 33-36.

Yadov, V. A. and R. Grathoff, eds. 1994. *Rossiiskaia Sotsiolgichdeskaia Traditsiia 60-kh Godov i Sovremennost: Materialy Simpoziuma*. Moskva: Nauka.

Yadov, V. 1995. "Dva rassuxhdeniia o teoreticheksikh predpochteniiakh." *Sotsiologicheksij zhurnal*. No. 2, http: //www.socjournal.ru/article/151.

Yadov, V. A. 2003. "Vozmozhnosti sovmeshcheniia teoreticheskikh paradigm v sotsiologii." *Sotsiologcheskii Zhurnal*, http: //www.socjournal.ru/article/563.

Yadov, V. 2005. "Nado po vosmozhnosti vliiat na dvizhenie sotsialnykh planet. . ." *Teleskop* 3: 2-11, 4: 2-10, http: //www.unlv.edu/centers/cdclv/archives/Interviews/yadov_2005.html.

Yadov, V. 2006. "Replika po povodu stati A. N. Malinkina "Poliparadigmatichskii podkhod I situatsiiq v rossiiskoi sotsiologii." *Sotsiologicheskie islledovaniia* 1, http: //www.isras.ru/files/File/Socis/08-2006/yadov.pdf.

Yadov, V. 2007. Dlia chego nuzhna segodnia natsionalnaia russkaia sociologiia? http: //www.unlv.edu/centers/cdclv/archives/articles/yadov_russocio.html.

Zaslavskaya. T. ed. 1997. *Rossiiskoe obshchestvo na izlome: vzgliad iznutri.* Moskva: VTSIOM.

Zaslavskaya, T. 1983. Novosibirsk Manifesto, http: //www.unlv.edu/centers/cdclv/archives/articles/zaslavskaya_manifest.html.

Zaslavskaya, T. 2005. "Chelovecheskii factor v tansformatsii rossiiskogo obshchestva," http: //www.polit.ru/lectures/2005/10/13/zaslavskaya.html

Zaslavskaya, T. & Z. Kalugina. 1999. *Sotsietalnaia traektoriia reforemiruemoi Rossii: issledovaniia Novosibirskoi ekonomiko-sotsiologicheskoi shkoly*. Moskva: Nauka, http: //www.unlv.edu/centers/cdclv/archives/articles/zaslavskaya_ch4.html.

Zdravomyslov, A. 2006. "Pole sotsiologii v sovremennoi Rossii: Dilemma avtonomnosti i angazhirvannosti v svete naslediia perestroika." *Obshchestvennye nauki i sovremennosti* 1: 5-20, http: //www.unlv.edu/centers/cdclv/archives/articles/zdravomyslov_russiansoc.html.

Zdravomyslov, A. 2007. "Natsionalnye sotsiologicheksie shkoly v sovremennom mire." *Obshchestvennye nauki i sovremennost* 5: 114-130, http: //www.unlv.edu/centers/cd-clv/archives/articles/zdravomyslov_nationalsoc.html.

Zhukov, V. 2002. Dukhovno-nravstvennye tsennosti sovremennogo rossiiskogo obshchestvo, http: //www.ispr.ru/Confer/confer4_1.html#v7.

Zhukov, V. 2007. Doklad na Uchreditelnom S'ezde Soiuza Sotsiologov Rossii, http: //www.mgsu.info/t/doklad-ssr/.

Name Index

Aaron, D., 39, 73
Abbot, Lyman, 43
Aboulafia, Mitchell, xiii, 119
Addams, Jane, 41-43, 47, 50, 59, 66, 7, 182
Adorno, Theodor W., 123-6, 135, 159, 16, 163, 351, 365; and the Frankfurt school, 123-6, 351; and administrated state, 123-4; and the irrational, 135
Agger, Ben, 175, 189
Akhmatova, Anna, 314
Albrow M., 354, 365
Alekseev, Andrey, 348, 354, 365
Alexander, Jeffrey C., 222, 224, 229-30, 233, 235-6; and cultural pragmatics, 229-30
Alexander, Thomas M., 119, 138, 154, 158-9
Aldington, Arthur, 80
Alterman, Eric, 326-7
Anderson, Nels, 92, 109, 113
Anonymous, 186, 189
Antonio, Robert J., xiii, 119-20
Apel, K-O., 128, 351, 365
Aquinas, 18
Aristotle, 18, 285-6, 295, 301-3, 310-2, 323, 325-7, 365; and law, 285; and pragmatism, 286; and democracy, 301-3; and education, 302-3; and music, 303, and anger, 310-11; and character, 312; and middle class, 301-2
Auden, W. H., 297
Augustine, 18
Austin, John, 132
Averintsev, Sergey, 365

Bach, Johann Sebastian, 145
Barbalet, J. M., 194, 222, 235
Barlow, A., 357, 365

Barnard, John, 39, 43, 73
Barthes, Roland, 173, 189, 210, 234
Barzun, Jacques, 2-3, 33
Bates, E. S., 70, 73
Batygin, Gennady, 333, 365
Baudrillard, Jean, 167, 169-71, 173-4, 178-9, 182-3, 189, 190, 212, 214, 234; and culture, 167; and Nietzsche, 167; and postmodernism 169; and sociology, 173; and symbolic exchange, 170; and the real, 170; and the power, 170-1; and Watergate, 171; and simulacrum, 171; and nihilism, 182; and objective chance, 183; and the evasion of embodied experience, 214
Bourdieu, Pierre, 205, 222, 224-9, 234, 235, 237
Bauman, Zygmunt, 175, 189
Bayle, Pierre, 137
Beilharz, Peter, 46, 326
Belcove-Shalin, Janet S., xiii, 37
Beliaev, Edward, xiii, 333, 349, 365
Belinkov, Arkady, 75
Bemis, 49
Ben-David, Joseph, 356, 365
Benhabib, Seyla, 120, 137, 158-9, 175, 189
Benjamin, Walter, 159
Berezovsky, Boris, 309
Berger, Peter, xiii, 1, 159 n. 7
Berlin, Isaiah, 3, 33, 270, 306, 326
Bernstein, Eduard, 48
Bernstein, Richard J., 120, 158-9, 161, 352, 366-7
Betz, J., 149, 159
Bliss, W. D. P., 39, 73
Blumer, Herbert, xiii, 79, 80, 101, 113 n. 6, 117, 143, 159, 189; and conceptual precision, 101; and structure, 113 n. 6; and joint action, 143

373

Subject Index

242; and legislative and administrative powers, 242, 274; and market place of ideas, 256; of rhetoric, 256; and its dispersion in the Constitution, 263; and ideal speech situation, 274; and Vladimir Putin, 309-10, 348; and hardman's propensity to seize control, 311; and civility as weapon of the powerful, 323; and anger as weapon of the powerless, 323; seized by Bolsheviks, 333; and Gorbachev, 336; as exercised by nationalist sociologists in Russia, 362-3, 264 n. 4. *See also* romanticism; pragmatism; postmodernism

Power-knowledge relationship, see power.

Pragmatic-discursive misalignment, 101-2, 154, 204-9, 212, 227-9; 280-1, 285; and Foucault, 212; and Goffman, 227-8; and Kant, 280, 285; and Dworkin, 280-1; and Swaggart, 205-6; and Haggard, 206; and Grass, 206. *See also* pragmatist hermeneutics; biocritique

Pragmatism, 119, 251; and Habermas, x; and indeterminacy, x; and law, xi; and interactionism, 79-112; and indeterminacy, 80, 91; and "world-in-the-making," 81-2; and symbolization, 83-4; and pluralistic universe, 84; and termination of indeterminacy, 85-6, 175; and the problem of universals, 88-91; and structure as processing, 89-90; and present as a seat of reality, 91; and knowing *of* and *about*, 97; as a "branch of Young Hegelianism," 128; and self-criticism, 131; and logic in use or logic of uncertainty, 143; and critique of postmodernism, 174-187; and meaning as feeling and action, 176; and Peirce's semiotics of triangulation, 176-7; and four stages of the act, 177; and self as ongoing accomplishment, 178-9; and self-identity as a moral project, 178-9; and science as a model of democracy in action, 180; and democracy as a historical mode of managing uncertainty, 181; and detaching truth claims from power, 181; and challenging entrenched institutions and authorities, 182; biocritique (biocritical hermeneutics), 202-4; and resistance to pragmatism, 349-54; and resistance to pragmatism in Europe,

350-1; and resistance to pragmatism in Russia, 349-350; and ethos of pragmatist hermeneutics, 232; 360-2. *See also*, Kant, Immanuel; Peirce, Charles; James, William; Dewey, John; Mead, George Herbert; Habermas, Jürgen; Shusterman, Richard

Pragmatist hermeneutics, 193-232; and termination of indeterminacy, 140-1; and signifying media, 203-205; and affect, 204-8; and ethos, 232; and Heidegger, 213-214, 232; and de Man, 214; and Saussure, 223; and the flesh of the sign, 199-200; and the sign of the flesh199-200; iconic, indexical, and symbolic signs, 199-204; and signifying media, 200-1; and symbolic-discursive signs, 200; and somatic-affective signs, 200; and behavioral performative signs, 200; and word-body-action nexus, 282; and critique of postmodernism, 209-216; and depth hermeneutics, 217; and surface hermeneutics, 217; and meaning of Christianity, 218-20; and meaning of Marxism, 219-20; and pragmatic-discursive misalignment, 219-20; and democracy as embodied phenomenon, 222; and critique of disembodied reason, 136, 222; and human agency, 223; and emergent grammar, 223; and reverse editing, 229; and reconstruction vs. deconstruction, 229; and its future research agenda, 232-3. *See also* embodiment; biocritique; embodied sociology; postmodernism; pragmatic-discursive misalignment; Heidegger, Martin; Shusterman, Richard

Pragmatism, resistance to, 349-54; in Europe, 350-1; in Russia, 349-350. *See also* nationalist sociology; Russian sociology

Pragmatist sociology, see interactionism

Pragmatic jurisprudence, see legal pragmatism; law

Pragmatist revival, 119-154, 351-2. *See also* pragmatism

Prejudices, 10, 197, 256; and hermeneutics, 10; and Marx's racial bias, 197. *See also* Gadamer, Hans-Georg

Progressivism, 37-71, 105; and Christianity, 39-42; and Social Gospel, 39; and socio-economic reforms, 40; and

For Product Safety Concerns and Information please contact our EU representative GPSR@taylorandfrancis.com Taylor & Francis Verlag GmbH, Kaufingerstraße 24, 80331 München, Germany

Batch number: 08158441

Printed by Printforce, the Netherlands